Adobe
Photoshop® 5.5
FUNDAMENTALS
with ImageReady™ 2

New Riders

Gary David Bouton

"Fireplug," "Bike," and "Pawn" (clockwise from top). In chapters 3, "Esoteric Selections," and 4, "Bouton's Bag of High-End Photoshop Tricks," you'll learn first how to create selections—from fairly simple to complex. Then, you'll apply filtering to the selected parts of an image to produce such things as a watercolor fireplug against a natural environment, a chessboard that you probably will *never* see for sale, and you'll learn how to make objects glow.

"A Fork in the Road." In chapter 1, "Interface Preferences and Photoshop Options," you can use this test image to compare different gamma settings. Chapter 1 is all about getting an image to look the same way onscreen as it does when you scan it and print it. If one image becomes your benchmark, all your images will come out balanced for screen and for print.

"Bon Voyage," "Nuts & Bolts Design." In chapter 4, you work on creating realistic shadows for selected objects. And in chapter 5, "Color and Tone Correction," you create the sunset picture above, by using silhouettes that began as a couple dancing, and then you play with the tones in the image to create a greeting card.

"Ball and Wall." This image is used a number of times in this book, but its basic purpose is to help you become handy with the selection tools in Photoshop. Chapter 2, "Straightforward Selections," shows how to combine simple selection areas, such as rectangles and circles, to produce more complex selections.

"Rickenbacker 481," "Flying Egg." Chapter 6, "Everything You Need To Know About Layers," takes you through clipping groups that can make this guitar appear with any finish you like. You can also create planes of depth by using layers; notice that the egg has clouds both in front and behind it.

"Fruit Puzzle." Knowing how to create selections isn't very rewarding unless you also know what to do with those selections. In chapter 2, you make a jigsaw puzzle from an image by creating selections, moving the selections to different layers, and then applying one of Photoshop's layer effects.

"Burger" and "Preserves." In chapter 7, "Retouching with the Rubber Stamp Tool," you'll learn to do the seemingly impossible. You will completely remove the burger from the image and replace it with a jar of fruit preserves.

"Rock." In chapter 8, "Working with Type," you will not only get hands-on experience with Photoshop 5.5's new Type tool, but you'll also learn how to bring type outlines into Photoshop and then add fills, as shown in this picture.

"Garage Sale." In chapter 8, you also learn the basic rules of good type design, so the signs for your next outdoor event don't send people running the wrong way!

"American Icons." Learn how to blend elements from layer to layer, using Layer Mask mode. If this picture looks complex, it really isn't. It was all done by using only three different layers.

"Happy Birthday." In chapter 6, you'll see how to create many birthday cards from a single background through the use of different names and the Layers palette.

"Lars Wuhdqax: Alien Hunter." In chapter 9, "Putting It All Together," you'll find out how to integrate everything you've learned in chapters 1–8 to create this fantastic, phony sci-fi poster.

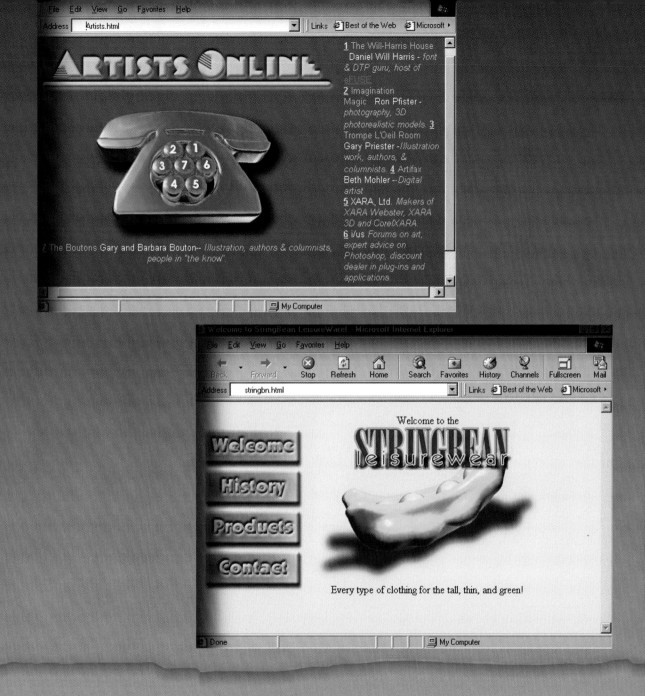

"Artists OnLine" and "StringBean LeisureWare." In chapter 13, you'll learn how to create *image map* buttons in ImageReady. An HTML element enables you to define several URLs on a single image.

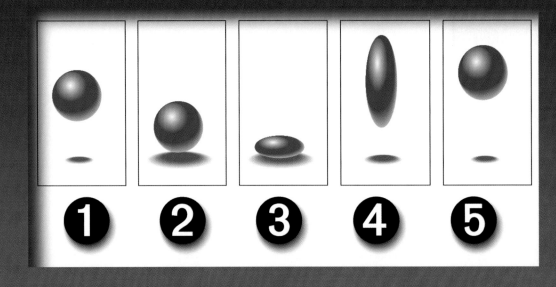

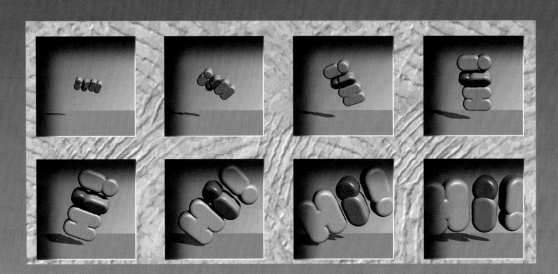

"Bouncing Ball" and "Spinout." Chapter 12, "Creating GIF Animations," is about ImageReady and animation. This chapter will show you the way to creating marvelous, miniature pictures that move.

Click here

"Susan's Susans." Chapter 15, "If You Read Only One Chapter…," puts together expert editing techniques and a lot of what you've learned in chapters 1–14, taking you on a ride from selections in Photoshop to creating JavaScript rollover buttons in ImageReady.

ADOBE PHOTOSHOP 5.5
FUNDAMENTALS WITH
IMAGEREADY 2

Gary David Bouton

201 West 103rd Street, Indianapolis, Indiana 46290

Adobe Photoshop 5.5 Fundamentals with ImageReady 2

International Standard Book Number: 0-7357-0928-9

Library of Congress Catalog Card Number: 99-066562

Printed in the United States of America

First Printing: December 1999

03 02 01 00 99   7 6 5 4 3 2 1

Interpretation of the printing code: The rightmost double-digit number is the year of the book's printing; the rightmost single-digit number is the number of the book's printing. For example, the printing code 99-1 shows that the first printing of the book occurred in 1999.

Publisher
David Dwyer

Executive Editor
Steve Weiss

Development Editor
Jennifer Eberhardt

Copy Editor
Gail Burlakoff

Indexer
Lisa Stumpf

Technical Editor
Gary Kubicek

Media Developer
Craig Atkins

Proofreader
Lisa Stumpf

Compositor
Gina Rexrode

Trademarks

All terms mentioned in this book that are known to be trademarks or service marks have been appropriately capitalized. New Riders Publishing cannot attest to the accuracy of this information. Use of a term in this book should not be regarded as affecting the validity of any trademark or service mark.

Photoshop, ImageReady, and Illustrator are registered trademarks of Adobe Systems, Inc.

Warning and Disclaimer

Every effort has been made to make this book as complete and as accurate as possible, but no warranty or fitness is implied. The information provided is on an "as is" basis. The authors and the publisher shall have neither liability nor responsibility to any person or entity with respect to any loss or damages arising from the information contained in this book or from the use of the CD or programs accompanying it.

Contents at a Glance

Table of Contents

About the Author

Gary David Bouton is a seasoned author and illustrator with a background of seemingly countless years as a print and film advertising art director. He has spent more than 20 years at a traditional drafting table, and hopes that by writing books like these he will help others with similar, traditional skills to bridge the chasm and become proficient with the digital equivalents of physical media. (Hint: typesetting is a lot easier to do on a computer than with dry-transfer lettering.)

Photoshop 5.5 Fundamentals with ImageReady is the ninth book about Photoshop that Mr. Bouton has written for New Riders. His other 15 books include *Inside Adobe Photoshop 5* (to be updated in early 2000 to include info on version 5.5), *CorelDRAW Experts Edition, Inside Macromedia Extreme 3D,* and *Multimedia Publishing for Netscape* (Netscape Press). The author is also a regular columnist for "eFUSE," a 'zine for Web site–design beginners (www.eFUSE.com) and Designer.com, a 'zine that provides high-end computer graphics advice. He is Moderator Emeritus of the CorelXARA discussion group on www.i-us.com.

In his spare time, the author is helping those like him to land and colonize this planet. In a friendly way.

The author can be reached at Gary@Boutons.com.

Dedication

This book is dedicated to my Dad, Jack Orvin Bouton, who thought he was doing me a favor when he bought me my first computer. I practically never see him anymore, what with the books, the CDs, the conferences, and what not! I'm trying to get him to buy a PC so we can do video-conferencing (yeah, right). Seriously, it's been my father's faith and occasional stubbornness (sorry, Pop, but you already know this) that have made the uphill climb that always accompanies learning a less-than-solitary thing. Thanks from the bottom of my heart, Dad.

Acknowledgments

If this book appears to be sung with a singular voice, it is only because the group that saves my hide book after book is chiming in with the same tune. I don't know how healthy it is for us all to think alike, but it *does* help to get what we want—what we insist on from ourselves and for our readers—done on time, and done right.

For those of you who have not met the folks who prop me up at the podium, I'd like you to meet, and me to thank:

- Gail Burlakoff, Editor. Gail is a very persuasive person; through her talent copy editing at least 10 of my books, she has me convinced that I am but a keyboardist in life, and it is *she* who tells the tale! Thanks for "thinking it my way" Gail, thank you for the incessant bail-outs you've performed in the past, and like you told me yesterday, I think we made this the best book ever on Photoshop.

- Developmental Editor Jennifer Eberhardt, who has been clicking along my train of thought (hint: never get tickets for this train) for at least four books now, and I never realized that we both really like *Star Wars* until I sent her a stuffed Jar Jar Binks. None of which has to do with the book, but let me tell you that all of us involved have used the telephone and the Internet, with an occasional assist from AirBorne, to get this book humming, cooking, and into your hands as quickly as we did.

- Technical Editor and a personal friend of mine, Mr. Gary Kubicek. Gare, I cannot believe you inspected every darned pixel in my screen caps to make sure they were accurate! That, and a thousand editor's suggestions, really helped to make this a book that will surely be distinguished from others due to sheer effort. And thanks for being a good sport about the unflattering images I use of you. My only excuse is that Dave was unavailable. Thanks, pal. Gary's site is at www.aiusa.com/gary/ and you can send him e-mail there.

- Mr. Ron Pfister of Imagination Magic (www.imaginationmagic.com/), for his work on accurately converting all the Boutons' fonts to the Macintosh platform, in both TrueType and Type 1. Thanks, Amigo. And, no, I did not forget to mention that you lent me that spectacular sunset image our readers use in chapter 5. Ron is a new addition to the "Bouton Family," and he certainly did rise to the occasion when we got tight on time creating this book.

- Mr. Ed Guarente (eguaren1@twcny.rr.com), a friend and dynamite portrait photographer who helped us set up Lars Wuhdqax's photo session one Saturday afternoon. Ed, I cannot tell you how much it meant that you schlepped lights and the whole nine yards over here for a goofy but totally professional session!

- Lars Wuhdqax, for flying in for the weekend and allowing us to do a photo session.

■ Mr. John Hall, CEO of Rickenbacker International Corporation, for allowing me to share with our readers the Rickenbacker 481 guitar photo we use in chapter 6. That image was taken from a 1976 catalog, and I own one of those guitars. I figure, if a Rick was good enough for the Beatles to use, it's certainly a welcome enough highlight to this humble tome. Thank you again, John.

■ Aren Howell and Louisa Klucznik, for making the book as fun to look at as it is to read!

■ Gina Rexrode, for hammering out very tough design problems and putting up with *me*!

■ Craig Atkins, for ensuring that the CD worked every ounce as well as we'd hoped.

■ Lisa Stumpf, for the wonderful index and the great proofreading.

■ Ron Pfister (again) and Robert Stanley, for being the Bouton QA (Quality Assurance) Group on the Companion CD. Ya go blind after looking at the same files 15 times, and Robert and Ron diligently did my work, ensuring that what you buy works right out of the sleeve. Thanks, friends.

■ Mark Thomas and the bunch at Right Hemisphere, for the wonderful offer (at the back of the book) and the trial version of Deep Paint. Just sneak a peek at the doodles I did in chapter 15½ with Deep Paint. This is a must for your Photoshop plug-ins collection.

■ Brian Jones at XAOS|tools, for the generous offer in the back of the book, and also for the trial versions on the CD. They are a stone-cold gas, Brian. Thanks!

■ JB Popplewell, Jeff, Scott, Skip, and all the wonderful aliens at Alien Skin, for a $40-off deal on their filters! This book practically pays for itself! Thanks, JB, and thanks to all for making me an honorary "Alien." Now all I have to do is worry about the Men in Black.

■ Carol DiSalvo, for providing the wedding pictures.

■ Spousal Consultant and Reality-Checker Barbara Bouton. Barbara, I can't thank you enough for putting up with me as I swung from the chandelier in the dining room while trying to type chapter 15 on a synthesizer keyboard (boy, they don't mark the keys all that well!). Thanks, hon'…as always.

■ Thanks to John and Susan Niestemski for their amazing offer in the back of the book! You won't find better prices for better quality film-recording work!

■ Thanks to Charles and Kate Moir at XARA, Ltd. for the demo program of CorelXARA 2 for Windows. I designed most of the ads and annotated all the screen figures with XARA, clearly a drawing app that came to us from the 23rd century.

A Message from New Riders

For those of you who remember Photoshop 3 (now almost three versions and several years ago), Gary Bouton was there with *Inside Photoshop 3*, followed by *Inside Photoshop 4*, *Inside Photoshop 5*, a couple of *Limited Editions* of *Inside Photoshop,* and a handful of other Photoshop titles. It's seems that Gary can't get enough of Photoshop, and we certainly can't get enough of Gary.

New Riders is proud to have worked with Gary Bouton—as well as his wonderful team, including Barbara Mancuso Bouton, Gary Kubicek, and Gail Burlakoff—over the past several years. What a wonderful group of people to work with. Now, we're proud to bring you Gary's latest book, *Adobe Photoshop 5.5 Fundamentals with ImageReady 2*. Let us know what you think...

How to Contact Us

As the reader of this book, *you* are our most important critic and commentator. We value your opinion and want to know what we're doing right, what we could do better, in what areas you'd like to see us publish, and any other words of wisdom you're willing to pass our way.

As the Executive Editor for the Graphics team at New Riders, I welcome your comments. You can fax, email, or write me directly to let me know what you did or didn't like about this book—as well as what we can do to make our books better.

Please note that I cannot help you with technical problems related to the topic of this book, and that due to the high volume of mail I receive, I might not be able to reply to every message.

When you write, please be sure to include this book's title, ISBN, and author, as well as your name and phone or fax number. I will carefully review your comments and share them with the authors and editors who worked on the book.

For any issues directly related to this or other titles:

Email: steve.weiss@newriders.com

Mail: Steve Weiss
                Executive Editor
                Professional Graphics & Design Publishing
                New Riders Publishing
                201 West 103rd Street
                Indianapolis, IN 46290 USA

Visit Our Website: www.newriders.com

On our website you'll find information about our other books, the authors we partner with, book updates and file downloads, promotions, discussion boards for online interaction with other users and with technology experts, and a calendar of trade shows and other professional events with which we'll be involved. We hope to see you around.

E-mail Us from Our Website

Go to www.newriders.com and click on the Contact link if you

- Have comments or questions about this book
- Want to report errors that you have found in this book
- Have a book proposal or are otherwise interested in writing with New Riders
- Would like us to send you one of our author kits
- Are an expert in a computer topic or technology and are interested in being a reviewer or technical editor
- Want to find a distributor for our titles in your area
- Are an educator/instructor who wishes to preview New Riders books for classroom use. (Include your name, school, department, address, phone number, office days/hours, text currently in use, and enrollment in your department in the body/comments area, along with your request for desk/examination copies, or for additional information.

Call Us or Fax Us

You can reach us toll-free at (800) 571-5840 + 9 + 3567. Ask for New Riders.

If outside the USA, please call 1-317-581-3500. Ask for New Riders.

If you prefer, you can fax us at 317-581-4663, Attention: New Riders.

Publisher's Acknowledgements

Without Gary Bouton, many of the New Riders Photoshop books could never happened. Gary, you're a true professional, even if you are a bit crazy at times (Lars Wuhdqax and the plummer in the bathroom sink!), and we can't begin to thank you enough for all you have contributed to our line of professional graphics titles.

Too, we can't thank enough Gary's readers, who write us time and again to tell us what they think about Gary's many books. Keep those e-mails, letters, and faxes coming. You're the reason we do this.

Introduction

Fundamentally Yours,

—Gary David Bouton

When this book was first dreamed up by my friends at New Riders, I had a lot of fun rolling the title of the book around in my mind. "Fundamentals?" What are fundamentals? Within the context of everyday life, I guess a couple of fundamentals would be "don't call a truck driver a sissy to his face" and "make sure you know where the ripcord is on a parachute." Life-saving basics, you know?

But I saw no reason whatsoever to make this a *beginner's* book—let's face it, you probably don't need any help in dragging an elliptical selection, using the Elliptical Marquee tool. And besides, there's already a truckload of beginner's books on Photoshop out there, so why kill one more tree?

"Okay, Gare," I hear from the balcony. "What *is* a fundamentals book on Photoshop?" I'm glad you asked.

I'd define *Photoshop 5.5 Fundamentals with ImageReady* as the quickest route to becoming proficient with the program, and as a result, beginning to make money using Photoshop faster than the next guy or gal. Time is money; with time you save, you can always make more money. This book is *the very least you need to know* to make Photoshop a worthwhile experience. There's no pandering, no long, drawn-out definitions, no examples of what is clear and apparent in a specific editing move within Photoshop 5.5 and ImageReady 2. No ambiguities, no insulting your intellect—just the best "boot camp" I could make this, while remembering that "Fun" is part of the word "fundamentals."

The distinction I need to make between a "basics" or "essentials"-type book, and this fundamentals book, is that a lot of the really cool and necessary-to-learn stuff in Photoshop is *not* always a basic topic. For example, holding down the Ctrl key when almost any other toolbox tool is selected will toggle the cursor to the Move tool. I think that's a time-saving morsel of info that is fundamental. But I also know that a good 50 percent of Photoshop's power lies in using image layers the right way, and this is not a basic concept. By the way, the other 49 percent of fundamental understanding of Photoshop lies in its selection capabilities, and that's why there are two chapters that concentrate on selection techniques. The other 1 percent of fundamental stuff in Photoshop is remembering to save the file, remembering that Ctrl(⌘)+Z means "Undo the last dreadful error I committed," and remembering the modifier keys (for example, Shift+F7 inverts a selection).

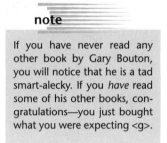

note

If you have never read any other book by Gary Bouton, you will notice that he is a tad smart-alecky. If you *have* read some of his other books, congratulations—you just bought what you were expecting <g>.

Is this really *all* there is to Photoshop? Not at all. But if you read straight through from chapter 1 to chapter 15½, you'll find that you can do a lot of amazingly complex and useful things without chipping a nail.

The Need to Grow, and the Hidden Aspect of this Book

I realize that a lot of folks might be intimidated by the size of the book, or some of the color plates. I also realize that experienced users might think that this is another beginner's book on Photoshop.

No. And no, most emphatically.

You are bound to get to a certain point in your Photoshop studies when you want to move from learning isolated bits and pieces to seeing where all these pieces fit together. That's why this book contains two chapters that lead you though the process of putting your newly learned "skillettes" (tiny skills) together to produce real, professional work.

When you finish these chapters, you *will be* surprised and delighted. Aren't you glad that this is not a conventional book?

I Won't Assume Anything

Whether you know how to paint masterpieces in Photoshop, or you're just learning where the Paintbrush tool is, *Photoshop 5.5. Fundamentals with ImageReady* doesn't gloss over something simply because I assume you already know it. Certainly, being proficient with a mouse or digitizing tablet would be a plus, and it wouldn't hurt if you knew a little Illustrator, CorelDRAW, or CorelXARA, but in your "experimental phase" with this new computer graphics stuff, you'll soon pick up on the obvious and this book will have you sailing through the ozone in no time.

Where Are the Keys to Success?

"Success" has been defined by about every modern millionaire and pundit today, and no one seems to agree on a definition. Failing a definition, how about an explanation?

First of all, *never give up*. It took me three months of day-and-night work to finally fig-ure out what Photoshop channels were good for when version 2.5 came out. And I cannot tell you the joys gained from hanging in there. If I had to describe "success" in a sentence, it would be "Being happy with what you've done." How about that one? No dollars or fame required. If I were asked to define "success" as an equation, it would be

Diligence + Perseverance = Success

You work at something in earnest, with no distractions, and you do it every day. In this mode, you cannot help but be a success at Photoshop or anything else.

How's the Book Organized?

As the flow of the book goes, I've provided information on core Photoshop features in the first chapters. We integrate techniques a little, and then move on to higher ground. Once we've been cooking on higher ground, we put all the pieces together to reach more complex image editing. Then we tip ImageReady into the formula, and by the end of the book, integrate its features into what you already know. *Everyone* is new to Photoshop 5.5; it's an adventure for the pro and the beginner alike, and I tried not to leave anything important out of the steps, the notes, the text, or the discov-ery process. Do not take the attitude of, "Yeah, yeah, I know about the Preferences in Photoshop, so I'll skip this section." There are *new features* in Photoshop's Preferences, you can customize this program more extensively than ever, and you'll be missing out on valuable information if you gloss over a chapter.

Instructions for Truly Accessing this Book

The examples in the book are documented in a step-by-step format. If you follow along, your screen should look exactly like this book's figures, except that your screen will be in color. Each chapter leads you through at least one set of numbered steps, with frequent asides explaining why I asked you to do something. The figures show the results of an action, and I explain what the effect should look like.

Occasionally, beyond the expected notes and tips that everyone puts in books, there are Photoshop Profound Wisdoms in *Photoshop 5.5 Fundamentals with ImageReady*. What are these? They are super-compressed bits of knowledge that, when ingested, will increase your Photoshop I.Q. by 25 points. Do not take them lightly. They will serve you well on a multitude of occasions, they will make you look smarter at company events, and best yet they contain no calories.

Most of Photoshop 5.5's tools have different, enhanced functions when you hold down the Shift, Alt, or Ctrl keys (Shift, Opt, Command keys, for Macintosh users) while you click with the mouse or press other keyboard keys. These *modifier keys* are shown in the steps as Ctrl(⌘)+click, Alt(Opt)+click, Ctrl(⌘)+D, and so on. *Photoshop 5.5 Fundamentals with ImageReady* is a multiplatform documentation of the application; Windows key commands are shown first in the steps, followed by the Macintosh key equivalent (enclosed in parentheses). UNIX users also will find the steps easy to follow; the primary difference in Photoshop 5.5 across platforms is the "look" the operating system lends to interface elements.

To show you how easy it is to follow along in this book, here's how I tell you to access the Feather command:

1. Press Ctrl(⌘)+Alt(Opt)+D (Select, Feather), and then type **5** in the pixels field. Click on OK to apply the feathering.

The translation? You hold down the first key while you press the second and third keys (then release all three keys to produce the intended result), or you can access the command the hard way through the menu commands in parentheses. I try throughout the book to get you comfortable with modifier keys rather than menu commands, because this constant reinforcement highlighted throughout the book will eventually make you work more efficiently in Photoshop 5.5. And you *will* work faster. Function keys appear in this book as F1, F2, F3, and so on.

If the steps in an application that's available in both Windows and Macintosh formats are significantly different, I explain the steps used in this book through the text and the annotated screen figures. But I'm going to show you exactly how different Photoshop 5.5 is when looked at through different operating systems.

Figure I.1 shows you the Windows Photoshop 5.5 Layers palette on the left; and on the right, the Mac OS 7 version of Photoshop 5.5's Layers palette. There really should be no questions about what to do with a given screen element when one is shown in this book—Adobe made this program as identical in look and feel as possible.

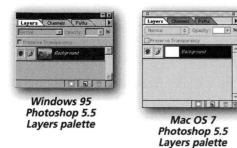

**Windows 95
Photoshop 5.5
Layers palette**

**Mac OS 7
Photoshop 5.5
Layers palette**

The figures in this book were taken in Windows 98; there simply isn't room in this book to show all the versions of Windows, UNIX, and Macintosh interfaces! Again, where there is a significant difference in the way something is accomplished on a specific platform, this book details the specific steps to be used.

Terms Used in this Book

The term *drag* in this book means to hold down the primary mouse button and move the onscreen cursor. This action is used in Photoshop to create a marquee selection, and to access tools on the toolbox flyout. On the Macintosh, dragging is also used to access *pull-down menus;* Windows users do not need to hold the primary mouse button to access flyout menus and main menu commands.

Hover means to move your cursor onscreen without holding a mouse button. Hovering is most commonly used in Photoshop with the Magnetic Pen and Magnetic Lasso tools, and also with the Eyedropper tool, when you're seeking a relative position in an image and the color value beneath the tool (the Info palette, F8, must be displayed to determine the values the Eyedropper reads).

Click means to press and release the primary mouse button once.

Double-click means to press quickly, twice, the primary mouse button. Usually you double-click to perform a function without having to click an OK button in a directory window. Additionally, when you double-click on a tool in Photoshop's toolbox, the Options palette appears.

Shift+Click means that you should hold down the Shift key while you click with the primary mouse button.

Nicknames Are Used for Well-Known Products

Photoshop 5.5 Fundamentals with ImageReady would be an even larger book than it already is if every reference to a specific graphics product or manufacturer included the full brand manufacturer, product name, and version number. For this reason, you'll usually see Adobe Photoshop 5.5 referred to here simply as "Photoshop." Similarly, Adobe Illustrator is referred to as "Illustrator," and other products are mentioned by their "street names."

New Riders Publishing and the author acknowledge that the names mentioned in this book are trademarked or copyrighted by their respective manufacturers; our use of nicknames for various products is in no way meant to infringe on the trademark names for these products. When we refer to an application, it is usually the most current version of the application, unless otherwise noted.

So, What's In Store?

Photoshop 5.5 with ImageReady is divided into five Parts (counting our marvelously compiled Appendix on the Companion CD). Here's a breakdown of what's in store:

Part I: Photoshop Basics

In Chapter 1, *Interface Preferences and Photoshop Options,* I'll show you how to change the appearance of the workspace to make it work better and more quickly for *you.* Also, I've got a handful of options you can change to suit your personal work style. And finally, we'll take a look at Photoshop's preferences so you can make your monitor show off images at their best (and most accurate), and see how to get memory assigned to Photoshop in the best and most realistic way. And I've a few tips that I don't think are documented anywhere except in this book.

Chapter 2, *Straightforward Selections,* uncovers the secrets to both advanced and elementary selection-making. If you casually glance at the toolbox, there seem to be about three selection tools. In reality, each selection tool has a modifier key or two that changes the way a current selection can be combined with a new selection you make. The possibilities are virtually endless, but the chapter's brief, terse, and occa-sionally silly.

Chapter 3, *Esoteric Selections,* is a comprehensive documentation of the "other" ways to select image areas—by color, by tone, by slopping on a coat of Quick Mask—and more. If you cannot handle the accurate selection of an image area, using the tools you know about, read this chapter for the Photoshop features you *don't* know about.

Part II: Working Smart in Photoshop

Chapter 4, *Bouton's Bag of High-End Photoshop Tricks,* is a payoff of sorts. Hey, you've just read three important but not awfully super-duper, let's-do-the-special-effects kinda chapters. This one *is* one of those (s-d-l-d-t-h-s-e) kinds of chapters. With what you've learned and what you are about to learn, you'll be making realistic shadows and glowing effects in no time. These can be your parlor tricks if anyone ever asks you, "Hey, do you know Photoshop?"

Chapter 5, *Color and Tone Correction,* is your introduction to correcting one of the most difficult aspects of a photograph that's out of whack. You'll see how to perform absolute miracles, specifically the type that photo-finishers charge beaucoup bucks for (if you're a photo-finisher reading this, I didn't mean most of it).

In Chapter 6, *Everything You Need To Know About Layers,* I leave no stone unturned as we explore ways that layers can cut down on your editing time, enable you to do things that are impossible without layers, and the special properties layers can offer. You'll know the Layers palette like the back of your hand in no time!

Part III: Moving Onward and Upward

Consider chapters 1–6 your limbering up. Now, for the workouts and the payoffs!

Chapter 7, *Retouching with the Rubber Stamp Tool,* is a glorious adventure in painting with parts of an image instead of colors from a palette. You can and will do the impossible in this chapter, like turning a hamburger in a jar of jelly preserves. Hey, *someone's* gotta teach you stuff like this!

Chapter 8, *Working with Type,* will get you up to speed with the Type tool and the Type Options dialog box. Creating wonderful text is easier than ever in a graphics program (except ImageReady, where type is always onscreen <g>). You'll also learn how to get your drawing application to display text in Photoshop, so you can do all sorts of neat special text effects.

Chapter 9, *Putting it All Together,* is a romp with fictitious alien hunter Lars Wuhdqax. Having learned a lot in earlier chapters, now you will put your skills to work creating a sci-fi poster with robots, a robe-clad hero brandishing a laser sword, the possibility of me getting sued, and more!

Chapter 10, *Output Essentials,* is a fancy way of saying, "What's the least you need to know to communicate with a laser printer and a commercial pressman?" This chapter not only takes you through the steps for getting the best output, but also contains some valuable math for making sure a camera-ready print from you gets into a flyer or newspaper exactly the way you want it to. This chapter is a real paper-and-nerves saver!

Part IV: Introducing ImageReady

Thought I'd forgotten about "the other" program, huh? Nope. We'll dissect this program like pros, and you'll see exactly how to create exciting Web media all by yourself.

In Chapter 11, *Photoshop, Meet ImageReady—Click!,* you're only a click away from having your image in Photoshop transported to ImageReady, and the bevy of optimization features covered in this chapter. Save the hi-fi, large images for Photoshop, but trust small JPEG and GIF files destined for e-mail or the Web to ImageReady, perhaps the most powerful stand-alone Web tool ever.

In Chapter 12, *Creating GIF Animations,* we create animated GIFs. Sorry. In this chapter, you will learn about how the Actions palette in ImageReady provides sample animation scripts that you use with your own images. You'll also learn three different eye-catching techniques for animation, as well as timing and optimization of these tiny gems.

Chapter 13, *Creating Image Maps,* shows you how to make multiple links—whether they are to other pages, other sites, or to a mail reader—all on the same graphic. Here's where ImageReady will write a few lines of HTML code for you. An image map is part illustration and part HTML—and you'll learn a little more of both in this chapter.

In Chapter 14, *Image Slicing and Rollovers,* two more New Media elements will become yours to add to Web sites. Image slicing is like image mapping, except the image is actually chopped up into pieces that you define, and any or all of the pieces can have a link, and any piece can be an animation. Rollovers are JavaScript elements that make the visitor to your site's cursor determine what image is displayed. It's cool and it's yours to use after you read this chapter.

Part V: Integrating the Whole Enchilada

It's nearly graduation time from this book, so the "big exams" are just around the corner. Don't worry, though; you are prepared by reading and working through the previous chapters. This book is not a school, however, and therefore we can make a round-up of all your newly acquired skills a challenge, and not a rote recitation of what I said on page 211, for example.

In Chapter 15, *If You Read Only One Chapter...*, almost every technique you've learned in the book is rolled into one easy, sophisticated assignment. I'd recommend that you *not* read this chapter first—it would be easier to step into a car that's going 75 mph. But chapter 15 sums up what you've learned, and reinforces your new skills by working through examples. It's a good refresher chapter.

Chapter 15½, *Is There Anything I Missed?*, doesn't have a lot to do with Photoshop so much as it has with the *way* you learn—what are your plans after the cover of *this* book is closed? Also, in this chapter I get to show off some of the really cool plug-ins I've found for Photoshop. You will find working demos of these programs on the Companion CD, and a few of the manufacturers have given us valuable coupons in the back of this book.

But Wait! There's more...

In the very, very back of the book is a CD. This is the Companion CD, which contains all the images and other files you use with the steps in any given chapter. There are four areas of the CD:

- **The Examples folder.** This is where all the resource files for the book assignments hang out. When you are asked in a chapter to load lugnutz.tif, you press Ctrl(⌘)+O (File, Open) and then scroll through the directory box until you find your CD drive, the Examples folder, the chapter number (such as Chap07), and finally, double-click on lugnutz.tif. And no, there is no such file as lugnutz.tif on the CD (but there *is* a nut&bolt.psd file).

- **The BOUTONS folder.** Gary and his spouse and co-conspirator, Barbara, have created in the spare time they do not have a wonderful collection of original typefaces for both Windows and the Macintosh, some seamless tiling images called Tilers (volume 4), and "Clipart for Photoshop." A whole bunch of neat 3D objects are perfectly masked on layers, so you can use 'em without having to first create a selection marquee.

  All of the contents of the BOUTONS folder are CharityWare. To find out what CharityWare is, and to comply with our licensed usage of the goods for public exhibition and for profit, please read the read_me.pdf file in the root of the BOUTONS folder.

- **The Programs folder.** It is here you will find limited editions of some of the funkiest, out-of-this-world plug-ins for Photoshop. If you read chapter 15½, you'll know exactly what I'm talking about.
- The **Reader4** folder. In this folder are Macintosh and Windows Adobe Acrobat Reader installation programs. I've used Acrobat technology quite heavly on the CD, so installing this reader is a sure way to get everything you paid for with this book.

Last (sigh) but certainly not least, "Where did those guys put the glossary?" Aha! The *Photoshop 5.5 Fundamentals* book has a 286-page glossary, but it doesn't add a millimeter to the thickness of the book because it's in Adobe Acrobat format, in the root of the Companion CD. Copy the p5fgloss.pdf file to your hard disk to make it run faster. There are links, full-color illustrations, and we think it's pretty handsomely organized.

No One is Perfekt

Forget the disclaimer in this book that says that the information is presented to you "as is." "As is" doesn't do you, the reader, any good if we've made a slip-up in this book, or other books by either of the Boutons. So we've created a branch of The Boutons' Web site that is exclusively devoted to corrections for all our books. The address is **http://www.boutons.com**, and when you get there, click on the Updates button. The corrections are posted as soon as we learn of an error and, as written on our site, the updates include text surrounding the error, so finding the error in the book is very easy. You might want to print the Updates page, fold the pages in half, and tuck them in the book.

All of this *does not* mean that New Riders and the author are going to leave corrections to their online format. We will get corrections into our books as soon as there is a future printing of a book. We simply want you to have the goods as soon as possible, and the Web makes this effort a reality.

About the CDs, Please!

If for some reason, the Companion CD in your book is dented, shaped like a triangle, or simply fails to read on your CD-ROM, please contact New Riders at (800) 571-5840 or go to www.newriders.com and click on the Contact button. Please have the ISBN number (0-7357-0928-9) of this book handy. Please *do not* contact Gary Bouton if your CD is broken. He does not own a warehouse, and will only pass your mail on to New Riders, so let's save a step in this unfortunate event.

It's for the Kid in All Of Us

More than anything else, I want you to have *fun* with this book. Fun is when you don't care that others stare at you when you giggle on the subway. Fun is when you can't wait to wake up your spouse and show her or him your latest creation. Fun is when you win a contest (this is how the author started his career in computer graphics). If it isn't fun, life's too short for it, right?

Electronic imaging is such a wonderful, magical thing that it's impossible to keep the child in us quiet. For that reason, many of the examples in this book are whimsical—they stretch reality a tad (okay, they stretch reality a lot), in the same way you'll learn to stretch a pixel or two, using Photoshop. I want to show you some of the fun *I've* had with a very serious product, and hope that perhaps I can kindle or fan the creative spark in you, as well.

So let the show begin...

PART I

Photoshop Basics

CHAPTER 1

Interface Preferences and Photoshop Options

Catchy title, huh? Okay, this is the "less than thrilling" part of the book, but *don't* gloss over it like an American Harvester parts catalog. Treat preferences and options like the specs, fuel, and options on the sports car of your dreams. And like a sports car (or any car, I've heard), you are not going anywhere without some gas.

So I will try very hard to make this chapter a gas.

Before You Install Photoshop

If there's a ghost of a chance that you have not yet installed Photoshop 5.5 plus ImageReady 2.0 on your machine...*stop right now!* And if you're already up and running with Photoshop, read on, and you might just decide to reinstall it.

By default, Photoshop and a lot of other software default to installing on your C drive, your "startup" or "primary" drive. The Adobe engineers have done this so they can feel fairly confident that every machine out there, Windows or Mac, has a primary drive—that Photoshop and ImageReady have a place to install.

What's *bad* about installing to your C drive is that every program wants to install in the primary drive. And your primary drive can be only so big. A lot of machines are coming prepartitioned: this means that a huge, say 23GB drive, is partitioned into 12 logical drives because the operating system can only handle a 2GB hard drive. So there are puh-lenty of places Photoshop can go other than your primary drive, where, by the way, printing jobs are spooled. And the hard drive spooling takes up a *lot* of hard disk space.

So when you install, choose a drive that has a lot of free space, and name the folder something succinct, such as PS55. Why do this when both the Mac and Windows can handle long file names? Because both the Mac and Windows have a 128-character limit to the path to an executable file. For example, D:/PS55 has five characters. On the other hand, there are 65 characters in D:/My all-time favorite programs/ Adobe/Photoshop 5.5 with ImageReady, and if you decide later that you want to create subfolders to contain work, it is conceivable that you will exceed the 128 character limit...and won't be able to write to disk where you'd *like* to write to disk!

Now that Photoshop and ImageReady are installed, you need to make sure they are optimized from a memory, a monitor-calibration, and a user-accessibility standpoint. Let's talk about displays first.

Files and Monitors Have Different Colors

This is bound to sound like a weird one to novices, but Adobe makes the distinction between color information as it's saved in a file, and color information as it's displayed on a monitor.

There are so many different makes and models of scanners, PCs, and output devices, that one would rightly think that there's no way you could ever get everything in synch. But at least the effort has been made by the International Color Consortium (ICC) to establish what are called *profiles* in Photoshop. *Profiles* are nuggets of information about a digital file, a monitor, and other devices, that in theory will translate accurately to someone else's system as long as they have the same color profiles installed.

In fact, Photoshop provides so many utilities that it begs the question, "How far do I take, and how much time do I spend on, this calibration stuff?"

note

Although this has probably been fixed (the author was working off an early copy of Photoshop 5.5), you might have a problem launching Photoshop if you install it on a drive other than the primary drive.

I must thank Mr. Shigenori Ohira at Adobe Systems for finding a patch for this problem.

First, find Cooltype.dll and remove it from your Photoshop folder. Hang on to it, though. Then, find a Cooltype.dll from a previous version of Photoshop that might be on your system (such as version 5.0.2), and put a copy of it in the Photoshop 5.5 folder. Then launch Photoshop, press Ctrl(⌘)+K to go to Preferences, and choose Plug-Ins & scratch disk sizes. In the First scratch disk box, choose a drive other than your primary drive. Chose Photoshop, and then swap back the Cooltype.dll files.

As far as jumping to ImageReady from Photoshop, you may have a problem because the Helpers folder is not in Program Files/ Adobe/Helpers when you install to a drive other than C. So what you do is locate the Helpers file under the Photoshop folder on drive x there, and drag an alias (a shortcut) to Photoshop 5.5 into the Helpers folder and put square braces around the name for the program, à la [Photoshop 5.5]. Then drag an alias (shortcut) from ImageReady to the Helpers folder and put curly braces around it, as in {ImageReady2}.

You're all set now, and again, I hope this note is not necessary after the shipping version has been released.

My own philosophy (which you'll be constantly subjected to in this book) is that you fix only what is broken. Chances are that you created or acquired images before you bought Photoshop, and you've probably tweaked them so they look good on your monitor. The real trick then, is how to avail yourselves of this new ICC technology without messing up the images that were created before the advent of ICC profiles.

The very first thing that happens when you launch Photoshop is that the Color Calibration and Gamma Utility pop up. Although it seems inviting to proceed with this cyber-eye exam, my advice is to hit Cancel until you know what you're goofing with. Contrary to Adobe's literature, I'd like us to start with the RGB Setup dialog box first, because this might very well be the *only* place in Photoshop where you need to synchronize colors.

Color calibration begins here with your monitor and the way it handles RGB color space images in Photoshop. The following steps show you how to tell Photoshop how to display images when an image's color mode is RGB (the most common type of digital images you will come across; there's more in chapter 5 about color space).

> ## *Profound Wisdom #1:*
>
> **The colors based on digital images are all relative.**
>
> This means that the image you scan probably won't look the same as it does displayed on a monitor, and it's pretty certain that the image as it's displayed on the monitor will not look like a color inkjet print of the work.
>
> This is not all bad news, because Adobe has done something in Photoshop to strive for color consistency across different mediums. Read on.

note

We need to assume that you're beginning the calibration adventures after the monitor has been on for at least half an hour, and there is ambient light in the room, but nothing bouncing directly off your monitor, like a tensor light or birthday candles or anything.

Defining Your Monitor in the RGB Setup

1. Choose File, Color Settings, RGB Setup. The default for Windows machines should be Adobe RGB (1998) in the RGB field, and Apple RGB for the Macintosh. Adobe RGB (1998) was created to improve upon smallRGB (sRGB) that came with Photoshop 5.0. The color space is a vast improvement over previous RGB settings.

2. For Windows users, type **1.8** in the Gamma field, as shown in figure 1.1. For Macintosh users, I would enter **2.0** to **2.2**, depending on the age of your monitor.

   I realize I'm going to get a lot of flack about my gamma recommendations, especially because Adobe's documentation insists that Windows gamma is 2.2 and Mac gamma is 1.8. It's actually the other way around, folks, and I know this from experimenting with both my Mac and my PC, side by side.

Macintosh display has a higher luminance, and therefore a higher midrange (gamma). Mac pictures appear darker on a PC because PC gamma is lower. And PC images, conversely, appear washed out on a properly tuned Mac. And I wouldn't be writing this if I didn't spend a whole Saturday going through SIGGRAPH and other online documents to confirm what I'm writing.

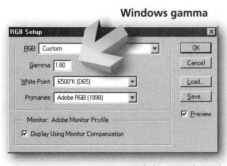

Windows gamma

Adobe RGB (1998)

Large color space, well-suited for images that will be converted to CMYK. Ideal for print production work. Some colors can't be accurately reproduced on all monitors.

FIGURE 1.1   *As soon as you enter a unique Gamma, the RGB field will switch from the set-ting you chose to "Custom." This is okay, though—you'll save this configura-tion to a unique file.*

3. Leave the White Point alone (because you might not know the White Point, and the default appears to work fine with no color casting).

4. In the Primaries field, choose the primary color combination that best describes your monitor settings. I chose Adobe RGB (1998) again, because this is a wide color space, and my monitor (an Ilyama VisionMaster Pro 17) has a reputation for being a very accurate proofing device—so it should be able to handle a wide number of colors (*color space*). Macintosh users should probably use Apple RGB. Adobe has worked with Apple longer than with Microsoft, and Adobe pretty much has the specs on Mac hardware defined.

5. Check the Display Using Monitor Compensation box. This option changes the way images are displayed in Photoshop, but it *does not change the image informa-tion in any way*. Adobe does have a facility that will actually convert image data to make it look right onscreen, and we'll touch on this in a moment.

6. Click on Save and then save your settings to a safe place on your hard disk. Name the profile MyPhotoshop55icm.icm (Windows users need the extension), or

something that'll remind you what this file is and does. Close the dialog box by clicking on OK.

For all the high-techy stuff we're going to get into to ensure that you know, fundamentally, what to do about calibration, I'm also tossing in a helping of common sense and "do what you eyes tell you to do." All the empirical data on earth isn't going to help you if you don't need help, or if there isn't any calibration mismatch.

Performing a Comparison

We haven't gotten to memory handling yet, but the following stunt is going to require that you have both Photoshop and an image-viewing utility open at the same time. This means—for both Mac and Windows—that you need at least 32MB of RAM to support Photoshop, additional RAM to support your OS, and additional RAM to support the loading of a small image-viewing application. If you have 64MB of physical RAM, everything is cool.

First, I am very happy to report that I did not need to perform additional calibration to my system because an image displayed in Photoshop looks identical to the same image loaded into an early version of Paint Shop Pro. In figure 1.2 (okay, okay, it's not in color), you can get the sense that Photoshop 5.5 is displaying the image almost exactly as Paint Shop Pro is, and I've used PSP for years to get accurate color inkjet prints.

To capture the screen used in figure 1.2, I pressed PrintScreen in Windows 98, and then dumped the clipboard into a new image window in Photoshop. Macintosh users can do the same thing: Press Command, Control, Shift, and 3 to send the current view of the desktop to the clipboard.

What I did after this was to press F8 to display the Info Palette, and I clicked the eyedropper in each image in exactly the same place. Consistently (I did this about five times in different locations), the Paint Shop Pro image was either identical in brightness, or was $\frac{1}{256}$ (one tick) off—certainly acceptable in most situations. The visual information being displayed was virtually the same in two different programs, so I guess there's no real disparity between image file colors and monitor reproduction of the colors.

PROFOUND WISDOM #2:

It is better to change viewing conditions than to change image data.

If your color calibrations are off on your PC, you can always correct them. But if you correct a picture to look right when your PC is miscalibrated, that image will never look the same again, because you physically changed the colors of the pixels in the image.

FIGURE 1.2   *Do some comparative shopping before you mess around with further calibrations in Photoshop. Does your current configuration provide you with a view that is consistent with other applications you've had for a while, or is it way off?*

To sum up this section, the RGB Setup might be all the setting up you need to do to make Photoshop a rewarding experience. If you're having problems with color consistency, check out the following section as I take apart the mysterious Adobe Gamma Panel and the Color Management Wizard (called the Assistant, on the Macintosh).

Accessing the Adobe Gamma Control Panel

Macintosh users are more accustomed to global changes made to gamma by Photoshop. Gamma, *verrrry* loosely defined, is the breadth of the midtones in an image, where the most visual detail takes place (such as facial features and nature scenes). Because the Macintosh does not use a "workspace" metaphor for Photoshop, whenever you make tone or color changes you generally see everything on the desktop change, too. This is called a global change: In addition to the application, everything else you see onscreen changes.

Windows users might need to get used to this phenomenon, because when you use the Adobe Gamma Control Panel, this sucker is going to change the gamma of your desktop and of every application in which you work. If this sounds like a bad idea to you, you're not obliged to tap into the Gamma Control Panel before you work in Photoshop and ImageReady. But for both Macintosh and Windows users who want a calibration system to control midtones in images, this one is free, and it goes something like this:

Setting Up the Adobe Gamma Control Panel

1. Click on Help, Color Management, and then click on Open Adobe Gamma. You have your choice of seeing several screens of options, or knocking off the gamma calibration in one fell swoop. Click on the Control Panel button, and then click on Next. All the options are neatly arranged and the Wizard can take the weekend off.

2. Adobe has placed a lot of ICC profiles for gamma in the System/Colors folder. If you spot your exact make and model of monitor, you might as well choose it. In figure 1.3, you can see the Adobe Gamma Control Panel, and if you click on Load (near the number 1), you'll get the directory box that contains all the profiles.

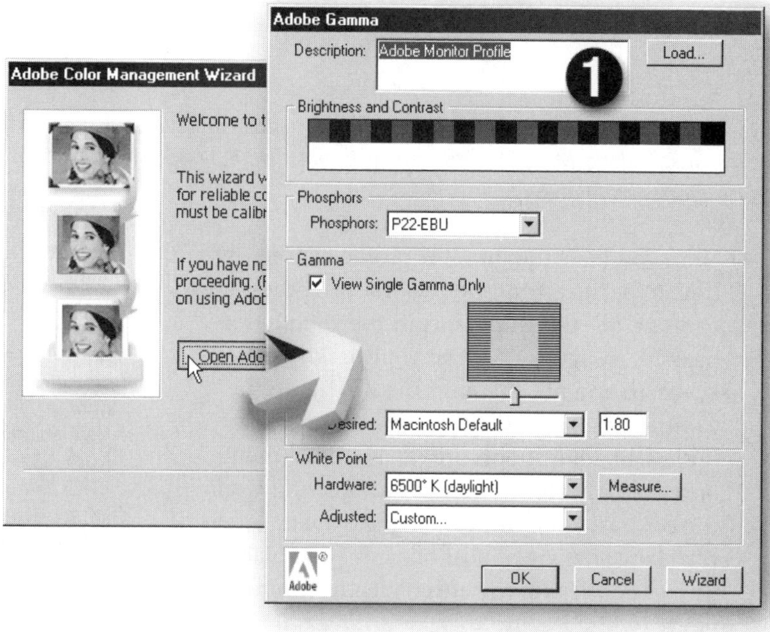

FIGURE 1.3   *Click on Open Adobe Gamma, choose the Control Panel button, and check out the Monitor Profiles that Photoshop has added to your system.*

3. If none of the monitor ICC profiles matches your monitor, leave the Description field at Adobe Monitor Profile. This is the default, and it works quite well, actually. However, if you want to thoroughly investigate the Monitor Profile folder, press the down arrow key to go through the profiles, as shown in figure 1.4. The Macintosh has all profile names completely spelled out, but Windows users will hit a few 8.3-named files (an eight-character name with a three-character extension). Look at the bottom of the dialog box, and if it says "The selected file is not a Monitor Profile," keep pressing the down arrow key.

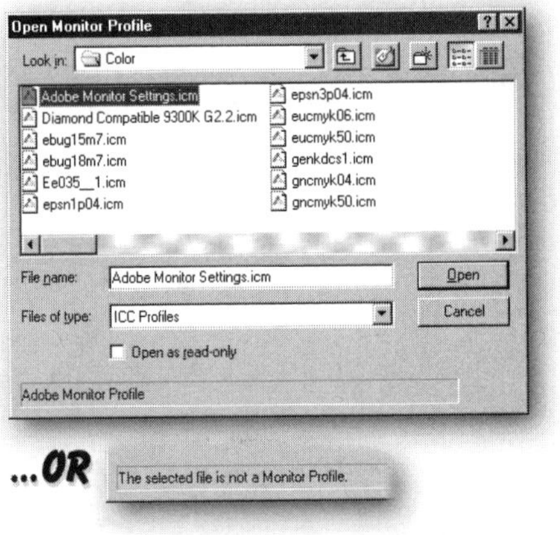

FIGURE 1.4   *You might or might not find the exact Monitor Profile of your monitor in this area. Adobe Monitor Settings.icm is the default, and works well, however.*

4. Once you have the monitor profile chosen, it's time to balance your monitor for brightness and contrast. See the strip beneath the Description box? It's in figure 1.5. Take your hands off the keyboard and put them on the Brightness/Contrast knobs on the front of your monitor (unless all adjustments are made from a menu onscreen; my monitor has no knobs). Now, turn the contrast knob until the lighter boxes between the black ones are almost but not quite black. Do this while keeping the area beneath the checks a perfect white.

tip

Take frequent glances away from your monitor while you do this stuff. Our technical editor informs us that the human eye and brain can perform adaptive chromacity. The HumanSpeak explanation of this is that our eyes sometimes lie to us after they've been tuned into a scene or a certain color for too long.

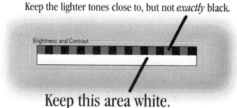

Keep the lighter tones close to, but not *exactly* black.

Keep this area white.

**Adjust the Brightness/Contrast dials on your monitor, and
not anywhere onscreen.**

FIGURE 1.5   *Keep the white white, and try to make the lighter checks almost, but not quite,
black.*

5. Phosphors? You can leave this box as is because the default setting will probably
   not impact on your monitor's color accuracy. But if you own an Apple monitor or
   one of many other makes or models, the manufacturers have turned to SONY to
   make the tube, so the correct selection in many cases is Trinitron, as shown in figure 1.6. Check your monitor's specs to make sure.

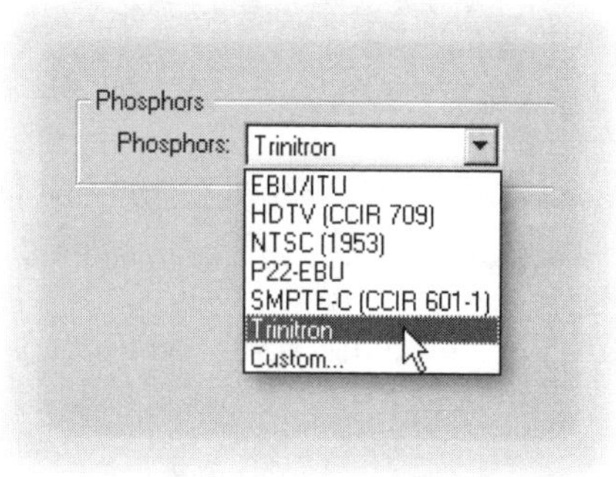

FIGURE 1.6   *SONY makes tubes for many monitor manufacturers. Check your monitor documentation; if it's a Trinitron tube, choose this setting from the Phosphors
drop-down list.*

6. Moving down a little on the dialog box, you have the Gamma knobs and dials.
   Now, you can set the gamma of each of the primary light sources a monitor displays by unchecking the View Single Gamma Only box here. My opinion is that
   if one or more of the channels is out of synch with the others, the monitor was
   either shipped to you damaged, or it's a 10-year-old monitor. You should be able
   to get correct gamma for display using the single box. Drag the slider ever so gently back and forth until you think you have the ideal density for the midtones on

your monitor, and the solid color in the center of the box matches the lines (if you squint a lot at the box). Performing this step is a lot easier when an image that you are very familiar with is loaded on the desktop; you then calibrate to the image.

7. The Desired drop-down list has Macintosh Default, Windows Default, and Custom. I believe Adobe has slipped up here and is titling the gamma reading incorrectly. In figure 1.7, you can see that I have chosen the Macintosh default on a Windows machine and the gamma, Adobe tells you, is 1.8. Guess what? Windows gamma is generally 1.8, and Macintosh gamma is 2.0 to 2.2, the amount specified for the Windows default. Advice? Do what your eyes tell you is right. I'm running Photoshop with the Macintosh default of 1.8 gamma, and my images are consistent across applications that can handle bitmaps.

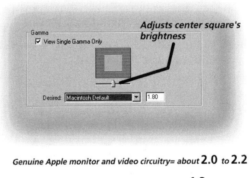

Genuine Apple monitor and video circuitry= about **2.0** to **2.2**

Average PC monitor and video circuitry= about **1.8**

FIGURE 1.7   *Let your eyes be the judge as to how dense you want the midtones to be in an image.*

8. The Hardware White Point is a utility within the Gamma Control that enables you to choose the most neutral color for the White Point. The utility negates color casting. This is another preference that you should leave alone if the default settings look good to you (6500° Kelvin is natural lighting—not really warm or cold on objects). Click on Measure, and then choose the most neutral-colored box onscreen until the utility has determined the closest match to your preference—it then ends the choice game onscreen, as shown in figure 1.8, and returns you to the dialog box.

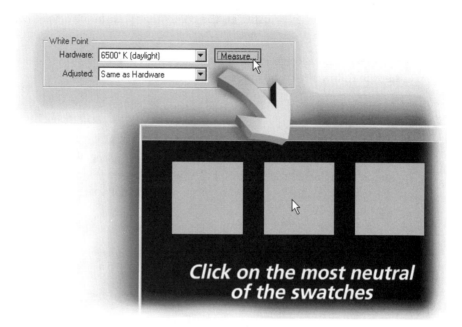

FIGURE 1.8 *Look carefully at the color casting on the neutral-colored boxes, and then choose a box by clicking on it.*

This concludes the gamma adjustment. Every time you start your computer, the Adobe Gamma Utility will set the screen to the gamma you've chosen.

Color Management

Color Management is different from the gamma calibrations you performed. If you want to allow Photoshop to run the color management show for you, click on Next in the Adobe Color Management Wizard dialog box, click on the Photoshop 5.0 default settings button, click on Next, read what Photoshop intends to do about color management, and then click on Finish. Although this sounds like a real time-saver, if you read the text in the second dialog box (the one that scrolls), you'll see that Photoshop will now use sRGB as the color space for

note

If you're happy with the colors onscreen, and your color prints match your screen fairly well, *skip over* the following section—you won't use Adobe Color Management.

Not using color calibration might draw stares from fellow artists, or it might not. The important thing is that once you've specified color controls, it is very hard to disable them permanently. So think twice before you take the plunge.

the screen. As mentioned earlier, this stands for **s**implified or **s**mall RGB color space. You might not even be using all the colors that your monitor has available to you. Who wants that?

If you want to calibrate your monitor to include the widest color space, here are the steps to follow:

Using Color Management

1. In the Adobe Color Management Wizard (Assistant), click on the Customize for prepress and other uses button, as shown in figure 1.9, and then click on Next. This choice enables you to work in the widest color space Adobe has to offer in Photoshop.

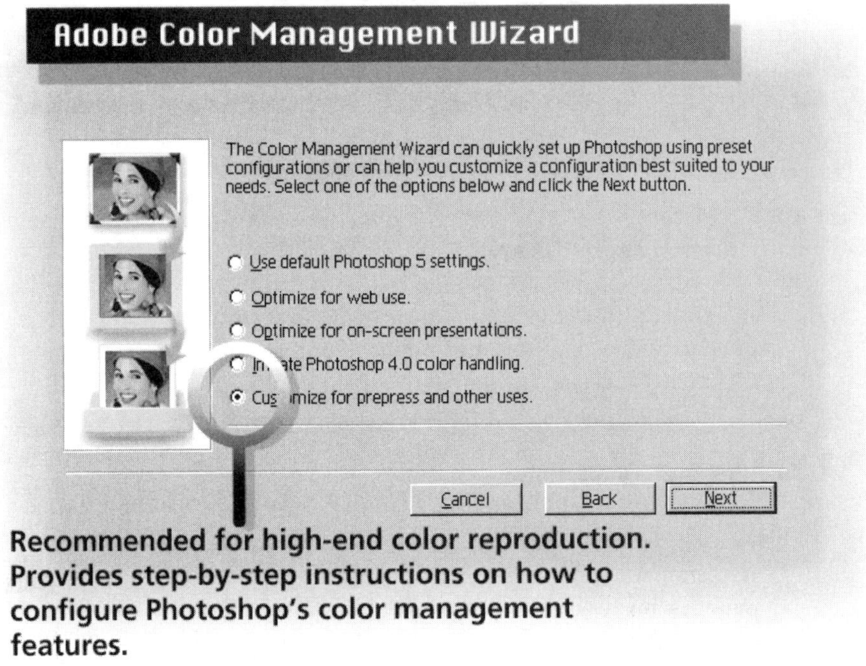

Adobe Color Management Wizard

The Color Management Wizard can quickly set up Photoshop using preset configurations or can help you customize a configuration best suited to your needs. Select one of the options below and click the Next button.

○ Use default Photoshop 5 settings.

○ Optimize for web use.

○ Optimize for on-screen presentations.

○ In. ate Photoshop 4.0 color handling.

● Cus mize for prepress and other uses.

Cancel   Back   Next

Recommended for high-end color reproduction. Provides step-by-step instructions on how to configure Photoshop's color management features.

FIGURE 1.9   *The prepress option gives you the opportunity to work in a color space so large, a few monitors out there might not be able to display all the colors in the color space.*

2. In the next box, you're asked to choose an RGB color space from a drop-down list. Windows users should probably choose Adobe RGB (1998), as shown in figure 1.10, because it shows colors very faithfully onscreen, and Macintosh users can choose from Apple RGB settings that correspond to their monitor size.

Adobe Color Management Wizard

Choose a working RGB space from the profiles below. The space you choose will determine the range of colors that can be represented in your documents.

Adobe RGB (1998)

Adobe RGB (1998)

Large color space, well-suited for images that will be converted to CMYK. Ideal for print production work. Some colors can't be accurately reproduced on all monitors.

Cancel   Back   Next

FIGURE 1.10   *For Windows users, Adobe RGB (1998) is a very good choice for monitor color space. The Macintosh has several color spaces designed exactly for your type of monitor.*

3. Click on Next, and the Color Management utility asks what you want to do with mismatched files. By "mismatched files," Photoshop means that Adobe RGB (1998) is new and unique, and that images you've had or created in the past almost certainly will not match the new color space. Click the Ask me what to do with mismatched files button. This way, Photoshop won't automatically convert an image you load into the new color space. Click on Next.

4. Like step 3, Photoshop wants to know what you want to do with images that have no ICC color tag within the file (which are most images on earth, because this ICC stuff is new). Click on the Ask me what to do when opening untagged files button, and then click on Next (see fig. 1.11). The next screen tells you you've finished, and you should click on the Finish button.

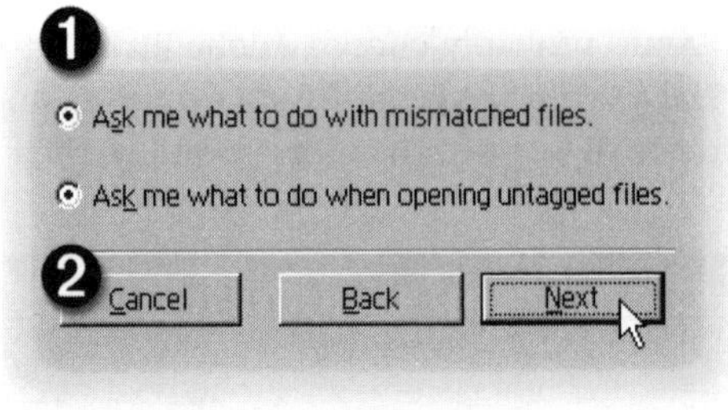

Figure 1.11   *Always have Photoshop ask you how you want color mismatching handled.*

If you're unhappy with what you see onscreen, you can always run the Color Management utility again, and choose a different option, such as Use default Photoshop 5 settings.

Now that your color calibration is securely stowed away, it's time to address the subject of memory—the physical RAM on your computer. Adobe has bent over backwards to make Photoshop work on even the most RAM-starved systems, but that's not the end of the story. Read on, and you'll see where to set up memory preferences, and what numbers you'll want to use.

Defining Memory

Photoshop requires not only a goodly amount of physical RAM, but also hard disk space where it puts bits and pieces of processes and images that will be used again. But wait—there's more! There are some things that Photoshop will and will not let you do, particularly on the Macintosh with virtual memory. Let's run down a list of things that will make Photoshop happy, because when *it's* happy, *you* will be happy<g>!

Defining the Recommended Amount of Physical RAM

The box in which Photoshop comes, and the spec sheets all tell you that 32MB of RAM is the minimum required amount to run Photoshop 5.5 only (forget ImageReady). This statement is true, if somewhat colored. Unlike other manufacturers who might make outrageous claims for minimum memory, Photoshop *will* indeed perform on 32MB of RAM. The only problem is that you will probably not be *happy* with Photoshop's performance with 32MB of physical RAM. One of the engineers (thanks, Marc!) at Adobe took the time to explain to me the following:

1. 32MB of RAM will keep Photoshop alive on both the Macintosh and Windows.

2. 64MB of RAM will make Photoshop sing on both the Macintosh and Windows.

3. 96MB dedicated to Photoshop and ImageReady will make the applications run fast enough on most computers.

So what we're saying here is that your system needs about 128MB or RAM to work with ease and comfort while both ImageReady and Photoshop are running. Why? Because your operating system needs RAM, too.

RAM goes for between $1 and $2 per MB as of this writing, and I'd suggest that if you've got the pocket change, buy two 128MB RAM modules, because you'll need extra memory in the future (at least the past 10 years have proven that to me), and frame or file any 64MB modules that might be in the sockets—or better yet, donate the modules to a charity or give them to a friend. You can't mix memory modules on computers: It's 32, 64, 128, or 256MB modules, straight across the board when you install memory in the slots in the computer's banks.

Windows does not handle memory in the same way as the Macintosh. On the Mac, you specify how much RAM is dedicated to an application by clicking on the application's icon and then choosing About this application from the Apple menu (see figure 1.12). Type **98000**(K)in the Preferred size box. Memory is actually 1024 Kilobytes per MB, not 1000 (we tend to round off stuff with computers), so a setting of 96MB would actually be 96×1.024, or 98.3MB.

For Windows users, you set the amount of memory for Photoshop in the Memory & Image Cache Preferences box in Photoshop (see figure 1.12). But before you do that, right-click on My Computer, choose Properties from the context menu, choose Performance, and then see how much RAM is on your computer, and *without* other applications running, see how many system resources are free.

It's recommended that you give Photoshop about 60 to 70 percent of your system resources in the Memory & Image Cache dialog box in Photoshop (press Ctrl+K for Preferences). Adobe says that NT machines might work even better with less than 60 percent resources dedicated to Photoshop, because Windows NT handles memory differently.

tip

Naturally, you don't want to memory-starve Photoshop, but if you are going to have an application open in addition to Photoshop, load the other application first. Photoshop will yield to the current available memory a lot better than other applications do. I know this for a fact after trying to load MS-Word *after* I loaded Photoshop!

Loading ImageReady, however, from the button on the toolbox in Photoshop does *not* impact on your system's memory if you have the allocations set up correctly.

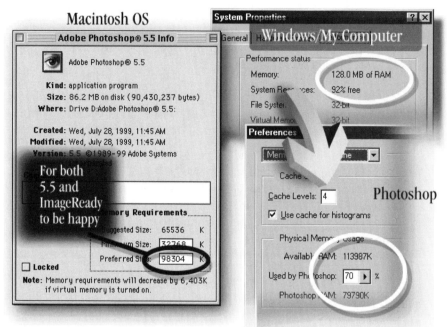

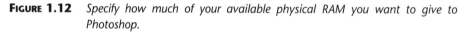

FIGURE 1.12 *Specify how much of your available physical RAM you want to give to Photoshop.*

Setting Up a Scratch Disk

A *scratch disk* is sort of like a temp file, except it contains only Photoshop info. You need exactly as much or more scratch disk space on the hard disk as you have memory. For example, if you defined your scratch disk size to be 64MB and have 128MB onboard your computer, Photoshop will only use 64 MB of your physical RAM.

Because hard disks are so cheap these days, I've created a Photoshop scratch disk drive on my machine. It's 1GB in size, and I never put any files on it. The drive is uncompressed and regularly defragmented for speed. Once you've decided on a scratch disk location, go to Preferences, Plug-Ins & Scratch Disks. There are four hard drive locations where you can assign scratch disks. And Photoshop will use these drive spaces when it runs out of memory, beginning with the first scratch disk you assign—so make the first drive a *big* one.

Restart Photoshop, and in the next section I'll show you how to tell what's going on under the hood without going to Photoshop Preferences all the time.

Checking Performance and Other Photoshop Issues

Adobe has given you a handy measure of several performance parameters right within the workspace. In Windows, what used to be called the Document Sizes controls are located on the left of the status bar, and on the Macintosh, the controls are on the bottom left of the current image's scroll bar.

If you click on the triangle next to the read-outs on the status bar (the scroll on the image window), you can specify what type of info is constantly being displayed. If you choose Scratch Sizes, the left number tells you how much of the scratch disk(s) is being used, and the right number tells you how much memory is allocated to Photoshop. Check out figure 1.13.

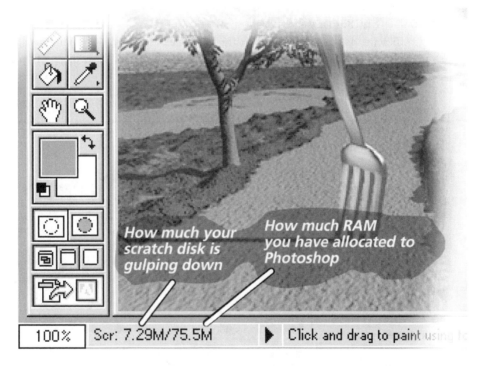

How much your scratch disk is gulping down

How much RAM you have allocated to Photoshop

100%   Scr: 7.29M/75.5M   ▶ Click and drag to paint

FIGURE 1.13   *You have a handy-dandy resource meter in Photoshop, right in the corner.*

I don't think you'll ever encounter a situation where the scratch disk size is 0%, but if the number stays at a steady low number, you can work with ease. If the scratch disk figure ever gets close to as large as the hard disk space you've allocated to Photoshop, you're in big trouble and heading for a crash. If you don't have a Mega-gizmo of RAM on your machine, practice a few of the following tips for keeping scratch disk sizes small:

- Use Edit, Purge, All, or Edit, Purge, (only one of the items that you do not need, such as the clipboard). This relieves your overall system from holding data you don't use in memory or on disk.

- Press Ctrl(⌘)+S at points in your assignment when you're committed to the way the image looks. When you save a file, backup copies on the scratch disk are deleted.

- Limit the number of Undos on the History palette. The default number is 20, and you specify this on the History palette in Photoshop by clicking on the menu flyout and choosing History Options. Do you really need to trace back a goof after 20 steps? I'd give the History palette 7 to 10 saved states and decrease my resource requirements for this valuable tool by 50%.

Photoshop Efficiency

Efficiency is another choice on the Document Sizes pop-up menu, as shown in figure 1.14. If you choose Efficiency, you'll be able to tell how often Photoshop needs to go out to scratch disk for data. I took this screen capture right after loading Photoshop and opening a window. So my efficiency read-out is at 100%—Photoshop's not writing to disk at all because I haven't done anything yet.

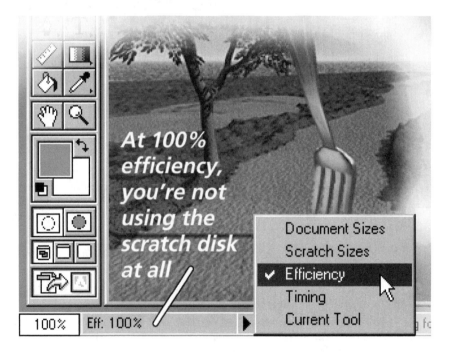

FIGURE 1.14   *Efficiency is a good setting to leave the Document Sizes box, because it tells you how clogged up your scratch disk might be getting.*

RAM is always better than hard disk as a savings place, because the speed of access is an order of magnitude in difference.

Okay, we did color management and memory. Now, it's on to some *fun* settings you can apply to Photoshop's tools and workspace.

Customizing Your Workspace

Upon opening Photoshop 5.5 for the first time, it looks like an apartment that has been burglarized, as shown in figure 1.15. Yeah, I can't believe all the cool tools and palettes, but what a mess! Adobe has no idea who you are, so it's done the next best thing for user customization—making it real easy for you to change things around.

Figure 1.15   *With so many palettes showing, there's hardly any room left for the image.*

A Hot-Key Cheat Sheet & Rearranging the Palettes

This section is part one of a two-parter. You'll see how to quickly access the most frequently used palettes by changing their grouping and location, and the second part shows you how to call these new things to the workspace with only a keystroke.

First of all, here's a cheat sheet that tells you how to hide and display the palettes and other things in Photoshop. This cheat sheet will change only slightly after you assign new keystrokes to things:

Key	Function
F1	Reserved for **help**, and it would be bad to change this guy.
F2	It's open, and you can assign anything you like to it.
F3	Same deal as F2. It's open, and you can assign anything you like to it.
F4	Assigned to **Paste Contents of clipboard as new layer**. I gotta ask ya, "What's wrong with Ctrl(⌘)+V?" This F key could be reassigned to something more useful, like the Select, Modify, Expand command.
F5	Assigned to **Show/Hide Brushes**. This F key isn't exactly necessary, but you'll see shortly that the Brushes palette can be moved for quicker access, instead of taking away its F key.
F6	Assigned to **Show/Hide Color**. Let's leave this one as is.
F7	Assigned to **Show/Hide Layers**. This is probably the first or second most important palette in Photoshop, so memorize F7=Layers!
F8	Assigned to **Show/Hide Info**. I like this keyboard shortcut right where it is. See upcoming Tip on a trick you can use the Info palette for.
F9	Assigned to **Show/Hide Actions**. Let's not tamper with this one.
F10	As with F2 and F3, it's open.
F11	This one's an airplane (and it's open).
F12	Assigned to **Revert to previously saved image**. I think that, given its position near the top center of the keyboard, you can make a terrible mistake with this keyboard shortcut—you can accidentally undo editing work and not know why. As you learn about less destructive commands, you might want to switch this one. I learned the hard way; I've got my screen-capture program set to go off when I press F12!

Now that we know which F key brings which palette to the list, let's see how we can bring together palettes with similar functions. Let's face it: You're going to use the Brushes palette a lot more often than the Swatches and Color—and the Options palette is dragging around dead weight with Info and Navigator tied to it.

I'm going to show you what we might call the Photoshop 3.0.5 classic arrangement of palettes. Version 3 had the palettes grouped dead-on, so you could work very efficiently. Follow these steps and I'll provide explanations for why you're doing this stuff along the way:

Grouping Your Palettes

1. Put an image in the workspace; it doesn't matter what image it is, but some of the options in Photoshop are not available when there's no image in the workspace.

2. Press F6 to get the Brushes/Colors/Swatches palette onscreen, and then drag the Brushes title away from the grouped palette so it is a stand-alone palette.

3. Press F8 to display the Info/Options/Navigator palette.

4. Drag the Options title on top of the Brushes palette, as shown in figure 1.16, and then let go. You now have a Brushes/Options palette, which will cover 90% of your painting needs, and can be called simply by double-clicking on a painting tool. No F keys to remember. Pretty high-tech, huh?

tip

Suppose you're the kinda guy or gal who needs to globally change units of measure from pixels to inches and back again. One short way is to show the rulers, double-click on them, and then choose the units from the Preference box. Then close the box and hide the rulers.

You can also do this: Press F8 to display the Info palette, click on the plus sign next to the XY position markers, and choose units. Then close the palette. I think this second way is quicker.

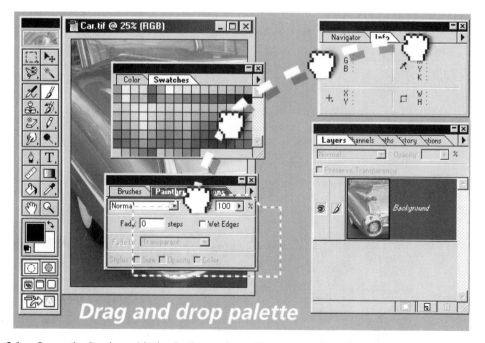

Drag and drop palette

FIGURE 1.16   *Group the Brushes with the Options palette. Chances are that whenever you need a paint tool, you'll need both palettes to customize the way you work with the tool.*

5. I think that the History and the Actions on the Layers palette is simply too much. Layers, Channels, and Paths are all ways of describing the outline of a shape, while Actions and History are not even remotely selection or painting tools. I say drag the History palette off the Layers palette, and group it with the Actions palette. F9 will still call the Actions palette (the History palette has no hot key), so this arrangement has uncongested the Layers palette, and you don't have to memorize anything additional.

6. This leaves the Info palette attached to the Navigator palette. The Navigator palette is only for times when you want to edit things at 1:1 and they are larger than your monitor can display. In other words, it's good for zooming around an image window, but you can bop around simply by holding the Spacebar to use the Hand tool for changing views. I say drag the Navigator palette off the Info palette, and access it from the Window main menu if you need it, or assign a hot key to it (we have four empty F keys).

We'll get to the F key assignments in a moment, but look at figure 1.17 for a moment. You can see the whole image, the Layers palette is showing thumbnails at maximum size (I'll show you how to do this later), and about anything you'd need to edit this image is right in front of you—*and this is a 640×480–pixel screen resolution*! Imagine how much more space you'd have with an 800×600 monitor viewing resolution!

FIGURE 1.17   *Everything you need at your fingertips. This is the way to work in Photoshop.*

Using the Actions Palette to Make New Hot Keys

note

If you become unhappy about the way I've recommended that the palettes are configured, press Ctrl(⌘)+K, and then click on the Reset Palette Locations To Default button in the General Preferences dialog box.

In addition to eliminating repetitive tasks, the Actions palette enables you to assign any of the F keys to a specific command in Photoshop. Now I personally hold a grudge against Adobe for taking away my Brightness/Contrast hot key and assigning it to the Color Balance command—Ctrl(⌘)+B has not been the same since. And I'm totally kidding if this has any impact on my professional relationship with Adobe Systems. But you know what? Instead of clumsily roaming through menus to get to the Brightness/Contrast command, I'm going to show you how to call up the command in one keystroke.

Here's how you use the Actions palette to do some keyboard enhancements:

Creating Hot Keys

1. Press F9 to display the Actions palette. Click on the Create new set icon. You can look to figure 1.18 for exactly where you click and type in these next four steps. In the Create New Set dialog box, type **my hot keys** in the text field and then press Enter (Return). The "my hot keys" set is the current set; any action you create will be located in this set.

2. Click on the menu flyout on the Actions palette and choose New Action. In the New Action dialog box, type **Brightness/Contrast** in the Name field, make sure that My Hot Keys is chosen for the current set, choose F11 from the drop-down list, and then press Record.

3. Brightness/Contrast immediately appears on the Actions palette as an action, as shown in #3 in figure 1.18. *Take caution not to touch* any of the controls in the interface, because you are in recording mode. Choose Insert Menu Item from the menu flyout on the Actions palette.

4. Type the first few letters of **Bri**ghtness, and then click on Find. As you can see in figure 1.18, Photoshop guessed correctly, and the Brightness/Contrast command is now linked to the F11 key. Click on OK. Then click on the Stop recording button on the Actions palette. You can close the palette now.

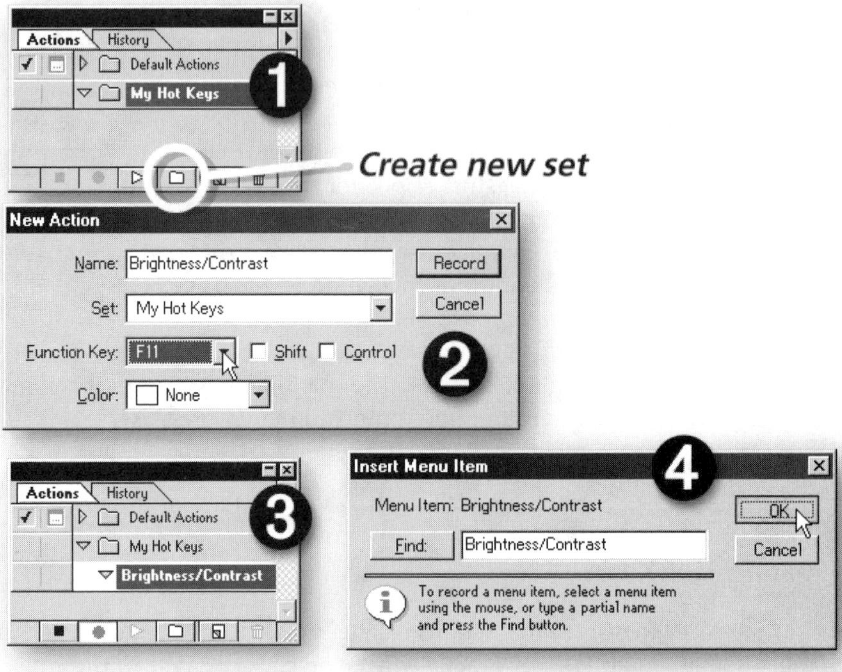

Create new set

FIGURE 1.18   *Creating a hot key for any command takes four steps. Why not try it?*

By the way, the New Action dialog box allows modifier keys to be used in combination with F keys. So now you know how to add the Variations command, for example, to a hot key—it can be Shift+F11. There are lots of commands you will use as you grow accustomed to Photoshop. There's no reason why you shouldn't spend about five minutes putting everything you'll be using within finger's reach.

Easy-Reading Thumbnails

The thumbnails that are on the Layers/Channels/Paths palette can be hard to see, especially when you have a complex scene with many layers going on. To specify where you want no thumbnail on a title on the palette, or an illegible one, a more sensible one, or a gigantic one, all you do is click on the palette's menu flyout, and choose Palette Options for all three of the palettes, as shown in figure 1.19.

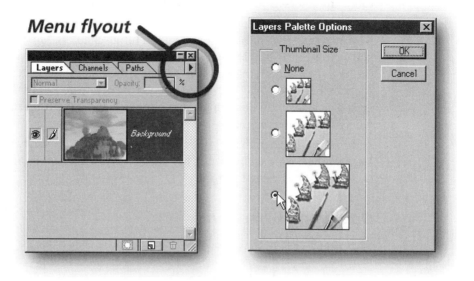

FIGURE 1.19   *If you're working at high screen resolutions, you might want to increase the size of the thumbnail images on the Layers/Channels/Paths palettes.*

Choosing Masking Options

The one thing that goofs up Photoshop newcomers the most is the terminology affixed to saved selections. The Quick Mask option (which you'll use in chapter 3) is exactly the kind of thing I'm talking about. Quick—what is a mask? Does it protect the area underneath, or does it select it and protect everything *except* the selection?

The wise-aleck answer is, "yes." The Quick Mask feature can either protect *or* expose an image area, and it's up to you as to what you're more comfortable defining Quick Mask as. In figure 1.20, you can see what the Quick Mask Options box looks like: You summon the box by double-clicking on the Quick Mask button at the bottom of the toolbox. Let's see here now, the first option says:

- Color Indicates: Masked Areas or Selected Areas, depending on which button you click. I have a strong preference for letting "color" indicate selected areas. In other words, wherever I apply Quick Mask tint, when I go back to Standard editing mode, the marquee selection is based on where I painted, and not where I *didn't* paint. It's simply more intuitive, right?

- Next, you get to pick a color and an opacity at which the Quick Mask tint is displayed in the image. For those of you who've never worked with Quick Mask, it's simply another "state" for a marquee selection. Quick Mask overlay will not touch the colors in your image, although it might *look* at first as though you're messing up your image.

Now, we have some tutorials coming up in future chapters. In one of them I ask you to select a fire hydrant. The default color for Quick Mask is red, and so's the fire hydrant. I guess it makes sense to change the color of the Quick Mask! Make it obnoxious green by clicking on the color swatch to go to Photoshop's Color Picker, or make it an obnoxious off-white (pick any color from the obnoxious family of colors except red).

As far as opacity goes, this is your call. I generally use 75% opacity for the Quick Mask so there is no ambiguity as to where an area's masked or only looks a little funky in the original picture.

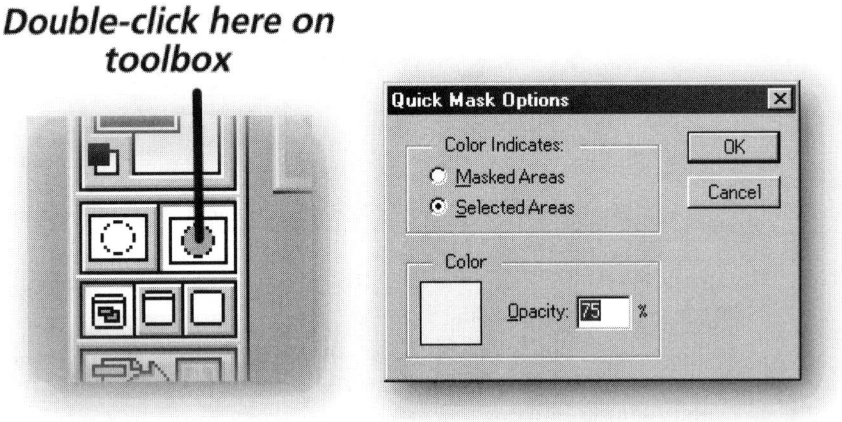

FIGURE 1.20   *Double-click on the Quick Mask icon on the toolbox to display the Options dialog box onscreen.*

Close out of the Quick Mask options box. You're in Quick Mask mode because you clicked on its icon, so click on the icon to the left of it—the Standard Editing mode icon, so when you paint, you paint, and you're not applying Quick Mask!

Channel Options

Like the Quick Mask options, an alpha channel you'll be creating in images in this book stores information based on grayscale color. At the extremes, there's

PROFOUND WISDOM #3:

It's very important not to let your settings for the Quick Mask be harmonious in any way with the colors in your image.

This is a common sense thing, like "Don't run with scissors."

black and white: one means total selection, and the other means total masking (protecting). After you create an alpha channel (fig. 1.21 shows a good example), you double-click on the title to display the Channel Options dialog box. Here, you can name the channel, and more important, like the Quick Mask, you can choose what color (actually there's no color; there are shades of black) represents a channel: masking or selecting.

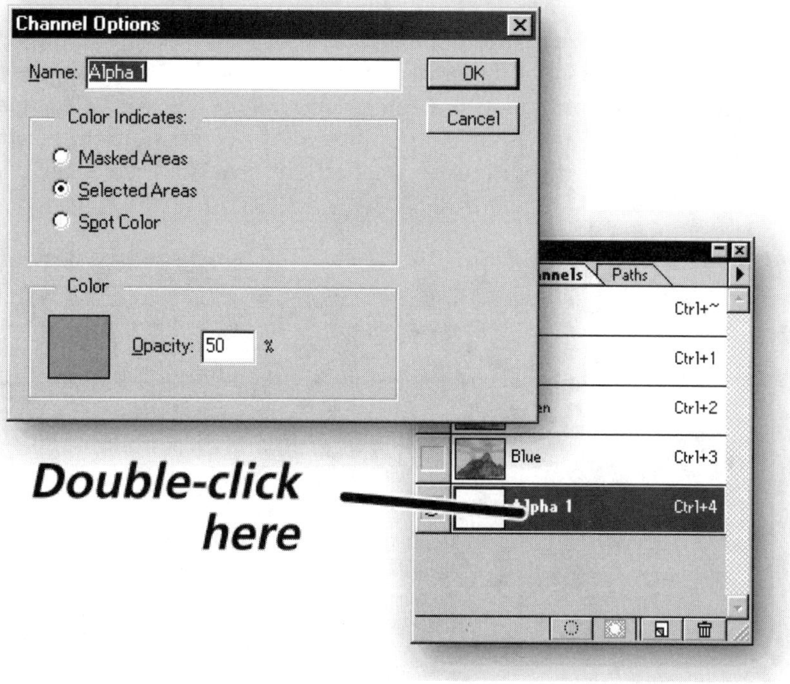

FIGURE 1.21   *Decide how you want an alpha channel to represent a saved selection: as black against white, or white against black.*

I usually opt for a black selection against white, because this reminds me of how I draw on a piece of paper. With selections as white, on the other hand, the channel takes on the appearance of a chalkboard, and I've always found chalkboards less than easy to read.

Darn! There are Even Brushes Palette Options!

Feeling optioned to death yet? Hey, all this stuff will serve you, given time, and the time to learn about it is before you have your first paying assignment, right?

Photoshop ships with five palettes of brushes: You're probably using the default set right now, and this set is hard-wired to the program, so you can never choose them or delete them from the workspace. You only restore the palette after you've had your fun changing the brush tips.

In figure 1.22, you can see that I've clicked on the palette flyout menu and chosen Replace Brushes. This is an Adobe-ism; I'm not replacing or trashing anything—I'm swapping the default set for any of the four sets that come with Photoshop. When you click on Replace Brushes, you're confronted with a dialog box. Choose Goodies, Brushes from the Photoshop folder on your hard disk. There are wild symbols, drop shadow brushes, natural brush tips that imitate real brush strokes if you use them thoughtfully, and square brush tips (for I don't know what). Load any of them, and when the novelty has worn off, choose Reset Brushes from the palette's menu flyout, click on OK, and your brush tip collection is back to the default.

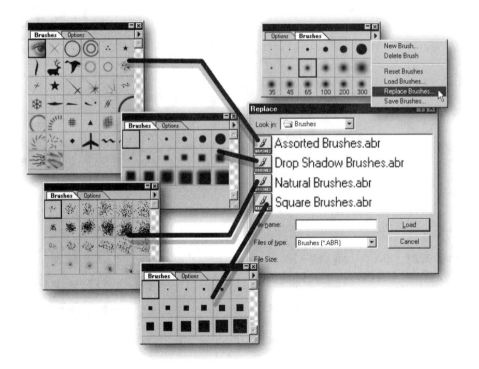

Figure 1.22   *You're not locked into a single look for brush tips. Photoshop ships with four exotic variations on the default palette.*

Want to make your *own* brush tip? It's easy!

Making Your Own Brush Tip

A brush tip in Photoshop can be a capture of a monochrome (grayscale) image from an image window. Let's say I work for a telephone company, and I want a brush tip that does silhouettes of telephones. Here are the steps to create a custom brush:

Creating a Unique Brush Tip

1. Open a new image window. It can be 100 by 100 pixels in Grayscale color mode. You'll be cropping the canvas later, so this is merely a comfortable size in which to work.

2. Press D (Default colors) and then choose the Type tool. Click on the canvas, and the Type tool dialog box opens.

3. Choose a symbol font such as Zapf Dingbats. If you choose this font, press Shift+5 (the percentage key), and you'll get a telephone in the Type preview and editing window in this dialog box. Highlight the telephone with your cursor, and then under Size, specify 55 points (about 3⁄4 of an inch). Press Enter (Return) to place the phone on the image canvas.

4. With the Rectangular Marquee tool (it's in with the Marquee tools at top left of the toolbox; drag on the face of the flyout until you select the Rectangular Marquee tool)—crop the telephone tightly, and then choose Image, Crop. Again with the Rectangular Marquee tool, drag an area around the telephone so there's practically no space left around it (see fig. 1.23).

5. Choose Define Brush from the Brushes palette's menu flyout, and you should see the telephone at the bottom of the current set of Brushes.

6. Let's test drive the new tip. Press Ctrl(⌘)+N to display the New (image) dialog box. Create a new image window that's 72ppi in resolution, 5 inches tall and 7 inches wide, with a white background color. Color mode can be Grayscale or RGB color.

7. Double-click on the telephone icon on the Brushes palette. This displays the options for the tip. Unlike the hard-wired soft tips on the palette, the tips you create can have only one option: spacing. So set the Spacing of the tip to 200%, press Enter, and then go skating along the image window using the Paintbrush tool as an application tool, as shown in figure 1.24.

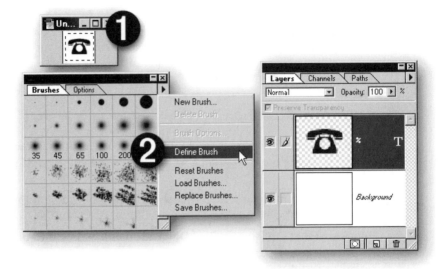

FIGURE 1.23   *Your imagination is the only limit as to what you can define as a Brushes palette tip.*

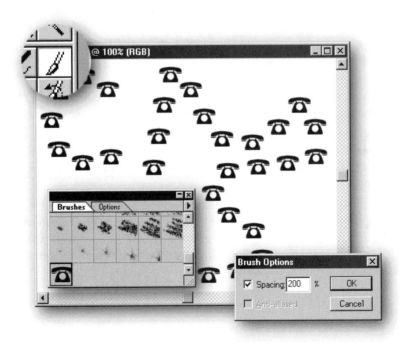

FIGURE 1.24   *Make your own Brushes palette tip from a symbol, a sampling of noise, or anything else you like.*

You can toss the telephone image now. By the way, you can also use the Pencil tool (which has hard edges—no anti-aliasing) or the Airbrush tool in combination with your new Brushes palette tip. The Airbrush option is particularly funky in the effect it leaves.

I'm leaving the easiest choices for last. Although Photoshop has eight Preferences screens, there are only two I think you need to know about as you begin learning the program.

The Two Last Preferences Boxes

If you've read through this chapter from the beginning, you already know about the Units & Rulers Preferences box, and the Plug-Ins & Scratch Disks and Memory & Image Cache preferences. But there are two more places I'd like us to visit, because knowing what these two other screens can do can have an impact on your work.

The Saving Files Preferences Box

Photoshop gives the Macintosh user and the Windows user two different sets of options in the Saving Files dialog box. On the Macintosh, you have the following Saving Files options for Image Previews:

- **Icon:** Saves the image with an icon preview of the image. Very handy on the desktop for quickly identifying files by sight, and this is on by default.

- **Full Size:** Saves a full-size version of the file at 72 pixels/inch in the file. This is for applications that can read full-size previews for placement purposes in, say, a PageMaker or Quark document. And yes, this does plump up the saved file size, so be forewarned.

- **Thumbnail (Macintosh and Windows):** Two separate check boxes. You'd want to use these for cross-platform visibility of a thumbnail image when you choose File, Open, and then click on a file. This adds about 50K to a file size, which is not much, so why not?

In Windows, the Image Previews box has the following options: Always Save, Never Save, and Ask When Saving. If you choose to save with the thumbnail,

note

As of this writing, it is an unwise idea for Macintosh users to save a thumnail preview to a GIF or JPEG format file, and then go placing it on a Web page. The problem lies with America OnLine's Web browser—the browser hits an image with a thumbnail embedded in it, it doesn't know what to do, and before you know it, you're staring at a blank screen.

Hopefully, this AOL browsing utility problem will be solved shortly.

not only is this a cross-platform nicety (as mentioned above), but a thumbnail of the saved image, along with the file name, will appear on your desktop. Or if you saved the file to a directory (folder) and choose the View, Large icons option from the Windows main menu, the thumbnails will appear in folder windows. Cool!

File Extension

For the Macintosh, this is called *Append File Extension*. Choices are Never, Always, and Ask when Saving. This is for cross-platform, Mac-to-Windows support, but the factory default is Never. Hey, with the Internet, GIF and JPEG files *always* need an extension for UNIX and NT servers to understand the file format. My advice is to choose Ask when Saving.

For Windows users, the choices are Use Lower Case and Use Upper Case. Without question, choose Use Lower Case. It's much easier on the eyes, and this is a feature Windows users didn't always have—so *use* it!

Include Composited Image With Layered Files

This option turns your artwork into a digital blimp! It saves a full-size, flattened image along with the layered image, simply so other applications and Photoshop 2.5 users can access the art information. The author's advice? Check around the shop if you work in a shop. If there are no other workstations running applications that claim they can open Photoshop files, then *don't* choose the option—and your hard disk will thank you for this. See the Windows Preference box in figure 1.25.

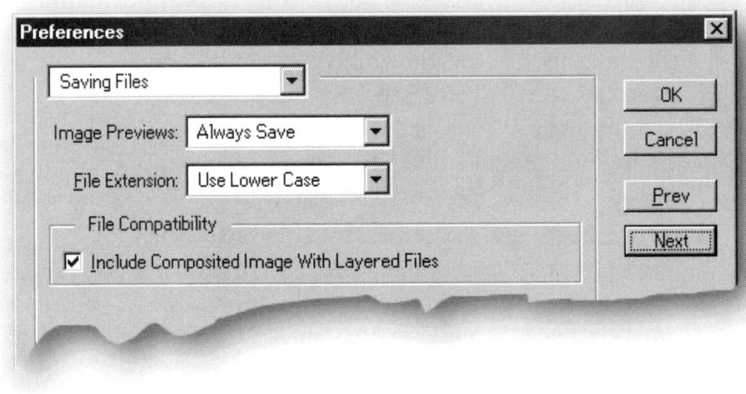

FIGURE 1.25   *Like to quickly glance at the contents of an image file? Then let Photoshop create a thumbnail of the image instead of displaying an eye icon above the title of your work.*

The Display & Cursors Preferences Box

It is here that you can specify the way you want cursors to look onscreen. By default, Brush size is the default for Painting Cursors, and I've got to tell you something, especially any experienced Photoshop users. The "drag" is gone on the Brush size cursors. For three versions I recommended against this cursor style because it was imprecise and slowed down your work. But these new Brush size cursors in version 5.5 are a charm to work with.

If you're just starting out with Photoshop, you might want to use the Standard cursors. Why? Because you can tell without looking at the toolbox which tool you're using.

The Precise cursors do not need to be chosen from this Preferences box. If you ever need a precise, cross-hair cursor, press Caps Lock and all cursors will be represented as cross-hairs.

The other cursors—those meant for measuring, creating paths, and selecting—can be left at their default of Standard. And again, press Caps Lock to turn these cursors, too, into precision cross-hairs. See figure 1.26 for the Preferences dialog box where all these changes can be made.

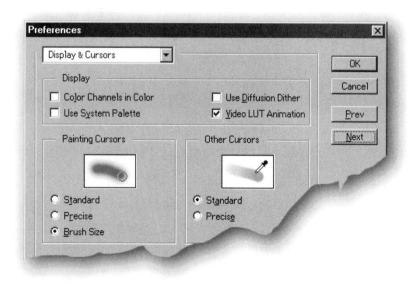

FIGURE 1.26   *Determine the shape of your cursor by accessing the Display & Cursors dialog box.*

It's obvious by now that Adobe has gone out of their way to make you feel at home in their program. Once you understand the ins and outs of preferences and options, you can pretty much call Photoshop your own. I have Photoshop so tweaked for my preferences that it takes me a while to grow accustomed to another user's PC and Photoshop! But after some days of practice, you'll find that Photoshop reflects your own sensibilities, and working in it will be at least 20 percent faster. (No, I don't have a gauge, but it sure feels this way!)

Summary

Clearly, if "discovery" was your sole intent with Photoshop 5.5, you could spend days and perhaps get lost! What I've done in this chapter is to call out the fundamentals of Photoshop—the least you need to know to make your experience with Photoshop a sophisticated, happy, and productive hands-on experience.

In chapter 2, we begin the journey toward understanding how to select stuff. You know, how you clip part of an image out and use it in a different image. An Adobe technician once told me that selection capabilities represents at least half of Photoshop's power. So I guess we ought to investigate and seize some of that power next, eh?

CHAPTER 2

Straightforward Selections

Ask anyone who has been using Photoshop for more than five minutes: *What's the most important feature in Photoshop?* The answer will almost certainly be the *selection* methods and tools. There is a method for selecting part of an image for everyone—there are 14 ways (or more) to select an image area in Photoshop.

This chapter doesn't deal with the fancy or advanced methods of selection, but instead concentrates on straightforward selection. Chances are you've seen lasso tools, rectangle and circular selection tools, and cropping tools in other image editing applications. Surprisingly, these tools in Photoshop are easy and straightforward to use, but their power is increased *enormously* when you, the designer, know the shortcuts and the modifier keys that change the way a selection occurs.

The following sections deal with each of seven tools used in straightforward selection:

- The Rectangular Marquee tool
- The Elliptical Marquee tool
- The Single Row and Single Column Marquee tools
- The Lasso and Polygon Lasso tools
- The Crop tool

Now, we're going to perform some *examples* using the tools, so this chapter isn't one large cheat sheet. My feeling is that cheat sheets encourage dependence on an external source for information. If you *memorize* shortcuts and modifiers, however, the cheat sheet is lodged in your noggin, and is a lot faster to retrieve. In one scenario, you've mastered some of the finer points of Photoshop, and in the other scenario, you always need quick reminders. So either way you like it, we're now going to get into the various ways a selection is created and modified, beginning with the Rectangular Marquee tool.

The Rectangular Marquee Tool

The Rectangular Marquee tool is located in the upper-left portion of the toolbox. Choose Window, Show Tools if the toolbox isn't onscreen, and refer to Chapter 1 on "Creating Keyboard Shortcuts" for toolbox access. If you click and hold on the tool, a flyout will appear with four other tools for selection—more on these tools later. The Rectangular Marquee tool might seem an odd name for something that produces square selections, but the name fits because the tool is not limited to square selections—you can make portrait or landscape selections of any size or shape, with 90-degree–angle corners.

Kick The Tires on the Tool

Try out this tool on a new image for a moment. Press Ctrl(⌘)+N, specify in the dialog box that the image is 400 pixels in width and 300 pixels in height, then press Enter (Return) to accept the other values at their defaults. Make a squiggle on the canvas using the Paintbrush tool to make this selection adventure more exciting. Press F5 to display the Brushes palette, and pick a nice, large brush tip, such as the far right, top row tip.

With the Rectangular Marquee tool, drag diagonally from the top left to the bottom right of the squiggle—this is called *marquee selection*. You'll see an animated dotted line (sometimes called "marching ants" in program documentation) in the shape you drew surrounding the squiggle you designed. Now, place the cursor inside the marquee and drag the marquee to the left or right.

The quickest and easiest way to access the Move tool is by holding Ctrl(⌘) when any tool you're working with is selected. With the exception of the Hand tool, all tools become the Move tool while you hold Ctrl(⌘). This method is better than selecting the Move tool from the toolbox because if you only hold Ctrl(⌘) you can switch back easily to what you were doing with the previous tool. If you clicked on the Move tool on the toolbox, you'd have to memorize all the tool shortcut keys if you wanted to run back to the previous tool.

Profound Wisdom #4:

A selection marquee is inert by default.
That is, it can be repositioned without disturbing the underlying image contents. If you want to actually *move* the squiggle, you need to use the Move tool to *cut it out from the background*. Figure 2.1 shows the difference between moving a selection marquee and actually moving an image area.

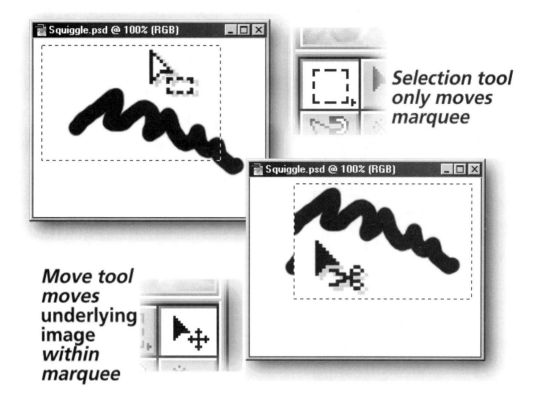

FIGURE 2.1   *Selections remain selections until you use the Move tool on them.*

Extending the Marquee Tools

In this section, you'll learn the extended features of both the Elliptical and the Rectangular Marquee tools. Because the modifiers of both tools are identical, only the Rectangular Marquee tool is demonstrated here (what works for it also works for the Elliptical Marquee tool).

As you saw in the previous section, by holding Ctrl(⌘) you can rip an image area off the canvas to reveal the current background color. But when you use additional keys, you'll discover a wonderful bevy of selection functions; these keys and functions are shown in use in figure 2.2. Here they are in cheat sheet format:

- **Hold Ctrl(⌘)+Alt(Opt).** This combination floats a copy of the selection area directly above the background of an image (see the upper-left illustration in fig. 2.2). Adobe's documentation has very little information on *floating selections* because they are trying to get us comfortable with layer functions, but this remnant of version 3 still exists. You can move the floating selection anywhere you want on the image without messing up the underlying image; then, when you click outside the selection, the floating selection replaces the image area over which it's lying. There's no retrieving the visual area underneath when you plunk down a floating selection (except by choosing Undo).

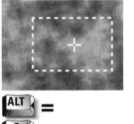
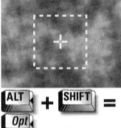

FIGURE 2.2   *Once you get the hang of them, modifier keys enable you to work the way you want (which is usually more quickly!).*

- **Hold Alt(Opt).** By default, when you drag with the Rectangular or Elliptical Marquee tools, the point at which you click is one of the corners of a selection. But if you hold Alt(Opt), you can draw a selection from the center outward. This is particularly useful when you want a selection centered, for example, when you want a perfect crop of an image area.

- **Hold Shift.** When you hold Shift, you constrain the selection tool to produce a symmetrical shape—for the Rectangular Marquee tool, that shape's a square, and for the Elliptical Marquee tool, it's a circle.

- **Hold Alt(Opt)+Shift.** Can you guess, based on the previous modifiers? You're right if you said, "This modifier draws a symmetrical shape, from the inside outward."

There are more straightforward selection tools you'll want to cozy up to, because they can do incredible things. In the following section, you'll get your hands on two different kinds of Lasso tools.

The Lasso and Polygonal Lasso Tools

The Lasso tool's name perfectly describes its action—you draw a loop around an area and then drag its contents or reposition the lasso selection. It's sort of a freehand tool, but it, too, has an extended use. If you hold Alt(Opt) while using the Lasso tool, it becomes the Polygonal Lasso tool; then all you need to do is to click on points on an image, and Photoshop draws straight selection segments between the points.

Alternatively, if you have a selection assignment that calls for more straight edges than freeform shapes, hold on the Lasso tool on the toolbox, and choose the Polygonal Lasso tool. Then, when you come to an area in an image that requires a flowing sort of outline, hold Alt(Opt) to make the tool toggle to the Lasso tool, as shown in figure 2.3. You can change tools in the middle of the selection-creation process. A tiny circle appears next to the cursor when you are about to close the selection.

Let's take the Lasso tool out for a test drive on an image, Star.tif, in the Examples/Chap02 folder on the Companion CD. Now, selecting an image area without having an idea for a different destination for the selection is a lot like tasting food without swallowing it! So the concept here is that you are going to select a shape and then move a copy of that shape to a different background. The images are weird-looking, too, so the upcoming steps will be fun to follow.

tip

If you release the cursor before you've completely encircled a selection area, Photoshop will automatically close the selection by drawing a straight segment between the first and last click points. This might or might not be what you want, so take it easy while mastering this tool, and make sure that *you*, and not an application, are designing stuff!

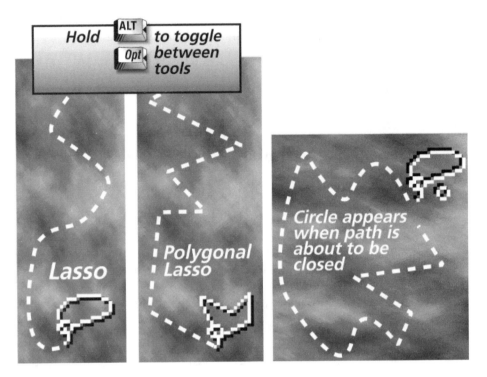

FIGURE 2.3   *The Lasso and Polygonal Lasso tools are interchangeable by holding Alt(Opt).*

Capturing and Moving a Straight-edged Image Area

1. Open the Star.tif image from the Examples/Chap02 folder on the Companion CD. Double-click on the Zoom tool to increase your viewing resolution of the image to 100%.

2. Choose the Lasso tool, hold Alt(Opt), and then start clicking points at the vertices of the star object in the image. This is a trial run. There's no "improper" way to do this—you're getting a feel for the accuracy of the tool. Stop whenever you feel like it; allow Photoshop to close the marquee if you haven't done this yet by letting go of the tool at the last vertex of the star.

3. Press Ctrl(⌘)+D to deselect the current selection.

4. Drag on the face of the Lasso tool and choose the Polygonal Lasso tool.

5. Click points around the vertices of the star shape until you come full circle to the beginning point. Single-click here, and the marquee will appear. See figure 2.4 for a view of what's going on.

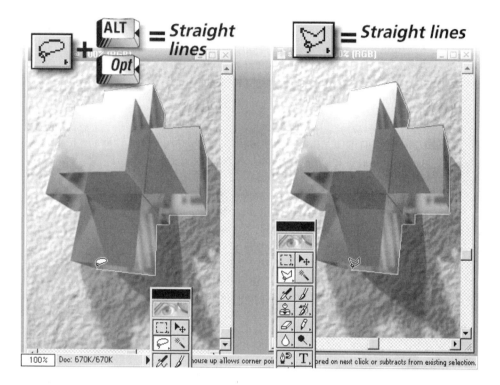

FIGURE 2.4   *Both the Lasso and the Polygonal Lasso tools can be used to make selection marquees composed of straight lines.*

6. Open the SunScene.tif image from the Examples/Chap02 folder on the Companion CD. Position the two images so you have a clear view of both. Zoom out of them if necessary; you can use Ctrl(⌘)+ the minus key for zooming, and then resize the window.

7. With the Move tool chosen, drag the marquee selection of the star shape into the SunScene.tif image window.

tip

After using the Polygonal Lasso tool, you might want to switch to a different tool, such as the Move tool. Why? Because even for advanced users, the Polygonal Lasso tool "feels" sticky—you can't accidentally single-click anywhere without starting (and Photoshop obliges you to finish) another polygonal selection marquee.

8. Position the shape anywhere you like, using the Move tool on the new layer that has been created for the copied selection, and then choose Layer, Flatten Image. Save the image to your hard disk as Sunset.tif, in the TIFF file format. You can close the images now at any time.

I think you've just done in seven steps what took me two hours to do when I first started with Photoshop 2.5! But now, it's on to fancier stuff in the following section.

Creating a Composite Selection

If you're not familiar with the term "composite selection," that's because I just made it up! Seriously, I don't think there's a proper term for beginning a selection with one tool, switching tools as you go along, and then switching back to the original selection tool. But this is what we're going to do next, and I think you'll agree that this is called "creating a *sophisticated* selection"—perhaps not a fundamental, but frequently a necessity in your cache of graphics tricks.

Using Both Modes of the Lasso Tool

1. Open the Star&Bal.tif image from the Examples/Chap02 folder on the Companion CD. Zoom into 100% viewing resolution.

2. Choose the Lasso tool, and then hold Alt(Opt).

3. Click points starting at the far left of the star shape. Work clockwise.

4. When you reach the edge of the ball, let go of the Alt(Opt) key and make a swooping (inaccurate) arc around the ball, bringing your cursor to the edge of the star (see fig. 2.5).

5. Finish up the selection marquee by holding Alt(Opt) once again and clicking to arrive at the beginning point of your selection.

tip

Pressing Ctrl(⌘)+D to deselect a selection is a very useful shortcut to memorize if you make the Polygon Lasso tool your selection tool of choice.

tip

The Move tool does not cut image areas out of an image when you are transporting the marquee selection to a *different* image window. Instead, it creates a duplicate.

tip

There's another way to move a copy of a selection to another document window, and probably you already know this one, but here goes: If you press Ctrl(⌘)+C in the window with the selection, you copy the selection to the clipboard. Then if you press Ctrl(⌘)+V while the "destination" window is in the foreground, you add a new layer to the image, the new layer containing the copy of the selection.

But the method you used in the steps above is easier and quicker, and doesn't add memory requirements to your system's Clipboard.

6. Right-click (Macintosh: hold Ctrl and click) and choose Layer Via Copy from the context menu. Your selection is now on Layer 1.

7. Save the image as Star&Ball.psd in Photoshop's native file format to your hard disk. You can close the image at any time now.

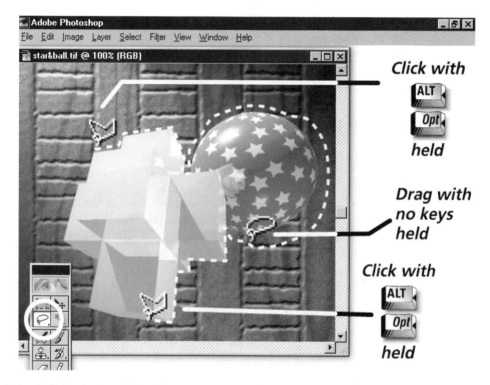

FIGURE 2.5   *Switch selection tools without stopping, by releasing the Alt(Opt) key.*

Yes, yes…we didn't get to the sloppy selection area to the right of the image. The ball is pretty ill-defined isn't it? Not to worry. Quite frequently, you will use a number of selection techniques to accurately describe an image area. There are at least two different ways to perfect the edge of the ball, and the quickest one is covered in Chapter 3, "Esoteric Selections." So you might want to come back to the Ball and Star image after you've learned some advanced selection features. For now, you're only beginning to learn the power behind Photoshop selections.

Repairing Images by Using Selections

Have you ever had a world-class system crash? I had a swell one back in 1995 while beta-testing Windows 95, and as usual, the first files to get "banged" were bitmap image files. I was heartbroken that a few of my designs were beyond repair, but elated that Photoshop has a selection tool which can help restore files that have suffered *minor* damage. On the selection tool flyout, you'll find the Single Row and Single Column Marquee tools. Their names sort of say it all; either tool will select the entire width or height of the image, but only by a pixel in width (or height). Do you have an image with corruption noise running through it? In the following steps you can take a whack at restoring an image file I've provided on the Companion CD.

Restoring an Image with the Single Row Marquee Tool

1. Open the BigTop.tif file from the Examples/Chap02 folder on the Companion CD. Double-click on the Zoom tool so that the image appears at 100% viewing resolution (1:1).
2. Drag on the face of the Marquee tool(s) and then choose the Single Row Marquee tool (see fig. 2.6). It does not matter if you can see the edges of the BigTop image; the Single Row tool will encompass the entire horizontal (width) aspect wherever you click, and the height will be but a single pixel.
3. Zoom into 300% viewing resolution for accuracy (press Ctrl(⌘)+ the plus key twice). Click the tool one pixel in height *beneath* the file-corruption line.
4. Press Ctrl(⌘)+Alt(Opt) and then press the Up-arrow key once. This makes a floating duplicate of the selection and places it on top of the corruption line (see fig. 2.7).
5. Press Ctrl(⌘)+D to deselect the floating selection and make it a permanent piece of the artwork. You can name and save the file to hard disk at any time and then close the file—or simply close the file without saving (it's an example image—it's not "High Art").

I've found this trick to be very useful and a sound one for presentation to even the most critical of eyes. In figure 2.8, the image is at 300% viewing resolution and you can't see a trace of retouching.

FIGURE 2.6   *The Single Row and Column Marquee tools enable you to precisely select a narrow region of an image.*

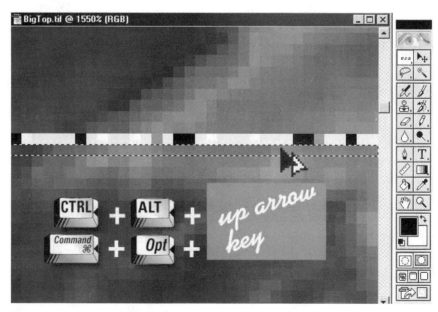

FIGURE 2.7   *Often, there is a great similarity in rows of pixels in large images that do not display a lot of color transition. In this case, the best way to mend a row of pixels is to copy a neighboring row.*

FIGURE 2.8   *The best retouching in Photoshop is that which goes unnoticed by the viewer.*

The Column Marquee tool operates exactly like the Row Marquee tool, except that its selections are up and down, not sideways.

It's time now to check out a tool that, unlike the others, has the capability to reduce or increase the dimensions and resolution of image areas—the Crop Tool.

Using the Crop Tool

Although you have the option of using the Rectangular Marquee tool in combination with the Image/Crop command, there's a more sophisticated way to trim your images. The Crop tool can help you make images all the same size, or simply enable you to frame part of an image before you make the crop.

PROFOUND WISDOM #5:

When you resize an image, you change the number of pixels in the image, and the image becomes a little blurry. When you trade image dimensions for the number of pixels/inch, the absolute pixel count in the image remains the same, and you have not altered the image's details.

In the following set of steps you'll take two images, get the physical size of one image via the Crop Options palette, and then apply these dimensions to the other image. Pretend you want consistently sized images for a gallery presentation.

This bit of wisdom is important to keep in mind. When you resize an image by using the Crop tool (or any tool), pixels have to be eliminated or added to the image, and even though Photoshop's a smart cookie, an application has no way of knowing *a priori* what the new values of the remaining pixels should be. So it simply averages pixel color according to the surrounding pixels. You can hide but not completely solve this blurring issue by using a sharpening filter as a final step.

The following simple example takes you through the controls for the Crop tool.

Working with the Crop Tool

1. Open 2Plums.tif and DukChart.tif from the Examples/Chap02 folder on the Companion CD (see fig. 2.9). You'll see that these images are clearly not the same size.

2. Press Ctrl(⌘)+ the minus key until you can see all of the duck chart image without scrolling. Drag the edges of the image window away from the center so you can see a little of the image window background.

3. Click on the title bar of the 2Plums image to make it the current image for editing. Double-click on the Crop tool (on the Marquee tools flyout) to display the Crop Options palette.

4. Click on the Fixed Target Size check box on the Crop Options palette. With the size fixed, if you don't specify a resolution the crop will not change the number of pixels in the cropped image. For example, a 2" by 2" image at 150 pixels/inch would become a 1" by 1" image if you specified these dimensions, but the resolution would then become 300 pixels/inch.

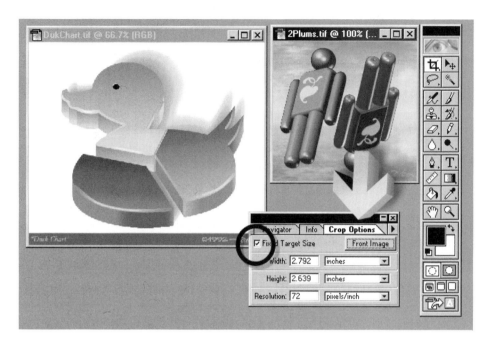

FIGURE 2.9   *The plums and duck chart images are not the same size.*

5. Click on the Front Image button on the Crop Options palette. Now, you have specified the dimensions and resolution of the 2Plums image, and can crop the duck chart image to be the same size (see fig. 2.10).

6. With the Crop tool, drag vertically in the duck chart image window from top right to bottom left (or as far as Photoshop will allow you to drag). As you can see in figure 2.11, the proportions of the duck chart image are a little wider than those of the 2Plums image. What you do about this is drag in the center of the crop marquee until the image is centered within the rectangle (see fig. 2.11).

7. Either double-click in the center of the crop marquee or press Enter (Return). Photoshop crops the image, and now you have 2Plums and DukChart at exactly the same size.

PROFOUND WISDOM #6:

Image size in inches (or cm or picas—whatever) is inversely proportional to the resolution of the image.

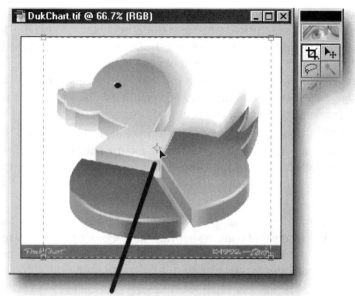

Drag with tool to reposition selection

FIGURE 2.10   *You can copy the dimensions and resolution from an existing image and apply them to a different image.*

FIGURE 2.11   *If you cannot crop all of the image, reposition the crop marquee to center the visual elements you'll crop.*

8. The only problem is that some text at the bottom of the duck chart image needs to be wiped out. Take the Rectangular Marquee tool, and press D (for **Default** colors) to make the background color white. Drag a marquee around the entire dark area where the text is. If your screen looks like figure 2.12, press Delete (Backspace). The enclosed image area will take on the same white as the rest of the image background. Save this image to your hard disk as Duck Chart.tif in the TIFF file format. Keep the image open.

9. Press Ctrl(⌘)+D to deselect the marquee in the image. Choose Filter, Sharpen, Unsharp Mask from the main menu. Forget about what the name of this tool suggests. It's actually the most sophisticated and "invisible" sharpening tool offered in any graphics software today.

10. You can play with the Amount (the strength of the effect), the Radius (the distance at which Photoshop compares neighboring pixels to add contrast), and Threshold (the amount of contrast between neighboring pixels). However, my recommended settings for images that are between 500KB and 3–4MB in file size are 40%, .9 pixels, and 1, respectively (see fig. 2.13).

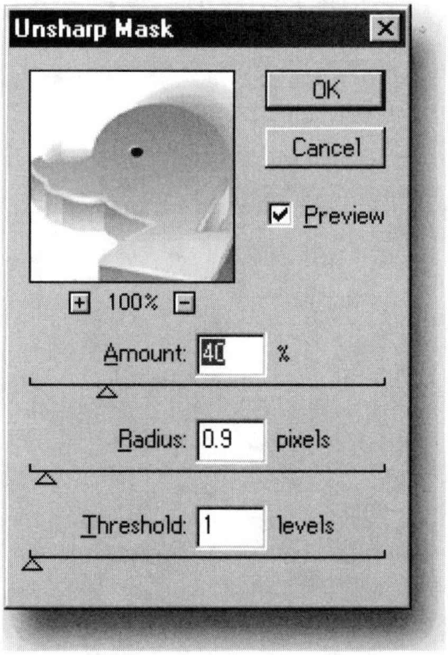

Figure 2.12   *Get rid of the author's signature (trust me, it's worthless) and the background area by deleting the encompassed area to the background color of white.*

11. Click on the OK button to apply the Unsharp
    Mask, press Ctrl(⌘)+S to save the image one final
    time, and you can now close the image.

I think it would be helpful here to reinforce the idea
that cropping can cause resampling. *Resampling* is the
changing of the number of pixels in an image, and as
a result, the application's reassigning of colors to the
pixels in the resampled image. The two Crop Options
palettes shown in figure 2.14 help illustrate the idea.
In the upper box, if you are measuring things in
inches, and you have not specified a resolution (pix-
els/inch), no pixels will be added or removed and the
image *content* will remain the same. Not so with the lower Crop Options palette. It
doesn't matter whether the Resolution field is filled in or not, because you are not
measuring in pixels/inch—you're explicitly measuring solely in pixels (*pixel count* as
it's called in the trade). Unless your image is 200 by 200 pixels, the Crop tool will
reduce or enlarge the cropped image to make up a total of 40,000 pixels.

tip

If you want to do some
before-and-after comparing in
dialog boxes that offer a preview window, click and hold
on the image to see the
"before" image. When you
release the mouse button you
will see the "after" proposed
changes without actually having applied them yet.

*This setting
will not change the
number of pixels in
the image*

*This setting
will change the
number of pixels in
the image
to 40,000*

FIGURE 2.13   *The Unsharp Mask offers more options for specifying the amount of sharpening than any other sharpening filter Photoshop has.*

By now you have a good working idea of what the various selection tools can do. The next section takes us one level higher. You'll learn how to combine different selections, and how to save a selection indefinitely by writing the selection to something called an Alpha channel.

Figure 2.14   *If you crop to inches, you either specify a resolution to change the cropped image, or leave the field blank and create no image-file change. Using pixels as the unit of measurement, your crop will contain exactly the number of pixels specified—and this can blur an image.*

Alpha Channels and Combinations of Selections

The term *alpha channel* has been tossed about in computer magazines as though everyone is supposed to know what an alpha channel *is*. Apparently, it's good when an application offers alpha channels—but what *are* they?

The bare-bones "techy" explanation is that *channels* were created as a means of storing color-component information for high-fidelity computer graphics and images. In RGB color mode, you have three channels to depict color. Each channel gets a primary *additive* color (*not* like primary *subtractive* colors of red, blue, and yellow—crayons are an example of subtractive colors), and mixtures of **r**ed, **g**reen, and **b**lue are used to depict all the colors you see onscreen. In commercial printing, CMYK-mode files have four channels—again, one for each color—**c**yan, **m**agenta, **y**ellow, and blac**k**.

But channels in an image are not constrained to holding color information. Channels above and beyond the color channels can hold bump-map information, information about the location of a saved selection, and more. We'll confine our discussion here to channels you add to an image file that represent *selection* information.

note

Bump-mapping is the computer process of defining elevations by using the brightnesses found in an image channel. Light areas tell the application to fake a 3D protrusion in an image; the darker the tone, the deeper the apparent dent in the image.

This bump-mapping is a Photoshop feature you'll use later in this book, and is quite a standard feature in modeling and rendering programs.

Also, you're going to learn the commands that enable you to *combine* marquee selections in different ways. You can add selections, subtract one from another, and even make an intersection selection from the place where two selections overlap. This is fun stuff, so hang on tight!

Multiple Selections All Over the Place

Look at figure 2.15 for a moment. "Hey, Gare, you didn't show nothin' like that in the first part of this chapter! These selections are way cool!" might be your reaction. Well, you'll see how to create all these selections, beginning with the water molecule selection (bottom right in figure 2.14), right here, right now.

Here's how to make a water molecule (two small hydrogen atoms and one large oxygen one, and yes, I had to look that one up) by using modifier keys and tools, and how to save your work.

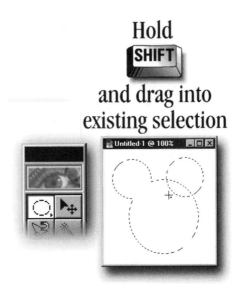

FIGURE 2.15   *Go way beyond simple oval and rectangular selections by combining, storing, rotating, and generally seizing some of the selection power that is in Photoshop.*

Adding Selections

1. Press Ctrl(⌘)+N to open a new document window. Make the dimensions of the window 7 inches wide by 5 inches high at 72 pixels/inch. (The screen figures in this section show isolated selections in much smaller windows, but this was done to focus attention on a particular technique.)

2. With the Elliptical Marquee tool, drag a circle of about 2" in diameter; it doesn't have to be a perfect circle—you don't have to hold Shift while dragging diagonally.

3. Hold the Shift key now, position your cursor slightly above and to the left of the current selection, and drag a circular shape from slightly outside of the first circle selection, *into* the selection edge by a fraction of an inch, until the second selection is half the size of the original. If you look closely at the cursor, it has a plus symbol in its corner. You've added a hydrogen atom to the water molecule.

4. Repeat step 3, adding a circular selection on the upper-right side of the original selection (see fig. 2.16).

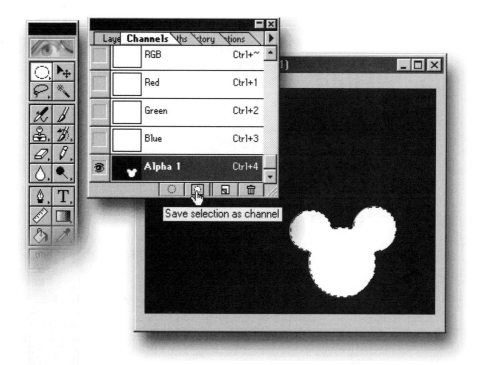

FIGURE 2.16   *When there's an active selection, holding Shift does not confine the selection to an equilateral one. Instead, the tool adds to the current selection in the image window.*

Now, a selection marquee this elegant deserves to be saved, and the easiest way is to...

5. Click on the Channels tab of the Layers/Channels/Paths/Etc. Palette, and then click on the Save Selection as channel icon, as shown in figure 2.17. By default, channels are displayed as black (depicting "no selection") and selections are white. You'll learn how to reverse this later in this chapter, but for now, just know that your selection of the molecule is safe and can be recalled at any time.

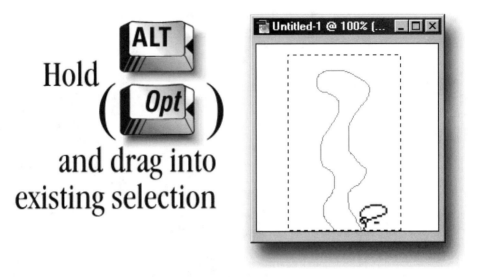

FIGURE 2.17   *Click on the icon on the palette to create a new channel—Alpha 1—and save your selection work.*

6. Press Ctrl(⌘)+D to deselect the selection. To test whether I'm fibbing about this "safe selection," press Ctrl(⌘)+ tilde (~) to return to the full color (the *composite* color) view of your work, and then press Ctrl(⌘) and click on the channel title, Alpha 1. The marquee's back, isn't it? Keep this image window open. You might want to save it as "Selections" in either the TIFF, Macintosh PICT (*.pct), or Photoshop PSD format. TIFF and PSD are the only file formats that can hold more than one alpha channel, and most graphics formats cannot hold even one alpha channel.

Okay, you paid good money for this book, and I think we can do a little better with these modifier keys than drawing a selection of a balloon at the Macy's Thanksgiving Day Parade. In the section to follow, you'll subtract a selection from an existing one, but you'll use two different tools.

tip

Adding selections to selections does not require that the shapes intersect each other (that they are *contiguous*). If you draw a circle and then draw another circle while holding Shift, and the circles don't meet, you'll wind up with one selection composed of two shapes that don't overlap.

Subtracting from a Selection

Quite often you'll find that there's a nice contrapuntal harmony in a design when hard right-angle edges enclose a soft, almost amorphous shape. This combination of shapes could make a swell Web button, in fact. Here's how to use the subtraction mode with the selection tools to achieve that which is better shown than explained <g>!

Removing Part of the Inside of a Shape

1. In a different area of the image window, with the Rectangular Marquee tool, drag a rectangle of proportions similar to a piece of paper, and make it about 3" tall. In figure 2.18, I've designed the rectangle to be flush with the bottom of the image window simply to show the versatility of what's going on here. You are not obliged to do the same.

2. Take the Lasso tool, and hold Alt(Opt). Now, draw a squiggle inside the rectangle; if your rectangle touches the bottom edge of the window, you'll have something that looks like figure 2.18.

   By the way, if your second (subtraction) selection doesn't touch the existing selection, no change is made in the original selection.

   Oh, yes—someday you will read books (if you haven't already) that talk about "Boolean operations," and this is exactly what you're doing in this section. Boolean operations consist of Unite (like the water molecule), Subtract (step 2 here), and Intersection (we've not gone that far yet; you haven't missed anything).

3. Now let's say you add this squiggle in a box to the water molecule selection you created. Hard? Hardly! You make the addition by editing the alpha channel. Click on the Alpha 1 title on the Channels palette.

4. Press D (**d**efault colors) so the background color on the toolbox is white. Now press the Delete (Backspace) key, and then press Ctrl(⌘)+D to deselect the marquee. Your screen should look like figure 2.19 before you deselect the box/squiggle. From now on, when you load the water molecule by Ctrl(⌘)+clicking on the title, you'll also load the squiggle in a box. If you don't want this selection to ever appear again, paint over the white area in the alpha channel with black color.

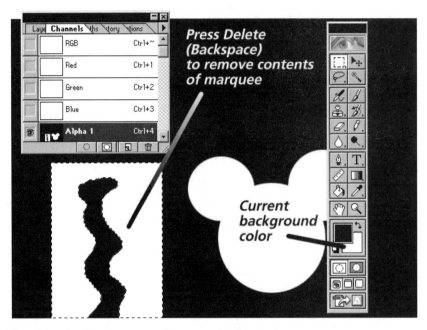

FIGURE 2.18   *Holding Alt(Opt) subtracts an area from an existing selection.*

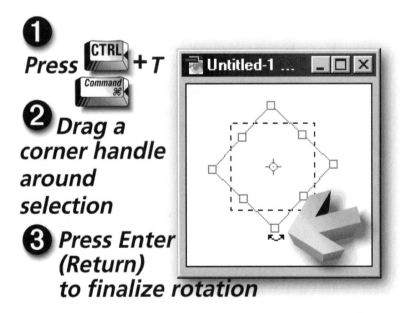

FIGURE 2.19   *Add your squiggle shape to the molecule shape in the same alpha channel.*

5. Press Ctrl(⌘)+S, and keep this image open.

Okay, you've worked with rectangular and square selections, but how would you go about making a square shape that's rotated by 45 degrees? Read on!

Rotating a Selection

Whenever you rotate a selection, there is some loss of detail in the selection's content. The solution to preserving detail in a selection that's diamond shaped is to create the selection marquee ahead of time, and then drag it over to the target zone in the image.

Here are the steps:

tip

The squiggle shape does not have to go in the same channel as the molecule. You can click on the Save selection as channel icon, and add a channel devoted to your squiggle, so that it can be loaded later, independently of the molecule shape.

Rotating Selection Marquees

1. Hold Shift, choose the Rectangular Marquee tool and draw a perfect one-inch square marquee someplace where you have high confidence there isn't an underlying saved selection in an alpha channel.

2. Press Ctrl(⌘)+T. The marquee now has a bounding box around it.

3. Hover the cursor over a corner handle on the box until the cursor changes to a bent arrow.

4. Drag to the left until the bounding box appears to be rotated by 45 degrees. Press Enter (Return) or double-click inside the square to finalize the rotation. See figure 2.20 for visual examples of the last three steps.

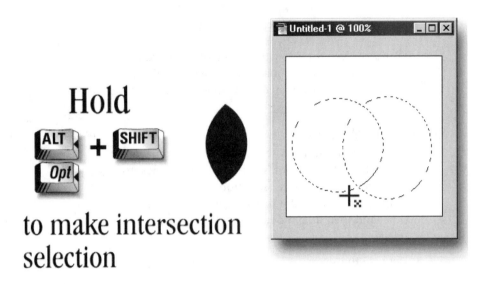

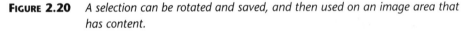

FIGURE 2.20   *A selection can be rotated and saved, and then used on an image area that has content.*

After the selection has been rotated and finalized, you have the following options:

- Save it to an alpha channel, either a new one or one that already contains selection information.

- Cut the contents and send the shape to another layer by a right-click (Macintosh: hold Ctrl and click), and choose Layer Via Cut (or Copy).

- Move the selection anywhere you like, using either selection tools or the Move tool, because this shape is a *floating selection*.

- Here's a *big* tip. You can move the selection marquee without moving the foreground white it contains if you right-click (Macintosh: hold Ctrl and click) in the selection, choose Fade on the context menu, and then choose 100% and click OK. This is the only way I know of to move a rotated selection to an area where there's image content *without* dragging white over it to replace it.

> **tip**
>
> In Photoshop, you must perform rotation work with some combination of 15 degrees—the number cannot be changed. Clearly, you can choose—multiples of 15 degrees—45 degrees is 15 degrees times 3.

I recommend saving the shape to an alpha channel right now, because we're moving on with this combination-selection stuff.

Creating Intersecting Selections

As you've seen, an oval is easy to create, as are shapes with straight edges. But what if you want to create a shape based on the intersection of two shapes? The string of shapes in figure 2.14 was accomplished by intersecting two circles, saving the shape to an alpha channel, and then moving the selection marquee in the alpha channel view and deleting the underlying alpha channel color. Here's how to create an unusual design:

Creating a "Cat's Eye" Selection

1. Toward the left and bottom of the selections image in Photoshop, create a circle by using the Elliptical Marquee tool.

2. Hold Alt(Opt)+Shift, and then drag another circle to the right of the first, into the first, so there's an overlapping area, as shown in figure 2.21.

3. On the Channels palette, click on the Save selection as channel icon, and then click on the title of the channel on the palette to display the channel's visual contents.

4. Hold Ctrl(⌘)+Alt(Opt) to float a duplicate of the selection's contents, and then move the duplicate above the original. Continue this process until you have a string of shapes, or until you get bored. You can close the file at any time now.

It should be noted that this Ctrl(⌘)+Alt(Opt) business has nothing to do with Boolean selections. This command, as described earlier in this chapter, can be of great use when you want to fill a canvas with the same pattern.

FIGURE 2.21   *You know a selection tool is in Intersection mode when a tiny "x" appears next to the cursor.*

Partial Selections

Here's one to ponder for a moment—you've seen that black can mean "no selection" within an alpha channel, and that white represents a "completely selected area." In art as in life, however, there are shades of gray. What happens when you put gray in an alpha channel and then load the selection?

The answer is that you *partially* select the color composite image—the area has partial opacity and you can do neat, creative things with this "ghost" of a selection. Photoshop's Feather feature uses the principle behind partial selections to make a smooth transition between an opaque interior and the transparent exterior of a selection edge. Let's get acquainted with this feature.

Feathering a Selection

What the Feather command does to a selection might not be completely logical or apparent, so here's the description in a (large) nutshell.

You create a selection, and this selection lies right on the pixel at any point around the selection edge. When you apply the Feather command to the selection, the selection edge becomes "wide"—it no longer lies over single pixels, but now it has a 100% opaque interior, a 100% transparent exterior, and in-between a wide path of pixels of different opacities. When, for example, you specify a Feather of 16 pixels, the selection is 100% and is 8 pixels inside the marquee. At the marquee, the selection strength is only 50%, and 8 pixels outside of the marquee, the selection tapers off to 0%. This is a lot more interesting visually than it sounds, so let's run through an example.

Feathering and Moving a Selection

1. Open the Fizz.tif image from the Examples/Chap02 folder of the Companion CD.
2. With the Lasso tool, select around some of the bubbles on the right side of the image.
3. Press Ctrl(⌘)+Alt(Opt)+D, or right-click (Macintosh: hold Ctrl and click) to get the context menu, and choose Feather. The Feather Selection dialog box appears.
4. Type **32** in the pixels field, as shown in figure 2.22. With this high amount of feathering, the selection will trail off very gradually to nothing, from its center to its outer extents.
5. Hold Ctrl(⌘)+Alt(Opt) and then drag inside the selection to the left, black portion of the image. Press Ctrl(⌘)+D to deselect. As you can see in figure 2.23, the copy of the bubbles makes a very gradual transition to background black.

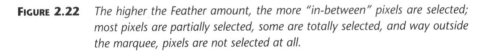

FIGURE 2.22   *The higher the Feather amount, the more "in-between" pixels are selected; most pixels are partially selected, some are totally selected, and way outside the marquee, pixels are not selected at all.*

6. You can close the file now, with or without saving it.

Imagine what you can do with portrait photos and the Feather feature; you can create cameos that look as though they were from the turn of the century (the turn of the *20th* century). If you were to save a feathered selection to an alpha channel, you'd see a shape with very diffuse, soft edges that make a gradual transition to the background color in the channel.

FIGURE 2.23   *There will be times when you do not want an image to have a hard crop around its edges. The Feather option is an easy, effective way of softening the border of a picture.*

As a splendid grand finale to this chapter you will edit an image to make it look like a jigsaw puzzle, using techniques you have practiced in this chapter—plus a special effect or two.

Ready to graduate to the next plateau of Photoshop expertise? Is this a rhetorical question?

tip

If you would prefer that white be the default color of alpha channels, and that black represent selection information, double-click on a saved alpha channel title to get the Channel Options box. Then click Color Indicates: Selected areas, and click OK to exit. Future alpha channels will be black on white, like most of the figures shown in this book.

Creating a 3D Jigsaw Puzzle

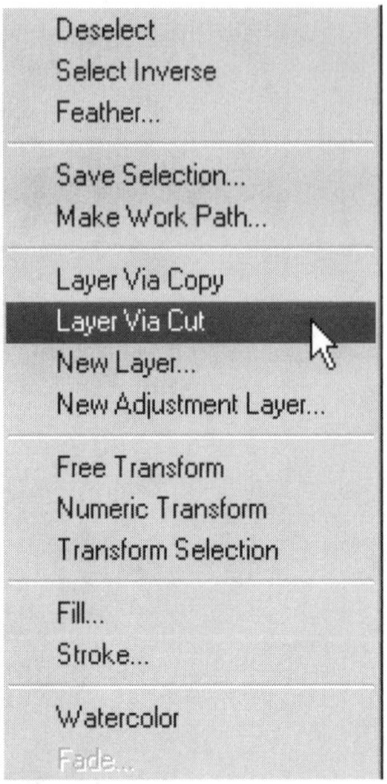

1. Open the Fruit.tif image from the Examples/Chap02 folder on the Companion CD. Type **50** in the zoom box in the lower left portion of the screen, and press Enter (Return) to zoom out of the image.

2. With the Rectangular Marquee tool, drag a rectangle on the image. Then choose the Elliptical Marquee tool, press Shift to add a rounded notch on one side of the rectangle selection, and then hold Alt to subtract a rounded notch from the rectangle. Your image should look like figure 2.24.

3. Right-click (Macintosh: hold Ctrl and click), and then choose Layer Via Cut from the context menu, as shown in figure 2.25. The marquee will vanish, but trust in the fact that the selection's contents are now on a new layer, Layer 1. And Layer 1 is now the current editing layer.

4. Choose Layer, Effects and then choose Bevel and Emboss. Choose Pillow Emboss from the Style drop-down list, and make the Highlight Opacity 100% by typing **100** in the box and pressing Enter (Return). As you can see in figure 2.26, you have a pretty credible jigsaw piece going on in the composition.

5. Click on OK to apply the effect, and then press Ctrl(⌘)+Shift+E to combine the layer with the Background.

Basically, steps 2 through 4 have been the Photoshop illusion you can reproduce, and the way to get an image that looks like figure 2.27, is to repeat steps 2–4. You will have to overlap some lines in the image. For this, I recommend the Lasso tool—it can be used in freehand mode to trace around the notches in neighboring jigsaw pieces. Then you can hold Alt(Opt) to toggle to the Polygon Lasso tool for the straight edges of neighboring pieces.

FIGURE 2.24

Use addition and subtraction modifiers and the Rectangular and Elliptical Marquee tools to make a jigsaw puzzle piece.

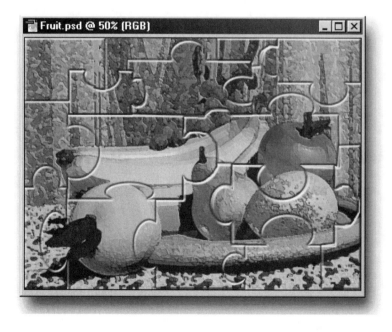

FIGURE 2.25   *Send the visual contents of the marquee to a different layer by using the Layer Via Cut command on the context menu.*

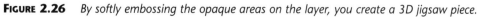

FIGURE 2.26   *By softly embossing the opaque areas on the layer, you create a 3D jigsaw piece.*

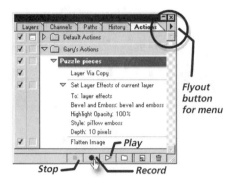

FIGURE 2.27   *Complete the design by repeating steps 2–4 on other areas of the image.*

If you're ready to take a gigantic (painless) leap in your Photoshop tutelage, I can show you a short way to automate the tasks of cutting out the pieces you define, applying the same pillow-emboss settings to each object, and merging the layers. You want to knock off this piece in five minutes? Then let's talk briefly about the Actions palette.

Let Photoshop Do the Actions for You

The Actions palette is a boon to anyone who has to perform the same commands over and over again; notice I said "commands" here—the Actions palette doesn't repeat paint strokes, although it *can* repeat selections.

This isn't the place for an explicit description of the Actions palette's inner workings, but if you follow these steps, you'll have programmed and used a *macro* (a batch of commands) that is saved on the Actions palette's list.

Speeding Up Your Work with Actions

1. Press F7 if the Actions palette's not currently onscreen, and then click the Actions tab on the palette.
2. Create a jigsaw selection in the image, but don't do anything to it. This is the only manual part of completing the design.
3. Click on the triangular flyout button to the right of the Actions tab, and choose New Set. In the New Set dialog box, type **Fred's Actions** (or whatever your name is), and then click on OK. You've created a new folder to contain the new actions you create, and now you won't disturb the Actions that come with Photoshop (Default Actions).

4. Again, click on the flyout button and then choose New Action. In the dialog box, name the action **Puzzle pieces,** and make sure that Fred's Actions is selected in the Set drop-down list; then, when you click on Record, every action you take in the image is recorded and saved. Click on Record now.

5. Right-click (Macintosh: hold Ctrl and click), and choose Layer Via Cut from the context menu.

6. Choose Layer/Effects/Bevel and Emboss, starting at Photoshop's main menu. Choose Pillow Emboss from the Style drop-down list, and make the Highlight Opacity 100%. Click on OK to make the pillow emboss.

7. Press Ctrl(⌘)+Shift+E to merge the layers.

8. Click on the Stop Recording button (the square icon) on the Actions palette. Keep the image open onscreen.

Now that wasn't a big deal, was it? About as easy as getting money out of an ATM, right? In figure 2.28, you can see the action "Puzzle Pieces" expanded; yep, all the moves you made were recorded—and now it's playback time.

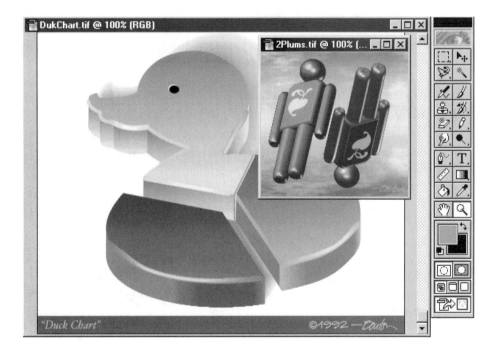

FIGURE 2.28   *The action you programmed should look like this.*

Ready to play?

Playing Back an Action

1. Make a puzzle-shape selection that fits the first piece.

2. Click on the title of the Action on the palette. In this case, it's labeled "Puzzle Pieces." If you click on a *component* of the action, and then press play, you'll play back only *part* of the action. So it might be a good idea to collapse the moves under Puzzle Pieces by clicking on the triangles directly to the left of them on the Actions palette's list. When a triangle is facing right, it contains hidden information. When you click on it, it turns downward, and unfolds the information stored under the step.

3. Click the Play button, and sit back. The Action will stop after the layer has been merged with the Background, and you only need to create another marquee selection and click on the Action title from now on to complete the design.

4. Save your work as Puzzle.tif in the TIFF file format to your hard drive. You can close the image at any time now.

Pretty cool, huh? The Actions palette is the fundamental way to take repetitive, sometimes irksome events off your hands in Photoshop.

Summary

If you walk away from this chapter saying to yourself, "Gee, Photoshop sure has some tools that integrate well with one another," then you've learned more than was taught in this chapter. Everything relates in some way to something else in Photoshop and ImageReady.

Now that you have straightforward selections firmly tucked under your belt, it's time to climb to Chapter 3's "Esoteric Selections." Ready to create a selection by painting over an image? How about a magnetic tool that creates a selection edge between colors in a picture? Or a smart Eraser tool that erases only the background of an image? To work faster in Photoshop, you need to learn about *all* the selection features, so you can pick an appropriate one (or a combination of several) for a specific assignment.

CHAPTER 3

Esoteric Selections

I chose "esoteric" as the title of this chapter because because books seldom offer beginners a satisfactory explanation of the selection techniques you are about to see. And this leaves a fraction of all Photoshop users—a select few—to reap the rewards gained by practice with the steps to follow in this chapter's examples. Photoshop's features were designed for *every* user, so by the end of this chapter

1. You'll know more than the average user about complex selections, and

2. I'll probably have to rename this chapter!

Among the tools you will work with in this chapter are the Paths tools, the Magic Wand, the Quick Mask feature, the Magnetic Lasso and Pen tools, and the Color Range command.

Masking Organic Stuff

Before we proceed, I'd like to make it clear that the selections you learned to create in chapter 2 aren't "real world" selections. I mean, how many photos do you take that contain perfect rectangles and circles? Straightforward selections were designed to help you create patterns and buttons and other shapes that cannot possibly describe with any accuracy, say, the subtle flow of a tree in bloom or the outline of a human. You'll work with photos of nature scenes and mechanical devices in this chapter, as you put more selection features at your command.

How to Work Best with the Pen Tool

The time to call on the Pen tool is when the object in a scene you want to isolate has geometry that's "hard" (as opposed to "diffuse," like the edge of a peach or a lawn). Path segments drawn by the Pen tool are not destructive to an image, and you can save and modify a path indefinitely without checking into an alpha channel.

In figure 3.1 you can see the flyout menu for the Pen tool extended, with all the names for the tools as callouts. The big trick you'll learn, whether you're an amateur or a pro, is that Adobe has redefined the keyboard modifiers for the Pen tool, so that everything you'll need to do to produce and modify a path can be accomplished without switching tools on the flyout.

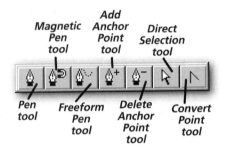

FIGURE 3.1   *There are many Pen tools on the toolbox flyout, and most of them can be accessed by using a modifier key in combination with the (regular) Pen tool.*

Only the Magnetic and the Freeform Pen tools need to be clicked on to use. They're covered as separate tools later in this chapter.

Creating Paths and Using Direct Selections

Why not open a new document that fills the workspace, so that you can test drive the Pen tool, with an emphasis here on how to draw path segments, how to change a curved segment, and how to move anchor points.

With the Pen tool, click a point on the blank image. Then click another point anywhere you choose. The points you are laying down are called *anchor points,* and *path segments* are created automatically between anchor points.

Now click, but also drag with the cursor somewhere on the image. You'll notice that you've created a curve, and that your cursor is no longer holding on to an anchor point. Instead, it's holding a *direction point,* one of two direction points on either side of an anchor point, which are connected and pass through the anchor point with a *direction line.*

If you hold Ctrl(⌘), your cursor will change to the Direct Selection tool, and you can twist the curve you've created by dragging on the end of either direction point. If you drag on the anchor point itself, you move it, and reshape the path segment that precedes the anchor point. In figure 3.2, you can see the four new techniques you've just practiced.

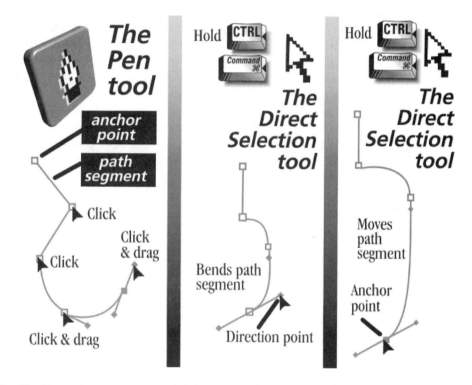

FIGURE 3.2   *The Pen tool serves many graphical purposes, depending on where you click and drag with the tool, and which modifier key you hold down.*

Converting, Adding, and Deleting Anchor Points

The Convert Point tool is particularly interesting and useful, and if you understand its "rules," you'll be designing complex, accurate paths in no time. If you hold the Alt(Opt) key, the Pen tool toggles to the Convert Point tool, and here's what happens, depending on how you use it:

- Clicking on an anchor point that's between two curved path segments will turn both of the segments into straight paths that have no direction points or lines.

- Clicking and dragging on an anchor point that's between either straight segments or curved ones will turn the segments that run through the anchor point into a smooth curve.

- Dragging on a direction point will turn a smooth anchor point into a cusp anchor point; the segments will no longer pass smoothly through the anchor. This is good, because you can then hold Ctrl(⌘) to access the Direct Selection tool, and drag the direction points in any direction or length from the anchor point. The direction points operate independently of one another when they have a cusp relationship. You'll often find that outlines of real-world things consist not only of many smooth connections, but also of plenty of cusp connections for path segments.

If you don't hold any modifier keys, there still are two important functions for the Pen tool: adding and eliminating anchor points. This, of course, presumes that you already have drawn a collection of path segments.

- If you click with the Pen tool on a path segment, a new anchor point is created, and the anchor has the property (smooth or cusp) of the segment to which you added the anchor.

- If you click on an anchor with the Pen tool, you remove the anchor point, and the path segments on either side of the anchor come together to form a single segment. The segment takes on the property of the segments that have been deleted; if the anchor bound two straight segments, the resulting segment will be straight, and if you knocked an anchor off a curve, the new single segment will be curved.

In figure 3.3 you can see a visual synopsis of the three other properties the Pen tool can have.

So, as you can see, there's little point (sorry) in changing Pen tools, even when you're creating a visually demanding outline. In the following section, you'll put all this theory into practice as you use the Pen tool to describe a challenging outline found in the real world.

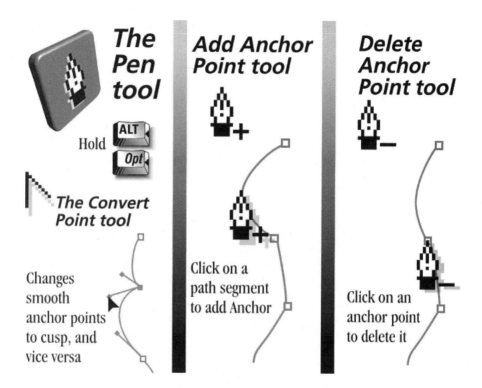

FIGURE 3.3   *The Convert Point, the Add Anchor, and Delete Anchor Point tools can all be accessed while you have the Pen tool chosen.*

Beautifying a Fireplug

Admittedly, having a fireplug on your property is about as aesthetic as having wood-peckers tearing down your Scotch Pine. In reality, there's not a lot you can do about either situation, but in Photoshop you can make that hydrant look fancy enough that you'll forget about adding a birdbath to your lawn.

This beautification is a three-step process:

1. You accurately define the hydrant, using the Pen tool(s).

2. You create a selection based on the path you draw, and then copy the interior of the selection (the hydrant) to a new layer in the image.

3. You apply an artistic filter to the hydrant, but not to the background layer.

This sounds simple enough, no? And it will really impress your friends! Here's how to begin the assignment.

Creating a Path Around the Fireplug

1. Open the Fireplug.tif image from the CHAP03 folder of the Companion CD. Double-click on the Zoom tool to bring your viewing resolution of the fireplug to 100% (1:1). Drag the window borders away from the image so you can see the whole picture, as shown in figure 3.4.

FIGURE 3.4   *Removing eyesores from a photograph begins with defining the outline of the offending object.*

2. Let's start at the top of the fireplug. Press Ctrl(⌘)+ the plus key twice so that you are at 300% viewing resolution and can make precise points. Hold the Spacebar to toggle to the Hand tool, and drag within the window so you have a clear view of the top of the fireplug. Choose the Path tool from the toolbox.

3. Click a point on the very top left of the fireplug, and then click another point on the right edge. This defines the very top of the hydrant with a straight path segment. Click down at the next corner of the outline of the hydrant, and continue to click on vertices (corners) of the right side of the hydrant until you come to the bell-shaped curve of the top. Here, click in the middle of the curve, and then drag until the curve you're creating with the Pen tool matches the curve of the hydrant. Do this again, as shown in figure 3.5; you're well on the way to tracing the hydrant's outline!

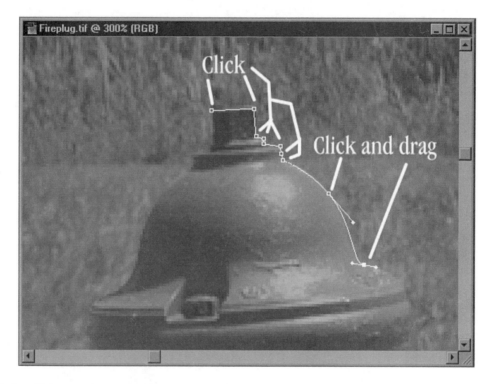

FIGURE 3.5   *Click around areas that have straight edges; click+drag in the middle of curves to create curves and to steer them so they accurately reflect the object's geometry.*

At a certain point, the curve of the hydrant's top will end, and a sharp turn is needed to connect the curved segment to a straight segment. As you'll recall, the Convert Point tool is only an Alt(Opt) key away...

4. Zoom in to about 600% viewing resolution (you can type **600** in the Zoom field at the bottom of the screen, and then press Enter/Return), and then hold Alt(Opt) and drag upward on the direction point to the right of the anchor point, as shown in figure 3.6. This breaks the continuity of the direction lines, the anchor becomes a cusp anchor, and you can release the Alt(Opt) key and click a point at the next vertex of the hydrant.

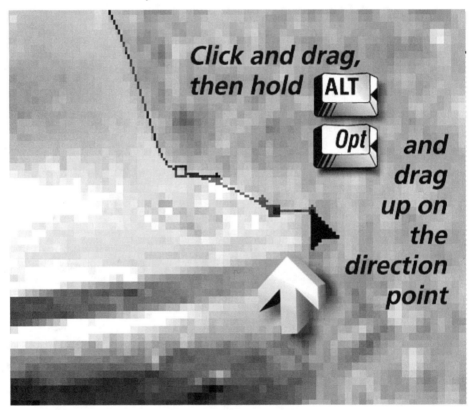

Figure 3.6 *Holding Alt(Opt) enables you to change the direction of the path and change the property of the anchor point.*

5. Work your way down the right side of the hydrant, include the outside edge of the chain, and when you come to the grass, draw long, loose path segments (see fig. 3.7). You'll need to blend the selected hydrant and some of the grass into the rest of the grass, using a new technique we'll cover shortly.

tip

If the curve does not fit the underlying geometry of the image, hold Ctrl(⌘) to toggle to the Direct Selection tool, and drag on one of the direction points surrounding the anchor until the curve has been refitted to match the hydrant's curve.

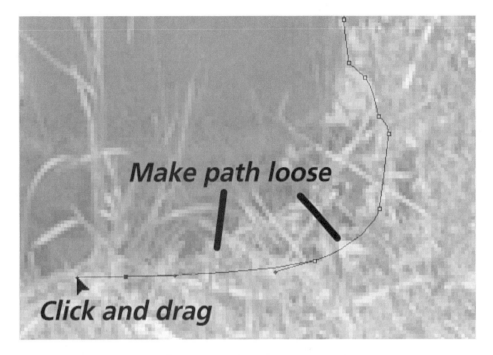

FIGURE 3.7   *Do not try to accurately draw a path around grass blades! Make a loose selection that will be modified later.*

6. Click and drag anchors and curved path segments around the left side of the hydrant, working your way up. When you come to the first anchor you clicked, a small circle will appear next to your cursor. This means you are going to close the path with a final click. Do it.

7. Double-click on the Zoom tool to reduce your viewing resolution to 100%. Press F7 if the Layers/Channels/Paths palette isn't currently on screen.

8. Click on the Paths tab, and then double-click on the Working Path title on the palette. The Save Path dialog box appears. Type **Outline of hydrant** or a similarly evocative name in the name field, and then click on OK to close the box (see fig. 3.8).

note

Although it might seem trivial, by naming the path, you have prevented it from accidentally being overwritten. No path is saved in Photoshop unless you explicitly save it.

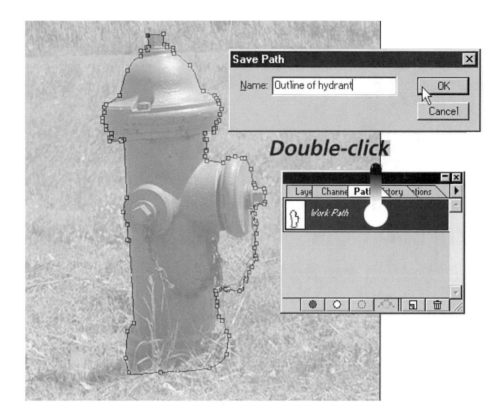

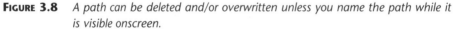

FIGURE 3.8   *A path can be deleted and/or overwritten unless you name the path while it is visible onscreen.*

9. Save the file to your hard disk as Fireplug.tif, in the TIFF file format; keep the document open.

As you progress through this chapter, you're going to see a new word, "contiguous," fairly often. In the context of working in Photoshop, *contiguous* means "something that is directly touching something else." Imagine a few game chips scattered near where you are playing. Some of the chips rest on top of others—their relationship is contiguous. But there are *other* chips that belong to you that do *not* touch the others. These are your *noncontiguous* chips: Although they do not directly connect with other chips, they still belong to the same group—specifically, *your* group of chips.

Boy, I'm glad we're clear on this one, because in the section that follows, you're going to design a *noncontiguous* extension to the path you just created.

Adding to a Saved Path

There are four *states,* visual representations of paths in Photoshop, that tell you what can and cannot be done with a path:

- **A path is invisible.** This means that you can't do anything with the path, and to make it visible in the image window, you have to click on its title on the Paths palette.

- **A path is visible, but you don't see anchor points.** This usually means that you're working on an area other than the path, or even that you're working with tools other than the Pen tool. However, this representation of a path means that you can load a marquee selection based on the path by Ctrl(⌘)+clicking on its title on the Paths palette.

- **A path is visible, and you can see empty anchor points.** This is usually the state of a path you're working on, or a path that you've clicked on with the Direct Selection tool. These paths can be loaded as marquee selections by clicking on the Loads path as a selection button at the bottom of the Paths palette. When you do this, there can be other paths that belong to the same saved selection (they can be seen in the same thumbnail window on the palette) that will *not* load as a selection.

- **A path is visible, and you can see filled anchor points.** This happens only if you marquee-select a path, using the Direct Selection tool, or if you click on the path while holding Ctrl(⌘)+Alt(Opt). What you can do with the path now is reposition it by dragging.

Now that the outer path of the hydrant has been saved, you can add to the selection, and this addition will also be saved automatically. As long as a path is visible and saved, all modifications are kept without alerting you. Now, if you were diligent ("patient" <g>), you drew a path around the outside of the hydrant's chain. To truly complete the description of the outline of the hydrant, you must now draw the inside edge of the chain. Aw, c'mon—you're getting to be a pro at this stuff and it'll only take a moment or two.

As you can see in figure 3.9, the original path is visible while I'm drawing the inside edge of the chain. The inside path does not touch the outside path, but the two paths will be treated as a composite path (a *noncontiguous* selection) once we're ready to load the path information as a selection marquee.

tip

If you want to *duplicate* and move a path, hold Ctrl(⌘)+ Alt(Opt)+Shift while you drag, using the Pen tool.

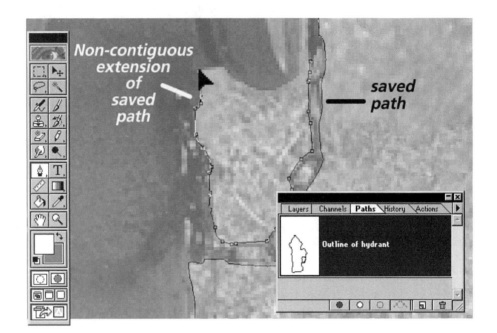

FIGURE 3.9   *The extension you make to the current path is saved as a single path on the Paths palette, whether the path touches the original path or not.*

Once you've closed the second path, you need to deselect the second path segment; unless you deselect the anchor points, only the inside path will be selected when you choose to base a marquee upon your work. This is simple enough: with the Direct Selection tool, click on an area of the image that doesn't contain a path.

Now come the fireworks. In the following section, you'll see your work pay off in a dramatic way as you convert a fireplug into a *painting* of a fireplug.

Loading, Copying, and Filtering a Selection

Both paths you have designed belong to the same path; you might call the smaller path a subpath, in the same way that the interior of the character "o" can be called a subpath, which belongs to the main path. The trick now is to load both paths as marquee selections because, as was mentioned earlier, paths are completely inert as far as designs in an image window go.

Once you have the marquee established, you'll save a copy of the contents of the selection (the fireplug) to a new layer. Then the fun begins, as you filter the fireplug to new artistic vistas for town utilities. Although the possibilities of layers haven't been thoroughly explained or covered in depth yet, they *will be,* later in the book. For now, accept the fact that Photoshop layers are like sheets of acetate you can place above an image, and you can put things on the acetate and move them around.

Here's how to turn a lowly hydrant into high art.

Working with Selections and Filters

1. Ctrl(⌘)+click on the title of the thumbnail on the Paths palette.

2. With a selection tool (such as the Lasso tool) selected, right-click (Macintosh: hold Ctrl and click) over the marquee and choose Layer Via Copy from the context menu, as shown in figure 3.10. *Hint:* if you don't have a selection tool at hand, right-click (Macintosh: hold Ctrl and click) over the title of the layer on the Layers palette. You'll get the same context menu as if you were right-clicking over a selection in an image.

3. Uncheck the eye icon for Layer 1 on the Layers palette to hide the copy of the fireplug, and then click on the Background title on the Layers palette to make it the active layer. You need to eliminate the original hydrant from the image. With the Rectangular marquee tool, drag to the right of the hydrant a rectangle that's about half the width of the hydrant, and is taller than the hydrant.

4. Right-click (Macintosh: hold Ctrl and click) and then choose Feather from the context menu. By feathering the selection you will create a gradual transition between the selection and the background (no one will notice that you've duplicated grass to cover the hydrant). Type **5** in the Feather dialog box, and then click on OK (see fig. 3.11). Although the marquee selection is usually a poor indicator of exactly where a selection exists, because you feathered the selection, 5 pixels inside the marquee represent 100% selection, whereas 5 pixels in diameter outside the marquee represent no selection. The concept of *partially* selecting something is a strange one, but you can make it work for you.

note

There is a second way to turn path shapes into marquee selections—by clicking on the Loads path as selection button at the bottom of the palette—and experienced users might tell you this is the way to go. *But*...if you click this button, the paths themselves, *in addition to* marquees, are visible and you can accidentally delete a saved path (by pressing the Backspace key a few times).

Ctrl(⌘)+clicking automatically hides the paths as marquee selections are created, so step 2 is the safest procedure for the novice (and the author!).

FIGURE 3.10   *Copy the selection of the hydrant to a new layer in the image.*

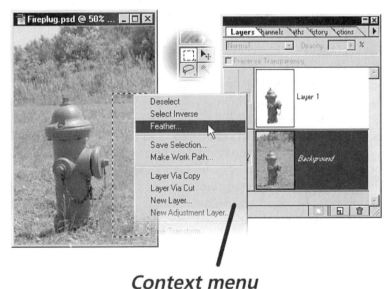

Context menu

FIGURE 3.11   *Partially select around the edge of the selection by using the Feather feature.*

5. Hold Ctrl(⌘)+Alt(Opt), and then drag a duplicate of the contents of the selection over the hydrant to half hide it, as shown in figure 3.12. Press Ctrl(⌘)+D to deselect the selection.

FIGURE 3.12   *Feathering the edge makes it nearly impossible to detect where the duplicate begins in the picture.*

6. Draw a similar rectangle on the left side of the page, and then repeat step 5. The background should now look like that in figure 3.13. Choose File, Save and save the image as Fireplug.psd in Photoshop's native file format; keep the image open. Press Ctrl(⌘)+D to deselect the selection.

7. Click on the Layer 1 title on the Layers palette to make the copied hydrant visible in the image. Double-click on the Quick Mask mode button, and then choose a color other than the default of red, as shown in figure 3.14. A red tinted overlay on a red hydrant would be unrevealing at best, so choose purple or some other clashing color. Click the Color indicates: Selected Areas button, and then click on OK to return to the workspace.

FIGURE 3.13   *The image looks as though a hydrant never was there!*

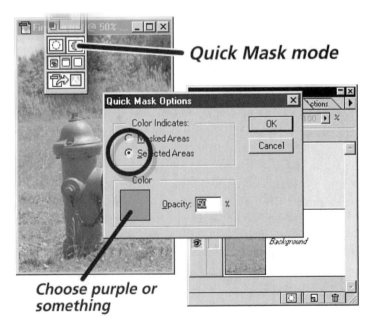

FIGURE 3.14   *Customize the Quick Mask mode to make it work better for you with this particular image.*

8. Ctrl(⌘)+click on the thumbnail image of the hydrant on the Layers palette. This loads the silhouette of the hydrant as a marquee selection. Press D to make the current foreground color black. Press Alt(Opt)+Delete (Backspace) to fill the selection with Quick Mask tint, and then press Ctrl(⌘)+D to deselect the marquee. As you'll note, while an image is in Quick Mask mode, selections can be made using the tinted overlay color, and operations on the image itself are impossible (you can't muck up the image in Quick Mask mode).

9. Zoom to the bottom of the hydrant where you created a real rough selection between the grass and the hydrant bottom. Choose the Smudge tool (it's on the Focus tools toolbox flyout—the icon looks like someone is smooshing an insect). Leave the options at their default (IOW, you don't need the Options palette onscreen), but double-click on the Smudge tool to bring up the Brushes palette, and then choose the second-row, fourth-from-left brush tip.

10. Stroke from the bottom of the selection to the bottom of the image, as shown in figure 3.15. You're smudging the selection of the hydrant from total selection at bottom to a gradual fall-off in the grass. Not many Photoshoppers realize you can smudge, blur, and perform a lot of regular operations on a Quick Mask.

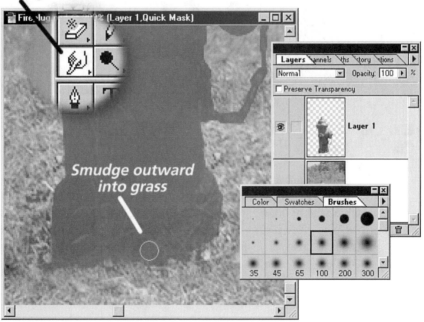

FIGURE 3.15   *"Push" some of the Quick Mask on the edge of the bottom of the hydrant away from the hydrant to make a smooth transition between selected and masked areas.*

11. Click on the Standard Editing mode button to the left of the Quick Mask button on the toolbox. The marquee reappears, except the bottom looks a little different than before (see fig. 3.16). This is good, actually.

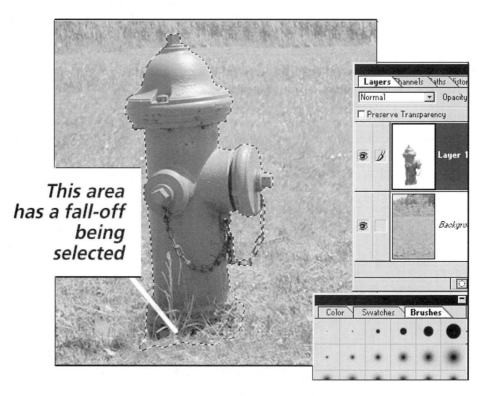

FIGURE 3.16   *The marquee selection looks a little different after it's altered in Quick Mask mode.*

12. Choose Filter, Artistic, Poster Edges. The dialog box appears for this filter. Choose 7 for Edge Thickness (this will create a pleasant, obvious drawn outline in areas where the hydrant has contrast). Choose 2 for Edge Intensity (how much contrast the edge shows from the non-edge surrounding areas of the image). Choose 2 as the Posterization level (few colors used to represent the hydrant). If your dialog box looks like that shown in figure 3.17, click on OK to apply the filter.

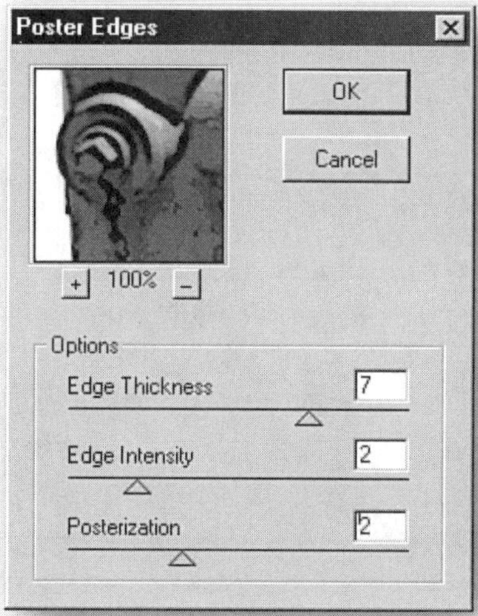

FIGURE 3.17 *Most of the effects you find under the Filter menu offer different options to customize the effect.*

13. Yay! You've done it! I originally thought that this was an advanced image-editing topic, but Photoshop 5.5 makes it easier than ever for first-timers to get professional quality results. Choose Flatten Image from the Layers palette's flyout—both layers are merged—and save the file as Hydrant.tif in the TIFF file format to your hard disk.

You might want to play around with different filters and the Fireplug.psd file in the future. Me? I'm going to frame the piece shown in figure 3.18. If anyone asks what it means, I'll simply say, "Ah, you must not understand the Expressionist Era in Modern Art."

You don't have to first establish a selection via the selection tools or the Pen tools to apply Quick Mask. If you feel comfortable creating a selection using digital paint (as I quite frequently do), then you can start using Quick Mask right out of Photoshop's jar, as it were. The following section takes you through image editing, using Quick Mask.

FIGURE 3.18　*If you have a painting of a fire, and a painting of a fireman, the fireman will naturally need a painting of a hydrant.*

Selecting, Using Quick Mask

My spouse's garden is a perennial topic of discussion at the dinner table, most of the chat being about how insects are destroying the (insert some Latin name here). So I must credit her with the next tutorial.

Photoshop's not necessarily all about serious, invisible retouching—it can be light-hearted, too. What I did to procure the photographic elements for this assignment was to take a close up of a picture of flowers with large buds, and a photo of a Volkswagen beetle from a distance, so the two pictures would scale correctly when combined. A beetle ruining a flower, get it?

Okay, in figure 3.19, you can see a fresh VW bug after being poured from a dump truck, and I'm using the top, second-from-last tip on the Brushes palette to apply Quick Mask to the inside of the beetle's silhouette. Open the VW_bug.tif image from the Examples/Chap03 folder, click on the Quick Mask mode button, click on the Paintbrush button, and re-create the masking work in figure 3.19.

FIGURE 3.19   *Treat the inside and the inside edges of a selection differently. You can zoom out and use a large brush for interiors, but for the edges, zoom in and use a small brush.*

Hmmm, this is beginning to smell like a numbered list of steps...

Using Quick Mask for Image Editing

1. After you have most of the interior covered with Quick Mask overlay, zoom into the image (you can press Ctrl(⌘)+ the plus key) to about 500%, and then choose the third-from-left, top-row tip on the Brushes palette.

2. Stroke around the inside edge of the beetle, connecting your Quick Mask strokes with the larger areas you previously painted (see fig. 3.20).

FIGURE 3.20   *Use the Quick Mask tint as though everything you paint should be selected in the future. That means getting to every nook and hubcap.*

3. Once you've completely outlined and filled the VW, open flowers.tif from the Examples/Chap03 folder on the Companion CD. Arrange the windows on your workspace so you have a clear view of both the bug and the flowers.

4. With VW_bug.tif in the foreground, press the Standard editing mode button, and then hold Ctrl(⌘) and drag from inside the marquee selection to the flowers.tif window, as shown in figure 3.21. When moving elements from window to window, Photoshop does not cut images; instead, it moves a *copy* of a selection.

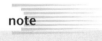

note

If you make a mistake, and overshoot with your painting, press X to invert colors on the toolbox. Now, everywhere you paint with white will erase the Quick Mask. But remember to press X once more to return to black foreground color.

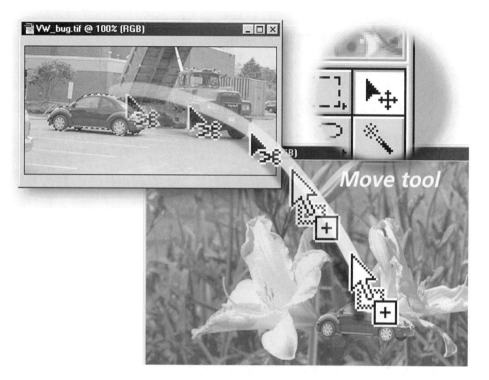

FIGURE 3.21   *Copying a selection does not change its size in any way, so make sure elements scale correctly before you start an assignment.*

5. Close VW_bug.tif now, without saving. Flowers.tif should be the only open document. Save the flowers image in Photoshop's PSD format, and keep it open.

6. Zoom out to 300% viewing resolution, and then scroll the window until you can see the leftmost petal and the bug in the window. If necessary, hold Ctrl(⌘) and drag the beetle so that it's on top of the flower, with its tail wheels almost touching the bottom of the petal (sneak a peek at fig. 3.22). Layer 1 is the current editing layer; whenever you paste or copy something to an image window, Photoshop automatically creates a new layer for the item.

7. Click on the Quick Mask mode button, and then paint a shape similar to that shown in figure 3.22. Notice that the Quick Mask shape describes the lower part of the car. In the finished composition, this part will be hidden by the flower petal, so you'll actually be deleting the area that the Quick Mask describes.

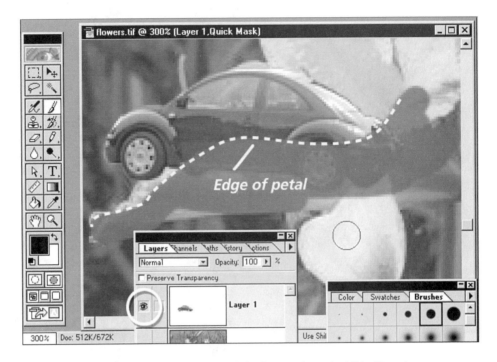

FIGURE 3.22   *With Quick Mask, paint over portions of the flower where the VW will not be seen.*

8. Click on the Standard editing mode button on the toolbox, and then press Delete (Backspace). Press Ctrl(⌘)+D to deselect the selection, and you're finished! You can either save this file in the PSD format, or flatten it and save it in TIFF format, JPEG, or whatever format you know your audience is capable of viewing. See figure 3.23 for the finished image—and if you know where to find a fly swatter the size of a Boeing 767, please let me know.

If you're reading this book from front to back, you may remember that we have some unfinished business with the star and ball image from chapter 2. Now's as good a time as any to flex your newly acquired techniques and perform more professional image editing.

FIGURE 3.23 *Playing with the size of real-world elements can be an engaging sport whose results are often real eye-catchers.*

Perfecting a Selection: Changing the Background

The image of the star and the ball floating in space was left unfinished in chapter 2 because you didn't know yet about the advanced tools in this chapter. The Pen tool seems an obvious choice for creating an outline that will trim perfectly around the outside of the ball.

So enough with the lead-in to this section!

Editing and Manipulating Complex Shapes

1. Open the star & ball.psd image you saved from chapter 2, or if you didn't read that chapter, open star&bal.psd from the Examples/Chap02 folder on the CD. Zoom into a 300% viewing resolution, hold the Spacebar to toggle to the Hand tool, and then drag in the window so you have a clear view of the ball.

2. Click on the eye icon next to the Background layer title on the Layers palette; Layer 1 should be the current editing layer. Choose the Pen tool from the toolbox and make a single click at the vertex between the 9 o'clock position of the ball and the edge of the star (or wherever you left background on Layer 1 from the previous chapter).

3. Click and drag your way around the outside of the ball. The ball is round, with smooth edges, and by dragging and clicking on the edge of the ball, you ensure that the path segments all have smooth connections.

4. When you reach the other side, the other edge where the ball meets the star shape, click. Then hold Alt(Opt) to toggle to the Convert Point tool, and drag the direction handle about ¾ of a screen inch away from the ball and star, as shown in figure 3.24. You've changed a smooth connection to a cusp, and now you can navigate the outside of the path without touching the ball or the star.

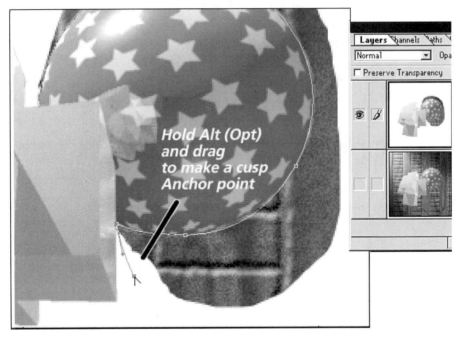

FIGURE 3.24   *Hold Alt(Opt) to convert the next path segment's connection to the previous path segment from smooth to cusp.*

5. Click single points outside the ball (you're working counterclockwise) until you come to the first point, where you should single-click to close the path. Then Ctrl(⌘)+click on the Work Path title on the Paths palette; the path will disappear and be replaced with a marquee selection. Press Delete (Backspace), and you'll have an image layer that looks like figure 3.25.

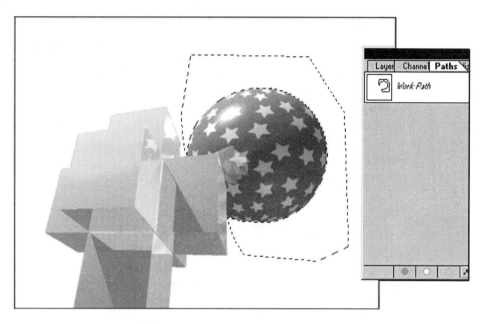

FIGURE 3.25   *Delete the remaining, unwanted areas on Layer 1.*

6. Press Ctrl(⌘)+D to deselect the marquee, and then open SunScene.tif from the Examples/Chap02 folder on the Companion CD. Click on the title bar of the star&bal.psd image to make it the current foreground image.

7. Hold Ctrl(⌘) and then drag the ball and star from its image window and into the SunScene.tif image window, as shown in figure 3.26. Continue to use the Move tool to position the elements on the layer so they're pretty much in the center of the image.

8. You can save SunScene in PSD image format to your hard drive and close the file at any time. We've demonstrated how a combination of tools can make accurate selections, and the file is no longer needed.

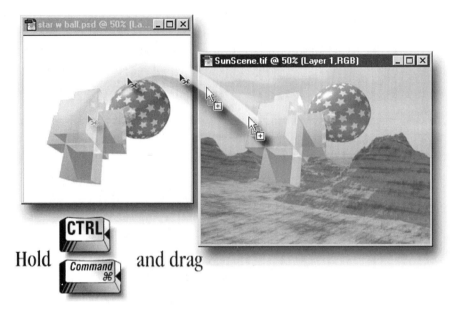

FIGURE 3.26   *Dragging a layer with the Move tool into a new window copies the contents of the original window.*

So far, you've had practice with Photoshop's Marquee selection tools, the Pen tools, and the Quick Mask feature. But there are still a few more ways you can select areas, and the nicest thing about them is that you don't have to know how to draw a straight line to use them effectively!

Selecting by Color

All bitmap images (you'll also hear them called *raster images* on occasion) are composed of building blocks known as *pixels* (for *pi*cture *el*ement). When you select pixels that are the components of an image area, using Marquee selection tools, you're actually gathering them by the *geometry* you've designed with the tool.

But you can also choose pixels by their *color* values. Think of it for a moment; if you go shopping for pretzels, for example, for a large party, you'll probably select the bags by their geometry—where the

note

There is a second way of copying a layer's contents to a new image window that does not require the Move tool. With your cursor, drag *the title of the layer on the Layers palette* into the new image window. Same difference!

bags are located in space (on the aisle, usually). But if you're a gourmet chef and you want to bake an apple pie, you'll probably pick the apples by their color. Admittedly, choosing by color is more time consuming, but only when humans do it instead of Photoshop. Let's look at the tools that take the tedium out of your hands and place it on the computer!

Introducing the Magic Wand Tool

The Magic Wand selects pixels based on color similarity. You click in a totally orange image, for example, and all the orange will become selected. But if there's some blue in the image, the blue pixels will remain unselected because you initially clicked on orange.

There are also shades of the same color which might or might not be picked up by the Magic Wand tool. The sensitivity with which the tool discriminates is called *Tolerance*, and it's an option on the Options palette. If you specify a tolerance of 255, you will be selecting all the pixels in the image, because 255 is the maximum value for tolerance. Usually, a comfortable Tolerance setting that will yield the best results is between 30 and 75.

You also have an anti-alias option when choosing areas with the Magic Wand tool. Anti-aliasing will be explained in detail in chapters to come, but for now, just live with this simple *tautology* (a numbered list that leads to a conclusion):

1. All pixels are rectangular in shape.

2. The Magic Wand tool only picks up pixels that touch each other on one of the flat edges. Pixels that meet at corners are not included in selections.

3. A selection by straight edge leads to phony, computery-looking selections, so something needs to be done on arcs and diagonal lines to hide the rectangular nature of pixels.

4. Anti-aliasing places around the outside edge of a selected area pixels whose color is a mixture of color from inside and outside the selected area. For example, an orange selection on a white background will contain anti-aliased pixels near the selection whose color is a light orange: a mixture of white and orange.

5. When the image has fine enough detail, the average viewer will not detect that "helper pixels," these anti-aliasing pixels, are smoothing the image and making it look more like traditional paint or pencil renderings.

The third option for the Magic Wand is a new Photoshop feature: the Contiguous option. Traditionally, a click of the Magic Wand in an area confined the selection to only those pixels that were bounded by pixels of different colors. This is contiguous behavior. But with version 5.5, you can uncheck the Contiguous option, click on a color in an image, and *every instance of that color* will be selected.

Hey, *I'm* interested in checking out this new stuff. Let's do a mock assignment where you need to select a specific color of chessboard tiles.

Selecting, Using the Magic Wand

1. Open the Pawn.tif image from the Examples/Chap03 folder of the Companion CD. Choose the Magic Wand tool from the toolbox by double-clicking on it. This not only selects the tool, but also brings to the front of the windows the Options palette for the Wand tool.

2. Type **75** in the Tolerance field. You're going to pick up all the purple tiles; because of the lighting in the scene, the purple tiles range from lilac to grape-colored.

   The Use all Layers option on the Options palette is only of use when you have a multilayered design and want to choose a color from *all* the layers, not simply the current, active one.

3. Clear the Contiguous check box if it's checked, and then click on a medium shade of purple in the image. As you can see in figure 3.27, the Magic Wand tool has pretty neatly picked up all the purple tile areas. But not quite perfectly. If you'd like to glance quickly at which areas have been chosen, click on the Quick Mask tool for a moment, and then switch back to Standard Editing mode.

4. To add to the current selections, you not only need to increase the Tolerance (because 75 didn't do the trick on the first click), but you also have to confine selections to the areas you click on—contiguous selections. Type **100** in the Tolerance field, check the Contiguous check box, hold Shift (to add to the existing selection),and then zoom into different areas of the image and click on spots that weren't selected, but should be (see fig. 3.28).

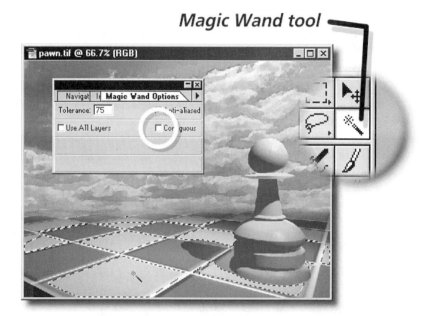

FIGURE 3.27 *Imagine how long it would have taken you to select by hand all the purple areas (shown here as light gray) that the Magic Wand tool selected in one click!*

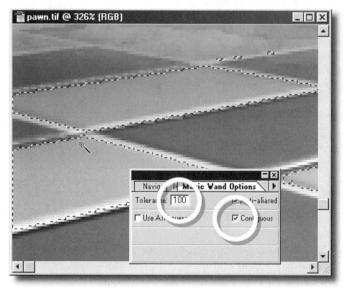

FIGURE 3.28 *A higher Tolerance admits more shades of purple to the current selection, but the Contiguous feature confines selected pixels to only the area in which you are working.*

Now that most of the purple tiles have been selected, press Ctrl(⌘)+H to hide the marquee lines. The image's areas are still selected—it's the indicator lines that are hidden. (Pressing Ctrl(⌘)+H restores visibility of the marquee lines.) Now you have an unobstructed view of a little magic...

5. Press Ctrl(⌘)+U to display the Hue/Saturation dialog box. This feature enables you to change certain color aspects of a selection without changing others. In this adventure, you'll change the Hue of the selected tiles. Drag the top slider to about +94, so the purple tiles are now a peach color (not shown in fig. 3.29, 'cause this is a black-and-white book. Bear with us <g>!)

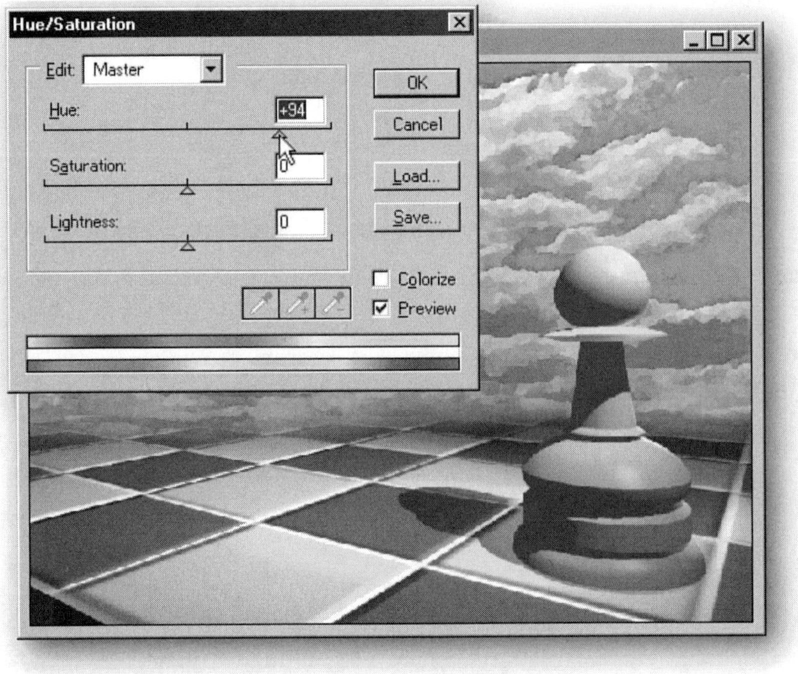

Figure 3.29   *Change the color of the selected tiles by altering only the hue, with the Hue/Saturation dialog box.*

6. You're on your own with this one; it's your call as an artist what you want to do next to the image. If you decide to make the changes permanent, save the file to a different name on your hard drive. You'll be using this image again in the next section in its unaltered state.

The Color Range command has been around since version 3 of Photoshop, and it's similar, but not exactly like the Magic Wand tool with its noncontiguous setting turned on. In the following section, you'll become acquainted with this time-saving selection feature.

Using the Color Range Command

The Color Range feature is straightforward, precise, and easy to use. You click on a color in the image, and then drag the Fuzziness slider to include areas not selected by your original click. *Fuzziness* is a fanciful term, and might better be described as "tolerance."

Once you've got the selection you want highlighted in the preview window, you click on OK and a marquee appears in the image.

In the following steps, you'll select the purple tiles in the Pawn.tif image.

Working with a Range of Colors

1. Open the Pawn.tif image from the Companion CD, and then move it to a corner of the workspace so you can see it as well as the Color Range dialog box (when you choose it in the next step).

2. Choose Select, Color Range.

3. Your cursor turns into an eye dropper. Click on a purple tile in the image window (not in the dialog box preview window), and then watch how the preview in the dialog box shows most of the purple tiles as white (meaning selected).

4. Drag the Fuzziness slider to the right until most of the tiles are selected but all other areas are black (not selected) in the preview window.

5. Choose the Eyedropper Plus tool from the dialog box, and then click on areas in the image window that were not selected by using the default selection eyedropper. You might want to turn the Fuzziness slider down a little after adding to the selections, because the Color Range feature will search the image for colors that are even remotely related to the area upon which you click (see fig. 3.30).

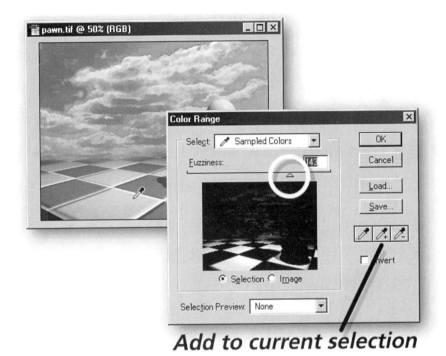

Add to current selection

FIGURE 3.30   *The Color Range command is an automatic way of selecting all similar colors in an image.*

6. Click on OK to create the marquee, and then click on the Quick Mask mode button on the toolbox to see how well the Color Range command did with selecting the purple tiles. Chances are that you selected the tiles better and more quickly than if you had used the Magic Wand tool. But then again, every tool serves a unique purpose in Photoshop, and the Color Range feature was not meant to replace the Magic Wand. You can clean up the selections now with the Paintbrush tool or the Lasso tool. To do so, you Alt(Opt)+click around an unselected area, press Alt(Opt)+Delete to fill the area with Quick Mask, and then press Ctrl(⌘)+D to deselect the marquee.

7. You can close the image at any time now. You might want to save the selection to an alpha channel to work with later. You do this by

tip

I frequently make scenes of clouds in the sky look more dramatic and appealing by selecting the midtones in the image, using the Color Range command. To do this, you click in the image on an area of cloud that's not white or dark. You click on OK, and then choose Feather—Ctrl(⌘)+zAlt(Opt)+D—and feather the current selection slightly. Then you use the Hue/Saturation command to turn the selected areas a peach/pink color. The transformation that takes place is incredible.

clicking on the Save selection as channel button at the bottom of the Channels palette *while the selection is a marquee selection.*

Both the Pen tools and the Lasso tools have a "magnetic" tool. The following section shows you how the Magnetic Lasso tool works (and in the process, you'll understand how the Magnetic Pen tool works).

Drawn to the Edges: The Magnetic Tools

One thing that Photoshop is particularly adept at is finding the edge in an image where one color begins and another ends. The Color Range command, the Magic Wand, and several other tools can detect, for example, where in an image area a deep burgundy starts and a pale violet ends.

Photoshop's Magnetic tools shave a lot of manual-labor time off selecting an area surrounded by a contrasting color. In the following steps, you'll use the Magnetic Lasso tool to select around some lettering.

Working with the Magnetic Lasso Tool

1. Open the Gear1.tif image from the Examples/Chap03 folder on the Companion CD.

2. Double-click on the Magnetic Lasso tool on the toolbox (you might need to select the tool first, as the tools are grouped and hidden); this chooses the tool and displays the Options palette for the tool.

3. On the Options palette, set the Feathering to 0 (you want a crisp edge to the logo in the Gear1 image). Click the anti-aliased box if it's not already checked (this keeps edge pixels smooth in appearance). Leave the Lasso Width at 10 pixels—this is how wide the path can be when the edge is being selected by the tool. Set the Frequency at 60. Frequency determines how often a "fastener" (a fastener looks like an anchor point) is placed along the selection edge. There are a lot of curves and twists to the gear path, so more fasteners ensure a more accurate selection. Finally, set the Edge Contrast to 30%. This determines how different in color the foreground and background have to be so the tool can find the edge. In this picture, the background is clearly a different color than the foreground lettering.

4. Start at the upper left of the first character in the image, and then *move*, don't drag, the cursor to the right *without clicking*, following the edge of the lettering (see fig. 3.31).

FIGURE 3.31   *Allow the tool to operate by itself; don't drag the tool, but instead, "hover" the cursor, don't click the mouse, and travel along the edge of the area you want selected.*

5. Okay, a quick lesson in using two different tools to create a single selection. Once you've moved the cursor all the way around the lettering to complete the outline, the selected lettering will become a marquee. Click on the Quick Mask tool to turn the selected area into an overlay color.

6. Use either the Paintbrush tool (with a small tip) or the Pen tool to encompass those areas shown in figure 3.32. Once they are selected, remove the Quick Mask overlay. With the Paintbrush tool, you remove the Quick Mask by applying white foreground color. If you use the Pen tool, Ctrl(⌘)+click on the Work Path title on the Paths palette to make selection marquees, and then press Delete (Backspace) while white is the background color.

7. Click on the Standard Editing button on the toolbox, and then right-click (Macintosh: hold Ctrl and click), and choose Layer Via Cut from the context menu.

8. Now you can fill the background layer with anything you please: a solid color, a gradient color, a repeating texture tile—you name it.

Remove Quick Mask from here

FIGURE 3.32   *Remove Quick Mask from the selection areas that you want to discard in the final image.*

9. This is all discovery stuff—there are no grades to be passed out—so you can close the image without saving at any time. Or save the image in Photoshop's PSD file format, for further goofing around.

Question: When is an eraser not an eraser? *Answer:* When it's a *Magic* Eraser! Okay, that was a pretty lame lead-in to the final section of this chapter—working with the Magic Eraser tool. This handy tool performs three functions at once—instead of selecting the foreground design from the image, the Magic Eraser:

1. Checks out where you clicked for color similarity.

2. It deletes as much of the background in the image as you specify.

3. It places the foreground element(s) on a layer.

Let's check it out.

Powers of the Magic Eraser Tool

The Magic Eraser, like other Photoshop tools based on color similarity, scouts the area in which you click, deletes all colors similar to that on which you clicked, and turns the background of an image into a layer. So your foreground object becomes an element on a layer, and you can stick anything you like on top of or behind this layer.

This is the easiest tutorial in the chapter, and yet it provides amazing results.

The Magic Eraser Tool and Solid Backgrounds

1. Open the Gear2.tif image from the Examples/Chap02 folder on the Companion CD.

   Note that the background is solid. Solid backgrounds might not cross your path in photographic image editing, but occasionally a model is photographed against a seamless piece of paper, and these steps will provide ideal results.

2. Drag on the face of the Eraser tool on the toolbox and then choose the Magic Eraser tool (the eraser with a sparkle next to it). Double-click on the tool to make the Options palette appear. Note that there are only three options, and you have experience with all three up to this point.

3. Type **1** in the Tolerance field. Such a narrow tolerance will allow you to choose only one color in the image, but, hey—the background is one, solid color, right? Check the Anti-aliased box—in addition to the background color, you'll want to remove some of the in-between colors at the edge between the foreground lettering and the background. Finally, make sure that Contiguous is unchecked.

4. Click on any area of the background, as shown in figure 3.33. Surprise! Not only has the background disappeared, but the lettering is now on a layer, saving you the trouble of an additional step.

5. Save the design in Photoshop's PSD format to your hard drive if you like. We won't be using the design again, so you might alternatively want to close the image without saving it.

note

There's a tool on the toolbox that has not been mentioned in this chapter: the Freeform Pen tool, located on the Pen tools flyout.

The operation of this tool is fairly straightforward. You drag with the tool; anchor points are added to the path whenever you make a sharp turn with the tool, and the tool's path is closed when you make a single click on the path's beginning point.

The Freeform tool is best used with a digitizing tablet, not a mouse, because a tablet offers more precision, and I can see no sense in making a rough path in an image. There are plenty of other tools that'll create a loose path.

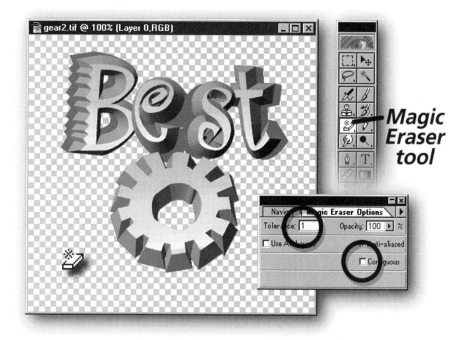

FIGURE 5.33   *The Magic Eraser tool can make quick work of erasing only the background of an image to transparency.*

You should congratulate yourself—or encourage others around you to congratulate you! You've made it through two chapters on selecting stuff, and you know how to use more than eight tools—probably more than someone with more experience than you. As you can see, different areas of an image, whether they represent a geometric pattern or they have colors in common, can be chosen in Photoshop when you pick the right selection tool. And you now know how to determine which is the best selection tool in your own work.

Summary

As mentioned earlier in this book, the art of selecting areas is probably the most important aspect of image editing, and Photoshop accommodates users of all levels with sophisticated tools for this chore. However, knowing how to select things isn't necessarily going to get you work! You need to know how to *manipulate* the things you select, and that's what chapter 4 is all about.

PART II

Working Smart in Photoshop

CHAPTER 4

Bouton's Bag of High-End Photoshop Tricks

It's only natural that when you see graphics tricks done, you want to know *how* the illusion was accomplished. More often than not I hear someone ask a graphics guru, "How did you do that???" and the answer is, "Photoshop."

"Yeah, okay, but what did you *do* in Photoshop to create the effect?" This chapter takes you through a handful of novel, eye-catching effects that are mostly created manually (we'll use a filter here and there). By the end of this chapter, you might just stop asking questions of the aforementioned graphics guru—and start providing the answers *yourself*, to others!

Creating Your Own Seamless Tiling Texture

There are many different uses for the right texture; you can use a texture for a Web page background, it can fill the background of a layout—you name it. But the most effective, useful textures have one thing in common—that they can repeat any number of times in any direction without displaying the seams that are the edges of the image.

Although you can create your own seamless tiling textures in any of several applications, this book is about Photoshop and what you can do with it. We'll focus on one—a brick wall—that can be used over and over again in your work, and *isn't* exactly simple to create. (Hey, as you read this book, you're gonna stretch a little <g>!) Let's get out the virtual mortar and trowel.

Setting Up the Document and Shading the Image

As we proceed, I'm going to toss some really good shortcuts at you so that, with a little practice, you'll be able to work with lightning speed in Photoshop. The first thing you need to do to make a brick wall tile is to open a new document, color it, and then filter it, so the individual bricks are not all a uniform color. Follow these steps and see how quickly you can get impressive results right from the beginning of an assignment:

Creating Brick Texture

1. Launch Photoshop. Once the interface appears, press Ctrl(⌘)+N.

2. Press Tab once to move from the title field to the Width field. Type **100** in the left field, press Tab, and then press the up- or down-arrow key to set the units to pixels. Repeat for the Height field.

3. Click on the drop-down arrow for color mode if it isn't already RGB Color, and choose RGB color. Press Enter (Return), and a new Untitled document appears in the workspace.

   These first three steps are pretty rote—you'll do this a thousand times in your years with Photoshop. Although this might not be the way *you* create new document windows, I've tried all different combinations of using the mouse and keyboard, or only the mouse, or only the keyboard, and these three steps are the quickest, if you'll practice using them all the time. My opinion is that (assuming you're right-handed) having the left hand on the keyboard and the right hand on your point-and-click device is the most productive way to approach designing in Photoshop. Now if there were only a way to incorporate our feet...

4. Click on the foreground color swatch on the toolbox, and in the Color Picker, choose a nice, medium brownish-red (R:167, G:112, and B:53 creates a handsome color). Press Enter (Return) to return to the workspace.

5. Press Ctrl(⌘)+A to Select All, press Alt(Opt)+Delete (Backspace) to fill the image window with foreground color, and then press Ctrl(⌘)+D to deselect the selection marquee. You can see the steps, and the result, in figure 4.1.

Perhaps the first time you perform these moves your hands will be in unique and uncomfortable positions. But with practice, you'll have anyone watching you work wonder how you set up a document so quickly!

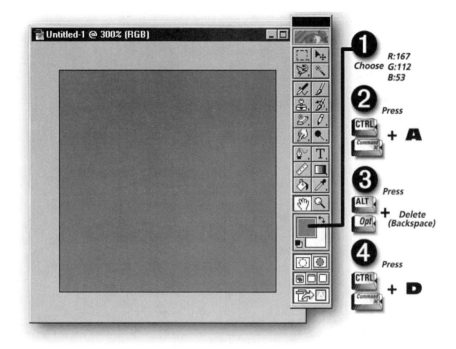

FIGURE 4.1   *Follow these steps to set up a document with the right foreground color in practically no time!*

6. Choose Filter, Artistic, Sponge. In the Sponge dialog box, choose 1 for the Brush Size, choose 12 for the Definition (the clarity of the border between colors), and then choose 5 for Smoothness (you don't want individual pixels to be evident in the image). Basically, you've defined a lot of detail in an area that now has smooth transitions between colors that the filter adds and the original solid color, as shown in figure 4.2. Click on OK to apply the filter.

   Although the Sponge pattern is a nice, organic one, it does not repeat precisely once across the image, and this means that a seam will show if you use it as a repeating pattern. This is not a big deal to correct—

7. Press Ctrl(⌘)+the plus key twice, and then drag the window edges away from the artwork; you're at 300% viewing resolution now. Choose Filter, Other, Offset.

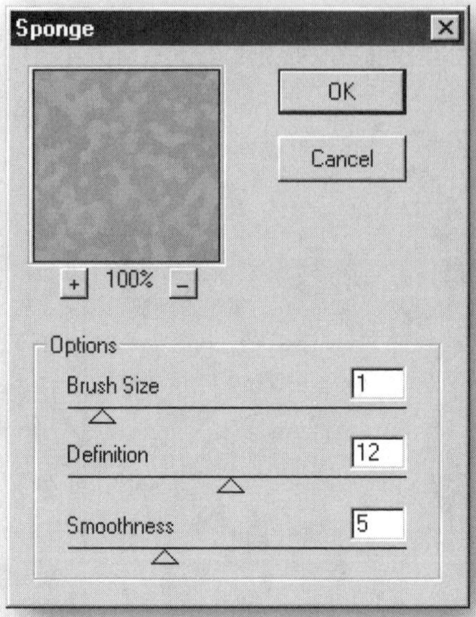

FIGURE 4.2   *Use these settings on a small image to create a good amount of detail in color transitions.*

8. In the Offset dialog box, type **50** in both the Horizontal and Vertical fields, and choose Wrap Around as the offset option, as shown in figure 4.3. You'll see hard edges starting at the center of the image, because you've used the Offset command to turn the image inside out, and the outside edges do not line up with each other.

9. Choose the Smudge tool from the Focus Tools flyout on the toolbox (the icon that looks like the "white glove" test), double-click on the Smudge tool if the Options palette isn't onscreen, set the Pressure to about 80%, press F5 and choose the second-row, second-from-left tip for the Smudge tool.

10. Stroke over areas that show the hard edges, as shown in figure 4.4. Yes, you are blurring the design somewhat, but a brick texture should consist of both pitted and relatively smooth surface areas.

FIGURE 4.3   *The Offset command can move the center of an image to the image window's four edges, and move the four edges to the center of an image.*

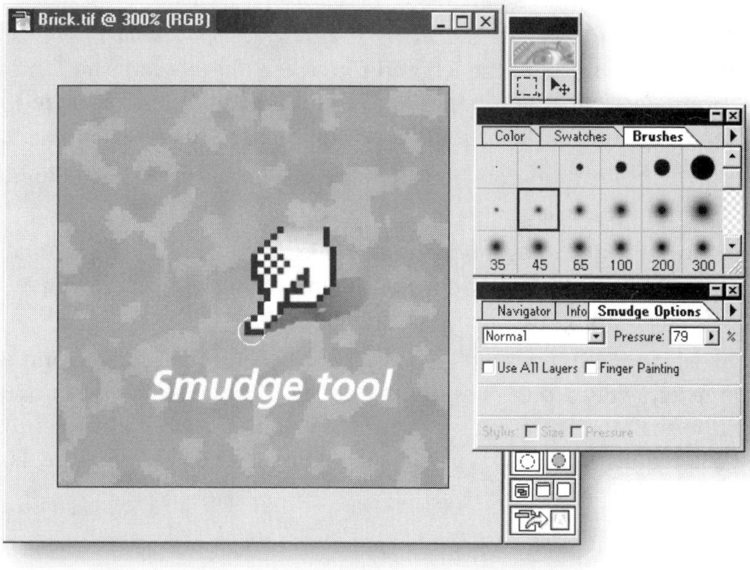

FIGURE 4.4   *The Smudge tool melds color areas together and blurs image content at the same time.*

11. Go to the Channels palette (F7) and drag the Green channel into the Create new channel icon at the bottom of the palette. This creates an alpha channel (a channel used by Photoshop for information other than color). Double-click on the title, and then type **Grouting & texture** in the Name field; then press Enter (Return).

12. Save this image to your hard disk as Brick.tif, in the TIFF file format, and keep it open. We're not done by a country mile.

In the next section you will design a mortar pattern on the brick texture, and then use the Lighting Effects' texture channel feature to make 3D recesses and protrusions across the surface of the image.

Setting Up Guides and Offsets for the Mortar

Like the Sponge pattern, the mortar in this tile also needs to be created in a way that repeats seamlessly. For this, we'll call on the Guides feature and the Offset feature (again) to ensure that the mortar repeats as seamlessly as the Sponge design. Here's how to push the design a little closer to realism:

Using Photoshop Guides

1. *(You're still viewing the* **Grouting & texture** *alpha channel.)* Press Ctrl(⌘)+R to display the rulers to the left and top of the image window. Chances are that the units aren't what you need (you want pixels, not picas or inches), so double-click on either ruler, as shown in figure 4.5, to go to the Preferences dialog box.

2. In the Rulers drop-down box, choose pixels, and then press Enter (Return) to return to the workspace.

3. Using any tool, drag a horizontal guide down from the horizontal ruler and place it at 50 pixels (half the width of the image). Drag a vertical guide to 50 pixels on the ruler, using the same technique.

4. Click on the foreground color selection box on the toolbox, and then choose a medium gray. Color does not matter; an alpha channel can handle only grayscale information. The grout on the bricks will produce a slight recess (because the color you chose is darker than the texture in the channel—the darker the color, the greater the recess).

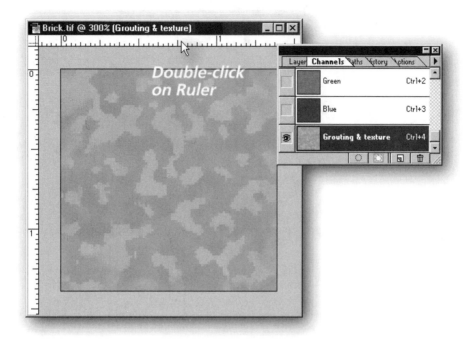

FIGURE 4.5   *To quickly access the Ruler Preferences dialog box, double-click on a ruler.*

5. Choose the Paintbrush tool, and then choose the top-row, third-from-left tip on the palette. Click at the left edge of the horizontal rule, and then hold Shift and draw all the way to the right. Shift constrains direction of the brush, but first you need to "tell" it where the beginning point is.

6. Click at the top of the image window, on the vertical guide. Hold Shift and drag down until the line meets the horizontal line, as shown in figure 4.6. Your effort so far has established half the bump map needed to make the brick texture dimensional.

7. Press Ctrl(⌘)+F. Offset was the last filter you used, right? Ctrl(⌘)+F applies the last-used filter, so the image becomes offset by 50 pixels, both horizontally and vertically, but the guides don't move (which is good).

8. Again, draw a straight horizontal line at the 50-pixel mark on the ruler, and drag a vertical line at the 50-pixel mark, a line that goes down from the top edge and stops at the horizontal line. For a better idea of what's happening, take a look at figure 4.7.

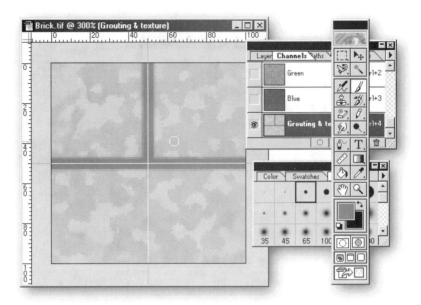

FIGURE 4.6   *Drag straight lines to form an upside-down T to create part of the bump map ("texture map," in PhotoshopSpeak) for the brick pattern.*

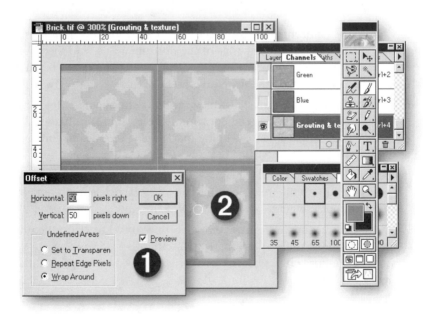

FIGURE 4.7   *After painting the first part of the mortar, use the Offset command to move the center of the image, and then apply mortar strokes again.*

9. Press Ctrl(⌘)+F so that the image has its original center in the center, and then press Ctrl(⌘)+tilde(~) to change your view of the image to the *RGB composite* (the normal) viewing mode.

10. Repeat steps 5–8 on the color view, except choose a lighter shade of gray for the mortar.

Now, we *could* be cyber-slobs about the guides. They can stay right where they are—you can hide them by choosing View, Hide Guides—or you can put the guides back into the rulers, or choose View, Clear Guides if you want *every* guide deleted. I prefer to put the guides back into the rulers (and so do you) because then other Photoshop users cannot open your file and exclaim, "Oh, what a sloppy user. He didn't clean up the file before sending it to me."

11. Hold the Ctrl(⌘) key and then drag the guides back into the rulers, as shown in figure 4.8. With the single exception of the Hand tool, every chosen tool toggles to the Move tool when Ctrl(⌘) is held. And only the Move tool can reposition guides.

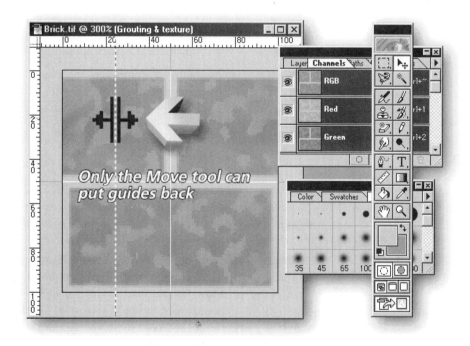

FIGURE 4.8   *Put the guides back in the rulers, using the Move tool.*

12. Press Ctrl(⌘)+S to save your work up to this point. Keep the image open in Photoshop.

We haven't used the alpha channel for anything yet, have we? This alpha channel is going to make the colors in your brick tile come alive as shading and highlights are added to the finished image. All it takes is a fundamental working knowledge of the Lighting Effects filter.

Using Lighting Effects to "Emboss" an Image

The Lighting Effects filter creates the illusion in an image that there is a light source in addition to the existing light in, say, a digitized photograph. I encourage you to play with this feature and experiment with the preset lights. Don't feel intimidated by the bevy of options in its dialog box, however—the Lighting Effects filter cannot truly *change* the existing lighting in a photograph, nor can it cast shadows in an image or correct a poorly lit photo.

The Lighting Effects option we're interested in is the Texture Channel option. This is Adobe's own name for something usually called a *bump map* in modeling and rendering programs. Briefly, the Texture Channel option works like this: a grayscale image governs the apparent height of all the areas in an image. When there's a transition from a dark area to a light one in the grayscale image, a "hill" is produced in the corresponding color image. Conversely, when the transition from light to dark occurs, a recess is suggested by the lighting in the corresponding color image.

You have in the Grouting & texture (alpha) channel all the visual information you need to create lines of mortar that dent inward, and sections across the brick part of the picture that look rough. Let's walk through the Lighting Effects features you can use to produce more realistic paintings:

Using the Lighting Effects Filter's Texture Option

1. Choose Filter, Render, Lighting Effects. The Lighting Effects dialog box pops up. By default, one Spotlight-type light is illuminating a *proxy box* (a thumbnail duplicate) of the image.

2. Click on the Light type drop-down box and change the default light to Directional. With the cursor, click in the proxy box on the end of the line farthest from the center of the image. You are controlling the strength and direction of the Directional light. You should place the light source end of the line a little outside the proxy box, resting about ¼ screen inches away from the upper-left corner of the proxy box (sneak a peek at fig. 4.9 for the exact location).

3. Set the Intensity to 35, set the Material slider to 0, choose Grouting & texture from the Texture Channel drop-down list, leave the White is high check box checked (light areas will protrude from the image), and then drag the Height slider to 18 (so the texture is obvious but not overstated). There are other parameters you can set when you create a lighting effect, but these are all you need for the brick texture. Think about the properties found in real brick, and you'll quickly understand why certain options were chosen in figure 4.9. Click on OK to apply the texture and return to the workspace.

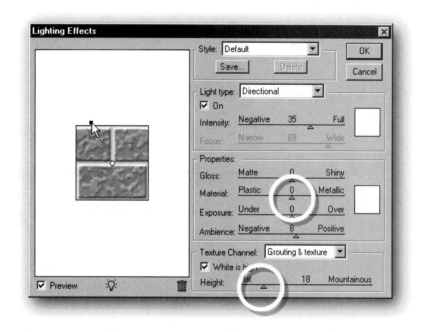

FIGURE 4.9   *The Lighting Effects dialog box offers many features, but you may only need one or two to create the texture you need.*

4. You can delete the Grouting and texture (alpha) channel at any time now, as it has served its purpose. To do this, you drag the title of the channel on the Channels palette into the trash can at the bottom right of the palette. Press Ctrl(⌘)+S now. Keep the image open.

Adding a self-created texture to the brick image was a piece of cake, right? Now, it's time to

- Test out the tile to make sure it's seamless (it is, but it's simply *fun* to check it out).

- Create a new image background that will serve as the test bed for the assignment in the following section.

Just follow these steps:

Checking Out Your Brick Work

1. To create a 640×480-pixel background texture, press Ctrl(⌘)+A to select the whole design, and then choose Edit, Define Pattern from the main menu.

2. Press Ctrl(⌘)+N to display the New image dialog box, and then enter **640** (pixels) in the Width field, and enter **480** (pixels) in the Height field. The Color Mode should be RGB color.

3. Press Enter (Return) to return to the workspace with an untitled new image. Press Ctrl(⌘)+R to hide the rulers.

4. Choose any selection tool. Press Ctrl(⌘)+A and then right-click (Macintosh: hold Ctrl and click) and choose Fill from the context menu. In the Use drop-down list, click on Pattern, and then press Enter (Return). Then press Ctrl(⌘)+D to remove the marquee selection lines.

   What you have now should look like figure 4.10.

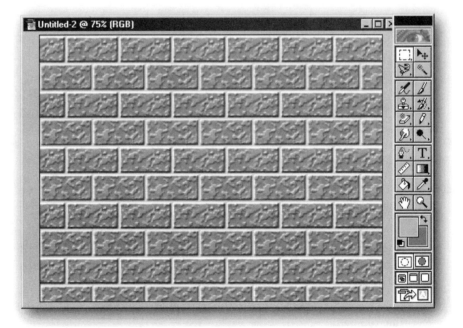

FIGURE 4.10   *A seamless tile can be used to fill an image canvas of any dimensions!*

5. Save this 640×480 image to your hard disk as Background.tif, in the TIFF file format. You'll use it next to add foreground interest and a very realistic shadow you'll handcraft.

Designing Shadows for Foreground Elements

Photoshop has a drop shadow filter for objects on layers (choose Layer, Effects, Drop Shadow), and Alien Skin's Eye Candy filters have a wonderful Perspective Shadow plug-in for Photoshop. However, shadows are not always straightforward enough to let a plug-in or a command do the shadow-creating work for you.

A shadow is a direct optical reaction to an object that either totally or partially obstructs the light cast on a surface. When the light source is located where the camera" is, the shadow drops beneath the object to create a *drop shadow*. And when an object is resting on a surface, and a wall or something is in the background, and the light casts on the wall, a *cast shadow* is created.

In this section you'll learn about a different type of shadow: a shadow that casts both down *and* behind an object, as though the light source were a spotlight. What shape will the shadow take? You'll see, in this set of steps:

Creating a Realistic Shadow

1. Open the Nut&Bolt.psd image from the Examples/Chap04 folder on the Companion CD.

2. Press F7 if the Layers palette isn't onscreen, and then drag the title of the layer into the brick wall image, as shown in figure 4.11. This is a shortcut for first choosing the Move tool, and then dragging from window to window. You can close the Nut&Bolt image at any time now to retrieve screen real estate.

3. Right-click (Macintosh: hold Ctrl and click) on the title of the layer, and choose Duplicate Layer from the context menu (see fig. 4.12).

4. In the Duplicate Layer dialog box, type **Shadow** in the As: field and then press Enter (Return).

5. The Shadow layer is on top of the image stack now, but shouldn't be. Drag the Shadow title on the Layers palette and drop it on the Layer 1 title. Layer 1 becomes the top layer.

   This last step might take a little practice. To reorder the layers, you need to click and drag the active layer and not let go of the mouse button until the layer you're holding directly covers the other layer title. Play with this technique until you've mastered it; your alternative is to memorize a really obnoxious pair of keyboard commands or to hunt through the main menu.

Figure 4.11   *To copy a layer, you can drag a title on the Layers palette into an image window.*

6. Click on the Shadow layer title to make it the current editing layer, and then check the Preserve Transparency check box. Press D (default colors), and then press Alt(Opt)+Delete (Backspace) to apply black foreground color to only the nontransparent areas of the layer, as shown in figure 4.13. When you're done, uncheck the Preserve Transparency check box.

7. Press Ctrl(⌘)+T to display the Transform bounding box around the shadow on the layer, and then right-click (Macintosh: hold Ctrl and click) and choose Distort from the context menu. With your cursor, create a diamond shape like that shown in figure 4.14. This distortion of the black area makes it look as though the light source in the scene is closest to the head of the nut, pointing both down and away from the viewer.

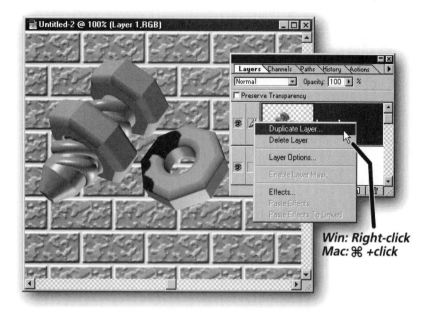

Figure 4.12   *There are three different ways to duplicate a layer. Approaching the command from the title on the palette is usually the quickest way.*

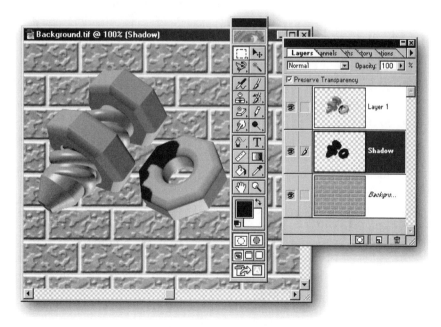

Figure 4.13   *Checking the Preserve Transparency box for the current layer prevents color or a pasted image area from entering the layer.*

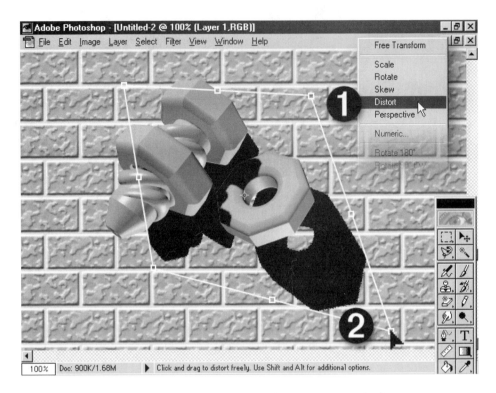

FIGURE 4.14   *The Distort mode of the Transform command enables you to move the four anchor points independently.*

8. Press Enter (Return) to finalize the distortion (press Esc if you don't like your work and want out of the distortion), and then choose Filter, Blur, Gaussian Blur.

9. In the Gaussian Blur dialog box, drag the slider to about 4.3 pixels, as shown in figure 4.15. To preview the area you propose to blur, place your cursor in the *image window* (it magically becomes a preview box); then find an edge to the shape and zoom in or out if you want to, using the plus and minus buttons in the dialog box.

10. Click on OK to apply the Gaussian blur, choose Multiply mode on the Layers palette to make the Shadow layer appear more dense, and then drag the Opacity slider to about 60% to allow some of the background brick to show through the shadow, as shown in figure 4.16. No shadow on earth is ever 100% opaque—there's usually a lot of ambient light in surroundings that illuminate the area partially hidden by shadows.

FIGURE 4.15   *It's usually a good idea to preview an effect before you apply it. IOW, it saves time.*

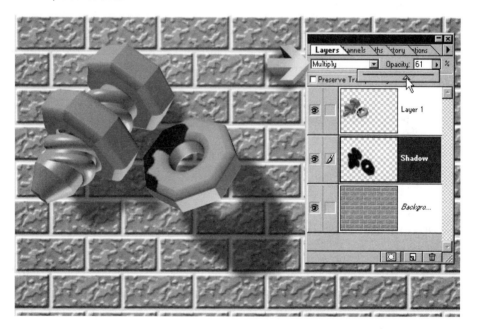

FIGURE 4.16   *Real shadows are not 100% dense. Use the Opacity feature on the Layers palette to "tune" your shadow.*

11. You can either flatten the image and save it in the TIFF format you started out with, or save this multilayered art as Brickwall (or some more inspired name), in Photoshop's PSD format. Keep this file open.

The brick-wall background image is quite large. If you wanted to post it on the Web, you'd use the small tile you created for the background—and people's browsing software would simply repeat the design. But the foreground elements—the nuts and bolt and shadow—are actually quite small. In the next section, you'll learn how to make Photoshop crop the foreground design to the smallest dimensions possible. This trick will make the graphic as compact as possible if you ever wanted to use such an image on the Web.

Using Photoshop's Calculations for Cropping

The programmers who create applications such as Photoshop tend to put into the program what is on their own personal wish list. And when you discover a gem like the one you'll see in this section, you'll be able to put it to good use as soon as you understand what's going on.

When you copy the contents of a layer, Photoshop will only copy pixels that have 1% or greater opacity. No totally transparent pixels are copied (how would anyone see them anyway?). Now, when a blurry background such as the shadow is copied to the clipboard, chances are you cannot tell where 0% opacity ends and 1% opacity begins (1% opacity is almost too faint for the human eye to see). But if you accidentally crop an image incorrectly by hand, you will definitely notice a shadow that has been cropped. Photoshop takes care of this potential problem automatically; it can tell total transparency from 1% opacity.

In the next set of steps you'll check out a maneuver that will create the smallest possible image whose dimensions include the nuts, bolt, and shadow:

Copying the Most Tightly Cropped Image

1. Uncheck the eye icon for the Background layer, as shown in figure 4.17. This makes only the Layer 1 contents and the shadow visible, and these are the layers you will merge to make one image area to copy to the clipboard.

2. Press Ctrl(⌘)+Shift+E (Layer, Merge Visible). Now, a single layer titled "Shadow" is visible.

3. Press Ctrl(⌘)+A, and then press Ctrl(⌘)+C to copy the contents of the Shadow layer to the clipboard. Close the PSD image without saving changes.

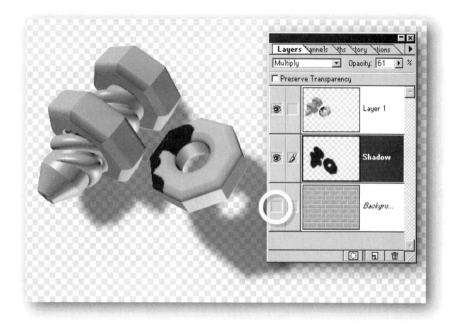

FIGURE 4.17   *Uncheck the eye icon to the left of a layer title to hide that layer.*

4. Press Ctrl(⌘)+N, and click on the Transparent button in the dialog box. Actually, you can press Enter right after this command, but I wanted to show you what the New dialog box will look like. Photoshop reads the information on the clipboard and offers a new canvas that is precisely the size of the outer extents of the clipboard contents (see fig. 4.18).

5. In figure 4.19, you can see the result of allowing Photoshop to calculate the perfect size image window for your nuts, bolt, and shadow.

6. You may choose to save this composition now, or you can close the image without saving; you no longer need the example image.

Now that you've learned the nuts and bolts of transparency selections, let's move on to creating a glow effect. It's a little like creating a shadow, but there are interesting things you can do to make the glowing effect your own—in a word, unique.

tip

If you do not want a new document to be automatically created with the dimensions of the contents of the clipboard, hold Alt(Opt) while you choose File, New from the menu.

Also, if you want a new image to be the same size as an image window currently in Photoshop's workspace, while the New dialog box is open, choose Window, and then the file name from the main menu.

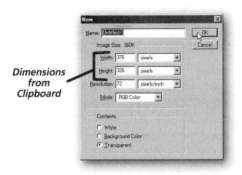

Dimensions from Clipboard

FIGURE 4.18   *Photoshop's New dialog box offers the dimensions, resolution, and color mode of the clipboard's contents.*

FIGURE 4.19   *With not a transparent pixel to spare, Photoshop's new image window perfectly encompasses the artwork from the clipboard.*

Creating a Glow Effect

Like shadows, glowing things in an image should have soft extremes, so the shape of the glow needs to be blurred. There's an important point I need to make here concerning the photorealism of the glows you will create. Anything like the sun or a light bulb gives off light and heat in a spherical shape, and part of that effect means that the front of the light-emanating object is partially hidden by the glow. I see little point in obscuring the front of the example image you'll work with, mostly because

- Artistically, you tend to ruin a piece when a glow not only outlines, but also fills the shape of the glowing object. Reality must yield to art once in a while to make visual communication direct and beautiful at the same time.

- The public is so used to seeing a CG (*computer graphics*) glowing outline on objects, your own creation in this section will be in keeping with the popular trend.

Let's begin with an object that would look cool if it were glowing—a 3D rendering of a bicycle:

Setting Up a Glowing Effect

1. Open the Bicycle.psd file from the Examples/Chap04 folder on the Companion CD. You might as well work with it at a 1:1 viewing resolution, so double-click on the Zoom tool, and drag the image window edges away from the image, if necessary. You can see in figure 4.20 that the file has one layer, no background, and that it's cropped too tightly to get a glow going around the bike. Choose Image, Canvas Size, type **600** (pixels) in the Width field, type **400** (pixels) in the Height field in the Canvas Size dialog box, and then press Enter (Return).

2. Click on the Create new layer icon on the Layers palette, and then click on the icon again. This creates Layer 1 and Layer 2 above the Bicycle layer.

3. Drag the Bicycle layer title on top of the Layer 2 title, and then release the cursor. The Bicycle layer is on the top of the heap now.

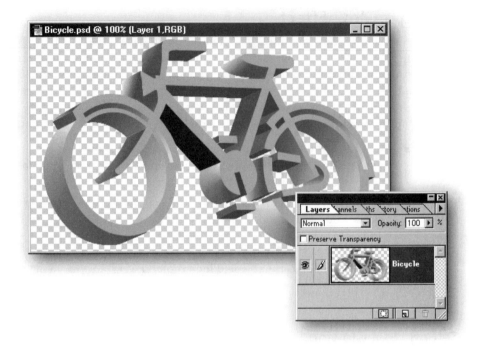

FIGURE 4.20   *Give the element on its layer some "breathing room" before you apply the effect.*

4. Click on the Layer 1 title to make it the active editing layer, press D (default colors), and then press Alt(Opt)+Delete (Backspace). Now Layer 1 is all black.

5. Double-click on the Layer 2 title on the Layers palette; then, in the Layer Options dialog box, type **Glow** in the name field, and press Enter (Return). Choose Screen from the Layers palette's modes drop-down list. Screen is exactly the opposite of Multiply mode, which you used earlier. In Screen mode, darker colors drop out, while lighter colors become intensely brilliant.

6. Ctrl(⌘)+click on the Bicycle title on the Layers palette. This loads the nontransparent areas of the Bicycle layer as a marquee selection (but the active, highlighted layer is still the Glow layer). See figure 4.21.

7. Choose Select, Modify, Expand. In the Expand Selection dialog box (see fig. 4.22), type **7** in the field and then click on OK. Click on the foreground color selection box on the toolbox, choose a lemon color, and then press Enter (Return).

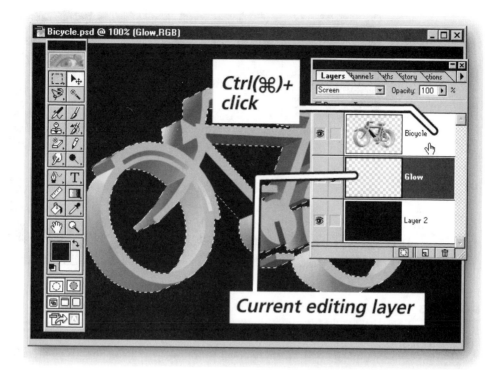

FIGURE 4.21   *You can load a selection marquee that is based on the nontransparent areas of an image layer.*

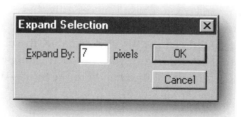

FIGURE 4.22   *The Expand command creates a new marquee that is a given number of pixels larger than the original, at every point of the original path.*

8. Press Alt(Opt)+Delete (Backspace), press Ctrl(⌘)+D, and then press Ctrl(⌘)+F. Ctrl(⌘)+F applies the last-used filter, and you used the Gaussian Blur filter last (if you read this chapter from the beginning. The value is 4.3 pixels). Your bicycle should now look like a shiny new one, as shown in figure 4.23.

Figure 4.23   *Apply the Gaussian blur filter to the Glow layer to make the color appear to glow behind the bicycle.*

9. Keep the image open. In the section to follow, you'll see how to create a variation on the glow effect.

Creating a Glow by Stroking a Path

A glow behind something doesn't necessarily have to touch the foreground element—you can have an outline of glowing energy that surrounds but never touches the foreground element (in this example, the bicycle). Although there are two ways to accomplish this effect, you will use the long way to your goal because it involves using a feature you'll find handy in the future—the option to turn a selection into a path.

Here's how to create a different type of glowing outline:

Creating a Path for a Glow

1. With the Glow layer as the current editing layer on the Layers palette, press Ctrl(⌘)+A, and then press Delete (Backspace). Press Ctrl(⌘)+D to deselect the marquee; the Glow layer is cleaned off and ready for a new application of "glow."

2. Ctrl(⌘)+click on the Bicycle title on the Layers palette to load a marquee selection, and then choose Select, Modify, Expand. Type **15** in the dialog box, and then press Enter (Return).

3. On the Paths palette, click on the Makes work path from selection icon, as shown in figure 4.24. At this point you could choose to stroke the marquee selection (Edit, Stroke), but I want you to work with more of the features, such as the Paths palette. "More is better," I read someplace…

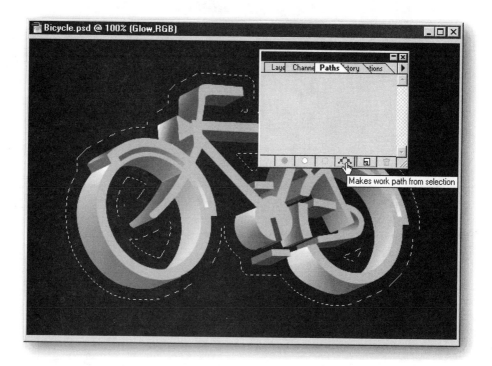

FIGURE 4.24   *When you click on the Makes work path from selection icon, the marquee is replaced with a fairly good approximation of the shape, made out of single or multiple paths.*

4. Get out the Brushes palette by double-clicking on the Paintbrush tool, and then choose the second-row, far-right tip from the Brushes palette.

5. Click on the Strokes path with the foreground color icon, as shown in figure 4.25, and then click on a vacant area of the Paths palette to hide the paths. Ta-dah!

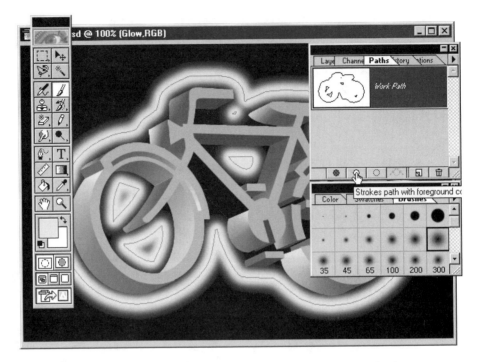

FIGURE 4.25   *You've created an eye-catching glow effect that does not touch the geometry of the object casting the glow!*

6. You can choose to save this piece or not. In your own work, you should buy the largest hard drive on earth and save absolutely everything as you begin with Photoshop. As you become more experienced, you can be more selective with what you keep. In any event, you are done with this image, so you can close it at any time.

An embossing effect can have several variations, and the good news is that Photoshop, starting with version 5.0, offers presets for embossing. So if you're new to this stuff, hang on, and we'll travel to the land of 3D Photoshop-created shapes.

note

If you ever want to stroke a path, but have no painting tool defined on the toolbox, the Stroke command on the Paths palette will default to the Pencil tool with a diameter of 1 pixel (a fairly pathetic effect). Always make sure you have chosen the tool you need before you use the Stroke path feature.

Using the Layer Effects Command

Adobe has gone out of their way to present a miasma (okay, a plethora, not a miasma) of variations on the plain, old emboss effect you might have seen with plug-ins or in other programs. This section is going to take you through the process of embossing, so all you need is a good piece of artwork and a few moments to create "art to go."

By the way, some of the example images you're working with came from the typeface Carta, which you probably own if you've bought an application that includes fonts. Zapf Dingbats is also an excellent resource for minimalist clip art. Don't underestimate how well you can embellish a well-designed, simple outline (the best symbols to use for extrusion and embossing are *stencils*—black shapes with no outlines).

Let's run through some of the creative possibilities of the Layer Effects command.

tip

This one will make advanced users wonder where you found this information! The Strokes path with foreground color icon on the Paths palette is a tad misleading—there are a number of *other* tools that can stroke the path, and these tools *do not* use the current foreground color. For example, choose the Blur tool and stroke a selection, or sample an area with the Rubber Stamp tool (press Alt(Opt)+click) and then stroke the path to get a *verrrry* weird effect!

Creating Layer Effects

1. Open Huey.tif from the Examples/Chap04 folder on the Companion CD. It's an enlarged symbol from Carta, and although the colors are black and white, this is an RGB color mode image (because you'll be adding color soon). Before you mess with an image, always check the title bar on the image window to see in which color mode you're working.

2. Press Ctrl(⌘)+A and then press Ctrl(⌘)+C, as illustrated in figure 4.26, to copy the image to the clipboard.

3. Click on the Channels tab of the palette (press F7 if the Layers/Channels/etc. palette isn't onscreen), and then Alt(Opt)+click on the Create new channel icon. In the New Channel dialog box, make certain that Color Indicates: Selected Areas button is checked, name the channel **Huey** (as shown in fig. 4.27), and then press Enter (Return).

   Okay, why did you choose Color Indicates: Selected Areas? Because what you have on the clipboard right now is a black helicopter against white, and shortly, you will want to load the color (the black) portion of the channel, but not the white.

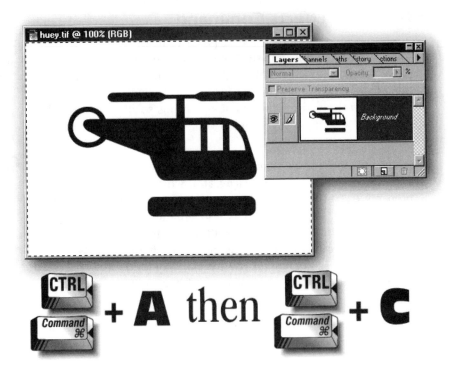

FIGURE 4.26   *Now do you see how useful it is to memorize some hot keys?*

4. Press Ctrl(⌘)+V and then Ctrl(⌘)+D. The copy of the copter is now in a new (alpha) channel.

5. Click on the RGB channel title on the Channels palette, and you really won't see a different view of the image window because the copter drawing is the same in both the alpha channel and the RGB view. Time to change that: click on the foreground color selection box to display the Color Picker.

6. Choose a nice military color, such as R:147, G:142, and B:129. Press Enter (Return).

7. Press Alt(Opt)+Delete (Backspace). The whole Huey image is a solid color now, and the drawing of the copter has been wiped out...sort of. It still exists as selection information in the Huey alpha channel.

8. On the Channels palette, Ctrl(⌘)click on the Huey channel title to load the outline of the copter as a selection. Click on the Layers tab to go back to the Layer options on the grouped palette. Right-click (Macintosh: hold Ctrl and click) on the Background title, and choose Layer Via Copy from the context menu, as shown in figure 4.28. You now have a new layer with a copter drawing filled in with the color you defined earlier, and a background that is the same color.

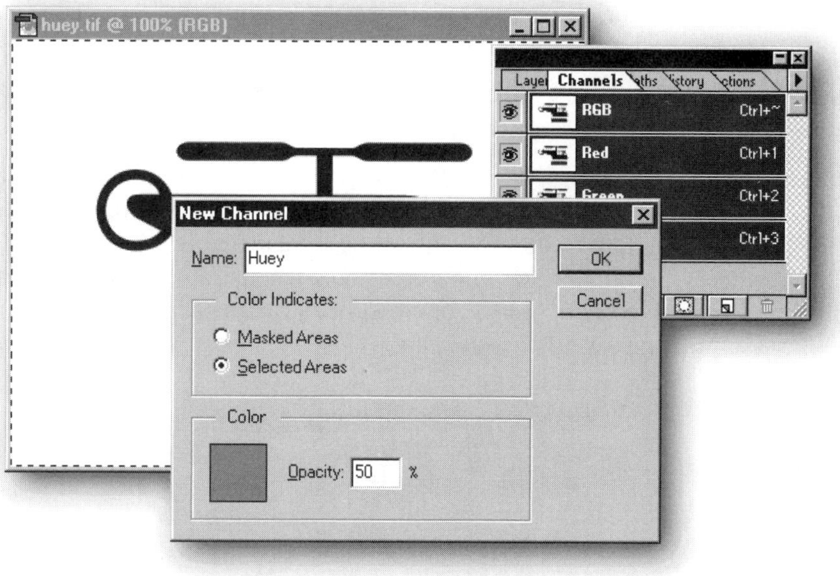

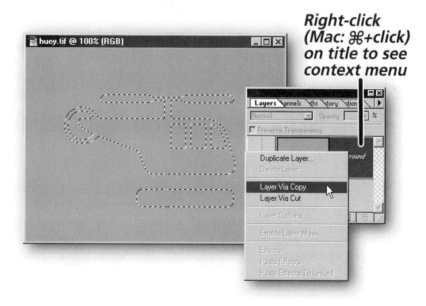

FIGURE 4.27   *Set up an alpha channel so that you will be able to load a selection that accurately describes the outline of the copter drawing.*

FIGURE 4.28   *Fill a layer with opaque pixels. Now you can use all of Photoshop's Layer Effects on the design.*

9. Choose Layer, Effects, Bevel and Emboss. Choose Inner Bevel as the style, as shown in figure 4.29. If you can move this slightly oversized dialog box out of the way, you'll see the Inner Bevel effect taking place on the layer.

10. Press Enter (Return) to apply the Inner Bevel command.

   At this point you can either save the file and call it quits, or...

11. Double-click on the "f" (for "filter") on the Layers palette. This loads the Bevel and Emboss dialog box. Guess what? You can change the emboss type ad infinitum! No emboss or other layer effect is permanent! Try choosing the Pillow emboss, press Enter (Return) and see how you feel about this variation. Continue to experiment now, or later, or close the file at any time, because you've now explored the Layer Effects feature.

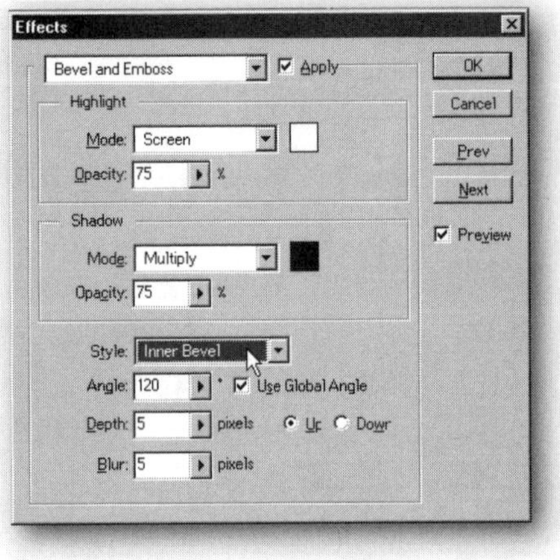

FIGURE 4.29   *Although the effect is always the same, you can change all the parameters of the Layer Effects to arrive at the embossing effect that most pleases you.*

In figure 4.30, you can see the four basic Bevel and Emboss effects. Again, by changing (light) angle and amount, and amounts of Highlight and Shadow (as well as their color), you can make an embossed design truly your own.

There's one last nugget on your way through Bouton's bag of tricks. Although this is a fundamentals—"the least you need to know"—book, a little polish applied to an effect can really make the difference between getting 10% out of Photoshop, and really using the program's graphics muscle. To conclude this chapter, let's look at fringing.

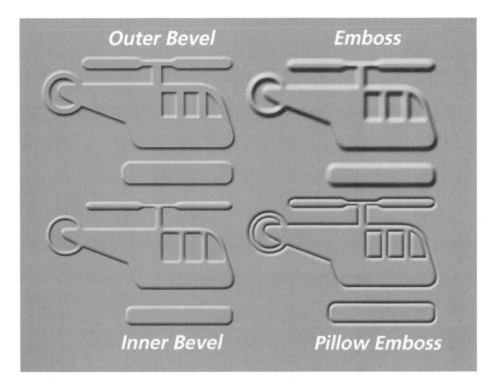

FIGURE 4.30   *Embossing is a valuable feature for Web work, or simply for making a card, using a color inkjet printer.*

Fringing is for Surreys, not Images

Because Photoshop offers anti-aliasing with most of its tools and commands, you're more likely than not working with image areas whose edges are smoothed through anti-aliasing most of the time. This can be swell if the area you're manipulating is destined for backgrounds that are the same color as the selection's *original* background. But more often than not, you're pasting a selection from an image with a dark background onto a background that's light, or vice versa. And upon close inspection, you will see what is called *fringing* (unwanted colored pixels) at the edges of the pasted selection.

The fringing problem is easy to fix; in fact, Photoshop has a command that's exactly for this use. In the steps to follow, you'll copy an area to a new background, and then solve the fringing problem:

Removing Fringing the Easy Way

1. Open the Greetings.psd file from the Examples/Chap04 folder on the Companion CD.

2. Double-click on the Background title on the Layers palette. This displays the Make Layer dialog box, as shown in figure 4.31. Press Enter (Return) to accept the default name for the layer.

FIGURE 4.31   *Double-clicking on a Background image puts you one step away from converting the image into a layer within an image.*

Now that the image is on a layer, you can use the Magic Eraser tool to eliminate everything but the text in the image.

3. To be able to detect the fringing that soon will occur in the image, the layer under the lettering should strongly contrast with the image's original background (white). Black is a good choice, so click on the Create new layer icon, drag its title to beneath the lettering layer on the Layers palette, and fill the layer with black (you *know* how to do this by now <g>).

4. Make the lettering layer the current editing layer by clicking on its title on the Layers palette. Choose the Magic Eraser tool from the toolbox, and then click on

the white on the layer. Poof! Nearly all the white is gone, exposing the black layer beneath the lettering layer. Press Ctrl(⌘)+ the plus key to zoom in to 200% viewing resolution. As you can see in figure 4.32, there are shades of white along the edge of the gold lettering. This marks image editing as amateurish, but the problem is very easy to fix when you use the right software.

FIGURE 4.32   *The white mixed between the gold edges of the lettering is due to anti-aliasing when the Magic Eraser tool did its thing.*

5. Choose Layer, Matting, Defringe. Type **1** in the field, as shown in figure 4.33, and then press Enter (Return). Also shown in figure 4.33 is what the edges of the lettering look like now. Pretty amazing, huh? The Defringe command selects, at the edge of a selection, pixels that are not 100% opaque (anti-aliasing pixels on layers are only partially opaque), and colors the pixels with the color that is on the *inside edge* of the selection border. In other words, Photoshop has taken white pixels and made them shades of gold like the rest of the lettering.

FIGURE 4.33   *The Defringe command is your ticket to more professional image editing...with basically no learning curve!*

6. Save the image in PSD format, or close the image now without saving. Again, all you've been doing is demonstrating a feature, using an example image. This stuff is not a candidate for the Louvre, right?

We've covered a lot of ground in this chapter. Many of the tricks are related to one another in one way or another; Photoshop's feature set—as I'm sure you've noticed by now—is tightly integrated. Anti-aliasing and feathering are different but share common aspects, selections can be made from layers or channels, and so on. Once you understand the relationship, graphics problem solving becomes a much easier task.

Summary

I know, I know...after two chapters on selecting stuff, this chapter on actually *doing* something in Photoshop was a welcome change of pace, right? The steps in this chapter that are used to perform *image editing* (I won't call them tricks anymore) are both hard and simple, and I chose the simple ones to share with you. Embossing, tile creation, shadow-making—none of this is difficult. But the big payoff is that now you've learned how to do it exactly like a Photoshop expert, and hopefully, the repetition of hot keys will make it quicker and easier for you in the future to set up a document and get right to work.

Chapter 5 concentrates on the photographic side of Photoshop. How do you correct that awful color in that photo of Grandma? How do you make the midtones lighter in an image without messing up the highlights and shadows? Good questions. And good answers right around the next page.

Color and Tone Correction

There are 1,001 things that can make the picture you take a clunker. You could have accidentally sheared off Aunt Bessy's forehead when you framed through the lens, or someone in the photo could have their eyes closed, or *you* could have moved and blurred the picture.

Even with today's high-tech image editors, such as Photoshop, there's not a lot you can do about visual information that is completely missing from a picture (except take the picture again). But—here comes the good news—there are a *lot* of features in Photoshop that can clean up a picture that's too dark or too light, or whose colors are cast in an unflattering direction (everyone in the image has the complexion of a smoked sausage or of an icicle).

Because this is a fundamentals book, we need to start at the root of color and tone corrections that computers enable us to do, and then quickly rise, taking this knowledge with us, to some practical examples of how to perform what folks on the street would call "miracles." Because tones are found in both color and black-and-white images, we'll explore tones and tonal correction first.

Working with Tones

Before talking about correcting tones, it might be nice to explain what a tone *is!* Tones are an image's brightness values. With computer monitors and adapter cards, what you see is generally broken down into three components—three channels of additive color: red, green, and blue. Hence the term RGB monitor. A combination of 100% intensity from all three guns in the cathode tube of your monitor builds a white tone, and when there is no signal through any of the guns, the monitor displays a black tone.

But RGB color is more than what your monitor displays; it's a color mode in Photoshop, a color space. A *color space* describes the limits to which any particular mode can express color. For example, all Indexed Color mode images, such as the GIFs people put on the Web, have a color space of 256 unique colors. If you want to add a color that's not in the color space, you need to first lose a color (and this process is called "messing up a perfectly good image"), or you can do nothing about the limitations of the color space. Fortunately, RGB color has a color space of 16.7 million possible unique colors. And because it's a fact that the human eye can only perceive a handful of colors at one time, the RGB color space ain't too bad.

RGB Equals HSB

The bad news (it's not all that bad, actually) is that if you work with colors in the RGB color space as combinations of red, green, and blue, you'll immediately find it almost impossible to define a color that you want. And if you have trouble finding the right *color*, you will almost surely find it impossible to tack down a specific *tone* and correct it.

One of the first people to see this problem is Dr. Alvy Smith (the founder of PIXAR). He, too, wanted a more convenient way to define colors as we see them, so he coinvented the HSB color space, which corresponds exactly to the RGB color model. (In other words, every color you can define using amounts of red, green, and blue can be identically expressed as degrees of **h**ue, amounts of **s**aturation, and amounts of **b**rightness: HSB).

Specifying a Tone

Okay, I feel like a fool illustrating the different mechanics of RGB and HSB color in a black-and-white book, but bear with me. Suppose you want to define 41% black to use in image retouching.

Profound Wisdom #7:

Because computers calculate colors digitally, all color components are measured in whole, discrete, limited numbers.

Huh? Okay—Photoshop's convention is to give 256 levels of intensity to each of the three color channels (red, green, blue) that make up the RGB color space. So the number 256 pops up a lot in calculations.

Why 256? Because to a computer, it's a nice, neat amount. It's actually expressed as 2 (on or off, in binary terms) to the 8th power (there are 8 bits in a byte of info), and 2 to the 8th power is 256. And because there are three channels, the number 256 to the 3rd power is 16.7 million and some change.

tip

For the same reason that no two people speak identically, it seems as though no two computer engineers will call the Brightness component of HSB color by the same name. Alternative names for Brightness are Lightness, Value, and Luminance.

What is the practical difference between the words brightness, lightness, value, and luminance? Answer: none!

Figure 5.1 shows how you'd do it in RGB color—with a lot of guessing and a lot of math. This figure also shows how you'd define 41% black using the HSB color model—not the same chore, eh?

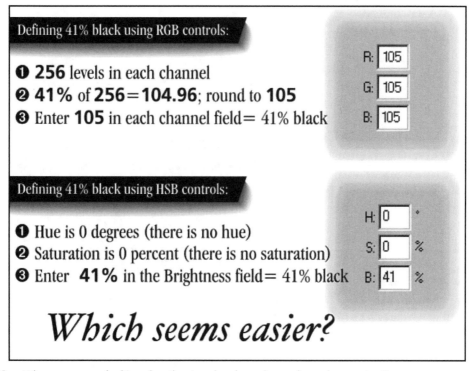

Defining 41% black using RGB controls:

❶ **256** levels in each channel
❷ **41%** of **256**=**104.96**; round to **105**
❸ Enter **105** in each channel field= 41% black

R: 105
G: 105
B: 105

Defining 41% black using HSB controls:

❶ Hue is 0 degrees (there is no hue)
❷ Saturation is 0 percent (there is no saturation)
❸ Enter **41%** in the Brightness field= 41% black

H: 0 °
S: 0 %
B: 41 %

Which seems easier?

FIGURE 5.1   *When you are looking for the tonal value of a color, why waste time calculating equal amounts of three colors? Instead, use the HSB color space to define the shade in 1-2-3.*

Being able to define a percentage of black is a good skill to have. Someday, someone is bound to call you on the telephone to ask you for art that has a certain tone in it, and you're now prepared to spec a tone. But the larger issue here is that brightness can be isolated from the other HSB components, which means that you can adjust the tones in an image without mucking up the saturation of colors or the hues. In the following section, first you'll correct the tones in a grayscale image, and then you'll try the same techniques on a color image. In both instances, what you'll be doing is a small sample of exactly what the pros do using Photoshop.

Examining an Image's Histogram

A *histogram* is a map. The map tells you at which brightness point pixels are located. For example, figure 5.2 shows an image and a histogram of the image. Let me explain what the histogram says about the image...

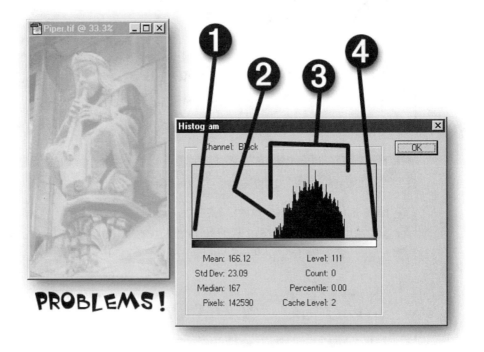

FIGURE 5.2   *A histogram tells you how many pixels are located at each point of the 256 brightness levels. In this image, there are too many pixels occupying neighboring values—and the neighborhood is crowded!*

1. At level 0 (zero) there are no pixels. That means that there is no true black in the Piper image (which you can detect also simply by looking at the picture).

2. There are very few pixels directly in the midtone region. A tip you can learn from a photographer (or from this book) is that the midtones are the location of most of the detail you see in many pictures. If there are not enough midtone pixels, or if they are bunched together, you are missing much of the image's content.

3. Most of the pixels are bunched around the upper midtones, which isn't necessarily a bad thing—but there is little or no contrast between adjacent levels. In

other words, level 112 should be markedly different in pixel count than, say, level 113. By staggering the amount of pixels at every other level (this is sometimes called "combing"), you increase the contrast without messing up image detail.

4. There are no whites in this picture, which accounts for a lot of the dullness of the image.

What can you and Photoshop do to correct this image? There are tools of varying sophistication, beginning with the Brightness/Contrast command, which you'll check out in the following section.

Adding Contrast to a Photograph

Brightness and Contrast do not need a fancy definition in this book. You adjust them in an image in Photoshop in much the same way you adjust them in an image on a TV set. We're particularly interested in the Contrast control on the Brightness/Contrast dialog box, because there's so little contrast in the Piper image.

When you add contrast to an image, it's almost as though you're commanding the pixels in the image to make a decision. You're telling the pixels in the lower end of the range to choose a value even darker than the current value. The converse is true with lighter pixels—by adding contrast you force lighter pixels to become lighter. This is why the Brightness/Contrast command is

- The simplest of the tone controls in Photoshop.
- The only tool you might ever need if your images have poor (but not disastrous) separations of tones.

Let's see what adding contrast alone can do for the Piper:

Using the Brightness/Contrast Command

1. From the Examples/Chap05 folder of the Companion CD, open Piper.tif in Photoshop.

2. Choose Image, Adjust, Brightness/Contrast; the dialog box floats above the workspace.

3. Drag the Contrast slider to +59, as shown in figure 5.3. As you can see, the Piper image definitely improves when contrast is created.

FIGURE 5.3   *A quick fix for a dull image is to increase the image's contrast.*

4. Save the image in Photoshop to your hard disk as Piper1.tif, in the TIFF file format. Keep it open; you can delete it from hard disk later.

So what does this improved image have in terms of pixel distribution? Let's check into the Histogram feature and find out. Choose Image, Histogram, and you'll see a graph that looks like figure 5.4. It's not a bad distribution of pixels. But your eyes and the histogram will tell you that you need something more sophisticated to push those pixels into the right levels!

You can close the Piper1.tif image now, and load again the original Piper.tif from the Companion CD. In the following section, we'll work with the Levels command (sounds ideal for setting brightness levels, huh? <g>), and see whether we can make this picture, um, "picture perfect."

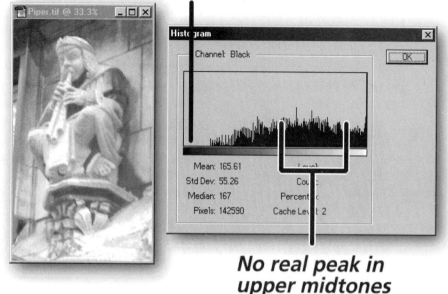

Still no black

No real peak in upper midtones

FIGURE 5.4   *The histogram (and your eyes) tell you that the picture still has no black point and the upper tones are still bunched together, obscuring image detail.*

Using the Levels Command

Photoshop's Levels command divides the histogram of an image around three distinct points: the *black point* (level of 0 brightness). The *white point* (level of 255 brightness), and a *midpoint* (level of 128 brightness). Although you can perform manual adjustments to an image, often you will find that clicking the Auto button in the Levels command's dialog box will dramatically improve an image. So much so that, after one step, you can call it quits!

Before you touch anything, try to envision the original histogram of an image as having an elastic band that encompasses all the levels. You can then stretch the band to make the levels proportionately spread out to the extent of the elastic band.

The Levels command dialog box consists of an Input area and an Output area, although even some pros (including *moi*) don't notice at first the controls at the bottom of the screen. In a moment I'll discuss these Output controls, whose sole purpose is to create *less* contrast in an image.

Let's test the Levels command now:

How the Levels Command Works

1. With Piper.tif as the current image in the workspace, press Ctrl(⌘)+L to display the Levels command dialog box. Not the current histogram that the Levels command is showing. It's very similar to what the Image, Histogram feature showed for the original image a while ago.

2. Click on Auto, as shown in figure 5.5. Wow! The image really snapped up, tonally, didn't it?

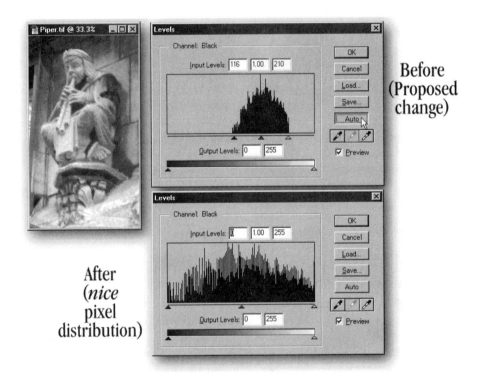

FIGURE 5.5   *Using the Auto button usually corrects the tones in color and grayscale images quite well.*

3. You can click on OK to apply the changes, and close the image, without saving, at any time.

Let us review exactly what the Levels command did, referring to figure 5.5, if necessary:

- The Auto feature, by default (you *can* change this; see the owner's guide), clips the upper- and bottommost pixels by 5 percent on the histogram. So when Photoshop defines the lightest and darkest pixels in the image, it ignores the first 5 percent of either extreme. This is done to eliminate any lone, errant pixel at an unrealistically high or low brightness value in the image, such as a reflection—a single pixel—off a far-away car.

- After the lightest and darkest pixels in the image have been defined as white and black, respectively, Photoshop redistributes the intermediate pixel values proportionately. If you look at the "after" histogram in figure 5.5, you'll see that Photoshop has not only stretched the area of pixels in the image to cover the whole tonal spectrum of levels, but has also gently increased contrast in the midtones by staggering each neighboring pixel's value. This is the comb effect I mentioned earlier, and it makes midtone detail easier to view.

The Auto feature is not a 100%, use-it-all-the-time panacea for poorly exposed images, however. There will be times when you want to increase or decrease contrast in the image selectively (in other words, by hand).

To do this on a muddy picture, follow these steps:

1. First, drag the black point slider (the far-left slider) to where there is a small number of pixels at the left of the histogram. Currently, the black point of your muddy image probably has no pixels at the absolute black point. This action redistributes all the pixels in the image (along a proportionate scale), so expect some differences in the overall shape of the histogram.

2. Next, drag the white point slider (the one on the far right) from its current position under no pixels to a position under several pixels. You've just added a lot of snap to the image, but you have one more control to adjust.

3. Take the midpoint slider (the middle slider under the histogram), and drag it slightly to the left, so the middle of the three Input fields at the top of the Levels dialog box reads about 1.2 or so. You've opened up the midtones by decreasing contrast, and now you might see more detail in the image's most critical zone: the midrange.

PROFOUND WISDOM #8:

Definitions of gamma by manufacturers, a lot of educated people, and sometimes the author, are usually imprecise. So don't get buzzed about the term.

The midpoint slider is sometimes called the *gamma* control, a mildly inaccurate term to describe the contrast in midpoint areas. Gamma is actually the nonlinearity of the monitor; as more voltage is supplied, the brightness of an image does not increase linearly—there's a dip in the 50% brightness area, and this "sag" in signal versus brightness is the true definition of gamma. We correct the sag by increasing the gamma.

4. If, on the other hand, the midtones in the image look wimpy and washed out, drag the Midpoint slider slightly to the right, until the middle Input value box reads .9 or so. It doesn't take a lot to dramatically change the mid-tone values.

Understanding the Output Controls in the Levels Command

You might never need to use the Output Controls in the Levels dialog box, unless you're making a camera-ready laser print (or film print) for a commercial printer.

Essentially, what happens when you drag to the right with the Output-Levels black point slider is that you tell Photoshop, "No, no—the black is too black in this image; only allow the lowest value to be (something such as) 95%. The converse is true of the white point Output slider. When you drag it to the left, you're telling Photoshop to ignore any information around the top percentile of the image, and absolute white shall fall beneath the new point. Why would you decrease contrast in an image? Isn't contrast good?

Hold the Presses

Yes, and no. For the human eye looking at an inkjet or laser print of your work, you want an image to be crisp and well balanced, tonally. But commercial print presses don't use ink jets or dots of toner to make an image. Commercial presses roll ink onto a very absorbent paper, and this ink *bleeds*. So to correct this problem, pressmen usually will tell you that their presses can hold 7% or 10% black and about 240% white.

The math is simple and you will get a positively crummy-looking, washed-out print from your laser printer that, in turn, will make a plate which will reproduce your work beautifully off a commercial press. Here's translation of what the pressman says:

Pressman: *I can hold 10% black.* You know that 10% of 256 (the number of levels of brightness in an image) is 25.6 (call it 26). So you need to set the Output black point slider to 26 for the image.

Pressman: *I can hold 95% whites.* This is the lightest area that is screened onto the newspaper. Anything higher results in no ink on the paper (and a glaring highlight is visible). You figure out that 95% of 256 is 243.2 (243). So you drag the white point slider to 243. Then press Enter (Return), and save your image as one that is destined for the commercial presses.

You know something? If this makes sense to you, this is more or less the same information I write for professionals in the *Inside Photoshop* series! So you're that much closer to the pros!

What Do a Good Color Picture's Tones Look Like?

On the Companion CD, in the Examples/Chap05 folder is a picture called 3Folks.tif. Open it in Photoshop; you're not going to do anything with it because it's already a good picture. You're only going to look at the color image's histogram.

Choose Image, Histogram now. As you can see in figure 5.6, the histogram tells you that the zones are well defined and separated. Your eyes naturally tell you this, too, but it's important to be able to read a histogram.

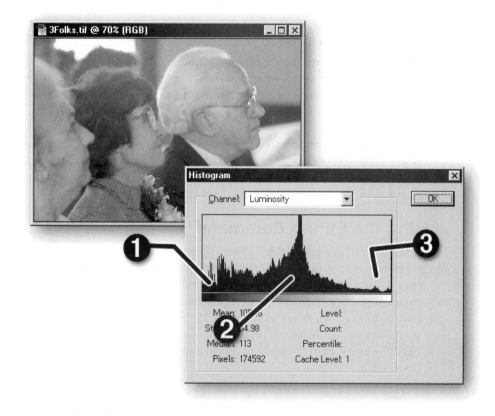

FIGURE 5.6   *Color images have hues, certain amounts of saturated color, and brightness values. The Brightness (also called Luminosity) affects the other two properties.*

Let me explain the callout numbers in figure 5.6:

1. There is a true black in the image's pixels—not only that, but there's a good amount of true black and dense-colored pixels. We can see this in the image in the middle woman's hair and the gentleman's jacket. Notice that there isn't a lot of detail to this navy blue jacket. This density is reflected in the histogram by the fact that there seems to be an even number of neighboring pixels in the low tones—there's no combing going on.

note

Notice that throughout this section, I've referred to tones as midpoints, black points, and so on. When you use the Levels command, you're only really moving these three points; Photoshop smoothly interprets the rest of the pixels to make smooth falloffs in the image.

2. There is a fairly steep peak in the midtones, and the midrange is where many pixels are located. This is good: this is where flesh tones are located, and this means that there's plenty of flesh tone value in the image. This is to be expected with a close-up picture of people's faces.

3. There's very little pure white in the picture, but there *are* some pixels in the upper register of this histogram, and that, too, is good. The man in the picture has a starched collar, and sunlight is streaming through the windows in the background.

In the following section you will work with the Curves command, the most sophisticated of the three tonal-correction tools. The Curves command goes beyond adjusting points on a tonal map.

Examining the Curves Command

Instead of a histogram, the Curves command presents you with a diagonal line that you can mold into a curved line, and in the process redistribute *groups* of pixels to reshape the tonal landscape of an image. You can lay down as many as 15 "anchors" on the Curves graph, reposition them, and as a result bend the curve until it makes an image look tonally perfect.

As I mentioned earlier, this is the most sophisticated tonal tool in Photoshop. As you begin your independent adventures with the program, the Curves command will be something you might want to

tip

Any time you get over your head in these dialog boxes and want to try again, but don't want to cancel out and then reenter the dialog box, hold down the Alt(Opt) key and the Cancel button becomes a Reset button. When you click Reset, every modification you made in the box returns to its original setting.

grow into, and not charge into head-first. Stick with the Levels command, and then get involved with some of the steps to follow here.

Here's a brief, hands-on experiment using the Curves comand:

Using Curves to Correct an Image

1. Open the Examples/Chap05 folder and then open Bride.tif from the Companion CD. It's a pretty crummy picture, as shown in figure 5.7—the text under the image explains the problem areas. Press Ctrl(⌘)+M to open the Curves dialog box.

tip

The left-to-right axis on the Curves graph is the original position of all tones in the image. The top-to-bottom axis represents changes you propose, so naturally the graph looks like a diagonal line when you begin. The left-to-right display goes from shadows to highlights you can manipulate.

Whites are dirty, midtones lack contrast, blacks aren't truly black.

Figure 5.7   *The midtones have no snap, and there is no true white or black in this image, but the Curves command will shake down this picture.*

2. Choose the Black Point Eyedropper tool from the eyedropper tools in this dialog box, and then click on an area you feel should be the darkest tone. I'd choose the shadow of the gentleman's tie or a shaded piece of shrubbery in the background as the target point for the tool.

3. Choose the White Point Eyedropper tool, and then click in the image where you think pure white should be. The bride's veil is an excellent place to click. In both steps 2 and this one, the Curves dialog box changes the preview image to reflect your changes, but the diagonal line will not change because you've not specified a point on it yet.

4. Click a second time on the White Point Eyedropper button to unselect it. Now you can use this tool to examine the tones in the image and it won't cause changes in the image.

5. Ctrl(⌘)+click on the gentleman's cheek. This should be the midpoint of the image's tones. A marker appears on the diagonal line on the graph.

6. Click and drag directly left in the graph. This increases contrast in the image without making the overall image brighter or darker. See figure 5.8 for the locations of the cursor in this example.

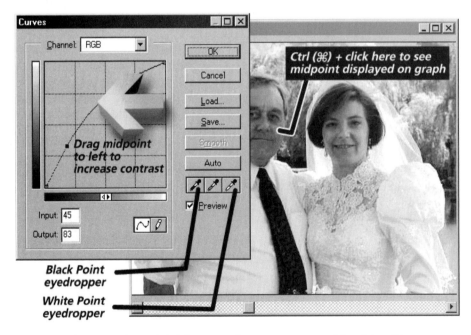

FIGURE 5.8   *You can change an image's brightness and contrast at up to 15 points with the Curves command. Or you can use the command exactly like the Levels command, and use eyedropper tools to set white and black points.*

7. Click on OK to apply the change. Then you can choose to save the image, or close it without saving.

We've spent some time taking bad images and turning them into well-behaved ones, but in the following section, you'll see how to take a lousy photo, make it *worse*, and then use certain areas of the picture to make an artistic element in a different photo. It's fun! C'mon...

Working with the Threshold Command

The Threshold command only works on the tones in an image. Expect all color to be lost in a picture when you use this command. The Threshold command forces pixels into one of two camps: black or white. This command can be very useful for determining the edge in a copy of an image, or for cleaning up a black-and-white drawing. However, we're going to use the Threshold command shortly as an artistic filter—to create silhouettes.

Here's the story: Suppose you have a nice sunset picture, but the photo lacks visual detail. The obvious thing to do would be to add elements, but be mindful that because it's sunset, these elements should have little or no detail—the lighting's too poor. Toss in text as an element, and before you know it, you've got a greeting card that'll floor Mr. Hallmark. The first step is to modify a crummy picture.

Working to Further Degrade a Poorly Exposed Photo

As mentioned earlier, the Threshold command makes a picture black or white at any given pixel, and there's a "break point" feature that enables you to control (to a certain extent) which pixels wind up being black or white. The Threshold command works best when there is a clear, unambiguous separation between light and dark areas, and the image you will work with—Candid.tif—is *nearly* perfect for the assignment.

The couple in the picture is definitely not illuminated (I think a flash didn't go off), and the background is. Unfortunately, there are medium to dark areas scattered through the photo. These areas need to be painted white to reinforce the edge of elements, and if you want to save time duplicating this example, make certain that the foreground elements are in the clear from a light background.

Here's how to prep the image for the Threshold command:

Retouching a Photo for the Threshold Filter

1. Open the Candid.tif image from the Examples/Chap05 folder on the Companion CD.

2. Choose the Paintbrush tool, and choose white as the foreground color. Then choose the fourth tip from the left in the top row on the Brushes palette, to help separate the foreground detail of the couple from the background. For example, the guy in the photo has the ceiling molding running through his head, and it's a medium color. Paint around his silhouette. Also, you can lose the side of his glasses to the far left (nobody wants a nice silhouette of themselves with glasses!). And the bride's veil can be deleted, as shown in figure 5.9. Bridal veils are not an everyday piece of apparel (although women get *married* every day), and we want a "generi-card," not one linked to weddings.

FIGURE 5.9   *Paint with white around certain areas of the couple's silhouette to make selecting the foreground easier, using the Threshold command.*

3. Choose Image, Adjust, Threshold. The Threshold dialog box appears; by default, it is set to 128 as the "break point."

4. Drag the slider in the dialog box to about 126, as shown in figure 5.10. It does
   not matter whether the interiors of the people are completely black or the room
   is entirely white. What you want is to be able to see the couple's *edges*, and 126
   appears to help you do that. Press OK when you've tuned the Threshold command.

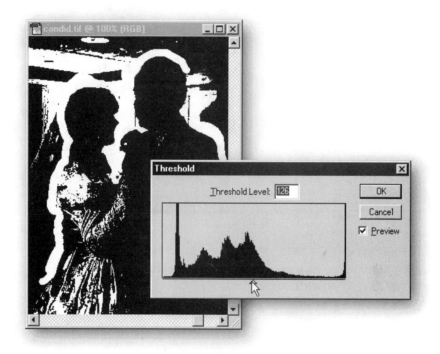

FIGURE 5.10   *Use the Threshold command to create edge work in the image.*

5. With the Paintbrush tool and the same tip you used last, start with white and
   paint away the areas that lie outside the couple.

6. After you've cleaned away the background, switch to black foreground color
   (press X)and and fill in areas of the silhouettes that didn't quite qualify to be
   turned to black, as shown in figure 5.11. More than likely, you'll find that the
   bride's white sleeve contains many areas of white among the shading.

Use the Paintbrush tool to fill in and trim edges

FIGURE 5.11   *Use the Paintbrush tool and white and black to retouch the photo so it truly is a silhouette image.*

7. Open the Palm_set.tif image from the Examples/Chap05 folder on the Companion CD. You might not have an image exactly like this in your collection of pictures (mostly because I asked a professional photographer to get me some coverage when he vacationed in Hawaii!), but surely you will come across a breath-taking sunset (and you should take a picture of it) regardless of where you live (except parts of Finland, and Syracuse, NY).

8. With both images in the workspace, and a clear, unobstructed view of both windows, use the Move tool to drag a copy of the Candid scene into the Palm_set.tif image, as shown in figure 5.12.

tip

If you want to do this with your own pictures, make sure that all the elements are the same scale. I was careful to blow up the Candid picture after I received the Palm_set image.

In this case, it doesn't matter that you lose visual detail when you enlarge a digital image—because the Threshold command is going to further mess up the image detail.

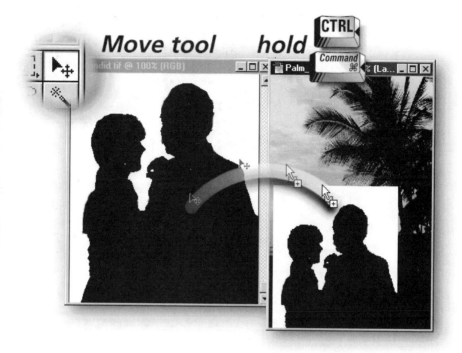

Figure 5.12   *Move a copy of the silhouettes to the Palm_set image.*

Now we have two problems: how to horizontally flip the image, because the guy's head is too tall and is sticking into the palm tree, and how to get rid of the white in the Candid layer of the image:

9. Choose Edit, Transform, Flip Horizontal, and only the contents of the Candid layer (and not the Background) are flipped.

10. Press F7 if the Layers/Channels/Etc. palette is not onscreen. With the Candid layer as the active layer, choose Multiply from the drop-down modes list on the upper left of the palette. Everything that is darker than 128 on a brightness scale will remain the same, but anything lighter will disappear. This is not a permanent state and you can switch back to normal layer-combining mode anytime you want (but doing this is not part of the plan here).

11. Open the Message.tif image from the Chap05 folder of the Companion CD. With the Move tool, drag a copy of the message into the Palm_set image, and then choose Screen from the modes drop-down list. With Screen mode, lighter colors remain and darker colors drop out, as shown in figure 5.13.

FIGURE 5.13   *Use different layer modes for combining elements whose background is a solid, contrasting color.*

12. Last step! Click on the "Candid" layer (Layer 1), and then choose Filter, Blur, and then blur. This takes the hard pixel edge off the couple's silhouette. The Threshold command doesn't know squat about anti-aliasing!

13. Save the layered image as Bon Voyage in Photoshop's native format, or flatten the image and save it in the TIFF file format. You're finished! Close the image at any time now.

Admittedly, the previous example is more of a design issue than the demonstration of a Photoshop principle, but you did use Photoshop in a creative way (this is good), and the product of a little experimenting is nothing short of a professional creation. I would not be ashamed at all to print a copy of this picture and sneak it into the card rack at the supermarket.

Selective Tonal Adjustments

All of what we've done with tone shifting up 'til now has been made with a global (the entire image) aspect. But all images are not 100 percent crummy across the surface. Sometimes only *parts* of an image are underexposed or generally less than wonderful.

Remember in chapter 3 how you used the Quick Mask feature selectively to encompass only part of an image (and then change only part of the image)? Well, there's no reason why you can't put one and one together here, and come up with a one-derful image. In the steps that follow, you'll take an image of a child, the right side of whose face is obscured by shadow. You'll create an extremely subtle transition between selected and masked areas, and then use the Levels command to even out her face.

Selectively Restoring an Image

1. Open the Smiley.tif image from the Examples/Chap05 folder on the Companion CD. As you can see in figure 5.14, it's a well-exposed image, and one side of the child's face is fine. It's the right side of the picture that falls into the shade.

FIGURE 5.14   *What do you do when only a part of an image is wrong? You only partially correct it!*

2. From the toolbox, choose the Airbrush tool, set the Pressure to 50%, press F5 to get the Brushes palette onscreen, and then choose the 100-pixel diameter brush. The brush size depends on the size of the image you're fixing: 100 pixels for the airbrush simply works in this example.

3. Press D (**D**efault colors), and then click on the Quick Mask button on the toolbox, as you have so many times before. Everywhere you paint will be selected when you switch back to Standard Editing mode.

   Fortunately, the Airbrush tool doesn't leave lines, so your selection work will be based on how you move the cursor around to apply the most Quick Mask to areas heavily in shade, and taper off your application of Quick Mask toward the edges of the shaded area, where the least selecting needs to happen. Now, in the following figure, I've specified a light white for my Quick Mask tint color. Do not be confused and think I'm whitewashing the image with actual color—it's purely for visibility's sake: you can use the default red if you like.

4. Click and drag around the area of the child's face that is most deeply in shadow, and then work your way outward to include the child's apparel and part of her hair, as shown in figure 5.15.

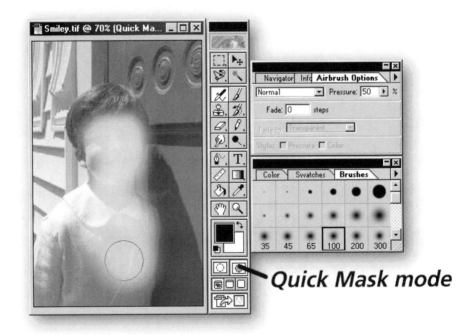

FIGURE 5.15   *Apply Quick Mask tint overlay to the areas that need lightening. The outer edges of the child need less Quick Mask than her face.*

5. Click on the Standard Editing mode button (to the left of the Quick Mask button), and then press Ctrl(⌘)+H to hide the marquee lines (the "marching ants"). The selection is still selected. Press Ctrl(⌘)+L to display the Levels command.

6. Drag the white point Input slider to about 144, and then drag the midpoint (okay, okay—the *gamma*) slider to about 1.4, as shown in figure 5.16. Then drag the black point Input slider to about 10, to subtly goose up the blacks in the picture. The whites are whiter on the child, and the midtones show more detail because you're lessening the contrast in the midtones. You know, I didn't even know which relative of mine this was until I performed these steps!

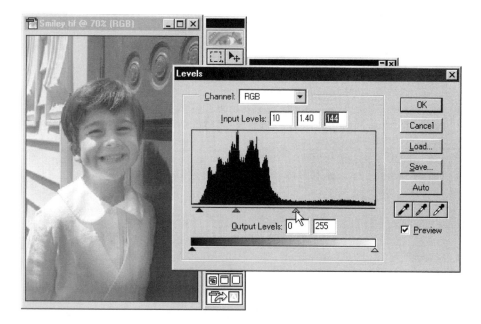

FIGURE 5.16   *Lighten the selected area by using both the white point and the midpoint sliders.*

7. Press Enter (Return) to return to a beautifully retouched image. Folks who don't use computers don't realize exactly how valuable and powerful tone and color manipulation is with Photoshop.

By the way, my own selection using the Airbrush tool was good but not perfect in figure 5.16. You can certainly do better if you spend some quality time with the image.

Tones, tones, tones! Everything has been about correcting tones and we've not yet talked about *color correcting*. Allow me to correct this oversight in the following sections.

Colors, Color Shifting, and Color Correcting

First off, forget everything you learned as a child in school about the "color wheel." This wheel was based on a Mr. "Roy G. Biv," which stood for "red, orange, yellow, green, blue, indigo, and violet." But within the context of our early education, this color wheel only worked for calculating color opposites (blue on the wheel is the opposite of yellow, for example), and basically told us nothing if we wanted to blend these colors together as subtractive pigments or additive colors. The progression of the spectrum was correct, I'll hand our teachers that much.

Ready for some new, improved color wheel stuff? Take a look at figure 5.17. Aside from the fact that New Riders saved readers some money and this is a black-and-white plate, you'll notice some new names for occupants of the color wheel. The spectrum progression in this plate is counterclockwise—the narrowest frequency is red (as measured in degrees) and cyan is the farthest away from red at 180°; then the color wheel decreases on degrees to offer us blue and magenta as we travel counter-clockwise back to red.

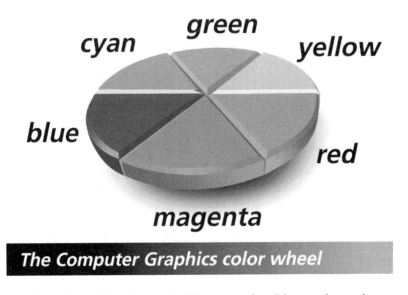

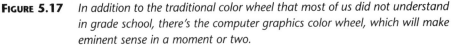

FIGURE 5.17   *In addition to the traditional color wheel that most of us did not understand in grade school, there's the computer graphics color wheel, which will make eminent sense in a moment or two.*

Every color on the computer color wheel has a complementary color; this is the color's opposite (and what you'd get if you painted a color, marquee selected it, and then pressed Ctrl(⌘)+I to invert the chroma of the color). Also, if you want to produce blue, you mix the neighboring (secondary) colors, cyan and magenta. Cyan, magenta, and yellow are secondary additive colors, and red, green, and blue (as in RGB color) are primary additive colors.

What does this mean to image color correction? Everything! If a color is casting way too red in an image, you introduce some cyan, the color opposite of red, to neutralize the red.

But enough theory. Let me guide you through color shifting a photograph whose colors are uniformly wrong.

Wielding the Hue/Saturation Command

The Hue/Saturation command is an excellent resource for changing one of the three properties of HSB color. In this next experiment, a little thought needs to back up your actions. Here's the story:

I deliberately messed up the Croquet1.tif image. *How* I did it is unimportant, but how to correct it *is* important.

What do we see in the image?

- The grass is brown instead of green.
- (You can't know this one, so I'll help you here.) The light blue ball farthest to the left is greenish cyan, and the ball to the right of the other one is red instead of yellow.

This strongly suggests that *all* the colors in this image are off. But by how much? Well, let's see. If the color wheel in figure 5.17 is to serve a purpose, we must use it for the basis of a calculation. Each pie wedge is 60°. Now if pale blue is posing as cyanish-green in this picture, this means that there is (approximately) a 40° to 60° positive shift in the Hue of the image. Try this one out:

PROFOUND WISDOM #9:

When retouching, detect before you correct.

Find out what's wrong with the image before you dig into your arsenal of tools. The more you learn about the image, the more precisely you can correct it.

Hi! How Are Hue Doing?

1. Open the Croquet1.tif image from the Example/Chap05 folder on the Companion CD.

2. Press Ctrl(⌘)+U to open the Hue/Saturation dialog box. Position the box so you have a clear view of the image.

3. Drag the Hue slider to about 40°, as shown in figure 5.18. Figure 5.18 shows nothing of the hue shift, but on your screen you will see a fantastic transformation. The image color becomes "correct." You can try 60° if you like, but basically, you've corrected a lousy picture in one step.

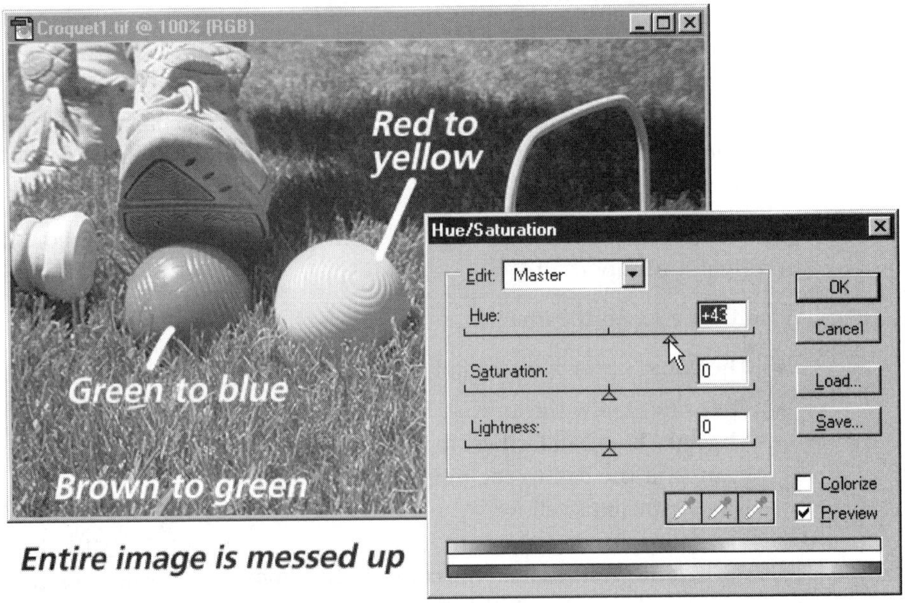

FIGURE 5.18   *Take a look at the colors in the image, envision what the correct colors should be, and then rely on the computer color wheel to guide you in the correction direction of the hues.*

4. Click on OK to apply the change, congratulate yourself several times, and then close the image without saving it, unless you're really into croquet and my wife's foot. (Hint: you're not.)

There's more mayhem afoot as I've goofed around with another version of the same photo. This time, only one color is really off in the image. Oh, what tool to use? Read on!

Using the Variations Command

You will probably adopt the Variations command a lot in future color correcting, because this command puts at your fingertips and eyeballs variations on how an image should look, based on hue, and range of tone. It even has an amount slider for subtle changes, and a clipping feature.

Let's walk through what to do with the Variations command and Croquet2.tif:

tip

Clipping is used by Adobe in the Variations command context to mean, "the pixels have 100% color, there's no room for any more color, you've gone off the scale, and a fat, monochrome color now takes the place of what used to be tonal subtlety." There are other places in Photoshop where "clipping" is used, but there it describes something other than color overload.

Working with Variations

1. Open the croquet2.tif image from the Examples/Chap05 folder on the CD. As you can see, the grass is either totally browned out, or the developing liquid used on this picture was from 1954.

2. Choose Image, Adjust, Variations. So you have a clue as to how to correct this image, crank the Fine/Coarse slider all the way up to exaggerate the colors in the examples within the dialog box.

   We can see two possibilities here for color replacement, and we might use both. Notice that the More Cyan thumbnail comes closest to a realistically lit outdoors picture. Cyan, if you treat the thumbnails like the color wheel, is the opposite of red, and red certainly predominates in the image.

3. Drag the Fine/Coarse slider to about one click to the right of the middle of the slider. Click on the More Cyan thumbnail. Surprise! The picture with the title Current Pick looks a lot more attractive, but the More Blue box looks better still. This is because you need to get rid of not only some red but also some yellow in the image. See figure 5.19 to see where this is leading.

4. Click on the More Blue thumbnail. The picture looks pretty perfect now, so click on OK to apply the changes.

5. You can save the image or simply close it without saving now.

You've experienced the thrill of hue shifting, and color opposite replacement so far. It's time now to introduce the third color-casting control feature in Photoshop.

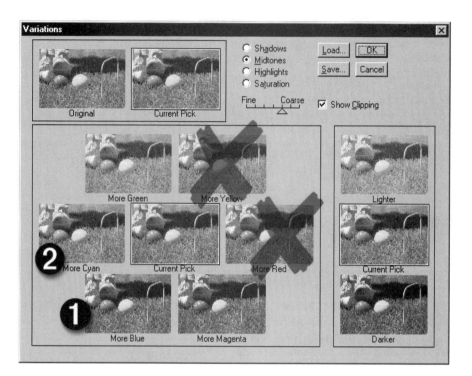

FIGURE 5.19   *Got a color casting problem? Solve it by introducing color opposites into the photo.*

Working with the Color Balance Command

My editor told me I had to start a new section with words instead of a Photoshop Profound Wisdom, but this wisdom is too important to keep quiet any longer:

Okay, the final color-correcting feature is called the Color Balance command. Unlike other color features in Photoshop, you can go back and undo a color shift, using this command. Why? Because you're changing the relationship between opposite colors—you're adding a little of this by subtracting an equal

PROFOUND WISDOM #10:

All changes you make to pixel color are progressive changes.

In other words, there's no way back to an original image to which you've applied three or four changes, except by using the History palette. Pixels by their nature cannot be restored by using an equal amount of opposite color. It's all change based on change based on change, as you saw in the previous section with the Variations command. You didn't know that you'd need to add blue until you'd first subtracted red (added cyan).

amount of that. So although this command might not be as intuitive as the Variations command

- There are fewer controls to mess with.

- Adobe gave us a hot key to display the command's dialog box immediately.

So without further ado:

Working with the Color Balance Features

1. Open the Croquet3.tif image from the Examples/Chap05 folder on the Companion CD. Unlike Croquet 2, this image appears to have been left near a sunny window for a decade, until there's no pigment left except shades of magenta.

2. Press Ctrl(⌘)+B to display the Color Balance dialog box.

3. Examine (*detect*) which tonal range is most affected by this bad color casting. It appears to be in the midtones, and by default, the Midtones button is already clicked, so this one's gonna be a breeze. This allows the highlight and shadow areas to be unaffected while you experiment (*correct*).

4. Drag the Magenta/Green slider way to the Green end, to about +95. The image looks a lot better now, but after removing this ton of magenta, we can see that the image is also too green.

5. Drag the Yellow/Blue slider to about –73, as shown in figure 5.20. You'll see that on your screen the image is looking very natural, very freshly taken instead of being mired in colors best suited for bicycle safety helmets.

6. Click on OK to apply the changes, and then either save the image to hard disk or close it without saving it.

This color and tone stuff wasn't too hard to understand, was it? As long as you understand *why* computer displays behave (or misbehave) the way they do, everything you need to change revolves around the RGB color space. And as we've gleefully ignored that color model in favor of HSB color space, we are assured that since RGB and HSB engender the same color space, we're not making weird demands of Photoshop or the system, and we're taking large strides toward improving the quality of poorly taken pictures. Do you smell a career in here someplace? You should!

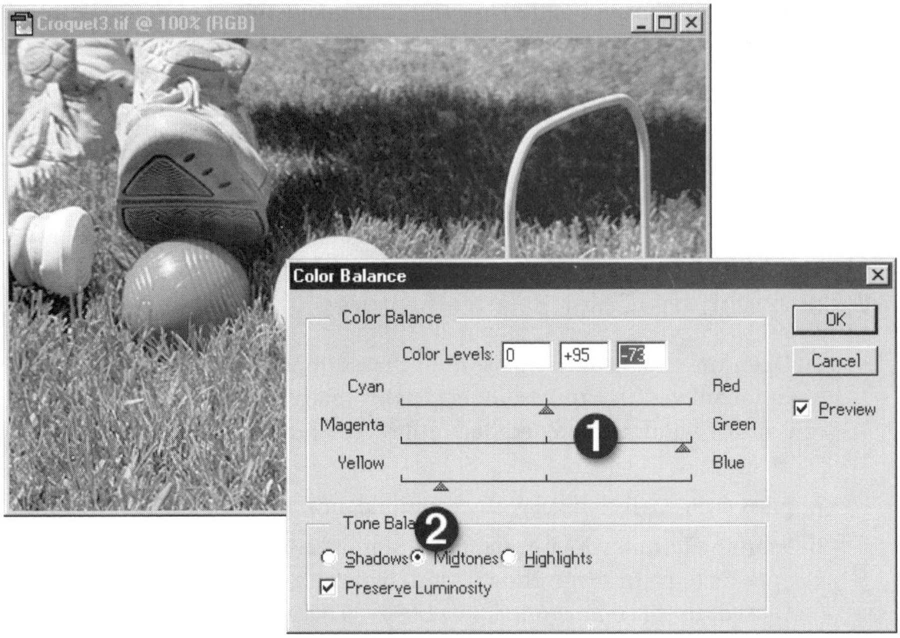

FIGURE 5.20   *Use the Color Balance sliders to shift a particular color in a particular range of tone toward its color opposite on the computer color wheel.*

Summary

Colors are as important an aspect of digital imaging as selections are. Manipulation of both can lead to stunning photographic retouching work. So now you've knocked off chapters 2, 3, and 5 on manipulating images according to their properties. Are you ready to examine the third dimension of image editing? Chapter 6 leads us into the wonderful world of layers, layer masking, and all sorts of ways you can perform photo-manipulation that can be surreal, can be accomplished in no time, and appears to be nothing short of magic.

CHAPTER 6

Everything You Need to Know About Layers

We've played with Photoshop layers in earlier chapters, but really have not made layers a focal point yet because they deserve their *own* chapter. Although we've done things with layers to make editing more convenient, there are unexplained properties and hidden features we'll address here and now—sort of like pawing over a sunken treasure!

Exploring the "Up Front" Layer Properties

Pressing F7 is your ticket to performing a lot of operations to change the appearance of a layer, operations that would have been impossible technologically only a few years ago. F7 Displays the Layers palette, and on it you will find controls that dramatically change nontransparent elements on the current layer.

To take a test drive of the more obvious layer properties, you'll work with a multilayered image in the next section.

Working with Opacity and the Modes

Every layer that is visible in an image window can be made less than 100 percent opaque, and can also visually blend into the underlying layer in any one of 17 ways. We'll keep our focus a little narrow in this section, because fundamentally there are only three modes that a beginner would tend to use to get stunning retouching results.

In the following example, you'll work with a 3D rendering of an egg with wings, a cloudy background, and a layer you'll add that consists of only clouds—this will be your "image sandwich."

There are six different ways you can move elements from somewhere into a Photoshop image window. I use the "tossing the Layers title" technique a lot in this book because it's the easiest way. But you might not always be able to access the layer title, so here are the other ways to add a layer to an image window:

- Use the Move tool to drag a layer from one image window to another. You don't even have to have the toolbox onscreen to perform this maneuver; simply hold Ctrl(⌘) and the tool you're currently using will toggle to the Move tool.

- To copy and paste from one window to another, Ctrl(⌘)+C, bring the target image to the front, and then Ctrl(⌘)+V. The only disadvantage to this technique is that it leaves elements— sometimes *large* elements—on the Clipboard. The solution to flushing the Clipboard after you've used it is to either copy a really small element to the Clipboard (thus eliminating the large element), or choose Edit, Purge, Clipboard from the main menu.

- Edit, Copy, make a selection, and then Edit, Paste Into. This creates a new layer with a Layer mask in the shape of your selection. We'll get to Layer masks a little later in this chapter.

- Drag a Layer title into the Create new layer icon at the bottom of the Layers palette. This does not create a layer with new visual content; instead, it creates a duplicate of the layer you dragged.

- Crop an element by using a selection tool, hold Ctrl(⌘), and then drag the selection into the target window. This puts a copy of the selection on its own layer in the current image editing window.

- There's the "toss the title" technique, used a few times earlier in this book, and it's what you'll use in the following example.

Let's get this egg and clouds composition cackling now:

PROFOUND WISDOM #11:

Above all things, Photoshop is the world's best integrator of media that might or might not have originated in Photoshop.

I would hate to mislead you in the upcoming example by not mentioning that the source materials for the example were not created in Photoshop. The flying egg was designed in Adobe Dimensions and the clouds were drawn in Fractal Design Painter 4. You'd be surprised at how many pieces of art are improved by passing them through Photoshop!

tip

Edit, Purge, Everything is a good candidate for an F key. Read chapter 1 for information on making your own hot keys from F keys. Window, Show/Hide Toolbox is another good candidate.

Fooling Around with Layer Modes and Opacity

1. Open the Examples/Chap06/Clouds.tif image in Photoshop.

2. Open the FlyEgg.psd image from the Examples/Chap06 folder.

3. Drag the "National Eggspress" title on the Layers palette into the Clouds.tif image, as shown in figure 6.1.

   You'll notice that if you are diligent about naming layers, when you duplicate them in other windows the name still "rides" with the layer. In this example, you now have a Background layer, and a National Eggspress layer, mostly because I'd get sued if I called the layer Federal you-know what!

   Layers always are added to on top of the current layer, so the National Eggspress layer is now on top of the background, and by default, it is the current editing layer.

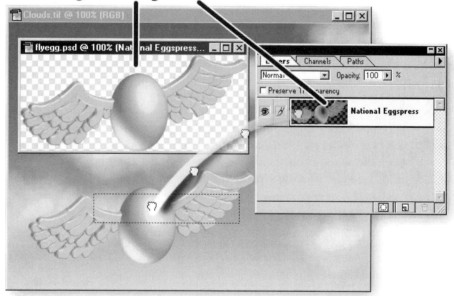

FIGURE 6.1   *Drag the layer title on the Layers palette to an image window (other than the current one) to add a new layer to the other image window.*

4. Click on the flyout triangle to the right of the Opacity number field, and then drag the slider down to about 45%, as shown in figure 6.2.

   As you can see, the flying egg now seems more integrated in the scene because it looks as though there are clouds behind the egg and haze in front of it. Figure 6.2 also displays the visibility icon and the editing state icon. When you see an eye icon to the left of a layer on the Layers palette, you know that layer is visible in the image window. The editing state icon takes on different appearances, as you will see soon. For now, the paintbrush icon tells you that the layer can be edited.

5. Click on the modes drop-down list and choose Screen. Now the egg is not only partially transparent, but it also appears to be glowing. Now you have a phantom, nuclear-powered egg, as shown in figure 6.3.

6. Choose File, Save As, and save the file as Flying Egg.psd, in Photoshop's native file format. Keep the image open.

Multiply, Screen, and Normal are the most used compositing modes for layers, at least in my own work. The other options on the modes drop-down list are exotic, artsy, and a little vertical in their effectiveness to change a layer's pixels in a realistic way.

note

Adjustment layers are not explained in detail in this book because they are designed for experienced users and photographers. Basically, when you add an Adjustment layer to a stack of image layers, you can tune the tones and colors using any of the Adjust commands by painting on the Adjustment layer. You first pick an Adjust command (such as Levels), adjust the image globally to a new setting, and then use black foreground color to restore areas that you do not want adjusted.

Or conversely, you can make no changes when the Levels dialog box is displayed, add the layer, make a few white strokes on the layer (you will see no change) and then double-click on the Adjustment layer title and perform a tonal change. You then close the Levels dialog box and paint away with different shades of black to modify, locally, tones in the image with any painting tool.

tip

A quick way to tell what the current editing layer is, is to look for bold layer title text on the Layers palette's list, with the text reversed out, and a paint brush icon immediately to the left of the layer title. You can see this in figure 6.2.

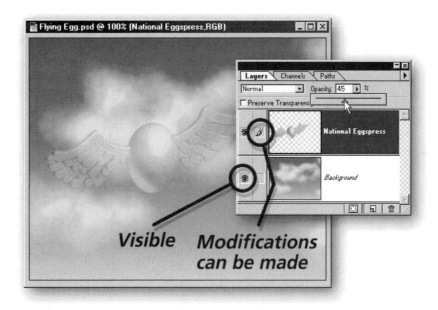

FIGURE 6.2   *Reduce the opacity on a layer to create a ghostly effect with the layer's contents. This example now has a phantom egg.*

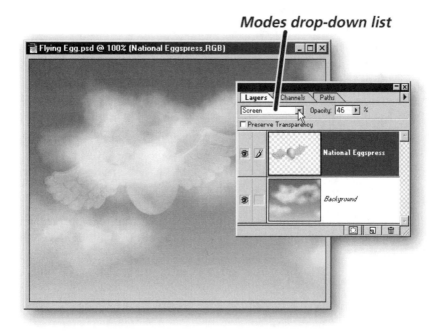

FIGURE 6.3   *Screen mode intensifies lighter portions of an image layer's contents, and tends to drop out tones that are darker than 128 on a 256 brightness scale.*

The Layer that's Larger than the Window

Photoshop 5.5 has the wonderful capability to allow you to shove nonopaque elements off the screen (making them invisible), to go about your business editing other layers, and then tow the opaque elements back into the window. The visual metaphor for this capability is that the image window extends beyond the window edges. The only times you would lose a layer's contents that are outside the window would be if you were to crop the image while the element was offstage, or if you flattened the image.

This presents yet another way to work with a better view of a document. Let's run through a very quick test example of how this "infinitely large" layer stuff works:

note

There is an Auto-Select Layer option on the Move tool palette that probably should be *un*checked as you learn the program. Double-click on the Move tool to bring up the Options palette, and then uncheck this feature. If this feature is on, whenever you click on an element in the image window, the current layer changes, to become whichever layer your cursor is over when you click.

See the potential for messing stuff up?

Testing Out a Huge Layer

1. Choose Normal mode for the egg layer, and then click on the Move tool on the toolbox.

2. Drag to the right, beginning anywhere on the layer. Hint: you do not have to click and drag on only the contents of a layer—dragging anywhere moves the nontransparent pixels on the layer, as shown in figure 6.4.

3. This one is your call. Do anything you like to the layer, add a layer and paint all over it, duplicate the layer where the egg is hidden—you name it. Tell me when this has stopped being fun, and we'll continue.

4. Okay, click on the National Eggspress title on the Layers palette to make it the current editing layer; then, with the Move tool, drag to the right in the window several times until you get your egg back. Keep the image open.

Pretty neat, huh? And you can save the file with the egg offstage, reopen the image at any time in Photoshop 5.5, and drag the egg back inside the window edges.

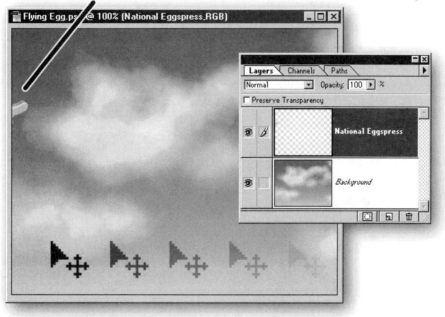

FIGURE 6.4   *Elements can be hidden by pushing them outside the visible range of the image window, and then they can be reeled back into the image window simply by dragging.*

Making a Multidimensional Design

In traditional animation, focal planes have been used in cartoon artwork to simulate depth. What the animators would do is create a background that might be simple and a little blurry (to imitate camera depth of field). The next layer would contain the hero (perfectly in focus), and then occasionally, you'd have (on top of the hero) a cartoon cell that was dark and slightly out of focus to make the star of the cartoon truly look as though it were *in* the scene.

You can create this same sort of effect with the Flying Egg composition because I've created for you an image with but a single layer, a layer of three clouds. In the following example you'll add a layer to the design, and explore what other hidden features on the Layers palette can prove to be handy:

Stacking Layers and Linking Layers

1. Open the 3Clouds.psd image from the Examples/Chap06 folder on the Companion CD.

2. Drag the Clouds, what else? title into the Flying Egg.psd image, as shown in figure 6.5. Although they might not be in a perfect position, you will soon see how placing partially transparent clouds in front of the egg truly makes the scene look more dimensional.

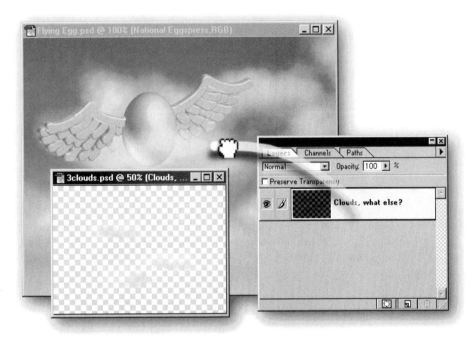

FIGURE 6.5   *Add some wispy clouds to the foreground of the design, and we're talking "3D" here!*

3. Click on the Background layer title on the Layers palette, and then click on the Create new layer icon.

4. Fill the new layer with black color. The simplest way to do this is to press D (default colors), and then press Alt(Opt)+Delete (Backspace). The clouds you've added and the egg are quite visible now!

5. Click on the Clouds, what else? title on the Layers palette to make it the current editing layer. Drag the Clouds, what else? layer around in the image window using the Move tool, until you think the clouds are positioned aesthetically in front of the egg.

   Now that these two layers are positioned nicely relative to one another, you need to position them against the background, but the two layers must move together. Here's the solution:

6. Click on the National Eggspress layer title on the Layers palette to make it the current editing layer.

7. Click in the box to the right of the eye icon on the Clouds, what else? layer, and with the National Eggspress title still highlighted, and using the Move tool, drag down and to the right, as shown in figure 6.6. Wowee! The layers are linked, that's why there's a little chain in the box to the right of the eye icon. Now, everywhere the egg goes, the clouds go, too!

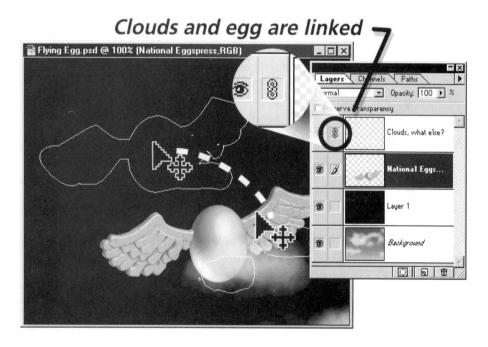

FIGURE 6.6   *You can link two or more layers when you want to move their contents but do not want to merge the layers.*

8. You can drag the Layer 1 (the totally black layer) title into the trash icon on the Layers palette to restore visibility of the cloud background. Press Ctrl(⌘)+S to save your work. You can close the image at any time now.

Hmmm. Layer opacity, layer linking, layer modes. What could be left? Plenty. Read on!

All About the Layer Mask

The Layer Mask feature in Photoshop is such a wonderful time-saver that Adobe Systems put the icon for it right at the bottom of the Layers palette. A Layer Mask is much like the Quick Mask feature you learned about in chapter 3, but applying the mask produces instant, visible results in the image window. When a layer is in Layer Mask mode, every area you paint a shade of black (or to which you apply foreground black by filling a marquee selection) becomes hidden, as though you had erased it. But nothing destructive has happened to your work: If you go over the same areas with white foreground color, you restore the hidden areas.

Before performing any surgery, I'll help you become acquainted with all the doodads you'll see when you use the Layer Mask feature, and with what every doo and dad does. Take a look at figure 6.7. This is the Bal&star.psd image we sort of left behind in chapter 2. And then I showed you in chapter 3 how to use the Paths feature to trim around the ball in the image—remember?

tip

I gave you the long way around viewing the egg and the clouds layer when I told you to fill a black layer and put it behind the elements. Actually, as you investigate Photoshop on your own, you'll find that you can press Ctrl(⌘)+K, and then press Ctrl(⌘)+4 to display the Transparency set of options. If you choose black or dark blue or something for *both* the lighter and the darker color check, essentially, Photoshop's display of transparency looks more like a layer of solid color.

And then you don't need to slip a solid layer into the stack to eggs-amine the top layers. You then hide the background layer by unchecking its eye icon on the palette.

Restoring the Transparency option to its default is very simple. In the Transparency preference box, you choose light from the Grid colors drop-down list.

tip

So how do you know *where* hidden areas are on a layer to which you've been applying Layer Mask color? You hold Alt(Opt) and then click on the Layer Mask thumbnail (*not* the image thumbnail—the *right-most* thumbnail on a layer title) on the Layers palette. This action moves your view to what has been painted in the image window, and a second Alt(Opt)+click on the Layer Mask thumbnail hides the view and returns you to the image in its apparent state of hidden areas all over the place.

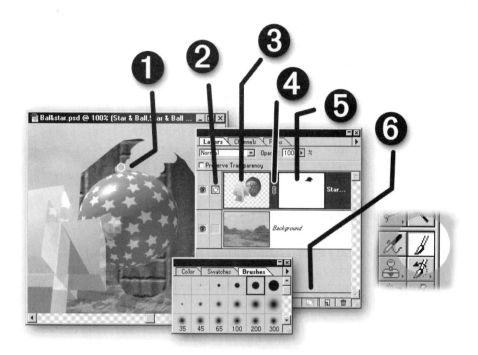

FIGURE 6.7   *There will be many strange icons on the Layers palette when you choose Layer Mode. Check out the following list against the numbered bullets here.*

Well, guess what? As you read, you grow, and you'll shortly see that using the Layer Mask feature is even better and quicker than defining a path in the design. First, here are the explanations for the bullets in figure 6.7:

1. **The Brush tip cursor:** In this figure, I'm using the Paintbrush tool (high-lighted on the right of the figure) to hide image areas. In Layer Mask mode, if you paint with black you hide image areas. You can also use the Pencil, the Airbrush, or the Gradient tool to apply percentages of color. For example, if you were painting with 60% black, only 40% of the area you cover would be visible—it would look like a semitransparent region in the artwork.

2. **The Layer Mask icon:** This icon informs you that you are painting on a Layer mask, and not on the image. If you see a paintbrush icon here instead of the mask icon, you need to click on the Layer Mask thumbnail (#5 in the list) to make certain you're hiding and revealing areas and not applying paint to a layer.

3. **The Layer thumbnail:** This is the image you'd usually see next to a layer title. The only difference is that in Layer Mask mode there is a highlight

around the Layer Mask thumbnail, and not around the Layer thumbnail. If you want to stop masking and actually change part of the layer, you click on the Layer thumbnail, the icon in location #2 turns into a paintbrush, and you can work on the layer. As you start out with Photoshop, I recommend *against* switching from editing a layer's contents to applying Layer Mask and back again. There's too much of a chance you'll not see the icon change.

4. **The Link icon:** *Don't* click on this icon, unless you want a weird masking experience. This icon means, "for every pixel on the layer, there is a corresponding masking pixel, to which you are assigning various degrees of opacity while in Layer Mask mode." If you click on this icon, your image and the Layer Mask are no longer bound to one another, and you can move your masking work all over the place using the Move tool. There *are* good uses for this feature, but I can't think of one for a fundamentals book.

5. **The Layer Mask thumbnail:** Always keeps updating to show you a teensy thumbnail of where you're masking in the image. It is this icon that you drag into the trash icon on the Layers palette when you want to finalize your masking work (make it permanent on a layer).

6. **The Layer Mask icon:** This is the guy you click on to place the currently highlighted layer title (and the corresponding image layer) in Layer Mask mode. Learn *not* to click on it unless you want to edit (it's proximity to the Create new layer icon is unfortunate).

With the bulleted list as your guide, you can indeed mask away the unwanted background areas on layer 1 in the ball and star image. I've added this file to the Chap06 folder for the sole reason of helping you try out different selection methods.

Using the Layer Mask

One of the first things I did when I got hold of the new Photoshop and the Layer Mask feature was to combine three image elements to make a surreal picture: a waving "ketchup and mustard" flag that dissolves into a beautiful cloudy sky, with three chrome frankfurters gliding across the scene (fig. 6.11 shows the finished image). I was hungry when I created the image, okay?

In any event, this is a very easy composition to create, using the Layer Mask. Now that you know everything about Layer masking, let's reproduce my fantasy image:

Creating a Layered Masterpiece

1. Open the Sky.tif image from the Examples/Chap06 folder on the Companion CD, and then open the Flag.tif image from the same folder.

2. Hold Shift and drag the title of Flag.tif on the Layers palette into the Sky.tif window, as shown in figure 6.8. Holding Shift centers the copied image element in the new window. You can close Flag.tif at any time now.

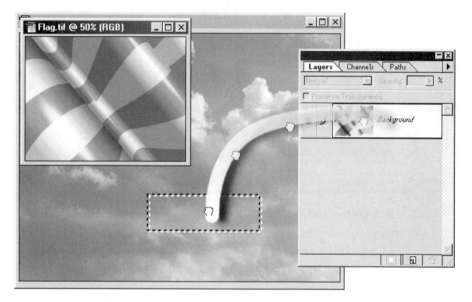

FIGURE 6.8   *The background of this composition will consist of a combination of both layers that you have in the window right now.*

3. Open the Wieners.psd image from the Examples/Chap06 folder on the Companion CD, and then drag its title, Franks, no sauerkraut, into the flag and sky image window, as shown in figure 6.9.

4. Close Wieners.psd, and then save the composition as American Icons.psd, in the Photoshop file format, to your hard disk.

5. On the Layers palette, click on the Layer 1 title to make the flag the current editing layer. Click on the eye icon next to the Franks, no sauerkraut layer to hide it for a while.

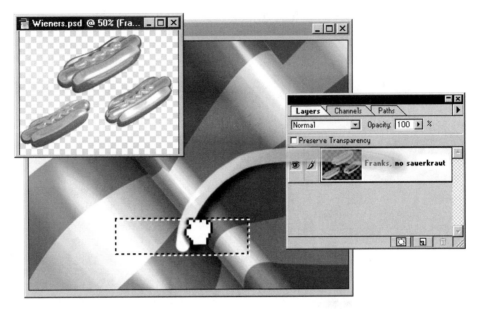

Figure 6.9   *Add a layer consisting of art and transparent areas to the existing composition.*

6. Click on the Add layer mask icon at the bottom left of the Layers palette.

7. Press D (default colors), and then double-click on the Linear Gradient tool on the toolbox. This chooses the tool, but also displays the Options palette. Make sure that Foreground to Background is chosen in the Options palette's Gradient drop-down list.

8. Look at figure 6.10 to get an idea of the direction and length of the stroke you should make with the Gradient tool now. Notice that you start so that a heavy concentration of black is placed at the top, making the transition to white fairly quickly, and at a slight angle, to give the background of the composition more visual interest.

9. Click on the thumbnail image of the gradient mask (not the flag thumbnail) to be absolutely certain that the mask is chosen right now, and then make a definitive dragging motion and drop the mask thumbnail into the trash icon at the bottom right of the palette. A dialog box appears, asking "Apply mask to layer before removing?" Your options are Apply, Cancel, and Discard. Click on Apply, and the areas that were masked are now deleted. Restore the eye icon and the visibility of the chrome frankfurters by clicking on the Franks, no sauerkraut area where there was an eye, as shown in figure 6.11.

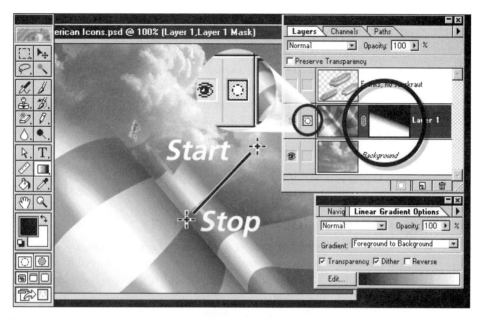

FIGURE 6.10   *Use the Linear Gradient tool in Layer Mask mode on a layer to create a transition between one image and the one beneath it.*

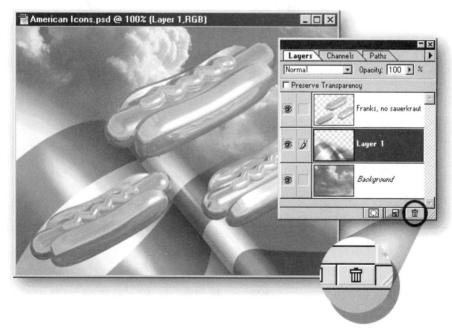

FIGURE 6.11   *No one application could create all three layers, but Photoshop alone can perfectly integrate them.*

10. Notice that the Franks, no sauerkraut layer looks a little washed out. "Detect before you correct" has been an ongoing nugget of wisdom throughout this book, and this means you aren't done with a composition until you've checked all the elements for correctness. The Franks... layer can have more punch if you press Ctrl(⌘)+L to display the Levels command, and then drag the black-point slider to the right so that the left Input level reads 245 or so.

11. Press Ctrl(⌘)+S; you can close the document at any time.

In the next section, you'll see how ingenious one can get out of desperation, and you'll create a dozen birthday cards from a single piece of artwork!

Leveraging the Hidden Layer Property

I got this idea about 10 years ago, and apologize to any of my friends reading this who received the birthday card you will build in Photoshop. It occurred to me that I was spending an awful lot of time designing the graphics for a card, and then putting a "Happy Birthday" (their name here) to complete it. And then it was off to hours *more* work designing the graphics for someone *else's* card.

The Modular Greeting Card

With the advent of layers in Photoshop 3.0.5 and later, I discovered that one piece of really nice artwork could be the foundation for a dozen cards. All one does is put a different name on a layer, and hide the other names—print, stick and lick, address, and mail the thing!

Let's walk through the steps for setting up a single name and title on top of a card graphic:

Combining Layer Elements

1. Open the Card.tif image from the Examples/Chap06 folder on the Companion CD. Position it to the right of the workspace, and scroll the image window so you can see all of the top of the image. You really don't need to see all the balloons right now.

2. Open the Birthday.tif image from the Chap06 folder on the Companion CD.

3. Double-click on the Eraser tool to bring up the Options palette, and then press Shift and press E (for eraser) until the Magic Eraser tool is the one chosen on the toolbox. You can toggle through any group of tools on the toolbox if you know the shortcut key and hold Shift while you tap the key.

4. On the Options palette choose 32 as the Tolerance for the Magic Eraser, and make sure the Anti-aliased box is checked and the Contiguous box is unchecked. Click in the Birthday image on a white background area, as shown in figure 6.12. The background and any nook or cranny within the lettering that was pure white vanishes. The image is now a layer image.

FIGURE 6.12   *The Magic Eraser tool removes the background color of an image to make the foreground visual content a group of opaque pixels on a transparent layer.*

5. On the Layers palette, drag the Layer 0 title into the Card.tif image window and position it toward the top of the image. You also might want to name the layer, so you can locate it more easily later. Double-click on the Layer 0 title (on the Layers palette) while the Card image is in the foreground in the workspace, and then type **Happy Birthday** in the Name field, and press Enter (Return).

6. Close Birthday.tif without saving it, and then open Bob.tif from the Chap06 folder. Use the Magic Eraser tool to make the name appear against transparency, and then drag its title from the Layers palette into the Card window.

7. On the Layers palette, drag the Bob layer (you will want to name all layers in this composition) and drop it on the Happy Birthday layer title, so Bob is beneath the Happy Birthday lettering. This is compositionally correct. Because the word "Birthday" in beneath the word "Happy," you can't see the top edge of "Happy." Using the Move tool, align the elements so that the text is centered in the window.

If your card looks like that shown in figure 6.13 (but it's in color on your screen), you can close the Bob.tif image without saving it, and save the Card image as Card.psd in the Photoshop file format, to your hard drive. Keep the image open.

FIGURE 6.13   *Drag the Bob layer to just below the Happy Birthday text.*

Okay, so far we have a card for Bob, but Lee and Chris both have a birthday this month, and Gail's birthday was two days ago. What are you going to do?

Layering Names in the Composition

In case you're wondering, the 3D plastic lettering in the examples in this book was mostly created in Adobe Dimensions (about $150 street price). It's highly compatible with Photoshop, and I recommend it as another useful print and Web utility.

If you're going to do this card yourself and send it to others, all the recipients' names have to be the same point size, to make the card look more personal. You've probably seen those "personal" letters for book clearing houses and such, and your name always appears in a slightly different typeface! This is why I took the time to provide you with alternative names for the Card.psd composition, names whose dimensions are proportionate to the existing 3D lettering. (See Chapter 8, "Working with Type," for the full scoop on Photoshop and typography.)

Let's add some more names to this single file:

Creating Different Versions of the Card

1. Open Lee.tif from the Examples/Chap06 folder on the Companion CD.

2. Use the Magic Eraser to remove the background, click on the Background layer title for the Card.psd image on the Layers palette, and then use the Move tool (hold Ctrl(⌘)) to drag the Lee name into the Card.psd window. You could have dragged the title on the Layers palette instead, but you need to see how the same thing can be accomplished in different ways in Photoshop. New layers always are created one layer on top of the current editing layer. Now, hide Bob's name by clicking on the eye icon to the left of his title, and position the Lee name so it looks as though it's right beneath the "Happy Birthday" lettering.

3. Perform step 2 with the rest of the name files in the Chap06 folder, or until you become bored doing this. Now, I owe a late birthday card to Gail, so I want to print her card first. This means unchecking the eye icons for all the names, so the Gail layer, the Happy Birthday layer, and the Background are all that's visible (see fig. 6.14).

4. I'd save the file one last time before closing it. In all seriousness, you can add your own list of names to this card (Adobe Dimensions export width is 270 pixels for the name), and if you have an inkjet printer, you might never have to be late sending cards again!

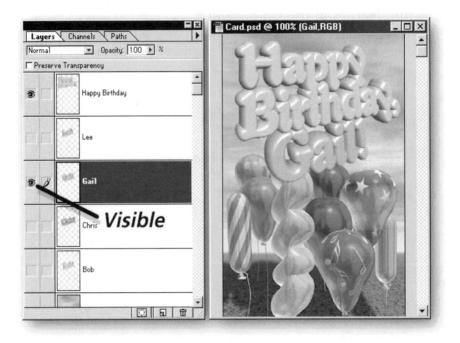

FIGURE 6.14   *Out of the stack of names, reveal only the one you want printed with the background and the Happy Birthday message.*

I mentioned integration a while back, and the files you'll play with in the next section are a perfect example of Photoshop as an integrating environment. Besides, I haven't talked about clipping groups yet.

Building a Clipping Group

A *clipping group* is a collection of layers that consists of a base layer (the background, for all intents and purposes), the *clipping mask* (a nontransparent area on a layer that defines the shape of what can be seen through it), and the element on the top layer that gets clipped. Using clipping groups is a wonderful way to show a multitude of different colored shirts with patterns, different colors, different cars, or—as in this example—different wood finishes on a Rickenbacker 481 guitar.

tip

In the ClipArt folder in the Boutons folder on the Companion CD are almost 75 objects that are CharityWare (read the read.me file). They are ideal for creating cards and snappy Web elements, with a little help from your humble author. Most of the images were designed in Adobe Dimensions (such as the flying egg, earlier in this chapter), and all the objects are on layers, so all you have to do is click and drag them into your existing compositions.

This is more than an exercise. I got the idea for the tutorial when I was about to buy the Rick 481 from a dentist I'd met on the Internet. The Rickenbacker catalog showed the model, but it showed it in red sunburst, and I was buying a natural maple finish guitar. So I needed to visualize what the thing would look like in maple, and hence, these sets of steps.

To build the clipping mask layer, I brought the image into Illustrator, and then carefully drew an outline around all the wooden areas of the guitar, as shown in figure 6.15.

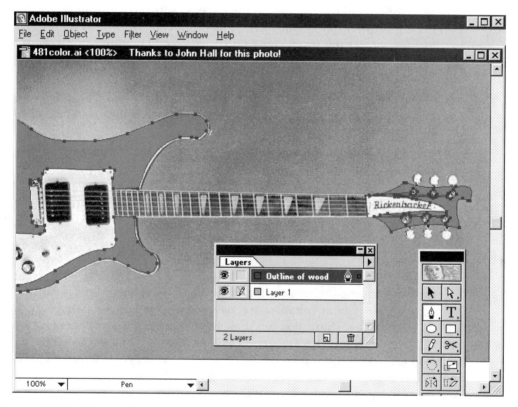

FIGURE 6.15   *I have nothing against Photoshop's Pen tool. It's simply that Illustrator's Pen tools are easier to use when you want to draw intricate paths.*

Notice that the image layer is locked, and I'm drawing on a new layer on top. If you own Illustrator, do this:

1. Import the Rick481.tif from the Examples/Chap06 folder of the companion CD by choosing File, Place.

2. Lock the layer, using the Layers palette's features, and then add a new layer, also using the Layers palette's features. The first thing you want to do is draw a rectangle with no fill that exactly matches the outer dimensions of the photo that's locked on the bottom layer. By doing this, you ensure that you can import the drawing you'll make into Photoshop at the correct size.

3. With the Pen tool, the Direct Selection tool, and the change Anchor tool (as you used them in Photoshop in chapter 3), carefully draw a noncontiguous path around the wooden areas of the guitar. Just to make certain my paths were correct, I filled the paths on the top layer with a color, as shown in figure 6.15. Upon exporting the paths, it makes no difference what color you use as a fill, because this will become a mask layer, and Photoshop only evaluates the layer for opaque pixels—it doesn't care what color the pixels are. One final note before leaving Illustrator: Do not stroke the paths. In other words, do not assign the paths a width.

4. Delete the layer that contains the image, and then save the file to hard disk as 481.ai, in Illustrator format.

5. With the Selection tool, marquee select all the paths in the image; then press Ctrl(⌘)+C, and then close Illustrator.

You have a PostScript file on the Clipboard right now, and I think that Illustrator and Dimensions for Windows are the only Windows applications that can put PostScript on the Clipboard. Do *not* copy anything to the Clipboard until I say it's okay! If you do, you'll lose the PostScript information about the paths you drew. Launch Photoshop.

For those of you who do not own Illustrator, you cannot simply copy paths from your drawing program as PostScript and have them paste into Photoshop. But you can do the next best thing: you can draw the outline of the wood areas over the Rick481.tif image in CorelDRAW, CorelXARA, or some other program that has a lot of export capability. Then export the paths (but not the image) to Illustrator file format. For example, I tried this same setup using XARA. I exported as an Illustrator file, and the masking information came into Photoshop flawlessly.

Also, I've tucked away an accurate selection in an alpha channel in the Rick481.tif image, so if you are not yet a whiz at path drawing, you can still follow along with the steps to come. And if you have no vector illustration programs, skip steps 1–6, and jump to step 7.

Making a Rickenbacker Sandwich

When you have a genuine PostScript collection of data on the Clipboard, Photoshop offers the following two ways to place the contents of the Clipboard:

- As anti-aliased pixels
- As a path, or a collection of paths

I'm taking the long way around stuff today, simply to show you the staggering number of different ways you can accomplish something in Photoshop. Did we honestly need to copy the Illustrator paths to the Clipboard? Nah. We can import the *.ai file as a bitmap to Photoshop, but you need to *see* this stuff, because someday you'll have a real need for it.

Here's how to get the clipping mask into a layer in the Rickenbacker picture:

Setting Up the Image for Clipping

1. In Photoshop, open the Rick481.tif image from the Examples/Chap06 folder on the Companion CD. You might as well zoom in to a 1:1 viewing resolution by double-clicking on the Zoom tool, but only if your monitor is set to 800×600 resolution.

2. Choose File, Paste. A dialog box appears, as shown in figure 6.16. Now, it would be a time-saver to paste the Clipboard's contents as pixels, but let's take an additional, exploration-oriented step. Click on Paste as Paths.

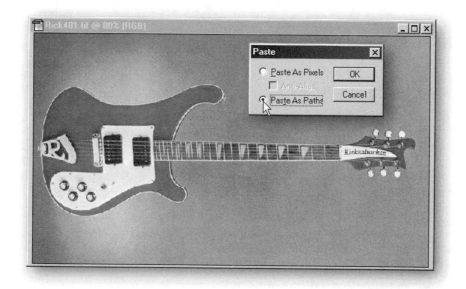

FIGURE 6.16 *You can paste vector paths from Illustrator to Photoshop. Vector paths are nonprinting, nondestructive descriptions of shapes.*

3. Press F7 to get the Layers/Channels/Paths palette onscreen, and double-click on the Work Path title on the Paths palette. Name the path **Wood Areas**, and then press Enter (Return) to close the dialog box.

4. You need to get rid of the rectangle (made up of paths) that was copied along with the outline of the wooden areas of the guitar. Drag the window edges away from the image so you see a little background gray.

5. Choose the Delete Anchor Point tool, and make a marquee around the upper-right anchor. This selects it. Now click on the anchor, to delete it. The image should resemble figure 6.17. Then (as shown in this figure), you click on the upper-left anchor, and then press Delete (Backspace) once to get rid of the remaining two anchors that describe the bottom of the image window with a path segment between them.

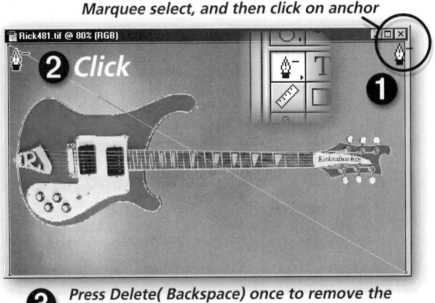

Figure 6.17   *Remove the outline that describes the extent of the image, and you'll be left with perfect selection information for the wood on the guitar.*

6. Press Ctrl(⌘)+click on the Wood areas path name to load the path as a marquee selection and hide the paths, as shown in figure 6.18. Then press Ctrl(⌘)+tilde (~) to return your view to the image.

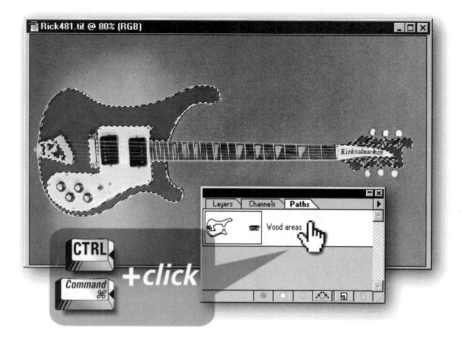

FIGURE 6.18   *Ctrl(⌘)+clicking on a path title not only loads the path as a selection, but it also hides the path(s).*

To catch up to this point if you did not use Illustrator: if you made and exported an Illustrator document, Choose File, Open and then choose the file. The defaults in the Rasterize Generic EPS Format are correct; this is why you traced the outline of the image in addition to the guitar...so press Enter (Return). In a moment, you will see an opaque shape of the guitar's wood areas. With the Rick481.tif image in the foreground, choose Selection, Load Selection, and then choose Rick481.ai as the Destination document, and choose the Layer 1 Transparency before exiting this box.

Finally, if you didn't trace the wood outline, Rick481.tif has an alpha channel hidden in it, so what you do to load the marquee is Ctrl(⌘)+click on the wood outline channel's title on the Channels palette.

7. Click on the Create new layer icon at the bottom of the Layers palette, fill the marquee selection with foreground color, and then press Ctrl(⌘)+D. It doesn't make a whit of difference what color the guitar wood overlay is. Your image should look like figure 6.19 now.

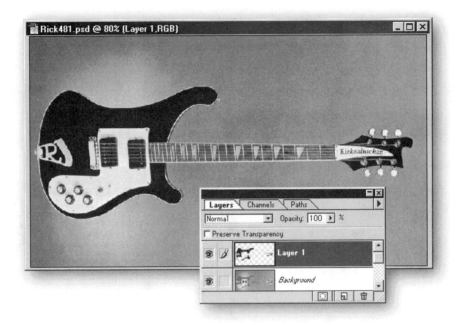

FIGURE 6.19   *The shape of the wood on the face of the guitar is now covered (you might say "masked") by the fill you applied in step 7.*

8. Save this image as Rick481.psd, in Photoshop's native file format to your hard disk, and keep the image open.

Depending on the fill color for the layer, you might already have an interesting-looking guitar color (turquoise is back in again), but it's still not a *maple* guitar. We need to mull over the following section to discover the power of clipping groups.

A Clipping Group Guitar: Some Assembly Required

Okay, here's the big artistic payoff. In the steps that follow, you'll add a layer of texture to the Rick481 image, and then clip the texture to the underlying layer. Only the areas outside the guitar will become transparent.

Here goes:

Creating a New Texture, Using Clipping Groups

1. Open Maple.tif from the Examples/Chap06 folder on the Companion CD.

2. Drag its title into the Rick481 image window, and then with the Move tool, position the wood texture so that it covers the whole image. Why? Because both the body and the head of the guitar need this texture (see fig. 6.20).

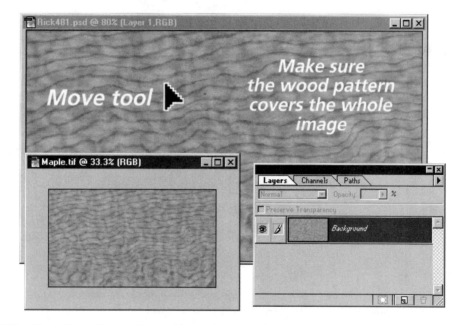

FIGURE 6.20   *Cover the entire new layer with wood texture after you drag a copy of it into the guitar window.*

3. Hold Alt(Opt) and place the cursor right between the mask layer and the wood texture on the list on the Layers palette. Then click. What happens is that everything outside the mask on the layer underneath becomes transparent, and the Rickenbacker 481 now has a maple finish (see fig. 6.21).

> **tip**
>
> Texture Creator, a program made by Three-D Graphics, was used to create all the textures in the Chap06 folder. A 30-day trial copy for Mac and Windows is available in the Three-D folder on the Companion CD.
>
> Buy it. It's fun and terrific!

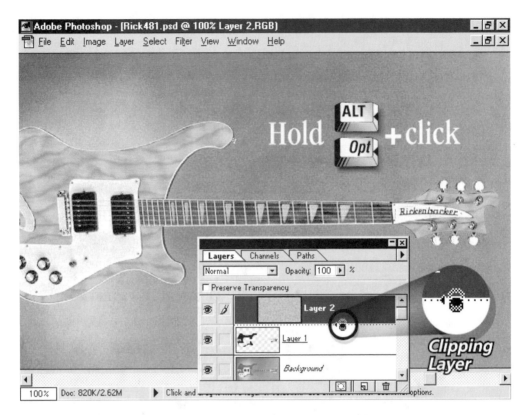

FIGURE 6.21   *When the wood part of the guitar is open for adding other textures, you can create an almost unlimited variety of exotic instruments. (The Rickenbacker International Corporation has a fairly good selection of finishes, too).*

4. To break the link between the clipping layer and the wood-texture layer, hold Alt(Opt) and click between the layers. Do this now to humor me. Notice that you can always spot a clipping group because the thumbnail for the clipped image is indented on the Layers list, and there is a dotted line between the clipped layer and the layer that's doing the clipping.

5. Open the Layer.tif image from the Chap06 folder, and then (using the Move tool) drag the image to the Rick481 window. Then, make this the texture of the guitar, as shown in figure 6.22.

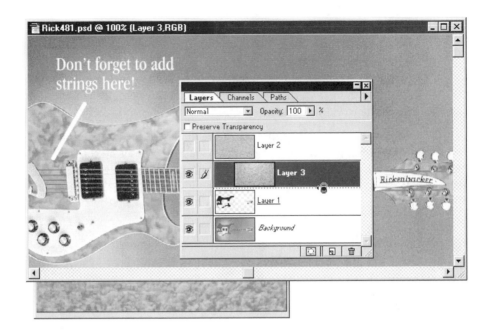

FIGURE 6.22   *Create a catalogue of guitars or anything else, in a wide variety of textures, by using clipping groups.*

6. (Optional, to become a pro): Create a new layer, drag on the Pencil tool on the toolbox to reveal the Line tool, double-click on it to reveal the Options palette, specify 1 as the weight of the line, and make certain that the Anti-aliased box is checked. Choose a light, neutral foreground color.

7. Make six strokes from the bridge of the guitar to the tailpiece (also shown in fig. 6.22). Perfect! Press Ctrl(⌘)+S and you can close (or play) the image at any time.

The clipping-groups feature is absolutely wonderful for accommodating clients who cannot make up their minds. Because this is a Photoshop-specific feature for images, images must be saved in the PSD format, and you can have a stack of images safely tucked away in the file for further experimenting.

Summary

Layers bring the traditional art tools of brushes, pencils, acetate, and a photocopy machine together in the form of one powerful feature that has a wealth of options. Experienced Photoshop users have come to *depend* on Layers ever since version 3 introduced them, and the sound of Photoshop 2.5 being deleted from hard disks all around the world was deafening <g>!

Chapter 7 concentrates on the use of the Rubber Stamp tool, perhaps one of the four most important features in Photoshop. Wait till you see all the fun and serious business this tool is used for!

PART III

Moving Onward
and Upward

CHAPTER 7

Retouching with the Rubber Stamp Tool

Part of mastering Photoshop means understanding how the Rubber Stamp tool works, when it is the appropriate tool to use, and developing a technique by which you work wonders in images with this tool. Unlike paint application tools, the Rubber Stamp tool samples image areas and feeds the graphical info to the tip of the tool, where you paint with a pattern of pixels. The action of painting with the Rubber Stamp tool is called *cloning*, because you usually duplicate something when you apply the Rubber Stamp tool.

The Rubber Stamp tool is a wonderful, high-tech, "we couldn't do this stuff a decade ago" part of Photoshop, and this chapter provides you with plenty of examples of how to best use the tool.

New to 5.5: The Pattern Stamp Tool

Experienced users of Photoshop will immediately recognize the Pattern Stamp tool as something that used to be an *option* with the *regular* Rubber Stamp tool. Now we have two *different* tools, so there are fewer accidental wrong decisions to make with the tool(s). Users who are new to Photoshop might get a little confused about how this Pattern tool works, because you aren't sampling data as you paint. Instead, you are applying parts of an image that is stored in memory—it can appear as though you're using an entirely different tool than the Rubber Stamp when your sampled image and the image you're working on are entirely different! But the capability to sample from X and apply to Y is actually part of the power of the Pattern Stamp tool. And it's a power we shall investigate right now.

Experimenting with the Aligned and Not Aligned Options

Let's clear the air and any preconceived notions of what a pattern is. A pattern, in Photoshop, is anything you've sampled using the Edit, Define Pattern command. It can be a selected area in an image, or it can be an entire image. The larger the sample, the more RAM you're going to ask Photoshop to tap into, but the following examples will show you a lot and are undemanding when it comes to file size.

First, a good question is, "What is an aligned pattern?" A pattern you paint with the Pattern Stamp tool with the Aligned option checked on the Options palette begins from the defined pattern's center, and as you drag the Rubber Stamp tool, the sampled image repeats in...well, a pattern! If you ponder this one for a moment, it is almost as though Photoshop has already created an image of tiling samples and is enabling you to apply this predrawn piece of art by pushing around the Pattern Stamp tool.

Let's try this one out:

Working with the Pattern Stamp Tool (Aligned)

1. Press Ctrl(⌘)+N and then, in the New dialog box, specify a new image window that's 100 pixels wide and 100 pixels high. You want a resolution of 72, the mode to be RGB Color, and the contents to be white. Press Enter (Return) after filling out this brief form <g>.

2. Double-click on the Linear Gradient tool to choose it and to display the Options palette. Choose Foreground to background from the Gradient drop-down box on the Options palette.

3. On the toolbox, click on the foreground color selection box, and then in the Color Picker, choose the color in the upper right of the color field—super-duper intense red. Press Enter (Return) to return to the workspace, and then click on the background color selection box.

4. Choose an orange-yellow color from the Color Picker, and then press Enter (Return) to return to the workspace.

5. Drag the (linear) Gradient tool from top left to bottom right in the image window.

6. Press Ctrl(⌘)+A (Select, All), and then choose Edit, Define Pattern.

Profound Wisdom #12:

With the Aligned option enabled, you will be painting a perfectly spaced, patterned image.

It doesn't matter where you begin, or whether you work on the left, then the right, and then in the middle of the image. Eventually, all the pattern strokes will appear evenly spaced and perfectly aligned.

That's why the option is called Aligned, and not "crochet an afghan" or "make some confetti."

7. Press Ctrl(⌘)+N, and then specify a 7" wide by 5" high image at 72 pixels/inch, in RGB Color mode with contents transparent. Press Enter (Return) to create the new image. Choose the Patten Stamp tool from the toolbox. The tool is fully loaded and ready to accommodate your every stroke.

8. Press F5 (or your Brushes palette might already be on the Options palette if you followed my advice in chapter 1), choose the second row, third-from-left tip, and then wail away! As you can see in figure 7.1, the pattern sampled is repeating, and can eventually fill the entire image window.

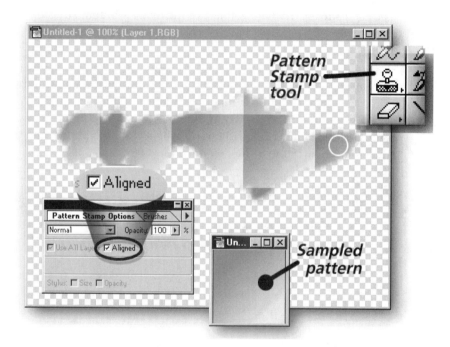

FIGURE 7.1   *Photoshop will tile the image held in memory for as far as the image extends, or until you run out of RAM!*

9. You can close the Untitled-2 image (the 5-by-7 one) at any time now. Or better yet, press Ctrl(⌘)+A and then press Delete (Backspace), and then Ctrl(⌘)+D. Now you can have a clean document window for the next section's experiment.

Without the Aligned option checked, something weird and potentially valuable in your work happens. Every time you start a new stroke with the Pattern Stamp tool, the image left under your cursor is the dead center of the pattern held in memory.

You can move the cursor anywhere you like, and when you click and drag, you'll still be beginning from the center of the pattern! Naturally, if you paint the canvas with one continuous stroke, you will not see the unaligned effect, but let's try this one out, because you'll use this option later.

Using the Pattern Stamp Without the Aligned Option

1. Uncheck the Aligned check box on the Options palette.

2. Click and stroke anywhere you like in the image window, and stop whenever the mood strikes you.

3. Pick a different section of the image area in which to begin stroking, but make it close to your first stroke so you'll be overlapping the first miniartwork you created. Surprise! The pattern is "broken"—you've disrupted the flow of the pattern as stored in memory because without the Aligned option, every time you start a stroke, you start it at the center of the small image held in memory. So it's not really a Pattern Stamp tool without the Aligned option; but you get the drift of what you can do without the option checked (see fig. 7.2).

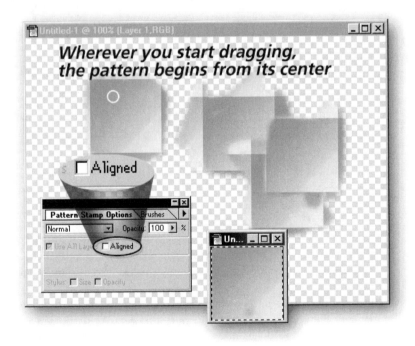

FIGURE 7.2   *By unchecking the Aligned option, you've freed yourself to start using the Pattern Stamp tool as a true imitation of a physical rubber stamp!*

The Rubber Stamp tool is like the Pattern Stamp tool, but it's much more powerful and flexible because it doesn't need a stored pattern to repeat image areas. And there is also what some people (such as the author) might see as a mistake. Adobe has slightly changed the way the Rubber Stamp tool works. It has the potential for fouling up the work of experts and novices alike, but I use the example in the following section to fully explain what to do and what not to do.

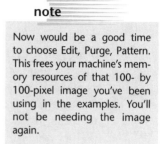

note

Now would be a good time to choose Edit, Purge, Pattern. This frees your machine's memory resources of that 100- by 100-pixel image you've been using in the examples. You'll not be needing the image again.

Starting Out with the Rubber Stamp Tool

In the 5,000 years that I've been using Photoshop, the Rubber Stamp tool with the Aligned option checked has been the most used configuration. Why? Because the Rubber Stamp tool is *excellent* at retouching pictures, particularly those pictures that have a corner missing from them or some other incompleteness.

In the steps to follow, I provide you with an image that is incomplete and show you how to fix it. But first, I need to discuss the "enhancement" Adobe Systems made to this tool.

Avoiding Unexpected Rubber Stamp Tool Performance

Up until version 4 of Photoshop, it was possible to create a "hall of mirrors" effect with the Rubber Stamp tool. In other words, if you set the sampling point directly behind the cursor, the Rubber Stamp would endlessly repeat the same image area, image area upon image area, due to the fact that you were basing a sample on work to which a sample applied had already been applied.

It really wasn't *that* irritating!

Now, you have to train yourself to keep your eyes focused in different directions. The Rubber Stamp tool will no longer sample an area that has just been cloned over unless you reset the sampling point to this exact area. This means that you can run out of good cloning resource material and accidentally start returning the image to its unedited state in a nutty mismatch of image locations within the image window.

The keys to success are

- to always sample as far away from the damaged area as possible in the image.
- to begin your cloning as close to the damaged area as possible.

Keep an eye on where the sampling point is traveling as you paint with the cursor, and life can be a peach.

With Align Activated, Are the Rubber Stamp and Pattern Stamp Tools the Same?

No. There is a fundamental difference between sampling with the Aligned option turned on with the Pattern and the Rubber Stamp tools. With the Rubber Stamp tool, the area that you sample in the image (or even in a different image window) travels as you stroke. Specifically, the sampling point travels at all times an equal distance from the Rubber Stamp tool—this is how you create effects. Figure 7.3 shows two scenarios for the Rubber Stamp tool, and also graphically makes the point about where you set your sampling point.

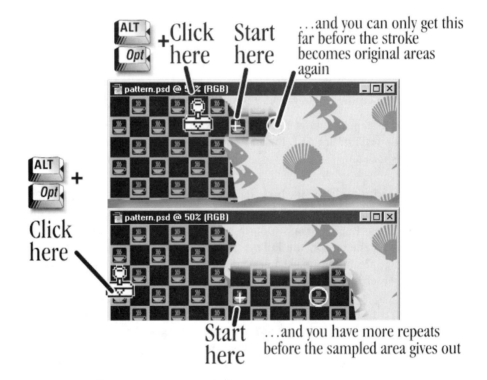

Pretend for a moment that you have a garden hose held precisely two feet away from your hand, and the garden hose is the sampling part of the Rubber Stamp tool. Your hand is the Rubber Stamp tool. Wherever you move your hand, the tip of the hose trails by an even amount at all times. Resampling is sort of like taking hold of the hose at a different distance, and traveling in a different direction with this lawn utility.

Now let's put this whole thing together, in a set of steps:

Retiling a Wall with the Rubber Stamp Tool

1. Open the abstract.tif image from the Examples/Chap07 folder on the Companion CD. A 50% viewing resolution is fine as you examine the image for damage. Uh-oh! There's a Profound Wisdom coming up to explain some stuff...

2. In figure 7.4, you can see that the tiles sort of fell off the right side of the image. Fortunately, all these tiles look nearly identical, so the repair work is fairly easy. Zoom in to about a 300% resolution of the tiles right next to the weird object at the left of the screen.

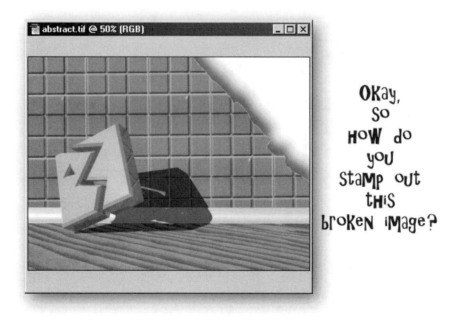

OKay, So HOW do yoU StaMp oUt tHiS broKeN iMage?

FIGURE 7.4   *Cloning efforts are the most rewarding (least flawed!) when the chore entails a regular repeating pattern that is busted.*

3. Drag on the face of the Pattern Stamp tool on the toolbox, and then choose the (regular, well-mannered) Rubber Stamp tool. On the Brushes palette, choose the middle row, third from left tip for the Rubber Stamp tool. Press the Caps Lock key. This toggles your Rubber Stamp cursor to a precise cursor, and you will be able to make out the exact center of the grouting where the tiles meet. Alt(Opt)+click on the center of the tiles, as shown in figure 7.5. By Alt(Opt)+ clicking with the Rubber Stamp tool, you set a sampling point. In this case, it's an aligned sampling point that will trail behind the Rubber Stamp tool. When you release the Alt(Opt) key, the tool becomes the Rubber Stamp tool.

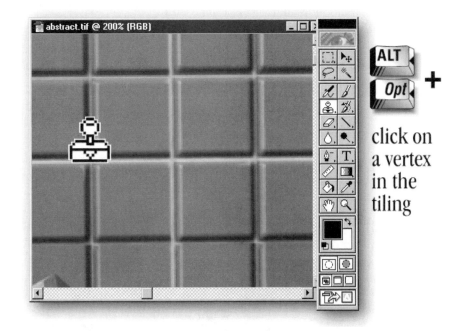

FIGURE 7.5   *This is what the Rubber Stamp tool looks like when you hold Alt(Opt) and click (the inside arrow is hollow). Generally, though, it's better to work with the precise cursors instead of the icon cursors.*

4. Hold the Spacebar and drag in the picture until you are at the intersection of tiles that border the damaged image area. Click on an intersection and hold up for a moment. You've just defined the spatial relationship between the traveling sampling point and the cursor, so anywhere you start painting, the pattern of the tiles will be aligned!

5. Back out of the image to about a 1:1 viewing resolution (double-click on the Zoom tool), choose the Rubber Stamp tool again, choose the 35-pixel tip on the Brushes palette, and then begin to repair the missing tile areas. In figure 7.6, I've created a callout to show you exactly how much latitude you have with the Rubber Stamp tool. If you have no more room to sample (if your sampling point is on the verge of where you started cloning), zoom in again to an intersection of tiles, hold Alt(Opt) for a second, and click on a new sampling point.

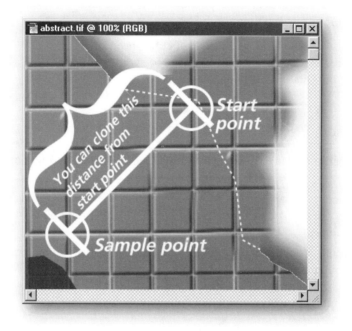

FIGURE 7.6   *When you set up the sampling point and the cloning point, there is a fixed distance of image area you can clone from before the sampling point hits the edge of where you began cloning. It's time, then, to respecify the sampling point.*

6. Hey, I personally like this picture, but that doesn't mean you have to. We're finished with the example, and you can close the image without saving it (sigh).

I think we did okey-dokey with the image of the gold icon and the blue tiles, but as I've observed, not everything in life is neatly tiled. In the following section, we get into the technique for cloning organic stuff that apparently has no flow or repetitive pattern.

Ready for an Easy Assignment? Clone *Coffee!*

Scenes that have organic elements—the waves in an ocean, the scattering of fall leaves, and a bag of coffee beans— all have visual detail that is sort of scattered all over and defies easy reproduction. But *mending* a damaged scene of nature is very simple. Why? Because there are no "hard and fast" edges to a clump of leaves—visually they blend together and the human eye gets more pleasure from the colors than from the geometry of the leaves.

The same holds true of a bunch of coffee beans. I've created yet another damaged image for you to correct, but this time, it's gonna be a piece of cake:

note

It is possible to have such a large tip size defined for the Rubber Stamp tool, and you can sample an area so close to the image window's border that you will leave edge marks when you clone. Be very careful where you sample, and pay attention to how close that brush tip is to the edge of the image window.

Coffee and a Piece of Cake

1. Open the Coffee.tif image from the Examples/Chap07 folder of the Companion CD.

2. Choose a larger Brushes palette tip, such as the 45- or 65-pixel tip. There is little need to approach this assignment with the precision you used for the blue tiles example.

3. Sample a point close to the bottom-left edge of the picture, and then start cloning at the edge of the damage in the image (see fig. 7.7). When you run out of cloning room, or the picture begins to look a little repetitive (phony), change sampling points.

Sample often from different areas

Figure 7.7   *By sampling often, you can avoid repetitive edges.*

4. Finish fixing the Coffee.tif image, as shown in figure 7.8, and then find a place on your hard disk where you might keep stock photography. I've used this coffee image at least twice in the Inside Photoshop books, and I'm passing the artistic torch along to you. Run with it!

Can you see any edges from cloning?

FIGURE 7.8   *Because organic matter has indistinct edges, you can get away with a minimum of precision when you use the Rubber Stamp tool on such images.*

Here comes the exciting part, where the author gets kicked out of his neighborhood for taking unflattering scenes of other people's houses. Sound exciting? It is! Read on...

Doing a Real-World Clean-Up

To be fair, the house in the picture you'll work with had just been sold, and the sofa on the front lawn was for the sanitation engineers to take away. But if you open Sofa.tif, ya gotta laugh a little. Not only does the sofa look inappropriate on a lawn, but they didn't straighten the cushions, either.

Here's where I get a little more demanding of your skills. You are going to remove the sofa from the image shown in figure 7.9. And as you can see, I've annotated this figure to point out that you don't have a whole lot of lawn from which to sample for the image repair.

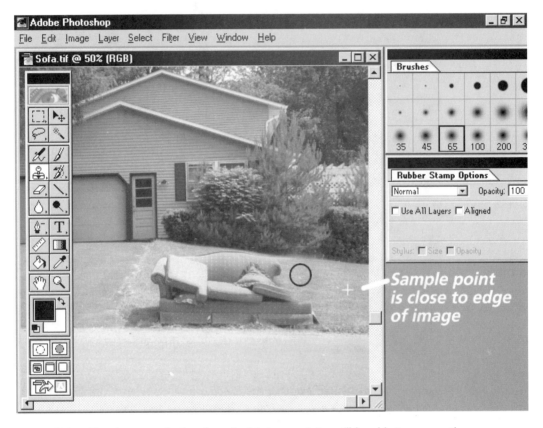

FIGURE 7.9   *There's more sofa than lawn in this image. But you'll be able to remove the sofa anyway, using Photoshop.*

Not to worry. We'll take it a step at a time:

Cloning over an Indoor/Outdoor Sofa

1. First, uncheck the Aligned check box on the Options palette. Why? Because you want to build up a significant amount of grass in the image (while cloning away the sofa), so that later you can use the Aligned option and smooth out any possible repetitions in the grass. The unaligned option always starts your cursor

in the same place, and with organic stuff such as grass, there's a tendency for patterning to show. And you don't want that. Also, set the Brushes palette's tip to 35 pixels in diameter.

2. After you've cleared the sofa away from about the right fifth of the image, check the Aligned check box on the Options palette, and then click a sample point on the right of the image.

3. Start dragging at the edge of the sofa, and don't stop until you see the sampling point approaching the Rubber Stamp tool's beginning point.

4. Continue with step 3, use different sampling points, and when you hit the edge of the lawn (where it meets the street), stop. You're probably nearly done!

5. The sofa cast a shadow on the driveway, and this is a telltale sign that the image has been goofed with. Choose the second row, second-from-left tip on the Brushes palette, Alt(Opt)+click on a piece of driveway, and then remove the shadow, as shown in figure 7.10.

tip

The default Brush Size cursor, when used with the Rubber Stamp tool, gives you a good, but not perfect, idea of how close the sampling point is coming to the image edge (and to a dead halt). Always plan on a little extra size with the soft-edge tips because the absolute extent of the tip is not indicated by the Brush Sizes cursor.

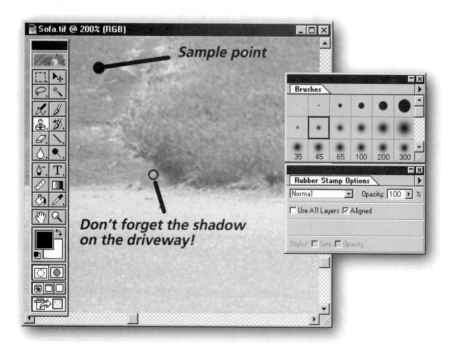

FIGURE 7.10   *Make your retouching work complete, and you've arrived at a different artistic vision of a photographed scene.*

6. You're finished! You can save the image to your hard disk, or try to sell it to a decorating magazine, like that shown in figure 7.11.

If you've gotten this far with the steps, you're no longer a beginner with the Rubber Stamp and other Photoshop tools. So in the section that follows, I'm going to play hardball with you, and toss you an image that would stump some Photoshop experts.

note

I pulled apart the Brushes and the Options palette in these screen captures so you can see all the settings I used. I usually have the palettes grouped (as recommended in Chapter 1), and they are easy enough to restore. You simply take hold of the title on a palette and then drop it over the palette with which you want the first palette grouped.

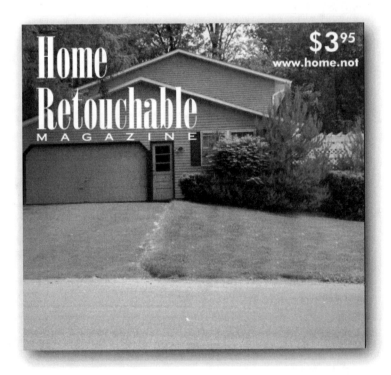

FIGURE 7.11   *Changing an eyesore of a scene into an eye-pleaser is sophisticated stuff. And doing it in less than 30 minutes is pure magic. Congratulate yourself as you grasp the power of Photoshop!*

The Banished Burger Affair

I created the composition by photographing a real burger, and everything else in figure 7.12 is a rendered 3D model, to demonstrate animation in *Inside Adobe Photoshop 4.* But there's more than a single use for almost everything one designs. I thought to myself, "How hard could it be to completely remove that stupid burger from an otherwise pretty kitchen scene?" I'll tell you right now that you'll probably need to set aside an hour to perform the burger-ectomy, but it'll be an hour well spent. In other words, you will learn much.

FIGURE 7.12   *Each of the four areas you need to retouch in this picture presents a different problem.*

Starting the Retouching Work

As you can see from the callouts in figure 7.12, there's a lot of area that needs to be restored and not a lot to work with. I'll tell you what: How about approaching this like the pros and depending on *a bunch of* Photoshop tools to retouch the image? The tools in Photoshop *integrate,* and that's why all sorts of image snippets can come together under Photoshop's roof.

Let's work on the problem areas in this image from the bottom up, starting with the countertop:

Restoring the Wood in the Image

1. Open the Kitchen.tif image from the Examples/Chap07 folder on the Companion CD. Zoom to 100% (1:1) on the image.

2. With the (normal) Lasso tool, create a selection area that includes the wooden countertop, but not the white trim or anything else in the picture. You're creating a dropcloth for use with the Rubber Stamp tool. Now the tool cannot wander accidentally into areas where you do not wish it to wander, and all you'll be retouching is wood.

3. With the 35-pixel tip, Alt(Opt)+click as far to the right of the image as possible, and then (with the Aligned check box checked on the Options palette), start making short, brisk strokes over the burger in the image, as shown in figure 7.13. I want you to make short strokes over the burger, resampling often so the viewer doesn't get the idea that the wooden countertop is covered with wood-grain contact paper or anything! Let's avoid obvious wood patterning.

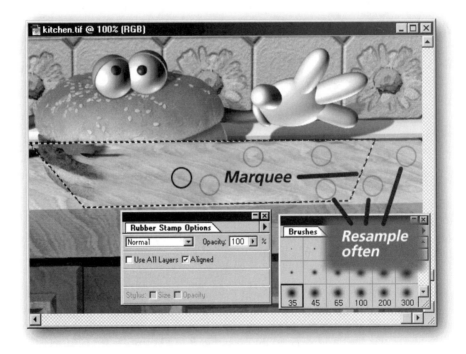

FIGURE 7.13   *Use the Lasso tool to describe the area that needs retouching, and then use the Rubber Stamp tool in Aligned mode.*

4. After you have one area covered, there's no reason to lose the marquee selection you've created, so simply move it to the left with the Lasso tool. Note for experienced users: Photoshop no longer moves the content of an image with a selection tool; you need to use the Move tool to do that. You merely move a selection area when you drag on it (see fig. 7.14).

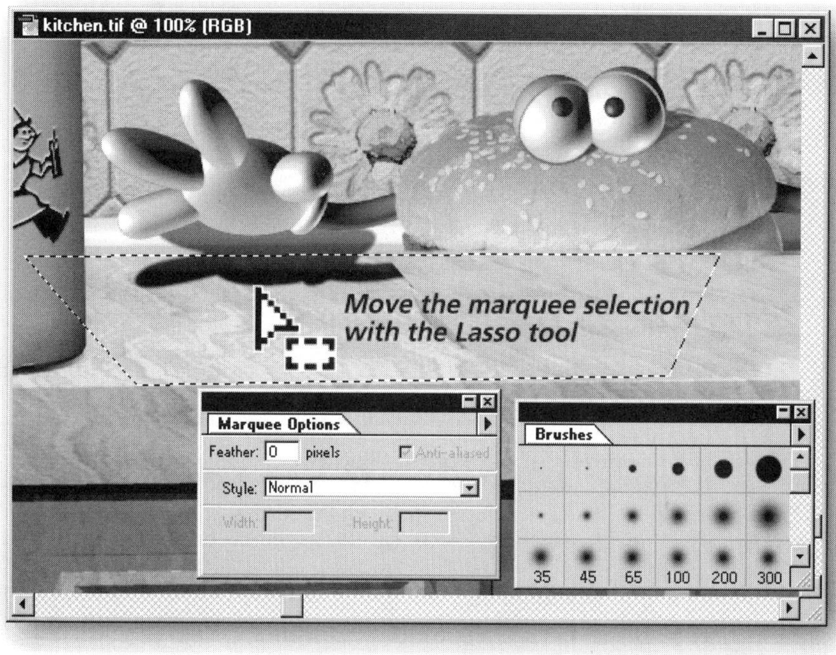

FIGURE 7.14   *Reposition the selection marquee by dragging on it with any selection tool.*

5. Keep setting those sampling points and clone the burger away, using wood samples as the replacement. You will find as you progress that you can use longer, fewer strokes, as the burger's bottom disappears.

6. When the wood has no more burger on it, stop, press Ctrl(⌘)+S, and save the image to your hard disk as Kitchen.tif, in the TIFF file format. Keep the image open.

Strategy Time for Restoring Molding

If you look closely at the molding that separates the tiled wall from the countertop, there's very little visual detail, and yet this area needs restoring. You do not have to use the Rubber Stamp tool (in fact, you'd get lousy results with it) to restore this area.

All you need to do is accurately define the areas with the Lasso tool and then use first the Eyedropper and then the Airbrush tool to re-create the molding (there are two parts to this molding if you look closely: the base, and then a scoop above it).

Let's walk through the necessary retouching steps for the molding:

Using the Airbrush Tool on Small Areas

1. Create a narrow, long marquee selection that encompasses the base of the molding. Hold Alt to toggle the tool to make straight marquee segments, and press the Spacebar when necessary to drag in the window and move your view of the molding.

2. Just to the left of one of the hamburger's hands is a piece of base molding that is in the clear. Choose the Airbrush tool from the toolbox, check figure 7.15 for the Options and Brushes palette settings, and then start retouching from left to right. The Airbrush might sometimes need to be used twice over an area to totally cover it because the tool produces an extremely diffuse color, with absolutely no brush lines (this is good.)

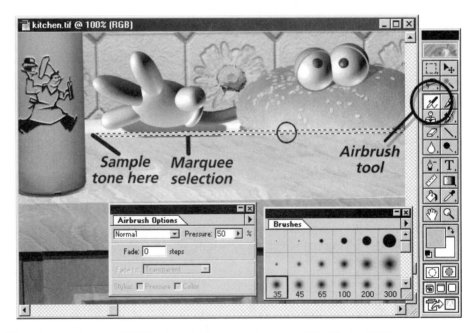

FIGURE 7.15   *Always ask yourself, "Which tools do I need to accomplish this task?" You will not always need the same Photoshop tool.*

You're going to run into a problem when you reach the right side of the image. The color at right is a little deeper than at left. Do this:

3. Hold Alt(Opt) to toggle to the Eyedropper, and then sample the color at the far right of the base molding. Then use the Airbrush tool to go over the rightmost area.

4. Choose the Smudge tool from the Focus Tools group on the toolbox, and briskly drag from right to left once (twice, tops). The Smudge tool blends the left color into the right color.

5. Press Ctrl(⌘)+S and keep the file open.

Although this image is mostly a modeling creation (I used trueSpace), the picture contains many photorealistic elements, some of them unwanted. For example, my virtual camera (when I was rendering the scene) was not perfectly perpendicular to the tiles, so everything on the counter moves uphill ever so slightly—by one pixel or so. You *will* encounter these less-than-optimal photographic challenges in your own work, so I'm getting you used to it right now. This is why you have to Lasso the molding instead of using the Rectangular Marquee tool.

Molding: Part 2

There's really no need for you to follow steps to get the scooped part of the molding retouched. The steps are the same as those you used to correct the base of the molding. You drag a marquee, you sample the color, and then you go over it with the Airbrush tool. Study figure 7.16, and it will all fall into place.

Aha! But here comes a monolith of a retouching effort. Can you use pieces of the tiles on the wall to get rid of the rest of the burger? Of course you can; that's why *I'm* here!

Industrial-Strength Cloning Power

In the next set of steps, it is not so much the tools that provide the results. Rather, your keen eyes should detect every opportunity to grasp cloning source material, and to use the right cursors and locations for applying the source material.

The very first place to work is the daisy tile that the burger's left (stage left) side is obscuring. ***Detect before you correct.*** There is a part of a daisy tile above, next to the light switch, that can solve part of the tile problem. Listen, with a scene as complex as this, you work in stages, and might not even get a whole tile restored in one step. In figure 7.17, the small, diamond-shaped blue tiles that are mixed with the octagonal tiles are perfect targets for the sampling point of the Rubber Stamp tool.

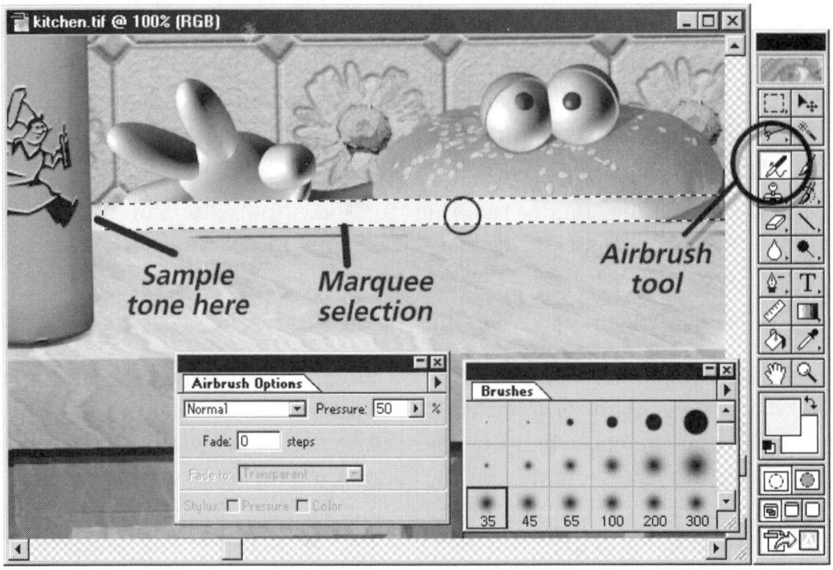

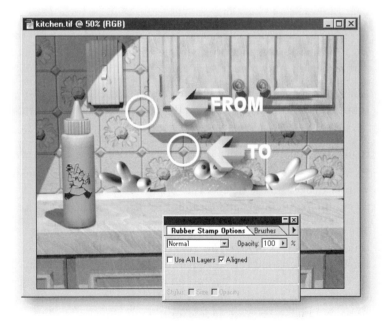

FIGURE 7.16   *It's only natural that an identical problem to the one you solved requires the same steps to fix.*

FIGURE 7.17   *What better opportunity to seize than to use the regularly spaced smaller tiles as reference points for the Rubber Stamp tool.*

Let's wrap up this assignment. Fewer tiles need correcting than you might think:

Cloning Tiles. What...Again?

1. With the Lasso tool and the Alt(Opt) key held, draw a marquee around the burger area, keeping the top of the molding precisely defined with the bottom of the marquee.

2. Choose the Rubber Stamp tool, change the size of the Brushes tip to 65 pixels in diameter, press Caps Lock to make the cursor a precise cursor, and then Alt(Opt)+click on the upper blue diamond tile that was circled in figure 5.17. Then, click on the blue diamond tile next to the burger's (stage) left eye, and stroke (carefully) down and to the left. Do not travel upward with the tool—there's a light switch near the sample point and there's a cabinet near the Rubber Stamp tool. Figure 7.18 shows where you should be by now in the assignment.

note

Watch *carefully* as you proceed. As I mentioned earlier, this is not a "dead on" camera view of the scene, and all the tiles might not be exactly the same width. So if you start seeing grout lines that are not lining up, *stop.* Find a good, clean grout edge and clone it into the lousy one.

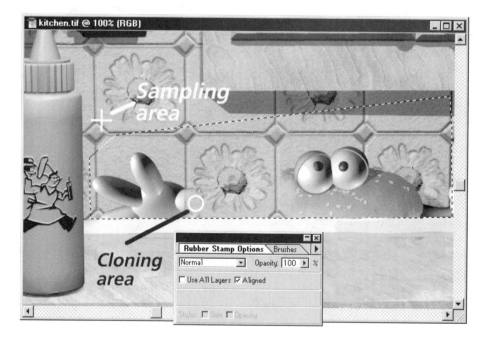

Figure 7.18   *You're removing the burger by aligning the sampling point with a tile of identical visual content.*

You should be able to restore the daisy tile, but the blank tile to the left of it presents a problem. There really isn't any suitable area from which to clone to obliterate the burger's hand. The solution lies a few chapters back—you *duplicate* a clean area:

3. The grain on the plain tiles really has no discernible pattern, so it's okay to copy one area and place it over an area containing the burger's fingers. Choose the Rectangular Marquee tool, drag a marquee containing only clean texture, and then hold Ctrl(⌘)+Alt(Opt) and drag a copy of the selection to below the original point. Do this four times, and you'll have a clean tile, as shown in figure 7.19.

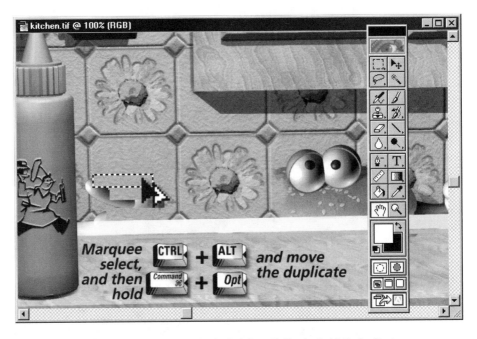

FIGURE 7.19   *In combination with the Marquee tools, holding Alt(Opt)+Ctrl(⌘) duplicates the selected image area.*

4. Re-establish that marquee whose bottom edge meets the top of the molding. Now you have a plain tile and a daisy tile that are in the clear. Start cloning to the right. In figure 7.20, I goofed, and the grouting lines don't perfectly match. No big deal: if this happens to you, line up the sampling point with a small blue diamond tile, and then clone downward over the awkward-looking grouting.

FIGURE 7.20   *Keep resampling as you clone, to ensure that everything visually lines up as it should.*

5. Um, I think you're finished! Press Ctrl(⌘)+S and keep the image open.

One of the rewards of working to retouch away things such as hamburgers with eyes and hands is that you now have a perfect kitchen setting for your own use. In figure 7.21, after taking the stupid hamburger out of the picture, I replaced it with a stupid-looking preserves jar. Much better, huh?

If you want to be as silly as I am, the Concord.psd file is in the Examples/CHAP07 folder and you can simply drag the preserves jar, shadow and all, into the Kitchen.tif window, and save the file in Photoshop's native PSD format.

I still get a kick out of dramatically retouching scenes for the fun of it, and time and again, I find that to do so I need to learn something new about the Rubber Stamp tool and special techniques. You know, you're walking away from this chapter with four different approaches to using the tool, each approach geared toward perfecting a certain type of image.

FIGURE 7.21   *If people ask what the mustard container is doing next to grape jelly, tell them, "It's not a mustard container. It's a toast container."*

Summary

Aside from the selection tools in Photoshop, the Rubber Stamp is probably the second or third most important tool you can master. You've seen how remarkably you can alter scenes, how to make them look plausible, and most important—

Hey, you know something? So far in this book it's been I who have been having all the fun with text! What do you say in the next chapter, we turn our sights to ways that Photoshop and *you* can handle text?

PROFOUND WISDOM #14:

The best Photoshop work is that which goes unnoticed.

You're not trying to make the image anything other than what you envision it to be. You're uncovering image potential, but you're not leaving your thumbprints all over your work.

Generally, when your re-touching work goes un-noticed, you should think of that as a personal award.

CHAPTER 8

Working with Type

In the world of electronic typesetting, the text you create on an application's page can be in either of two formats:

- **Text as a graphic.** We generally think of a text graphic as a bitmap of some text that has been converted to pixel format.

- **Text as (editable) text.** This sort of text formatting belongs to the vector family of computer graphics. For example, InDesign and PageMaker use Adobe Type Manager's outline representation of text to offer type that scales smoothly, unlike what you'd get if you tried to scale a bitmap of some 12-point type into 72-point type.

Photoshop 5.5 brings to the party a hybrid of vector and bitmap text. The text in Photoshop is rendered as a bitmap, but until you explicitly command Photoshop to do this rendering, the text stays *editable*—which is one of the prime reasons designs use DTP (desktop publishing) and vector drawing programs to create text.

By the end of this chapter, you will know more text tricks in Photoshop than you might need to in a year's worth of working with the application!

Examining the Types of Type with the Type Tool

Photoshop offers not one, but four entry points for adding text to an image window. This gives the user a good amount of flexibility and decision-making when it's time to add text to a graphic. Let's cover what a tool *does* before you start working with type.

The Type Tool

This tool has been around since Photoshop offered text as a feature (I'm putting the date at around 1989), but significant power has been added to the tool to make it more user-friendly in version 5.5. When you click an insertion point in an image window with the Type tool, the Type Tool dialog box pops up, and it is here that you enter text and specify the various styles of the text (you'll be using this tool extensively in this chapter).

The text is immediately displayed in the image, even while you're working in the dialog box; you can "step outside" the dialog box, your cursor becomes the Move tool, and you can reposition the text for instant feedback. For example, if the text is proving to be too large, you highlight the text you've entered in the Type Tool dialog box, and then pick a smaller font size. You can also pick any color you like for the text before putting it in the image. The color box icon in the Type tool's dialog box displays the Color Picker, and there you go.

As soon as you've entered your text, you click on OK, and the text appears in your image on a new layer, whose name is what you typed. There's a large "T" to the right of the title to remind you that the text is editable. When you double-click on the title of the text layer, the Type Tool dialog box pops up again with the text you typed.

The Type Mask Tool

This tool is more like the traditional Photoshop Type tool because it

- Does not create a new layer for entered text.
- Does not even lay down text with the current foreground color. All you wind up with, after working in the Type tool box and clicking on OK, is a selection marquee.

Although the chance of accidentally deselecting the text is always present, the Type Mask tool has a number of advantages over the Type tool:

- You can fill the selection marquee with a gradient blend of many different colors, as well as transparency between colors.
- You can reposition the text before adding color to the marquee selection of the text by dragging inside its outline. (Recommendation: Use the Lasso tool for repositioning the text, because this cursor's "sweet spot" is at the end of the Lasso icon and it's easy to locate and place inside the text.)
- You can add a layer to the composition at any time, and then fill the text marquee, and you essentially have done what the Type tool does.

- You can cancel your text work *after* clicking on OK by simply clicking outside the Type Mask marquee borders.

Check out the results of working with all four Type tools in figure 8.1. We'll cover the other two variants in a moment.

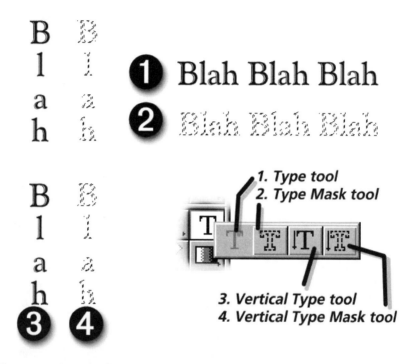

1. Type tool
2. Type Mask tool
3. Vertical Type tool
4. Vertical Type Mask tool

FIGURE 8.1   *The Type tool is actually a collection of tools whose purpose is to enable you to create variations on text placement and appearance.*

The Vertical and Vertical Mask Type Tools

These tools, as shown in figure 8.1, create text that is vertically stacked, much like the neon on a hotel or motor court sign. If you forget about the direction the type is laid down, the Vertical Type tool operates identically to the Type tool. By the way, the align-middle, left, and right buttons do nothing to the intercharacter alignment of text you specify. Instead, these text controls determine the location on the image of the text (in other words, to the left of the insertion point, to its right…you get it).

A question that immediately sprang to my mind as I examined this feature was "What's it good for?" I think I'd be correct in saying that the Vertical Type tools are not every day tools (just as the CMYK Gamut Preview is not a feature you constantly use in Photoshop). But when you want to design a magazine cover, and the title of the 'zine is to be on the left, you have your choice of rotating text after placing it, or using the Vertical Type tools (which produce text that is oriented in a conventional way, and hence is more legible than rotated text.)

The Vertical Type Mask tool creates an outline of the text you type in the image window. No extra layer is created, and layer naming according to what you typed will not appear on the Layers palette.

So, text placement has taken a big step forward with Photoshop 5.5. You no longer need to perform the mental gymnastics of converting pixels at a given resolution to inches to know that the text will fit on the page—you simply type it, and then drag the text around in the window. If it doesn't fit, you highlight the text in the Type tool box and specify a different size for the text.

A Bevy of Text Effects

In the same way that an idea can have widely varying graphic executions—from photorealistic to abstract—*text* can also communicate a message on both a literal and an artistic level. In the sections to follow, you'll see text used for a lot of different purposes...purposes that you'll definitely want to adopt.

Titling and Autographing Your Work

One of the most common questions readers ask is, "How do I protect my work on the Web?" The answer is, "You can't—not with 100% certitude." But you can make it darned hard for a would-be graphics pirate to commandeer your work.

I have to admit that I've occasionally entered some data into the File Info box while creating the images for this book. The File, File Info dialog box was originally created for magazine and newspaper photographers who transmit their images electronically, and want to tag credits to the image. This is a nice feature for yourself to make notes that will travel with the file, but here are some caveats:

- Using File/File Info with an image requires that you load an image and then go to File, File Info each time you need the information. Essentially, the embedded information is invisible unless you have Photoshop 3 (or a later version) around to read it with.

- File Info is totally inadequate for "branding" your work that you put up on the Web. Anyone who owns Photoshop can easily change the File Info because

File Info does not hard code itself into the image. If you want something that's nearly foolproof for branding your files, check out DigiMarc (www.digimarc.com). The plug-in comes with Photoshop 5.5.

Nope, if you want instant info, and if you want to sign your work, you need to use the Type tool, plus a little trick I'll show you that involves the Illustrator format for signatures.

Let's begin by titling a piece of artwork, through the following steps:

Adding a Title to Your Work

1. Open the HoleHead.tif image from the Examples/CHAP08 folder on the Companion CD.

   Notice that I've left some white space at the bottom of the image for a title and a signature. Background color doesn't really matter here, but you should create enough space at the bottom for legible but subtle text. In other words, 24-point type reads beautifully on the Web, and would require no more than .4 inches of background space. If you make text larger when you title a piece, and you overwhelm the audience with the signature, then you don't wow them with your art. This is text meant for the Web, and not a Piggly-Wiggly 18-wheeler.

2. Click an insertion point with the (regular, normal, well-adjusted) Type tool at the bottom left of the image, and then pause for a moment as Photoshop pauses to poll your system as to how many hundred fonts you have installed (see fig. 8.2).

3. In the top field of the Type Tool dialog box, there is a drop-down list of the fonts currently installed on your system. My (artistic) suggestion is to choose a font that is delicate but not fragile. Hoefler Text, Cataneo Italic and Swash, Esprit Italic, Giovanni Italic, and even plain old utilitarian Times Roman Italic make nice titles for your artwork.

4. Type what you like in the text field, and then with the cursor (which is a text cursor as long as it's in the dialog box), highlight the text, as shown in figure 8.3. If you forget to highlight the text, you cannot apply a font size or any other text attributes such as style (bullet 4 in fig. 8.3) or specify how tall the text should be (bullet 3 in fig. 8.3).

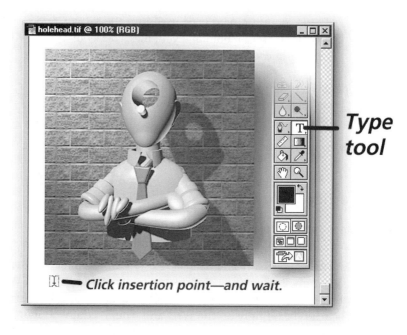

FIGURE 8.2   *Click where you want the text in the image to begin.*

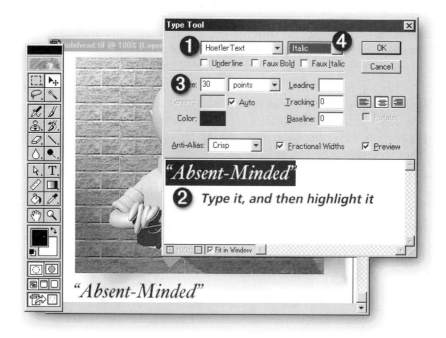

FIGURE 8.3   *You can choose, from within the Type Tool dialog box, all the parameters of the text.*

5. Choose a font style (bullet 4), click on the align-left button in the dialog box, make the text about 30 points (I know I told you 24 points, but this image is a little on the large side), and then press OK to apply the text.

6. Save the piece as HoleHead.psd in Photoshop's native file format to your hard disk, and keep the composition open.

Now, it's time to sign the image, and this also means a change of scenery. For Illustrator owners, we move from Photoshop to Illustrator to accomplish a natural-looking digital signature.

Creating the "Hand-written" Look

I know what some of you are going to say: "Mr. Bouton, I own a digitizing tablet, so why would I need Illustrator to create my signature? I can do the signing right there in Photoshop."

You sure could. In fact, after I was introduced to a digitizing tablet, I didn't want to work any other way. However, there are catches:

■ If you sign your name with a digitizing tablet, you cannot guarantee that your signature will always be the same in every saved file.

■ And after you sign the work, you have no way to scale the signature up or down without losing the signature's focus.

That's why I think that if you're serious about Photoshop, you need to also get Adobe Streamline (if you own CorelDRAW version 7 or better, skip this comment—you already own CorelTRACE, an imitation of Streamline). With Streamline or CorelTRACE you can make a vector copy of the bitmap signature you scanned into your computer, and then save the file as an Illustrator file, which Photoshop can scale to any size before rendering the signature to bitmap format.

Here are the steps to take to get your signature into the proper digital format for Photoshop to accept:

note

Although I've recommended pressing Enter (Return) in many of the steps in this book as a quick way to apply an effect or other command, you might not want to do this in the Type Tool dialog box.

You see, the Enter (Return) key is not only used for executing a command, but it also puts a hard break in text. Now, if you want to break lines while you're typing in the text field of the Type Tool dialog box, Windows users should use the (big) Enter key, and Mac users can use the Return key. Do *not* use the Enter key on the number keypad—when you do, you tell Photoshop, "OK, apply the text and close."

On second thought, perhaps you should only click on the OK button when you are finished in the Type Tool dialog box. Hey, doing this is a 100% error-free move.

Creating a Digital Signature

1. Buy a scanner and install it, if you haven't already. A decent flatbed scanner can be had for around $200 if you shop smart (like shopping on the Web).

   If you don't have a scanner, I'd suggest you add one to your graphics hardware—Photoshop and a scanner were meant for each other. For this assignment here, I've provided you with a signature in the Chap08 folder that's ready to go, and I'll reference it in the steps when it's time to use it.

2. Use a felt-tipped, nonpermanent marker (okay, a Flair® pen—Gillette, you can thank me later).

3. Write your name a number of times on a piece of white paper. You might want the paper to be thin so you can put a ruled piece of paper behind it. Hint: downhill- or uphill-running signatures look unprofessional.

4. Scan the signature at 1:1 size at about 150 pixels/inch in grayscale scanning mode. This is one of those "magic numbers" I've discovered through the years. It works with digitized signatures and not much else.

5. Save the scanned signatures to the TIFF file format, and then decide which one you like best. Crop it out of the page and save it as MyName.tif in the TIFF file format.

6. Import the MyName.tif file to Streamline or CorelTRACE, and then have the program trace a vector copy of your signature. Windows users, be sure to add an ".ai" after the file name, as in Dilbert.ai.

7. Now, if you own Illustrator, you can tweak the signature, and add a copyright date to it in a relaxed-looking typeface such as Tekton (David Siegel, you can thank me later. In figure 8.4, you can see my signature in Illustrator, and I'm simply cleaning up the handwriting. Streamline has a good, but not a comprehensive set of editing tools for this particular task.

8. Load Photoshop and the HoleHead.psd image, and then choose File, Place. Then pick the Illustrator file on your hard drive. If you don't have a scanner or Illustrator, use the FredSign.ai file in the Examples/CHAP08 folder on the Companion CD.

9. What happens next is that a preview-quality signature appears in a box with an "X" running through it. The signature is at its default size, that is, the size at which you created it. And it's probably misplaced in the image, and way too large.

10. Click inside the bounding box of the signature, and then drag it down to its final position, as shown in figure 8.5.

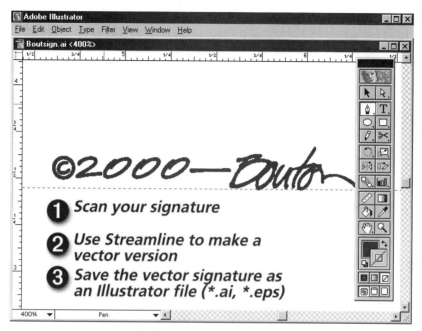

FIGURE 8.4 *Get your signature into Adobe's native vector file format, and you'll be able to work with it more easily in Photoshop.*

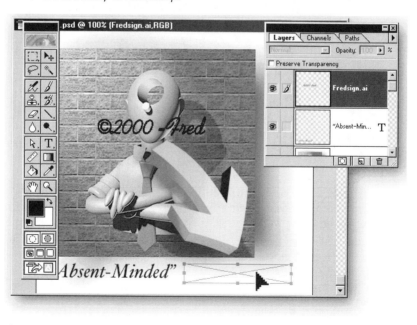

FIGURE 8.5 *A placed EPS or *.AI file (they're virtually the same format) can be enlarged, distorted, or moved, and always comes into the scene on its own layer.*

11. Hold Shift, hold one of the corners of the signature's bounding box, and then drag toward the center of the placed file (see fig. 8.6). The Shift key is constraining the placed Illustrator file to proportionate scaling.

You might want to zoom in to 200% or 300% viewing resolution while you do this, but you cannot use the Zoom tool from the toolbox. Instead, hold Ctrl(⌘)+ the Spacebar and click on the signature. This move toggles whatever tool you're using to the Zoom In tool in a way that Photoshop permits—you haven't really changed tools before finalizing your editing—you've merely used modifier keys to access the Zoom In tool.

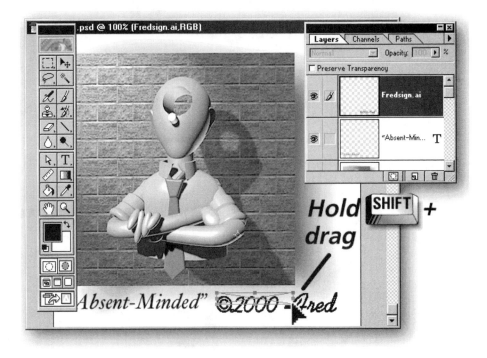

Figure 8.6   *To scale the Illustrator file of your signature, hold a corner handle while you hold the Shift key—and drag.*

12. Press Enter (Return), or double-click inside the bounding box to finalize the rendering of the signature to bitmap format. Keep the file open.

Far out! Way cool! Photoshop rules!

Okay, in our next section, you'll see a short, simple trick for foiling the most stubborn of Web art thieves.

Put the Signature *in* the Image

Before the invention of white space below an image, it was a tradition to actually write your name *on* the artwork you drew. Your success as an artist was directly proportional to how small you could sign your masterpiece, and how harmoniously your signature blended into the finished artwork. For example, someone who signs their name in 2" letters on a canvas that's 11"×14" has serious self-image problems and should probably seek a career as a graffiti artist.

tip

If you want the Zoom Out tool while all seven of your hands are busy doing other things, Press Ctrl(⌘)+ Alt(Opt)+ Spacebar, and then click in the image window.

You can also simply hold the Spacebar to toggle to the Hand tool without ruining the Illustrator file that has yet to be converted to pixels.

If you've followed the steps so far, you currently have a black signature on its own layer in the HoleHead.psd image. How hard would it be to move the signature up *into* the image, and change the signature's color to something that contrasts against the dense shades in the lower-right corner?

I don't know. Let's try it out and see.

Recoloring a Signature

1. Press D (default colors) and then press X (switch foreground/background colors). The current foreground color is white.

2. Press F7, in case the Layers palette is not onscreen, and zoom in to about 200% viewing resolution so you have a good, unobstructed view of the signature.

3. On the Layers palette, with FredSign.ai (or your own signature) highlighted, click on the Preserve Transparency check box. Only nontransparent areas can be edited now.

4. Choose the Paintbrush tool, choose a Brushes tip size from the second row, in the middle of the row, and then paint over the signature, as shown in figure 8.7.

5. You can save the composition one last time, and then close it. In chapters to come you'll see how to optimize a copy of this work so it'll display on the Web quickly and with clarity.

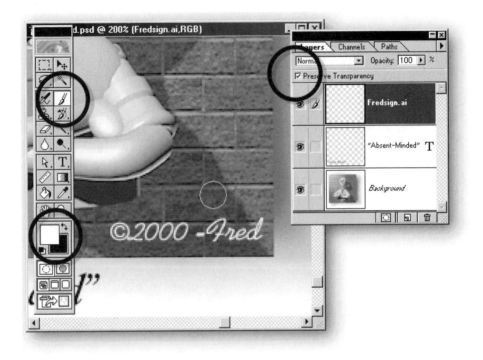

FIGURE 8.7   *With Preserve Transparency turned on, only the signature can be colored in on the signature layer.*

Protecting their work on the Web is only one reason people want to put text in an image. In the next section, you'll see how you and Photoshop can accommodate your e-mail attachment needs.

Creative a Captivating Caption

I don't know how many times I've wanted to embed information about a picture I've downloaded from the Web, or somehow attached an e-mail message to an image that came along with the e-mail. Because text travels the Web as editable text, and graphics travel along as graphics, there doesn't seem to be a time or place to meld the two.

So I've decided on the best method, and in the steps that follow, you'll see how to add a caption to an image. This is not as simple as it seems, and I'd like to call out various points here that you can follow to make this your *best* captioned image:

■ When you add the background area, first sample a background color from the image itself. This is an ancient trick that picture-framing folks have used to ensure that you're not introducing an odd new color to the overall composition. In short, if you sample from the image you aren't adding a new color to the composition.

- The text should be as small as possible while still being legible, and it should be aliased—that's right, folks—*aliased,* as in, "this text has a rough outline." Why, especially when Photoshop is a wizard with pleasing-looking anti-aliased text? This is a simple one: When a character consists, for example, of only a stem that's one pixel wide, anti-aliasing surrounds the stem, makes it appear bolder than it really is, and the following anti-aliased character will surely blur its *own* anti-aliasing into the first character.

- To reduce the harsh appearance of aliased text, and also not to call too much attention to the text (hey, it's *supporting* the image, not dominating it), I heartily recommend using an off-white color for the text, something like a 30% black. The text will be legible, but subdued.

I think that's the complete list of caption caveats. Let's work on titling an image now.

Building a Caption into an Image

1. Open the Lou.tif image from the Examples/Chap08 folder on the Companion CD. This isn't simply an "anybody" in the image; it's the Boutons' Uncle Lou, and we need a caption pertaining to the event and the activity shown in the image.

2. Choose the Eyedropper tool from the toolbox, and then Alt(Opt)+click on the lighter part of Lou's sports coat. Alt(Opt)+clicking designates the current background color.

3. Choose Image, Canvas Size, and as shown in figure 8.8, make the height of the image 350 pixels (it's originally 304 pixels high), and be sure to click the top center chiclet in the Anchor field. This forces the new canvas to go at the bottom of the newly sized canvas.

4. Click on the Type tool, and then choose a clean sans serif typeface. Helvetica, (Macintosh) Chicago, and Tekton seem to read very well without anti-aliasing at small sizes.

5. Type whatever you like in the text field, but make the text 8 point, centered, with no anti-aliasing. Specify 10-point leading for the text—this creates two pixels between lines of text. Then, choose a color for the text. Now that the text is appearing in the image, as shown in figure 8.9, it's a simple matter to click on the Color box in the Type Tool dialog box, and pick a color that's about seven or eight shades lighter than the background color. The important thing is that white is out of the question for text. It's way too harsh, due to the contrast between it and the background.

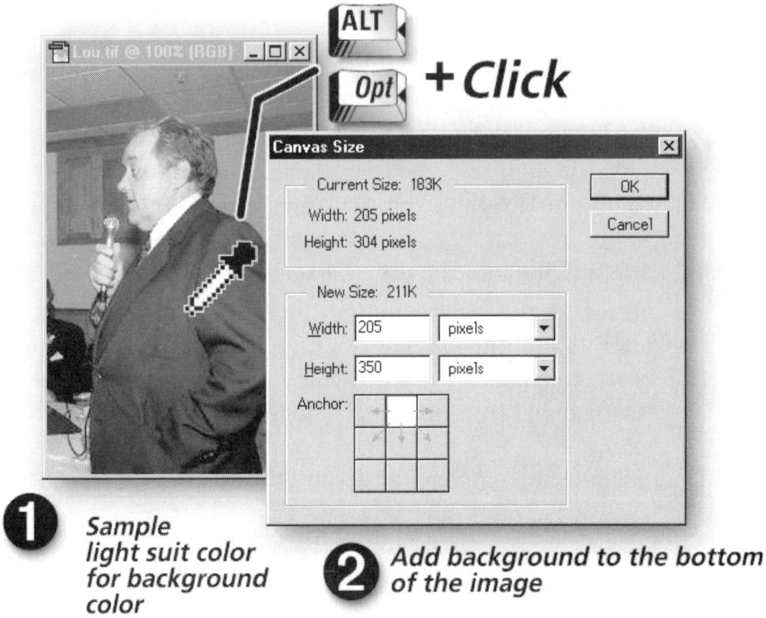

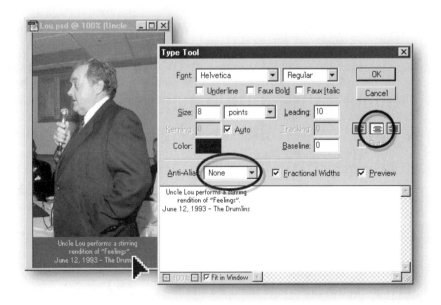

FIGURE 8.8   *Choose a background color sampled from the picture, and then use the Canvas Size command to add a colored background to the image.*

FIGURE 8.9   *Once you have the font, the font color, the size, and anti-aliasing turned off, step out of the dialog box and drag the text around until it is centered.*

6. Choose Flatten Image from the Layers palette's flyout menu, and save the image as Lou.tif to your hard disk. When we get into ImageReady later in the book, you'll see how you can optimize your captioned image for fast download and good fidelity. You can close the image at any time.

Coming up is a neat trick by which you integrate text with the image. You actually see part of the scene through the text, as though the text were frosted glass.

Creating Subtle Text

You can do something very creative when an assignment calls for medium- to heavy-weight text. You can run a headline across the image (almost as though the text were subliminal advertising). The text is harmonious with the image, yet holds its own as an attention-getter.

It's a little less than thrilling that this new version of Photoshop will not let you preview text placement in an alpha channel, but the workaround is easy. In the next set of steps you'll create the text in an alpha channel, load it as a selection and position it, and then save the new position to a new alpha channel.

Creating a Glass Text Look

1. Open the W_Cake.tif image from the Examples/Chap08 folder on the Companion CD.

2. On the Channels palette, Alt(Opt)+click on the Create new channel icon. Then, in the dialog box, choose Color Indicates: Selected Areas, and press Enter (Return).

3. Choose the Type tool, and then click an insertion point in the alpha channel to the far left.

4. When the Type Tool dialog box is displayed, click on the aligned-left button, choose a font size of approximately 1 inch (there are 72 points to an inch, so type 72 to 75 here for text of the correct height). Choose black as the color of the text before leaving the dialog box. Because the type is not previewing in the alpha channel, I had to guesstimate to define the right-sized text.

5. Type **Wedding Cake** in the text field, highlight the text, choose Crisp from the Anti-Alias drop-down list, and then find a nice script font from the list of installed fonts. I'm using Vivaldi, but Snell, Signet, Palace Script (Bold), or Kunstler Script (Kunstlerschreibschrift) can work here (see fig. 8.10). Click OK to apply the text.

Figure 8.10   *Use a font size that you've predetermined will work well with the image.*

6. Press Ctrl(⌘)+D to deselect the text, and then press Ctrl(⌘) and click on the Alpha 1 title to load the black text as a marquee selection.

7. Press Ctrl(⌘)+tilde (~) to move the view in the image window to the color channel in the image. Your view of the palette should still be on the channels, but the selection is now floating over the wedding cake scene.

8. With a selection tool (such as the Lasso tool) drag inside the marquee to position the text where you want it. Then click on the Save selection as channel icon at the bottom of the Channels palette, as shown in figure 8.11.

9. Ctrl(⌘)+click on the Alpha 2 title on the Channels palette to load the text as a selection, and then click on the RGB channel title to move to the color view of the cake.

10. Press Ctrl(⌘)+H to hide the marquee lines, and then press Ctrl(⌘)+L to display the Levels command.

tip

Once a text object has been deselected in an alpha channel, you can no longer edit it by displaying the Type Tool dialog box. Editable text can only be found on image layers.

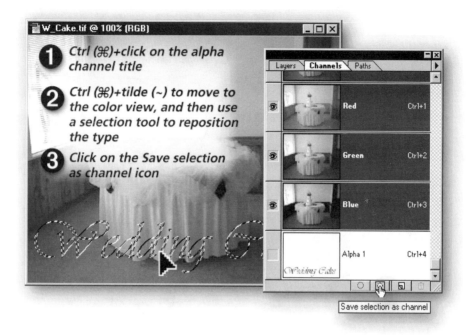

FIGURE 8.11   *You need to load your text as a marquee selection and then reposition it, when writing text to an alpha channel.*

11. You can either enter the following values directly into the number fields, or drag the sliders to create the necessary tonal changes here. The white point input should be about 172, and the midpoint input should be about 1.12. In the output fields, the black point should be at about 48, as shown in figure 8.12. What you're doing is lightening the interior of the text but keeping the hues and a lot of the detail beneath the text.

12. To add a professional touch to an already glorious composition, while the marquee selection is still active, press D (default colors), switch to the Move tool, and press the down arrow once and the right arrow once on the keyboard (not the numeric keypad). When a selection is active, only the Move tool can move the visual contents. As shown in figure 8.13, you've added a subtle, one-pixel highlight to the top and left edges of the lettering.

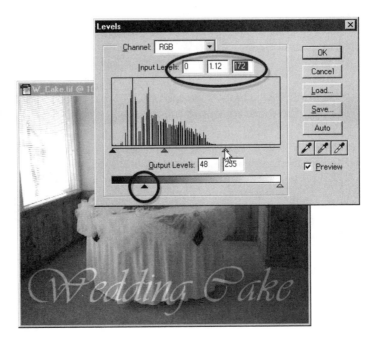

FIGURE 8.12   *The Levels command only changes the density of pixels in an image. It does not change hue or saturation.*

FIGURE 8.13   *Semitransparent text adds a touch of class to an image as private and ornate as a wedding cake.*

13. You can save and close the W_cake.tif image at any time. And the alpha channels can be trashed to make the image's saved file size smaller.

In the past sections we've been getting precariously close to working with text on the Web. So, in the next section, we're going to flat-out explore how to do nifty text things to a Web site.

Going with the Flow: Creating Today's Web Text Elements

I'm going to show you two or three things in this section that are not original—actually, they have been lying around the Web for a year or more. These elements are

- **3D text.** If you don't have embossed text on your site, you probably wear reasonably priced sneakers. I'm kidding! Seriously, everyone loves 3D text, so I'll show you the best way to create it.

- **Text as a graphic.** You can really amaze and confuse visitors to your site by including *reserved* characters (characters that stand for something in HTML—you can't use 'em) such as slashes, fractions, greater-than and less-than signs, and em-dashes (those funny hyphens that are twice the width of normal ones). You do something called rendering the text you want for the site as a one-color graphic with a transparent background. And you can do this all within Photoshop. As we progress here, you'll be able to see exactly what the difference is between HTML text and text as a graphic.

- **Anti-aliasing large text.** When text is 12 point, you generally have no problem reading it on the Web. But a 24-point headline that has aliasing is an eyesore—it can really hinder your reading and influence how you feel about the site's creator! So anti-aliasing is shown in the following sections.

Ready to join the gang of professional Web designers out there? I thought so!

In the Beginning, There was Alien Skin

I promised myself not to get into third-party plug-ins in this book, especially since Photoshop now does just about everything you need to make attractive Web sites. But for history's sake (and the product is still sold today), I thought I might show you how the first extruded Web text was created. And if you like this effect better than Photoshop's Layer Effects, then at least I've steered you in the right direction.

There are no steps to follow in this section, because you might not own Eye Candy version 4000.0 (the tentative name as of this writing for the January 2000 release of the new Eye Candy). But you can try them out, if you like, with the (free) limited editions of Eye Candy for both Windows and the Mac, which you'll find in the A_Skin folder on the Companion CD.

In figure 8.14, you can see that I've typed the first few words of "The Watching Grass Grow" home page. A selection needs to be active for Eye Candy's Outer Bevel effect to work. So you type the text, and then press Ctrl(⌘) and click on the title of the channel to load the marquee.

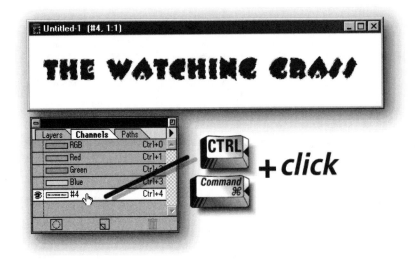

FIGURE 8.14   *Create text in a channel and then Ctrl(⌘)+click to load it as a marquee so Eye Candy's Outer Bevel filter can extrude the text.*

You then return to the color channel of the image, and choose Filter, Eye Candy, Outer Bevel. As you can see in figure 8.15, you have complete control over the glossiness, the depth, the light direction, and other parameters, and a preview is shown.

As I mentioned earlier, the extruded-text preview in figure 8.15 should look very familiar; for at least a year, no one had a product even remotely similar to Eye Candy (originally called the Black Box filters).

Okay, end of historic digression. If you like the look of Alien Skin's extruded text, get the collection of plug-ins.

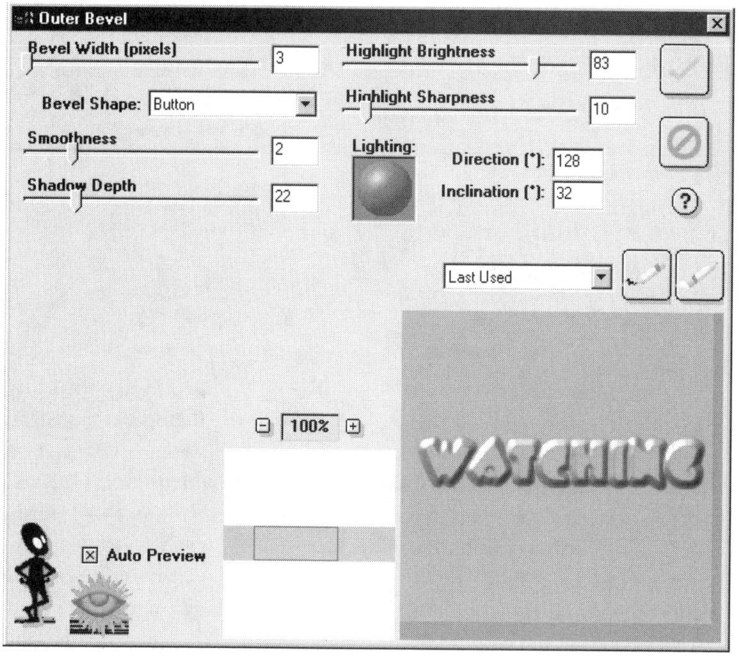

FIGURE 8.15   *The Outer Bevel interface gives you a lot of control over the appearance of extruded text, symbols—you name it.*

Flying with Photoshop Text Effects

No matter how heavy and how legible a typeface is to begin with, an effect will make it *less* legible. So choose your font carefully when you're extruding or drop-shadowing text. In figure 8.16, I've used both a Pillow Emboss and a Drop Shadow for the headline, which was created on a layer and could be used in combination with Photoshop's Layer Effects. The text was done in ITC Beesknees, and the file size it adds to the overall page is quite small, because I told Photoshop to use a minimum of colors when exporting the file to JPEG format.

It is the second element in this Web page, the body text, that is of most interest here. On the left in figure 8.16 is text that was coded in an HTML editor. On the right—and you'll notice that I've used every HTML-restricted character on earth here—is a small (2K) bitmap version of the text. Creating body-text-as-a-graphic will probably be the most demanding of your skills, and there will be literally scores of occasions when you want a graphic to masquerade as text. So I can't think of a better place to resume the decompiling of the Watching Grass Grow home page.

FIGURE 8.16   *The Web was designed for graphics—even graphics that are impersonating text!*

To see how you can create text as a graphic for Web pages, follow these steps:

Creating Body Text as a Graphic

1. Press Ctrl(⌘)+N and create a new image window, 260 pixels wide and 188 pixels high. These measurements are good for the page I show you how to produce, but aren't necessarily the dimensions you'd use in your own work. Choose RGB color mode, and Contents: White. Press Enter (Return).

2. Our client wants a pale violet background for the text, so click on the foreground color selection box, click on the Only Web Colors check box, and choose Brightness as the sorting order for colors, as shown in figure 8.17. "Legal" Web colors (see upcoming Wisdom #15) are limited to 216, and that's why the Color

Picker looks funky. Click on the closest thing to pale violet, write down the HTML code for the color you chose (it's 9999CC in fig. 8.17), and then press Enter (Return) to return to the workspace.

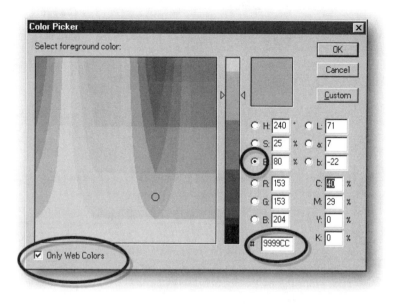

FIGURE 8.17   *Web colors are those that do not display dithering when viewed in 256-color mode by visitors to your site.*

3. Fill the image with the foreground color [Alt(Opt)+Delete(Backspace) is a good filling method], and then click on the Type tool and click an insertion point at the top center of the image window.

4. I did my research, so you don't have to. The default font in Web browsers is Times New Roman, and it's 14 points tall and has 19 points of leading between lines. Let's make our text-as-a-graphic black (choose black from the Color box in the Type Tool dialog box), choose Times New Roman from the Font drop-down list, make it a bold font (so it really stands up to that pale purple background you've got there), choose the correct font Size and Leading, and choose None from the Anti-Alias drop-down list. Finally, click on the Centered button for the text you'll type. See figure 8.18 for the placement of elements in Photoshop's workspace.

This is *not* a book on learning how to type. Therefore, in the Chap08 folder I have a file called Text.txt, which contains everything you see in the body copy onscreen. To save on the typing, load this file in a text editor, copy the text, and then press Ctrl(⌘)+V to paste the text into the Type tool's text field.

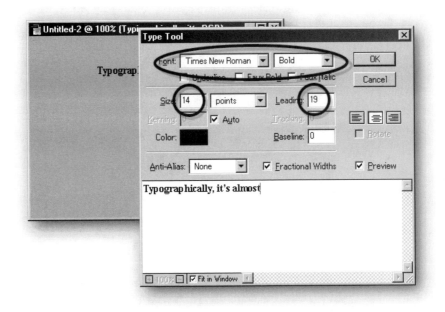

FIGURE 8.18 *Not one person on the Web—okay, except perhaps Daniel Will-Harris—will notice that this text is not actual HTML code. The font size and leading are correct, and there might even be a little better kerning (intercharacter spacing) with the text as a graphic.*

5. Click on OK to add the type to its own layer in the new image window. You'll need the Move tool to center the text in the window. Give or take 5%, your image window should look like that shown in figure 8.19. Notice that the layer has a "T," indicating that this is editable text, and that the name of the layer is what you have typed (at most, the first 31 characters).

6. Press Ctrl(⌘)+A to select all the text, press Ctrl(⌘)+N to make a new image window, and then press Ctrl(⌘)+V to plop the text from the Clipboard into this new window.

   In figure 8.20, I took the liberty of using color number 9999CC for the background layer, to see how the text reads. And you might be wondering why I copied text (destroying its editablility—you can't copy editable text to the Clipboard) and put it in this teeny image window. I did it because the less padding surrounding a graphical element, the smaller the saved file size. As you can see in figure 8.20, the Clipboard knew exactly how large the copied graphic had to be, and Photoshop (having read the Clipboard), offered a window not one pixel larger than it needs to be.

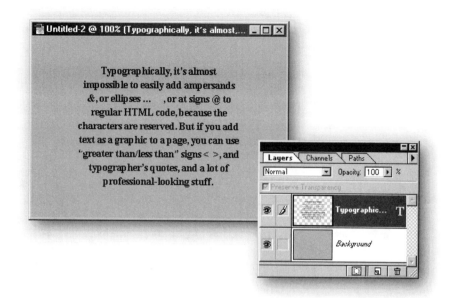

FIGURE 8.19   *If you made a typing error, no problem. Double-click on the "T" on the layer title, and the Type Tool dialog box will pop up with the current text you've typed. Fix the error and you're home free.*

7. Okay, to export the text as a graphic for a Web page, you do not need ImageReady. First, you trash the background layer; then choose File, Export, GIF89a Export.

8. Click on the (Default) Transparency Color box, choose color 9999CC from the Color Picker, and then press OK.

9. The Palette field should be Exact. Why? Because you picked a Web color for the background (the transparency color), and foreground black is also a Web palette color. So, additionally, the number of colors you are exporting is 2, as shown in figure 8.21. Click on OK, name the file Text.gif (Macintosh users must use the three-character extension because that's the way the universe of UNIX servers understand files. It's not just a Windows convention.)

10. Click on OK in the GIF89a Export Options box, and then save the file as text.gif to a special place on your hard disk where you can copy other Web files later. Save and close the original at any time.

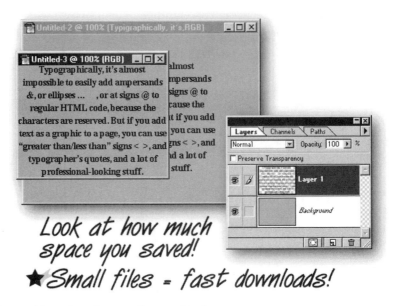

FIGURE 8.20 *Make graphics only as large as they need to be.*

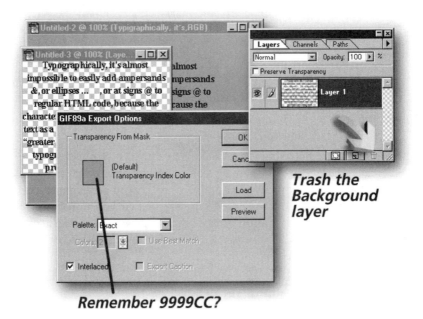

FIGURE 8.21 *Export a transparent GIF image with only two colors, and you have yourself a nice, small file that'll download quickly.*

In the Examples/Chap08 folder on the Companion CD is a folder called HTML. Within this folder are three graphics and an HTML document that will assemble the graphics into a Web page (refer to fig. 8.16). You can substitute your text.gif file for the text.gif file in this folder (copy the folder to your hard disk), and you can double-click on Index.html to launch this page in your favorite Web browser. I think you will find that the text-as-a-graphic will load almost exactly as quickly as the editable text on the left of the screen.

As long as you don't go off the deep end and do *all* your text as a graphic, you've now discovered a very powerful way to communicate on the Web, using all the typographic conventions you'd expect in a type-set document.

As for the text at the bottom of the page, probably the best way to export it is as a GIF, interlaced, exact color mapping, but with a maximum palette of no more than about 17 colors. If Photoshop offers you many more colors than 17 for exact mapping, choose Adaptive from the Palette drop-down list, and then specify 16 colors in the Colors box. Photoshop will use error diffusion to create the appearance of other colors outside the 16 you have.

When you're working with a solid-color text against a solid-color background, the palette colors should come from the *exact* palette rather than the Web palette because you almost certainly will not be able to match the anti-aliased fringe pixels by using only Web-safe colors. It might bum out a few visitors to your site who are running 256 colors, but most will not see the dithering in the fringe zones of the text, and those who are running 16.7 million colors (24-bit) on their monitor will see no dithering at all.

The Web isn't the only place where text should look professionally laid out and legible. In the next section, I'm going to show you how to make-over one of the most common pieces of display text in America—the garage sale sign.

Profound Wisdom #15:

Web browsers that cannot show more than 256 colors on your monitor will dither the site's graphics.

Dithering occurs when an application weaves available colors together to create a simulation of colors that are not available, due to insufficient RAM on your video card, or the Web browsing software is incorrectly set up.

You, as viewer, have some control over the way the "Big Two" browsers display images, using limited colors. In MS-Internet Explorer, choose View, Internet Options, Advanced; then, under Multimedia, check the Smart image dithering check box. In Netscape (AOL) Navigator, choose Options, General Preferences, and on the Image tab, click on the Dither button.

As a creator of graphics, you'll want to limit the colors on your monitor to test pages. The more Web-safe (Web palette) colors you use in a design, the less dithering will be performed by your audience's browser.

Creating a Garage Sale Sign

I picked a garage sale sign for the following tutorial because there's something intrinsically funny about most of these signs (to a designer, I guess), and because there's a shipload of typographic *faux pas* that folks commit. In the course of this make-over, I will point them out and help you avoid the same errors. We will work with a garage sale sign from concept straight through printing it, so you'll have a good idea of how to create oversized signage, using the equipment you own.

Six Pretty Large, Avoidable Sign Mistakes

I drove out the other day with my camera, and took about a half-dozen pictures of garage sale signs. The worst offender in the typographics/sales arena is featured in figure 8.22. I explain the callouts in the list that follows the figure.

FIGURE 8.22   *You can't sell something if your audience can't read your sign!*

1. **Placement of your ad is important.** Both of these signs are the same, but the one on the far side faces the traffic in the far-right lane (too far away to be read) or points *away* from traffic.

2. **Choice of fonts is important.** Apparently, the folks who are holding this sale used a worn-out felt-tip marker to create the sign. Only the first car in the lane facing the sign can read it.

3. **Poorly placed text is a bad reflection on the designer's sense of planning.** The folks having this sale wanted to reuse the sign, so they put carton tape over the original date and hastily scrawled "today" on the sign. Fine. What day is "today," folks?

4. **Revisions to the sign should be definitive.** You'll notice that you can still read "Sunday" on the sign, even after the folks taped over the word. This makes me feel as though the people don't know where to get more cardboard and create a new sign. I'm aware of at least three revisions on the sign, and all three "cover-ups" were done inexpertly.

5. **Direction markers should be correct and well thought out.** I admit that I've tampered with this photo, disguising the *real* address so my neighbors don't drop by and kill me. But I can tell you right now that the arrow on the sign is pointing *away* from, and not toward the address.

6. **Try to compose all the physical elements of your sign to withstand the weather.** These signs are taking more of a bruising than necessary from the wind and weather. Why? Because the paper is slightly larger than the cardboard backing. Folks? Get a can of 3M Spray-Mount, a utility blade, and a metal ruler, and do the trimming on the garage floor. If you don't have these materials, perhaps *I'll* run a garage sale soon and offer them!

Okay, I've been negative far too long here. In the following section, you'll see how to set up and begin the document that will become a professional garage sale sign.

Page Setup and the Importance of the Text Elements

It is unfortunate that Photoshop, unlike its sister program PageMaker, does not offer tiling when outputting to a personal printer (or any output device). *Tiling* is when a page is too large to fit on an 8 ½ by 11" page, so the application creates several pieces of the file output from a personal printer, so you can then paste together the pages to make a big sign. Without tiling, we need to tile the sign manually, which means we have to begin with calculations.

First, a 16" by 20" sign with the appropriate weight of font will definitely reach the reading audience from their cars. Coincidentally, four 8 ½" by 11" pieces of paper collectively measure 17" by 22", so printers—none of which print right to the edge of the paper—will leave room for you to overlap the tiles on paper.

Conceptually, the most important thing your sign must communicate is what event is going on. Follow these steps to get on your way to professional sign creation:

Beginning a Garage Sale Sign

1. Press Ctrl(⌘)+N and then, in the New dialog box, specify a size for the sign that is 16 inches high by 20 inches wide. Make the resolution 72 pixels per inch, Grayscale color Mode, and a white background. Press Enter (Return) to create the new document.

2. Create a black rectangle that is 19" wide and 3" tall. Press Ctrl(⌘)+R to display the rulers if you don't want to ballpark the dimensions of the rectangle. Use the Rectangular Marquee tool and a black foreground fill, as you've done in other steps in the book. Press Ctrl(⌘)+D to deselect the rectangular marquee.

3. Click the Type tool in the image window. Choose a sans serif font for the headline. Why? Because serif fonts look stupid when you use all caps, and without serifs on a font you can tighten the space between characters and not sacrifice legibility. In figure 8.23, you can see that I've chosen Olive Antique. Futura, Arial, Helvetica, Compacta, and Balloon Bold are also good choices. Choose white as the color in the Type Tool dialog box, and choose a size of about 211 points. As you know, 72 points equal one inch, so you're creating text that's a little less than 3", and it will fit in the rectangle. Click on OK to add the text to the image.

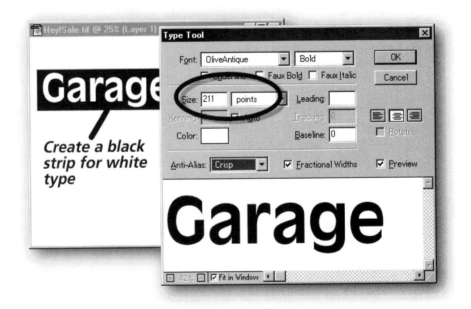

FIGURE 8.23   *Reversed-out text—text that's light against a background that's dark—is great for getting attention, but don't over-use it.*

4. With the Move tool, drag the white text and visually center it within the black rectangle. Click the Type tool in the image again.

5. Let's say that the sale is for the weekend—Saturday, August 25th and Sunday, August 26th. These elements need to stand out, but also to be subordinate to the "Garage Sale" text. As they say in the ad biz, "something's gotta give." The dates can be slightly subordinate and still be legible. In the Type Tool dialog box, type **Saturday, August 25th** in 150-point text. Then, press Enter (Return) and type **Sunday, August 26th**. Choose black as the color of the text.

The words in the date are not of equal importance. "August 25th" and "August 26th" will resonate with viewers—especially if they have a calendar wristwatch—more than the days of the week do. Happily, you can mix fonts in the Type Tool dialog box, so:

6. Highlight "August 25th" and make it a bold font, as shown in figure 8.24; then do the same with "August 26th."

PROFOUND WISDOM #16:

Don't waste image resolution no one will ever see.

The reason the document's resolution is only 72 pixels per inch is that no one is going to stick his or her nose directly on the sign and critique its lack of image resolution. Seventy-two pixels per inch will print just fine to a 300dpi laser printer, and your goal is to attract someone who will never see it from closer than a car's length away.

You can change text anywhere in the sentence by highlighting it, and then choosing a different font.

FIGURE 8.24 *You can make a font bold, or choose an entirely different font by highlighting it in the text field.*

7. Click on OK to add the text to the image. Then, with the Move tool, drag the dates to beneath the "Garage Sale" lettering.

8. Choose File, Save As, and then save your work as Hey!Sale.psd in Photoshop's native file format to your hard disk. Keep the image open.

Now let's think about the relative importance of the rest of the sign's text.

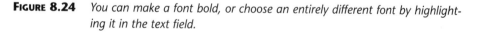

Sizing Up the Rest of the Text

The following elements are missing from the sign:

- The address of the garage sale. This is an important selling point.

- The hours for the sale. This is a throw-away line in terms of selling importance—its type size can be small. People are going to come to the sale any darned time they feel like it. It's America.

- If these signs are to be hung on telephone poles and street lamps (which is technically illegal in most states, but no one seems to care), then you should create an equal number of signs with left-facing and right-facing arrows, and make the arrows *big*. Then your hired help (most likely your son, daughter, or the neighbor's kids) can choose which way a sign's arrow is to face when they get to a pole.

Additionally, and optionally, you might want to sprinkle one or two subtle prompts to attend the sale on the sign—but *not* at the expense of cluttering up the sign. My experience in sign-making has uncovered these two truths:

1. People will read the lettering inside arrows. So you can make a large arrow for the sign, and put a selling point, such as "All sane offers accepted," inside the arrow in white text. This will make bargain hunters feel as though they're on easy turf.

2. Regardless of how small you print your sign, people can read the words "Free," "New," and "Save" with both eyes closed. So without messing up the various weights of text on the sign, you can run "Save $" five or six times across the top of the sign at about 24 points and it *will* get read.

I'm going to leave you alone while you create the arrows, the text in the arrows, the street address, the hours, and the "Save $" elements. Because text is always rendered to a unique layer, you should have no problem (and actually a lot of fun) pushing the text around until it looks like a well-composed sign. We used to do this in the advertising trade with print layouts, but we used pieces of paper. You've got it easy—we'd occasionally lose a headline or misplace a graphic!

If you'd like to follow my layout (laying text upon it to see whether it's a good size), Hey!Sale.tif is in the Examples/Chap08 folder on the Companion CD.

Merging and Aligning Text

Photoshop 5.5 has a feature that you'd normally expect to find in a vector drawing program such as Illustrator. You have an Align command at your cursortips. And that means that all the text you've laid out in the image window can be perfectly aligned—yet another touch that'll attract attention.

Also, it would be placing less of a stress on your computer's hard disk and memory if this sign were smaller in file size. So in the steps to follow, you'll merge the layers to a single layer after everything has been laid out correctly.

Finalizing the Sign

1. Click on the Garage Sale text layer's title on the Layers palette, and then press Ctrl(⌘)+E. This key combo activates the Merge Down command. Now, the Garage Sale text and the black rectangle are on one layer.

2. Save a copy of the arrow you created, copy it to a new image window, and then flip it (Image, Rotate Canvas, Flip Horizontal). Save this arrow for the time when the entire sign is composed on one layer, and then you can copy all the elements (except the arrow on the original) to the new image window to make signs whose arrows point in opposite directions.

3. Choose the text layer above the arrow, and then press Ctrl(⌘)+E to merge the arrow with the text.

4. Click on the right column check boxes (on the Layers palette) for all the layers. All the layers are now linked.

5. Choose Layer, Align Linked, Horizontal Center, exactly as you see it in figure 8.25. This aligns all the elements, and you're just about finished with the sign.

6. Choose Flatten Image from the Layers palette's flyout menu.

7. Save the file as Hey!Sign.tif, in the TIFF file format to your hard drive. Keep the image open in Photoshop.

This concludes the composition of the garage sale sign, but we aren't done by a country mile. You still need to chop the sign into four pieces that can be sent to a laser printer. And this requires a little planning and still more of Photoshop's features.

FIGURE 8.25   *Linked layers can be aligned. Try saying that twice, fast.*

Creating a Tiling Sign

Before we go any further, go to Staples or Office Max and get fluorescent laser paper. Hot lemon and hot pink are very obnoxious colors, sure to attract attention as garage sale signs, and you can use the rest of the paper for wrapping presents. Before you leave, pester the clerk for some cardboard, ideally the cardboard that filing cabinets and knock-down furniture came in. The larger the cardboard, the less you compromise the signs' appearance.

The Rectangular Marquee tool can be set to select areas for cropping at almost any specified height and width, as measured in pixels. We don't know how many pixels are in 16" or 20" at 72ppi, but this is the discovery part of the following steps. Get ready to get those lamps, the bike training wheels, and that velvet painting out of the basement and into the garage!

Cropping and Assembling the Signs

1. At 25% viewing resolution of the sign, drag the image window borders away from the sign so you can clearly see the file's background.

2. Alt(Opt)+ click on the document sizes area, as shown in figure 8.26. You can see that 20" at 72ppi is 1440 pixels, and 16" at 72 ppi is 1152 pixels.

3. Double-click on the Rectangular Marquee tool to display the Marquee Options palette, and then choose Fixed Size from the Style drop-down list. In the Width field, type **720** and in the Height field, type **576**. Why these amounts? Because you're going to bisect copies of this document so they will output to a personal printer. And the Options palette will only measure in pixels, not in inches.

4. Click in the upper left of the image window, outside the live area. The marquee will snap to the upper-left corner and create a perfect selection of one quarter of the sign.

FIGURE 8.26   *You can crop an image by setting the Marquee tools' Options palette to Fixed Size.*

5. Press Ctrl(⌘)+C and then press Ctrl(⌘)+N, and accept the defaults by pressing Enter (Return).

6. Press Ctrl+V and then press Ctrl+E to make the image a single-layer image.

7. Press D (default colors) and then choose Image, Canvas Size from the main menu.

8. In the Canvas Size dialog box, type **11** (inches) in the Width field, and then type **8** (inches in the Height field, as shown in figure 8.27. Although the live area of the quarter of the sign is smaller than these dimensions, Photoshop will want to output to standard paper size—and besides, you will need to overlap the quarters to build the entire sign.

FIGURE 8.27   *Create a border around the original pasted graphic by increasing the Canvas Size.*

9. Repeat steps 5–8 on the other three quarters of the sign. In figure 8.28, you can see the trim areas colored in. Naturally, you do not want to color in your own images; I illustrated it this way to show you how this jigsaw of a sign will all fit together.

Inside areas should be
trimmed on one side...

and overlap the trim
area on the facing tile

FIGURE 8.28   *When these page-size graphics are printed, there will be trim space around*
all four sides of each quarter-document.

10. Print several copies of each quarter of the sign (it also might be a good idea right
    now to save each piece as 1.tif, 2.tif, and so on). Every printer is different, but I'd
    recommend printing to 300 dpi, using non-PostScript rendering technology—only
    because Hewlett-Packard's Resolution Enhancement Technology delivers a decent
    print very quickly, and these prints do not need to be half-toned or to experience
    any other process that PostScript technology affords.

11. Work in the garage with the doors open. Trim the inside edges of alternating
    pages (in other words, only trim inside edges on 1 and 3, or 2 and 4), match up
    the four pieces, glue them together and...what am I *talking* about?

None of this stuff has *anything* to do with Photoshop!

Lesson is completed!!!

Whether it's a For Sale sign or your first retouched picture, it's sort of fun to follow
through with the process. I have tried to make this book as comprehensive as possible, and that means that occasionally we need to talk about output. You'll get your
share of printing tips in chapter 10.

Have you ever wanted to really distort text in Photoshop? It might have come out crummy looking because when you stretch a selection too much, Photoshop is less capable of guessing which colored pixels need to be added to the image. But I've found a way around fuzzy-looking distorted text. It's right below this sentence.

Creating Text for Distortion

If you're familiar with Illustrator, CorelXARA, or CorelDRAW, you probably already know how to distort text, and have it stay sharp and print clean. Well, you can sort of do the same thing in Photoshop, using the Pen tools and the Paths palette. The Pen tool is based on vector curves that need to be stroked so the paths will become printable.

I'm going to show you two different techniques that enable you to create text that has an incredible perspective—but the text is sharp and legible. The first method requires a little skill on your part, but does not require any other program.

Tracing Text

1. Open the RockWall.tif image from the Examples/Chap08 folder on the Companion CD. You need something to play against the text you'll create. A 50% viewing resolution is good for the RockWall.tif image.

2. Click the Type tool in the image window, and in the Type Tool dialog box, type **ROCK**. Highlight the text, type **200** in the points field, make the text white, and then specify the boldest sans serif font you own. Me? I used Futura Knockout in figure 8.29. I've also included a font called Kibbutz in the Boutons folder on the Companion CD, and you are free to use this font to create super-bold lettering if you don't already own a hefty-looking typeface.

3. What you'll do is trace over the text, using the Pen tools, and then distort the paths by using the Free Transform feature in Photoshop. I promise you that you'll go to the head of the class in graphics if you get comfortable with the Pen tools. Not enough people practice with the tools.

4. Zoom in to 100% viewing resolution (press Ctrl(⌘)+the plus key until the title bar on the image says 100%), and then click on the Pen tool to choose it.

5. Start tracing. If you picked up this book at this chapter, please go back and read chapter 3 on the Pen tools before proceeding. You sort of need to build on your past experiences to make new ones in Photoshop. In figure 8.30, you can see that I've got most of the "R" character outlined. Once you've completed a character (and characters sometimes do have subpaths, such as the center of the "O" in ROCK), press F7 to display the Layers/Channels/Paths/Etc. palette, double-click on the Work Path title on the Paths palette, and name the path "Rock." This saves the path indefinitely, so you can take breaks more often!

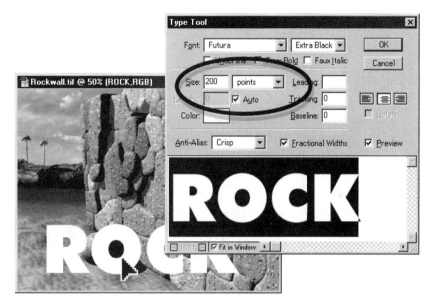

FIGURE 8.29   *Make the text all caps, sans serif, extremely bold, and about 3" tall (200 points is about 3").*

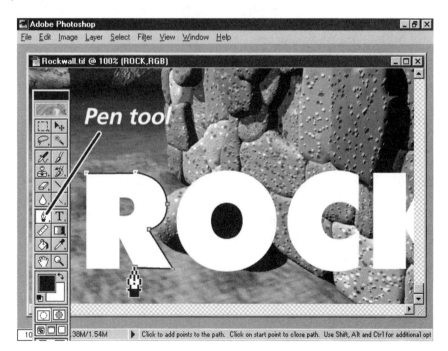

FIGURE 8.30   *Use your skills from chapter 3 to create the outline in this chapter.*

6. Press Ctrl(⌘)+S and save this image as RockWall.psd in Photoshop's native file format to your hard disk. Keep the image open.

The Second Way to Add Paths

If you've read earlier chapters in this book, you already know that if you own Illustrator, the most practical way to draw paths for this text is to create the text in Illustrator, convert the text to curves, and copy it to the Clipboard. Then you press Ctrl(⌘)+V in Photoshop, and Photoshop gives you the option of pasting the Clipboard's contents as pixels or paths (you choose paths and click on OK).

So if you're doing this mock assignment manually, or you tapped into Illustrator to provide accurate font outlines, we should be in the same place before continuing. In other words, you need an outline of the word ROCK, created by using paths. And if you did this by hand, delete the layer with the text.

Distorting a Collection of Paths

The interesting thing about the way Photoshop handles paths (either imported or drawn by the Pen tool) is that everything that is represented on a Paths palette's title is considered to be one path, even though there can be totally noncontiguous components to the path. This means you can scoop up all the path segments on a single path layer, and use the Free Transform tool on them.

Here's where the assignment gets interesting:

Distorting and Filling a Path

1. Create a new layer in the image by Alt(Opt)+clicking on the Create new layer icon (on the Layers palette). Name the layer **Rock**, and then press Enter (Return).

2. With the Direct Selection tool (on the Pen tools flyout on the toolbox), marquee select all the paths in the image, and then drag the rock lettering outlines to a place on the rock wall in the image, as shown in figure 8.31. The idea here is that you will create perspective text that matches the perspective of the stone wall.

3. Press Ctrl(⌘)+Shift+T to make the Free Transform bounding box surround the selected paths, as shown in figure 8.32. Then, right-click (Macintosh: hold Ctrl and click), and choose Distort from the context menu.

FIGURE 8.31   *All the anchors on a path must be selected (they will appear filled) before you can move a path, using the Direct Selection tool.*

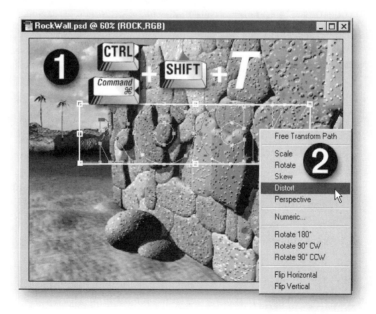

FIGURE 8.32   *The Free Transform feature will surround with a bounding box anything that's selected...even vector paths.*

4. With the cursor, click and drag on each corner anchor, one at a time, until you've distorted the lettering so that it pretty much shares the same perspective as the wall (see fig. 8.33). Then press Enter to finalize the new shape for the text paths.

FIGURE 8.33   *Create a perspective identical to that of the wall in the image.*

5. Double-click on the Gradient tool to display the Options palette, and choose Foreground to Background from the drop-down list as the kind of gradient. Make sure Linear is the type of gradient. Choose a maroon for the foreground color and an orange-yellow for the background color (on the toolbox, from the Color Picker).

6. Ctrl(⌘)+click on the Rock title on the Paths palette. This hides the path lines and creates a marquee selection in the shape of the paths.

7. Using the Gradient tool, drag from the top of the lettering to the bottom. You can see the result in figure 8.34.

FIGURE 8.34   *Fill the lettering with an exciting blend of colors.*

8. Press Ctrl(⌘)+D to deselect the selection marquee. The color fill is now on the Rock layer on the Layers palette, and you should probably press Ctrl(⌘)+S. Keep this file open, because I'm going to show you how to *over*work the graphic. It'll be cool—trust me.

Here's the score in the ninth inning: The image looks dimensional because I used a modeling program to make it that way. The lettering's *geometry* is dimensional, because you added perspective to it. But the lettering looks flat because it is not interacting at all with the wall.

Here's the quick fix:

Adding a Drop Shadow to the Wall

1. Drag the Rock layer into the Create new layer icon on the Layers palette. This creates a Rock copy layer, and makes it the top layer.

2. Click on the Rock title on the Layers palette to make it the current editing layer. Press D (default colors), click on the Preserve Transparency check box, and then press Alt(Opt)+Delete (Backspace). Uncheck the Preserve Transparency check box.

3. Choose Filter, Blur, Gaussian Blur, specify 7 pixels, and then press Enter (Return).

4. Choose the Move tool. Press Shift+down-arrow twice and press Shift+right-arrow twice. When you hold Shift you move elements by 10 pixels at a time instead of the usual 1 pixel.

5. On the Layers palette, drag the Opacity slider down to about 65% for the Rock layer. Now you ought to have a 3D image like the one shown in figure 8.35.

FIGURE 8.35   *There are many ways to cast a shadow in an image, but most of them use the Gaussian Blur command at some point.*

6. Press Ctrl(⌘)+S. You can close the image at any time now.

Don't you wish the figures in this book were in color?

Summary

Text is always a graphic when you work with it in Photoshop, but that does not mean you can't have fun with it. You can edit text after you've added it to a picture, and you can stretch and scale text when it's based on a path. There's a place for anti-aliased text, and there will be times (such as with Web work) when you absolutely don't want anti-aliasing. Photoshop has grown a lot since version 4, and the embossing effects in combination with the right font can make your work look at least as good as that of the next guy—even if the next guy has been using Photoshop for quite a while! I hope you treated this chapter as a discovery chapter, and that the assignments spawn a score of original ideas for your next (paying!) assignment.

In chapter 9, we grow up a lot. Yes, I realize that this is a "Fundamentals" book, but no one ever said I wouldn't ask you to grow while you work. Take a talent test (and win!) by following along with me at about 200mph (miles in pixel hours) in the next chapter.

CHAPTER 9

Putting It All Together

For eight chapters now, you've thoroughly familiarized yourself with

- Selecting stuff
- Layers, channels, and paths
- Masking

and the other staples—the fundamentals—of Photoshop 5.5. Wouldn't it be a kick if you were to combine all you've learned and a little ingenuity (the problem-solving kind), and actually witness what you can do at this point?

I'm not kidding when I tell you that if you've worked diligently through the previous chapters, you are now capable of professional-level image manipulation. The only difference between you and the person who gets $200/hour for doing this stuff is that people know him or her but don't know you.

Yet.

I'm going to present you with three challenges in this chapter. Each assignment, done correctly, will produce a commercially salable piece. Naturally, I'm here on the sidelines for advice and coaching, but remember the Profound Wisdom as we begin:

Enough pep talk. You have the skills to make some powerful imaging right now.

Profound Wisdom #17:

> **Photoshop means nothing without a master at the helm.**
>
> Neither does any other program. If you bring junk to the party (attitudinally), you wind up with junk. It is *you* who drives Photoshop, and not the other way around. Come to think of it, when you're good, it is *you* who makes Photoshop look good to others!

Grafting Together Photographs

It is the sport of every advanced Photoshop user to bring together photographs from different sources into a seamless whole. You know, the placing of different heads on people's bodies, the addition of a building, or the removal of a person from a family photo.

Your first challenge will demonstrate the eminent practicality of being good at bringing together photographs. Its inspiration came to me when I worked in advertising. A location scout used to go out with a Polaroid, take several pictures of a vista, and then staple them together to show the commercial crew what we had to deal with. I always used to be the picky one and think to myself, "Why does this composite photo look phony?"

I answered my own question about three weeks ago while biking. I saw a beautiful ranch house facing the street, and the camera I took along with me was begging me to take a photo of it. The only problem: To take a good-resolution image of the ranch house in its entirety, I'd have to use a wide angle lens (and wide angle lenses distort perspective), or I'd have to stand on the roof of the house on the other side of the street.

Hey, Bouton, you wood head. You've got several exposures on your film roll—why don't you take multiple pictures of the house and then stitch the images together in Photoshop? In figure 9.1, you can see the *correct* way to take multiple pictures that you know you're going to meld together in Photoshop. You do *not* stand in one position and pan the camera—if you do that, every image will have a different perspective. You click, take three or four steps to one side, and click again, making sure of the following two things:

1. Keep the *vertical perspective* (the top-to-bottom visual information) in more or less the same place from frame to frame. You can be a little off, but if your aim is not consistent, vertically, from pic to pic, you'll have to do a lot of unnecessary cropping to the final image. Also, keep the same distance from frame to frame between you and the house (or whatever you're photographing).

2. Overlap the image edges a little. This allows you to match up different pictures easily from within Photoshop.

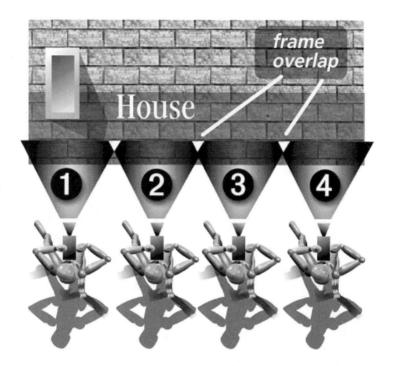

FIGURE 9.1   *Either get a tripod, or very carefully photograph the house, maintaining a consistent height from frame to frame.*

Let's inspect before we detect and correct.

Sizing up the Photographs

Let me tell you right now that this section is not going to go on forever as I show you how to match four images together. We're going to concentrate on matching the first two of four; the other two are on the Companion CD, and if you do two right, doing four requires no extra education—or paper!

We're not into the tutorial phase just yet. For now, in Photoshop, open images House01.tif and House02.tif. Then zoom in or out (I zoomed to 33%) of both image windows and drag the first house image slightly over the left edge of the second house, as shown in figure 9.2. The match between the two pictures is good, but not perfect. And that's fortunate, because if the images lined up perfectly, I'd have nothing to teach here!

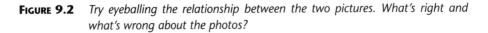

FIGURE 9.2   *Try eyeballing the relationship between the two pictures. What's right and what's wrong about the photos?*

It's time to perform the coarsest sort of image manipulation—building the foundation of your retouching work here by getting both images into one image window and aligning them as best as possible.

Setting Up The House Collage

1. Press D (default colors), so the current background color is white.

2. Choose Image, Canvas Size. It would probably be good to increase the width of the image by 200% or more.

3. In the Canvas Size dialog box, click on the drop-down Width increments box, choose percent, and then type **225** in the Width field as shown in figure 9.3. Click on the chiclet in the 9 o'clock position, and then press Enter (Return).

4. Expand the resized image window so you can see the new, empty area, and then move the image window so that both images can be seen. Hold Ctrl(⌘) to toggle to the Move tool, click and hold on the image in House02.tif, and then drag it to the House01.tif image, toward the extra area you created (see fig. 9.4).

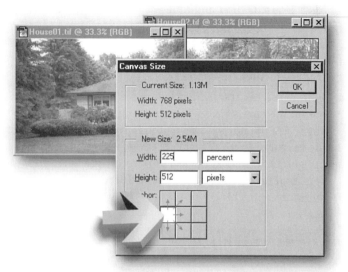

Add canvas to accomodate additional image

FIGURE 9.3   *Create more room than you'll need to add the second photo to the image window of the first house image. You can always crop the extra pixels out of the image later.*

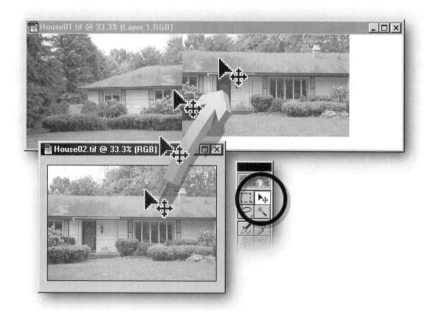

FIGURE 9.4   *Add a copy of the second house image to the first by dragging it, using the Move tool.*

5. Close House02.tif at any time without saving. With the Move tool, move the second house image (which is on a layer) until the left edge more or less aligns with the visual information on the bottom picture's right side. Now, choose the Zoom tool and marquee select around this edge between the two pictures. I zoomed to 169%, which proved to be a good percentage of "zoominess."

6. With Layer 1 as the current layer (it is, but it doesn't hurt to check these things out on the Layers palette—by pressing F7), and the Move tool as the active tool, press 5 on the numeric keypad to decrease Layer 1's opacity to 50%. Then, use the keyboard (not the keypad) arrow keys to nudge Layer 1's contents—as shown in figure 9.5—so that objects in both images begin to line up. Perfection is not your goal here, nor is it possible with these two images. You're simply trying to minimize retouching work.

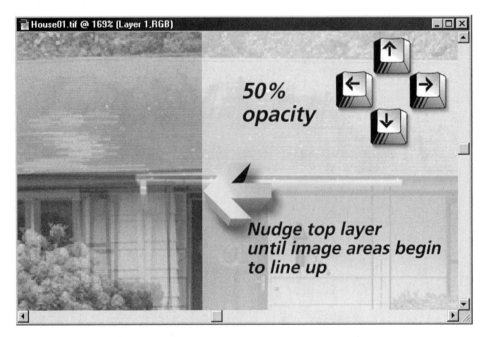

FIGURE 9.5   *Drop the opacity of Layer 1, and then nudge the layer's contents by using the arrow keys.*

7. Press 0 (zero) on the numeric keypad to restore Layer 1 to 100% opacity. Save the image as Home.psd, in Photoshop's native file format, and keep the image open.

Once again it's time to follow the maxim, "Detect, then correct." This is going to become your Photoshop mantra. In the next section, you'll analyze the composite image to see what needs to be done. We'll take it a little at a time, in an orderly fashion, so the chore(s) don't seem overwhelming.

Assessing the Aligning Work You Need To Do

In figure 9.6, you can see a line I've created to show you where the two house images meet (and where the match is close, but not perfect).

FIGURE 9.6   *There are some challenges to fixing this image, but nothing requires a technique you haven't practiced earlier in the book.*

Before you start learning the correction techniques in numbered-list style, study the following list of home repairs you need to make:

- **The roof is not aligned.** I took picture #1 at a slightly rotated angle (because I don't usually tote around a tripod...and I'm *not* being defensive!) and to get most of the image elements to align, the roof is also about 5 pixels higher in the second image than the first.

- **The rain gutter and the top of the window are misaligned by only about 1 pixel.**

- **The top of the hedges in picture 1 are rotated and misaligned by several pixels.** This is a snap to correct, because organic elements can be blended to even the most discerning eye's satisfaction by using the Rubber Stamp tool.

- **The bottom of the hedges—hoo, boy!** There is a serious alignment problem with the bottom of the hedges, but again, the Rubber Stamp tool will work wonders.

Additionally, the tree tops are misaligned in the image. This is obviously not a problem with the house itself, but if you don't correct it, the house will have a weird view of the back yard from the kitchen.

Retouching the Composite House in Stages

Let's begin retouching the image, first the tree tops, and then the roof. The roof calls for rotation as well as alignment, and the amount of rotation is so small, you do not want to do it manually. Instead, you'll use a Photoshop command—one not yet used in this book—from the context menu. You'll be surprised at what one degree of rotation does to correct things.

To begin...

Aligning the Elements of the Two House Images

1. Double-click on the Zoom tool to reduce your viewing resolution to 100% (1:1).

2. Choose the Rubber Stamp tool, and then on the Brushes palette (F5), click on the 65-pixel-diameter tip.

3. Alt(Opt)+click a sample point to the right of the mistake with the trees here, and make sure the sample point is close to the top of the trees, as shown in figure 9.7. Then make a stroke or two where the trees aren't aligned.

4. Click on the Background layer title on the Layers palette to make this the current editing layer.

5. With the Lasso tool, drag a selection around the corner of the roof (sneak a peek at fig. 9.8). This is the area that needs rotation.

6. Press Ctrl(⌘)+R to display the rulers, and then drag a horizontal guide out of the top ruler and align it with the roof toward the right of the image. This is the "correct" angle of the roof in the finished image.

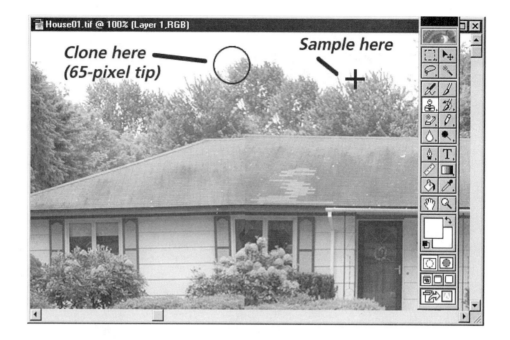

FIGURE 9.7   *Before you graduate from novice to professional, you need to address every aspect of the image you're retouching. And tree retouching is easy to do.*

7. Press Ctrl(⌘)+T to put the selection in Free Transform mode, and then right-click (Macintosh: hold Ctrl and click) to access the context menu. Choose Numeric from the list, and type **1** in the Angle box of the Rotate area, as shown in figure 9.8. Unfortunately, Photoshop doesn't offer a preview of the transformation while in the Numeric Transform box, but instead you can see a low-resolution picture of the proposed change (in the house image window) after you type a value in the dialog box and then click on OK to return to the work. If this were the wrong amount (hint: it's correct), you can always cancel the transform operation by pressing Esc. Press Enter (Return) to apply the rotation.

8. With the Move tool, move the selection so it touches the roof area on Layer 1. Then press Ctrl(⌘)+D to deselect the selection.

9. Press Ctrl(⌘)+S; keep the file open.

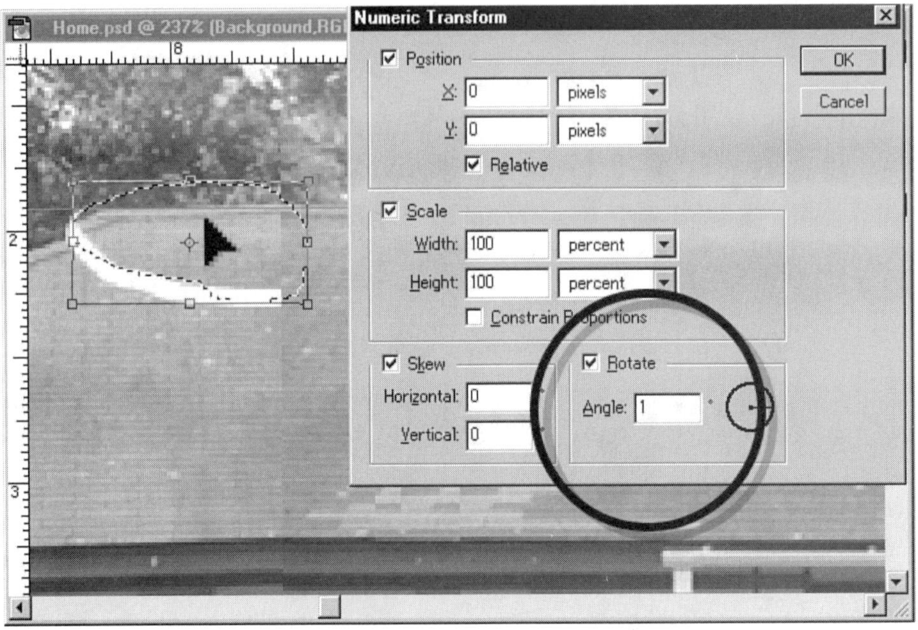

FIGURE 9.8   *Apply a very minor amount of rotation to the roof selection, to get it to line up with the Layer 1 roof.*

We're now left with a lined-up roof, but we also have a gaping sore on the roof, and the far, diagonal edge of the top of the roof doesn't look too swift, either.

Fixing a Hole in The Layer

Repairing the roof is a two-step process. First, you need to get the left side (the slope) whole again, which can be done with the Rubber Stamp tool. And if you clone too far, you can easily add foliage to cover the mistake. The second step also involves the Rubber Stamp tool, but you will be working across layers to blend the roof tiles into a harmonious patchwork quilt of slightly different colors.

Let's get back up on the roof again:

Cloning Repairs onto the Roof

1. Zoom in to 200% or more resolution of the damaged area of the roof.
2. Choose Layer 1 from the Layers palette to make this the current editing layer.

3. Double-click on the Rubber Stamp tool, to both select it and to bring forward the Options palette. Check the Use All Layers check box. Now you can clone from both layers.

4. Alt(Opt)+click a sampling point on the bottom, left part of the diagonal roof line. Then, with the second row, third-from-left tip on the Brushes palette, drag straight along the line of the roof until its edge meets the horizontal part of the roof. Stop here; you're done. If you overshot your mark, clone some tree samples into the area where the goof occurred.

5. Clone sparsely from left to right across the roof front, where the tiles do not seem to be the same color. Leave a dappled look to the roof, so it looks as though there's been uneven wear on the roof, as shown if figure 9.9.

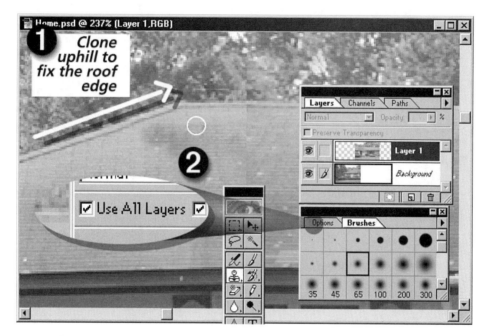

FIGURE 9.9   *Get the left edge looking correct, and then apply mottling to the roof where you see the edge, to make this look more like one roof!*

6. Go into Layer Mask mode on Layer 1 by clicking on the icon on the Layers palette, and then set the opacity of the Paintbrush tool to about 70% (this is done on the Options palette). With black as the foreground color, make a few strokes here and there to expose roof detail on the background layer, as shown in figure 9.10. When you are happy with the roof's patchwork quilt look, drag the Layer Mask icon into the trash icon to finalize the editing work, choose Apply from the query box that appears, and then press Ctrl(⌘)+S and keep that image open.

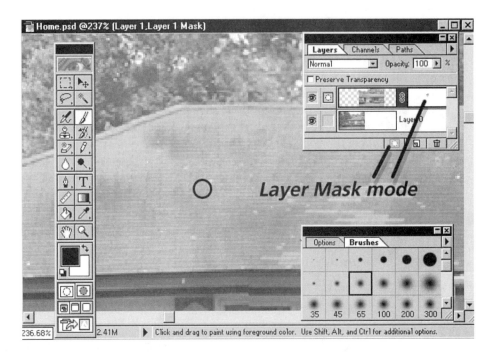

FIGURE 9.10   *Use the Paintbrush tool to expose the roof's detail.*

The preceding set of steps were probably the most demanding so far of your skills. From here on in, every technique should seem familiar and you should feel right at home tampering with a $140,000 house.

Mending the Gap Between Foliage Areas

Let's move down in the composition and tackle the easy stuff—the hedgelines that are far from aligned. Starting with the bottom, where the hedge meets the grass, you'll make a swooping motion with the Rubber Stamp tool to suggest that the hedges were actually planted that way. But here's the twist—to make the hedge look as though it has sprouted in totally random directions, you'll set the Rubber Stamp tool to partial opacity, and then resample hedge areas frequently. The effect will be one of newly redesigned hedges that look convincing and authentic. Here's how to fix the bottom of the hedges:

Blending the Two Hedge Areas

1. Press Ctrl(⌘)+E to merge the layers so you have only a Background layer. You no longer need separate layers.

2. Choose the Rubber Stamp tool, then pick the 45-pixel-diameter tip from the Brushes palette.

3. Zoom in to about 150% viewing resolution. This can be done quickly by typing **150** in the Zoom field at the lower left of the screen, and then pressing Enter (Return).

4. Alt(Opt)+click a sampling point to the right of the sharp hedge edge in the photo.

5. On the Options palette, drag the opacity slider to about 57%, and then make a few brisk, swooping strokes over the hedge edge, as shown in figure 9.11.

tip

For novices and experienced users alike: surprise. The Opacity slider on the Options palette doesn't exist until you click on the right-facing arrow to the right of the numeric field.

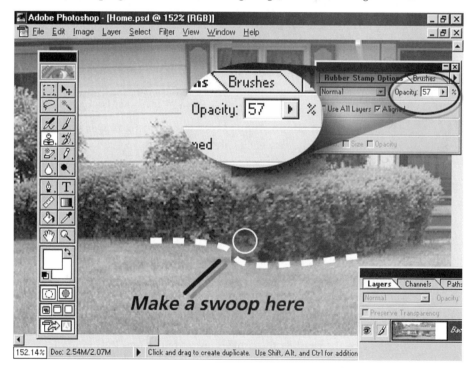

FIGURE 9.11   *Add to the hedge's bottom by making swooping motions, but don't try to completely cover the error in the image.*

6. Set a different sampling point by Alt(Opt)+clicking elsewhere in the image for some good hedge samples. Then continue to build the opacity of the hedges where you're mending the edgework, until all traces of photo-phoniness are gone.

7. Press Ctrl(⌘)+S; keep the file open.

Piece of cake, right? Now, on to the top of the hedges and the flowers.

Blending the Tops of the Hedges

The top of the hedges doesn't require as much work as the bottom did, mostly because the hedges sort of meld into the flowers above them. Let's take a quick moment and make the necessary changes in the image.

Up into the Hedges and Flowers

1. With the Rubber Stamp chosen, pick the Brushes tip at the far right of the second row.
2. Alt(Opt)+click on a hedgetop area that is at least 2 screen inches away from the area that has a sharp vertical edge; then press 0 on the keypad to increase the opacity of the Rubber Stamp tool to 100%, and go over the edge with swooping motions similar to those you used on the bottom of the hedges. The vertical edge is less prominent along the top of the hedges, so you don't need the fancy partial-opacity trick to integrate the left and right sides of this image.
3. With the same small brush tip, Alt(Opt)+click on a flower sample and then stroke over the edge in the flowers, as shown in figure 9.12.
4. Press Ctrl(⌘)+S; keep the file open.

There are only two more spots where the house halves need to be integrated: the window, and the gutter directly above it.

Finalizing the House Blending—Window and Roof Gutter Time

You are going to use a technique that you've learned but might not have considered using to mend the left and right halves of the left window in the image. What you're going to do is *extend* the window upward by a pixel or two, and nobody is going to notice this architectural shortcut. As for the gutter, a simple cloned replacement from a sample to the right of the broken gutter will mend it.

Here are the blueprints for the finishing touches:

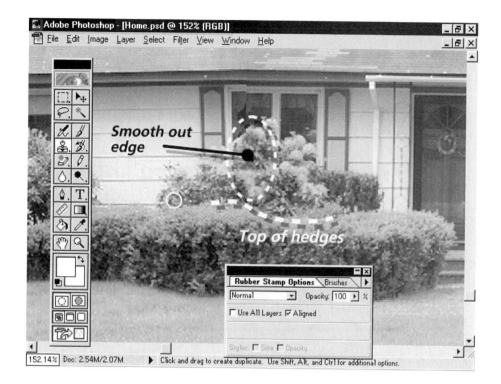

FIGURE 9.12 *The smaller the flaw, the smaller the brush you can use, and the less fine detail you need to add to a photo-phlub.*

Fixing the Window and Cleaning the Gutter

1. Zoom in to about 300% viewing resolution on the window that's cracked in the image.

2. With the Rectangular Marquee tool, draw a selection, starting at the top left of the window; make the selection about ½ screen inches wide and 1 screen inch high (working down and to the right).

3. Hold Ctrl(⌘)+Alt(Opt). This action toggles the Marquee tool to the Move tool in its "float a copy" mode. Press the up-arrow key once—the selection is now floating and you no longer need to hold the Alt(Opt) button. Press the arrow keys, as shown in figure 9.13, until the window selection lines up with the rest of the window.

4. Press Ctrl(⌘)+D to deselect the floating selection when it's in place. On to the gutter now.

5. Scroll the window up slightly so you can see where the bottom of the gutter is broken.

6. Keep the same brush-tip size, and Alt(Opt)+click to the right of the break in the gutter, on the very bottom edge.

7. Stroke, starting where the bottom edge of the gutter should be, along the edge where the two images were blended. You only need one or two strokes to fix it, as shown in figure 9.14.

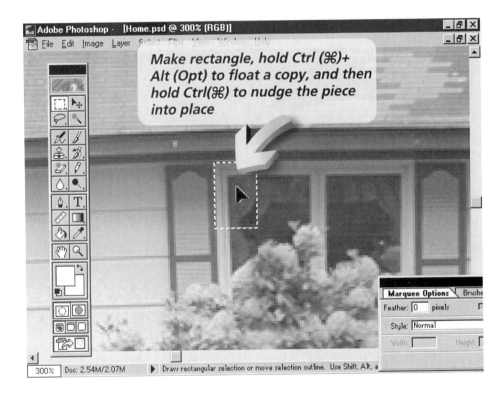

FIGURE 9.13   *Don't cut in an image when you can copy. Float a copy of the window area to mend the area directly above it.*

8. You've finished putting the two images together! You can close the file at any time after saving it, or keep it open. The House03 and House04 images are still in the Examples/Chap09 folder!

Seriously, nobody gets to Carnegie Hall without practicing, and to rise to the top of the heap of Photoshop experts requires a little quality time with the program, too. I recommend that you finish the house piece (see fig. 9.15), using the same techniques you used to meld the first and second pictures.

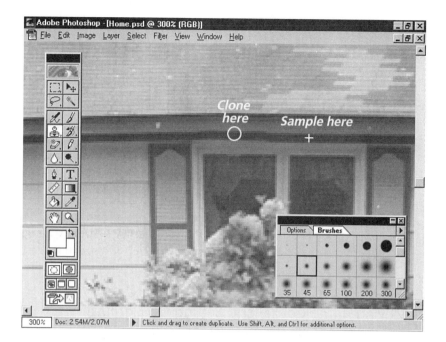

FIGURE 9.14   *Elements that are only a few pixels in width or height are easily mended with only one or two strokes.*

FIGURE 9.15   *If you have the spare time, I've got just the tutorial for you!*

The next section deals with controlling the focal point of a composition through the use of shading and focus. You'll be using tools you're already familiar with, but they will be used in a unique way!

Flying a Cookie Through A Kitchen

Face it; we're all attracted to things that are flying around—logos, paper airplanes, black-headed chickadees, and kites, to name but a few items. Perhaps this is why, when we were two or three years old, we liked being tossed in the air by a family member with good catching skills.

In the next assignment, you're going to make a cookie appear to be flying through the kitchen, and the image represents a split second in time. Now, how can a humble cookie become the star of the composition? Partially because of its design and perfect focus (the cookie is a rendered model) and size, but also because you're going to dim the lighting in the kitchen and gently throw it out of focus.

Moving In the Cookie and Setting Up Lighting

We're going to be doing a lot of work with layers for the remainder of this chapter. If you are not familiar with Photoshop layers, check out chapter 6 before you begin the work.

First, you need to move an image of a cookie into a kitchen scene. Then, to emphasize the cookie, you'll create a subtle spotlight effect by adding black to a layer, blurring the layer, and putting the layer in Multiply mode at a partial opacity.

Let's begin:

Adding the Cookie, Shading the Scene

1. Open the Kitchen.tif file from the Examples/Chap06 folder of the Companion CD. A 33.3% viewing resolution is good for this image; type **33.3** in the Zoom field (at the bottom left of the screen), and then press Enter (Return).

2. Open the Cookie.psd file from the Examples/Chap09 folder on the Companion CD. Then, using the Move tool, drag the contents of the Cookie layer (look at the Layers palette) into the Kitchen.tif image, as shown in figure 9.16. Position the cookie so it's in the vertical middle of the image, and about half of an inch (on your screen) from the right side of the image window. You can close Cookie.psd at any time now.

3. Save the file to your hard disk as Cookie scene.psd, in Photoshop's PSD format. Keep the file open.

4. Drag the edges of the image window away from the image so you can see some background to the image window. Click on the Background layer, and then click on the Create new layer icon at the bottom of the Layers palette. The new layer is just above the Background, and below the cookie layer.

5. With the Polygon Lasso tool, drag a spotlight shape that falls on the cookie. Then, press Shift+F7 to invert the selection. Everything *but* the spotlight area is now selected and the cookie area is masked, as illustrated in figure 9.17.

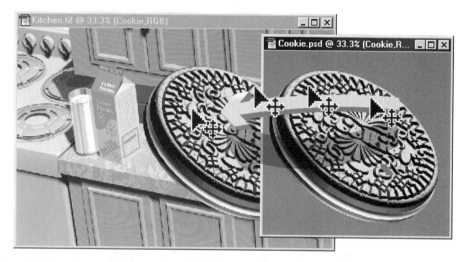

FIGURE 9.16   *Let's keep the cookie from a lot of the visual complexity in the scene, by keeping it to the right of most background objects.*

6. Press D (default colors), press Alt(Opt)+Delete (Backspace) to fill the selected areas with black, and then press Ctrl(⌘)+D to deselect the marquee.

7. Choose Filter, Blur, Gaussian Blur. A processor-intensive step is coming up, so don't expect results immediately.

8. Drag the pixel slider to about 33, as shown in figure 9.18, and then press Enter to apply the blurring effect to the black pixels on Layer 1.

9. On the Layers palette, drag the Opacity slider to about 59%, and then choose Multiply mode to create the final shading in the image, as shown in figure 9.19.

10. Press Ctrl(⌘)+S; keep the file open.

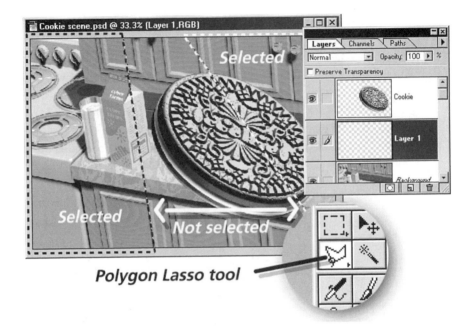

FIGURE 9.17 *Create a spotlight shape starting on the left of the image and casting down and right in the image, using the Polygon Lasso tool.*

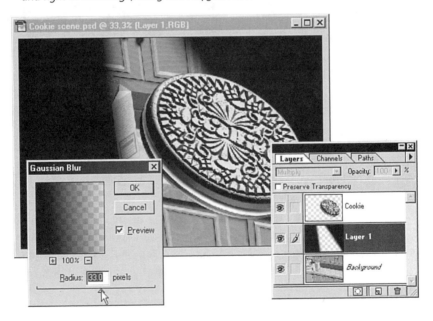

FIGURE 9.18 *Apply a whopping amount of Gaussian blur to get a very soft transition between shaded and unshaded areas in the image.*

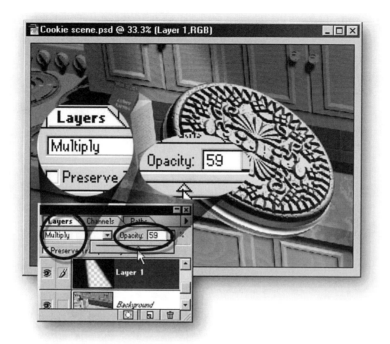

FIGURE 9.19   *Lighten the background by choosing partial opacity for Layer 1. Multiply mode only allows pixels on a layer darker than those in the scene to appear— so the shading, although not dramatic, is dense in the image.*

In the next section you're going to do something weird and wonderful. Using Quick Mask mode and image blurring, you will make the background of the composition gradually come into focus from back to front.

Creating Transitional Masking

In traditional photography, you have an aperture on a lens that determines the depth of field—how deeply into the three-dimensional world things are in focus. We generally see a medium depth of field—the frontmost and backmost areas are slightly out of focus—because the photographer wants to isolate something in the midground of the scene.

You'll notice that the kitchen scene is perfectly in focus, and it looks phony because of the focus, but this could not be helped because many modeling/rendering programs put the entire scene in focus.

Your mission in the next set of steps is to make the very farthest point in the scene extremely out of focus, and then, as the eye moves toward the front of the scene (to the right), to bring the background more into focus, a focus similar to that of the cookie.

We haven't covered a handy shortcut yet, but there's a very easy way in Photoshop 5.5 to make sure that the Quick Mask overlay represents either selected areas or protected areas. You'll be using the Linear Gradient tool to create a mask in the following steps, so take a look at figure 9.20 right now.

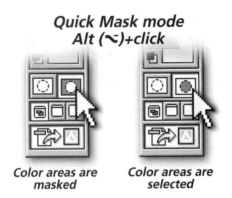

Quick Mask mode
Alt (⌥)+click

Color areas are   *Color areas are*
masked   *selected*

Figure 9.20   *You decide what the Quick Mask overlay represents before you apply the Quick Mask.*

When you enter the image into Quick Mask mode, holding Alt(Opt) and clicking on the icon toggles between selected and protected mask areas. The shaded circle in the icon means that Quick Mask tinting is selecting areas, and another Alt(Opt)+click makes the background shaded on the icon, meaning that tinted areas are exposed and that no overlay is on selected areas. We want to add to the scene a tint that most strongly selects the upper-left corner and diminishes to nothing at the lower-right corner. Then let the blurring filter do its thing.

Here's how to add realism to the scene:

Making a Linear Gradient Mask

1. Make sure you can see the entire image. If you're running a low screen resolution, you might want to reduce the viewing size of the image by typing **33** in the Zoom field, and then pressing Enter.

2. Press Ctrl(⌘)+S. Hide Layer 1, as the shading will interfere with your perception of the Background layer.

3. Click on the Background layer title on the Layers palette, and then Alt(Opt)+click on the Quick Mask icon until color represents selected areas. Press D and then press X to make the current foreground color white.

4. With the Linear Gradient tool set to Foreground to Background, drag diagonally in the image, as shown in figure 9.21, starting at the lower right of the center of the image, and ending somewhere toward the top left. Everything that is tinted will be selected, and the selection will taper off to 0% when you see no mask in image areas.

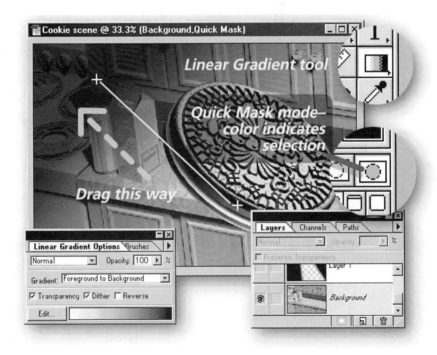

FIGURE 9.21   *You're creating a mask that has a transitional property. Some areas will be totally selected, some partially, and some not selected at all, but the transition will be smooth and seamless.*

5. Click on the Standard Editing mode icon (to the left of the Quick Mask icon), and then press Ctrl(⌘)+Alt(Opt)+F to display the dialog box of the last-used filter without applying the filter. Drag the slider to about 5, as shown in figure 9.22, and then click on OK to apply the filter.

FIGURE 9.22   *A mild amount of blurring, which disappears gradually to a sharp image, is a visual clue that a photographer took the image with an aperture of f8 or less. The important fact is that we've added reality—there is now a hint of photographic realism in the image.*

6. Press Ctrl(⌘)+D to deselect the marquee, unhide Layer 1 (the shading), and you now should have a finished image, as shown in figure 9.23.

7. Press Ctrl(⌘)+S. You can close the image at any time now.

Are you ready for a little science fiction bonanza? Read on, and you'll learn how to integrate even more of your skills in a single composition.

FIGURE 9.23   *Shading and focus are two photorealistic properties that you can add to any type of scene.*

Introducing Lars Wuhdqax

Any guy who romps around outer space in a karate outfit waving a glowing sword is bound to attract attention, especially the attention of Mr. George Lucas. So the following example is *nothing* like any movie you've seen, okay?

We're going to build a composition starring Lars Wuhdqax, Alien Hunter, along with his molecular spaceship and his trusty mechanical assistant, TechBot Y2K.

Let's begin at the beginning, with a photo from long ago.

Masking the Hero From the Background

In figure 9.24, you can see the primary image of the composition being turned into a layered image. To do this, you open the Lars.tif image from the Examples/Chap09 folder of the Companion CD, and double-click on the Background title. A dialog box appears, in which you can name the layer. I suggest you name it "Lars Wuhdqax" because there will be several layers to this image.

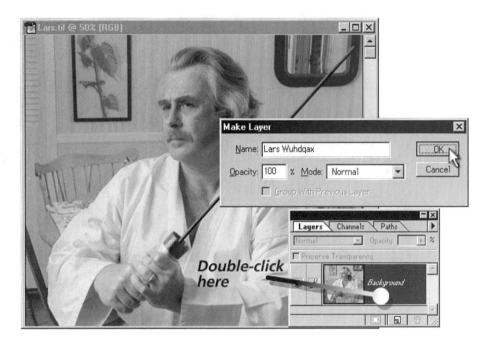

FIGURE 9.24   *Convert this ordinary image into a layer image so you can get rid of the breakfast nook in the background.*

Instead of tutorial steps on how to separate Lars from the breakfast nook, the following steps are intended as hints on what to do, and which tool to use around the various parts of Lars' silhouette. You probably have already read two chapters about selecting stuff, so you don't need that information here!

Tips for Isolating the Hero in the Image

1. Click on the Layer Mask mode icon at the bottom of the Layers palette. Press D (default colors) so you're working with black paint, which hides areas on a layer.

2. Zoom in to about a 200% viewing resolution at the bottom right of Lars' karate outfit, choose the upper-right tip on the Brushes palette, choose the

note

This composition can and will rise to about 12MB as you add layers, although its final saved size will be between 2 and 3MB. You really should have between 48 and 64MB of RAM on your system and just as large a scratch disk (see chapter 1 for scratch disk configuration) to work easily and quickly with the image elements.

This composition will be of sufficient resolution to output at 8" by 10" from a midpriced color inkjet printer.

Paintbrush tool, and start working carefully on the outside edge of Lars' karate outfit, as shown in figure 9.25.

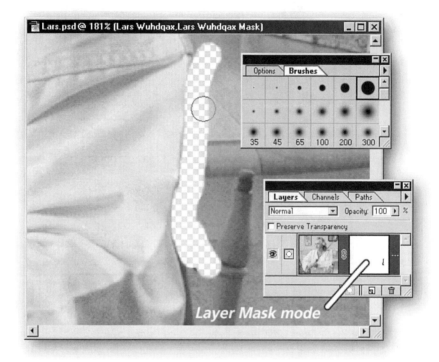

FIGURE 9.25   *The easiest way to create a character on an empty layer is to hide everything except the character.*

3. Work your way up the right side (stage right) of the karate outfit until you hit the plant stake that is sticking out of a flashlight, as shown in figure 9.26. The plant stake was a deliberate prephotography addition to the image. It is meant to describe the angle of the laser coming out of Lars' weapon, so that creating the laser effect will be easy as pie (or a piece of cake) later.

4. At this point, it might be good to remove large areas from the image. You've created a path between the karate outfit and the background, and you can run the Lasso tool along this "gutter" (the Layer Mask path), and close the selection to the *outside* of Lars. Then press Alt(Opt)+Delete, and then Ctrl(⌘)+D to hide large areas.

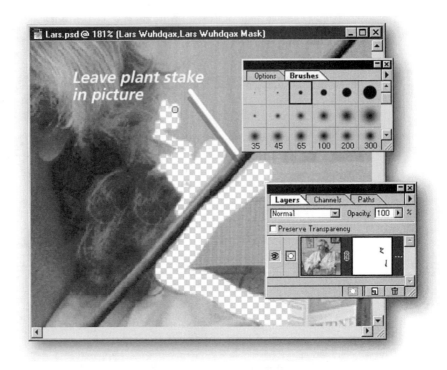

FIGURE 9.26   *Leave the plant stake in the selection; you'll paint over it to create a laser effect later.*

5. When you reach the hair, use a small tip, making precise stroke beginnings at the hair, and getting looser in precision as you complete a stroke. Doing this will enable you to use the Lasso tool more easily around the outside of the hair areas.

6. Over on the left side of Lars (stage left), you can switch back to a hard, large brush tip to finish separating the karate outfit from the background.

7. Finally, use the Lasso tool on large areas, fill the selections with foreground color to hide them, and then deselect the marquee.

8. Drag the Layer Mask thumbnail into the trash icon, and click on Apply in the query box. Keep the image open and save it to your hard disk as Lars.psd, in Photoshop's native file format.

PROFOUND WISDOM #18:

Use the tip size and tip hardness that correspond with your masking chores.

Tip size is sort of an obvious thing—you don't mask out an elephant with a 3-pixel-diameter brush. However, if there is a clear, clean dividing line between objects in an image, you use a hard tip (top row on the Brushes palette). Lars' karate outfit clearly contrasts against the background in the image, so a hard masking edge is used. On smaller, softer parts of the image, such as Lars' hair, you will want to change brush tips to small and soft.

It's my belief that this book should give you a workout of sorts—that strange new things on your computer screen will become second nature to manipulate. But I *don't* believe that failing on one part of this book's tutorials should bring your need to work and learn to a screeching halt.

For this reason, I've created an alpha channel in the Lars picture that I didn't tell you about until now, because I really wanted you to practice your skills. If, on the other hand, your selection skills aren't terrific, you can still work through this epic assignment by Ctrl(⌘)+clicking on the alpha channel icon on the Channels palette, and then right-clicking (Macintosh: hold Ctrl and click) and choosing Layer Via Copy from the context menu, as shown in figure 9.27.

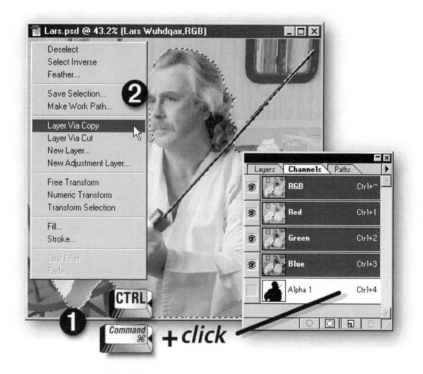

FIGURE 9.27   *If your selections skills aren't quite ready for prime-time, simply choose Layer via Copy from the content menu after Ctrl (⌘)+clicking on the alpha channel icon.*

If you choose the short route here, make sure you've named the layer "Lars Wuhdqax," and that you've dragged the Background layer into the trash icon. So users with some experience and those with none are in the same place now in the assignment.

Making Room for the Other Elements

The Lars image was cropped to cut down on file size while you worked—the complete image simply contains the rest of the breakfast nook. But you need more room than is currently in the image to add the molecule starship, the robot buddy, and perhaps a little text later.

In the steps to follow, you'll enlarge the canvas, and actually learn a new trick with background composition. You see, the background I rendered for the scene is a little too small (I misplaced my calculator)—it won't fill an image of the size you will create. So you'll enlarge the image (thus seriously hurting the focus and adding pixelation to the background), but then you'll use the Gaussian Blur filter. This not only helps make the hero of the composition stand out more, but it's photographically correct to have an out of focus background when there's not a lot of light pouring into the image.

Here goes:

Enlarging the Composition for Other Elements

1. Choose Image, Canvas size.

2. Choose pixels as the unit of measurement in both the Width and the Height drop-down boxes.

3. Type **1296** in the Width field, and type **981** in the Height field. You cannot guess these numbers by yourself because you haven't run through the entire tutorial to arrive at the correct size for the canvas. But *I* did, and these numbers work best for this piece.

4. Click on the bottom-right chiclet in the Anchor area. This expands the canvas horizontally and vertically from the anchor area you specified, as shown in figure 9.28.

5. Open the Tundra.tif image from the Examples/Chap09 folder on the Companion CD. Position it in the workspace so you have a clear view of both the Lars image and the tundra. With the Move tool, drag the tundra image into the Lars image, and then press Ctrl(⌘)+Left Brace ([). This command sends the current layer one layer backward, so the tundra is now behind our hero, as shown in figure 9.29. Name the layer "Tundra" when you get a chance, to avoid future confusion. You can close the Tundra.tif image at any time now.

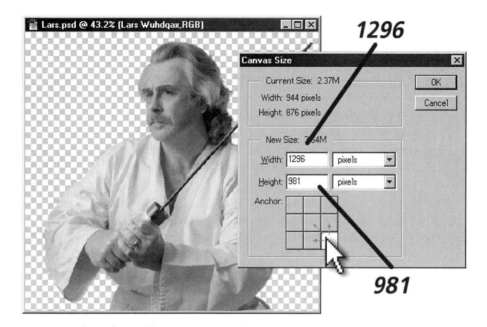

FIGURE 9.28   *Add canvas area to the left and top of the existing image.*

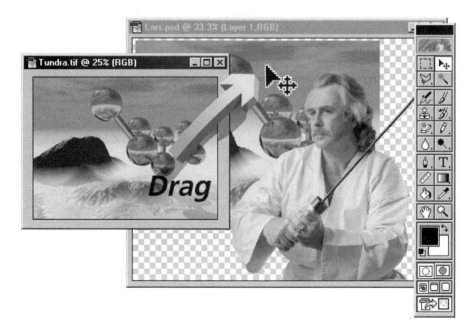

FIGURE 9.29   *Copy the image to a different image window, using the Move tool, and then send it behind the Lars layer.*

6. Widen the image window so you can see lots of image window background. Windows users can use the Maximize/Restore button to make the window take up the entire workspace in Photoshop.

7. With the Move tool, position the image on the Tundra layer in the upper right of the image window and then press Ctrl(⌘)+T to put the Free Transform bounding box around the image.

8. Right-click (Macintosh: hold Ctrl and click) on the image and then choose Scale from the context menu. Then, hold Shift and drag the bottom-left bounding box handle to just slightly outside the image area, as shown in figure 9.30.

9. Press Enter, or double-click inside the bounding box to finalize the transformation (the scaling). The image of the tundra looks pretty crummy, right? This sort of thing happens when you dramatically change the size of a bitmap image, whose pixels are finite, and Photoshop is left to "guess" what the new, additional pixel colors should be. But you're not quite done yet.

10. Choose Filter, Blur, Gaussian Blur. Choose 4.5 pixels in the Gaussian Blur dialog box, as shown in figure 9.31, and then click on OK.

FIGURE 9.30   *Holding Shift keeps the image you're scaling equal in proportions to the original dimensions.*

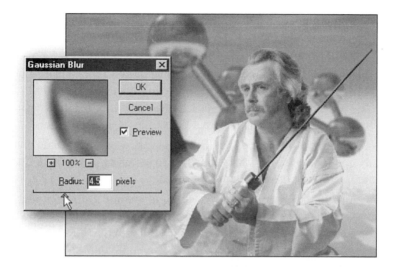

FIGURE 9.31   *If you scale an image too much up or down, you will see harsh edges in the image. But this is okay if the goal is to have a background such as this one, which is out of focus in the finished composition.*

11. Press Ctrl(⌘)+S; keep the file open.

In the next section, you'll add a spotlight in front of the tundra and behind Lars, using the technique you learned earlier with the flying cookie.

Adding a Touch of Spotlight

Okay, Lars is the hero of the image and the imaginary film, so we could justify putting a spotlight on him for that reason alone. But have you noticed also that there is really not much visual business going on in the background? There's only the molecule ship. From a compositional point of view, you can make the top of the image a little darker and let the lightness open up the image toward the bottom, where Lars and the molecule ship are located. Then, if you decide to add text later, the top of the image will hold reversed (white on black) text.

Here's how to add subtle shading to the scene:

Highlighting a Hero

1. Hold Alt(Opt) and click on the Create new layer icon. Doing this displays the Options box for a new layer, so you can name the layer and create it in one fell swoop. Name the layer Spotlight, and click on OK. You now have a spotlight layer on top of the previously used layer, the Tundra layer.

2. Zoom out of the image and drag the window edges away from the image so you can see the background. With the Polygon Lasso tool, create a polygon around Lars, suggesting a spotlight that broadens at the bottom. Press Shift+F7 to invert the selection, press Alt(Opt)+Delete (Backspace) to fill the selection, as shown in figure 9.32. Press Ctrl(⌘)+D to deselect the selection marquee.

3. Press Ctrl(⌘)+Alt(Opt)+F to display the last-used filter's dialog box without actually applying the filter. Drag the slider to about 23 pixels, click on OK and wait a moment, even if you have a fast machine.

4. Choose Multiply from the Layers drop-down list for the Spotlight layer, and then drag the Opacity slider down to about 53%. If you don't have a lot of RAM and hard disk space, you can press Ctrl(⌘)+E to merge the spotlight layer down into the background layer to conserve resources. If you've got a fast, powerful machine, you may care to keep the Spotlight layer separate from the background.

5. Press Ctrl(⌘)+S; keep the file open.

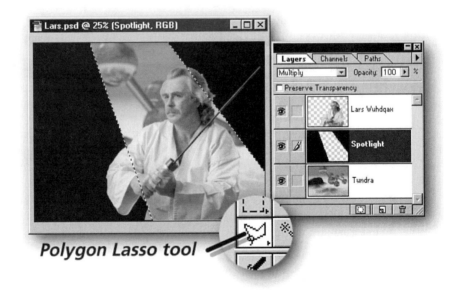

FIGURE 9.32   *Create a spotlight by inverting the shape of a spotlight, and then fill the selection with black.*

Next on the agenda is adding TechBot Y2K at Lars' side. In the next section, you'll not only place Y2K in the scene, but selectively blur him/it so he/it is also truly *in* the scene and not on top of it.

Adding a Robot to the Composition

You're confined a little with regards to Y2K's placement in the scene—I only rendered Y2K's hips and a little of the legs, so the bottom of the image must be placed at the bottom of the Lars.psd image.

But you know something? Y2K is so rich in detail (it's a rendered model), that to try to pack more attention into the scene would be overdoing it. Lars is going to get his laser sword soon, and it's actually a fun tease to your audience to hide some of the detail of the robot. It makes the scene look more like a photograph—people with cameras are incessantly cropping scenes ineptly...we're used to it <g>!

Here's how to place and blur a robot in the Lars composition:

Adding Y2K to the Scene

1. Open the TechBot.psd image from the Examples/Chap09 folder on the Companion CD. The robot is on its own layer.

2. Drag the TechBot Y2K title on the Layers palette into the Lars.psd image window, as shown in figure 9.33. You can close the TechBot image at any time now.

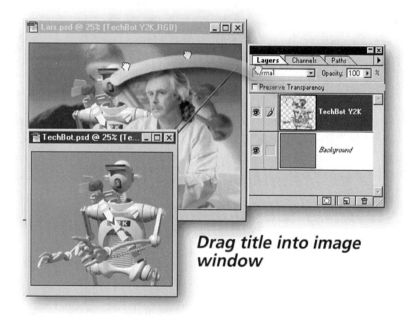

Drag title into image window

FIGURE 9.33   *Dragging a layer title into an image window puts a copy of that layer on top of the current layer, which is what you want to do in this example.*

3. With the Move tool, drag the TechBot Y2K layer until the TechBot is behind Lars and its right hand is slightly out of frame. Again, clumsy cropping adds photo-realism.

4. Choose the Radial Gradient tool from the toolbox. What you're going to do here is mask the robot so its hands (which are closest to you) are in focus, and focus gradually decreases as you come to view the edges of the TechBot.

5. Press D and then press X to make white the current foreground color. Double-click on the Radial Gradient tool (if necessary) to display the Options palette. Make sure the gradient type is Foreground to Background on the drop-down list.

6. Alt(Opt)+click (if necessary) on the Quick Mask icon, so that color indicates selected areas in the image and your image is now in Quick Mask mode.

7. With the Radial Gradient tool, click between the TechBot's hands, and then drag as far away with the tool as shown in figure 9.34.

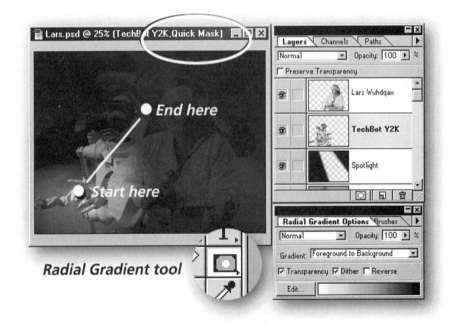

Figure 9.34   *The Quick Mask starts at 0% strength at the hands of the TechBot, and increases to 100% at the edges of the TechBot.*

8. Click on the Standard Editing mode icon to the left of the Quick Mask button, and you now have a selection marquee in the image. If you like, press Ctrl(⌘)+H to hide the marquee lines, so you can better see the transformation that is about

to take place. The selection's still active; it's the dotted line "reminder" on the screen that's hidden.

9. Press Ctrl(⌘)+Alt(Opt)+F to display the last-used filter's dialog box.

10. In the dialog box, decrease the blurring strength to about 2 pixels, about half of what you used to blur the tundra.

11. Press Ctrl(⌘)+D, and then press Ctrl(⌘)+S; keep the file open.

note

Why half? Actually, this is sort of a silly, logical decision: The tundra is twice as far away from Lars as is the TechBot, so the TechBot is half as sharp in focus. Is this scientific? Not in the least, but it does give the image a number of focal planes, and heightens the interest and realism of the picture.

Avast! I have no idea what that means, but pirates in movies seem to say it a lot. Are you ready to get involved in some high-tech swordplay?

Creating Lars' Laser Light

Remember how to create a glowing effect around stuff? (You learned how earlier in the book.) Well, to create a shaft of laser light you make a minor modification to those steps. In the steps you'll perform momentarily, you'll create an open Pen tool path, stroke it with a fat, semitransparent foreground color, and then stroke the path a second time with a brighter, more opaque color to represent the core of the laser light.

And for accuracy's sake, you should be aware here that laser hits in the motion pictures look absolutely *nothing* like a real laser in action! Here's how to make a *theatrical* laser:

Leaping Lasers!

1. Click on the Lars Wuhdqax title on the Layers palette, and then press Alt(Opt)+click on the Create new layer icon. In the New Layer dialog box, type **Laser** in the name field, and then click on OK to exit the box. The Laser layer is the top and current editing layer. Choose Screen mode for the layer from the drop-down list on the Layers palette.

2. Zoom to about a 50% resolution of Lars.psd, hold the Spacebar to toggle to the Hand tool, and then drag in the image until the plant stake in Lars' hand is in the center of the window.

3. Choose the Pen tool from the toolbox, and then click an anchor at the bottom part of the plant stake, and another at the top of the stake.

4. Click on the foreground color selection box on the toolbox, and choose a brilliant green in the Color Picker. Click on OK to return to the scene.

5. Choose the Paintbrush tool, and then on the Brushes palette, choose the 100-pixel tip. On the Options palette, lower the Opacity for the Paintbrush tool to about 65%.

6. Click on the Strokes path with foreground color icon on the Paths palette, as shown in figure 9.35. Pretty cool, huh?

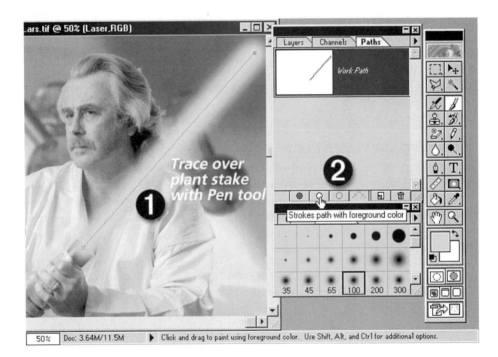

FIGURE 9.35   *Stroking a path with a wide, diffuse color while a layer is in Screen mode does indeed produce a light- or laser-type effect.*

7. Click on the 35-pixel Brushes palette tip, click on the foreground color selection box, and pick a lighter green color (more white in the color) than you currently have selected. Click on OK to get back to the action.

8. Click on the Strokes path with foreground color icon on the Paths palette. You can drag the Work Path icon into the trash icon at any time now.

9. You need to clean up the bottom of the laser light so it appears to be coming *from* a source and not lying on top of a source. Choose the Eraser tool, choose Airbrush from the Options palette's drop-down list, and drop the Pressure down to about 25%. Choose the 65-pixel tip from the Brushes palette, and then press D (default colors).

10. Make a curving stroke or two at the bottom of the laser light, as shown in figure 9.36. Press Ctrl(⌘)+S; keep the file open.

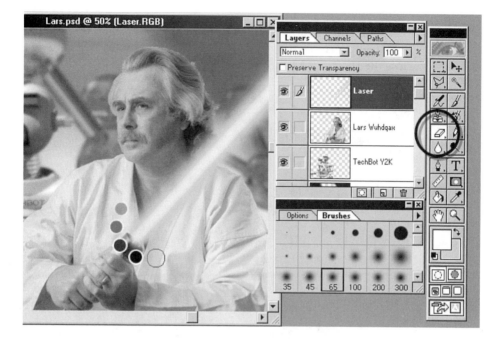

FIGURE 9.36 *Remove some of the light from the bottom tip of the stroke by using the Eraser tool in Airbrush mode.*

The Airbrush tool, even when it's used only as an Eraser tip, is a powerful retouching tool. Even at partial strength, it gives you a great deal of control over the amount of erasure or paint you're applying. And unlike other tools, the Airbrush tool leaves no edges. Your work is always undetectable if you practice with this tool/setting.

Adding a Suitable Handle to the Sword

Okay, I'm sure you were waiting to see what I was going to do with the stupid-looking plastic flashlight that Lars is brandishing. If you were doing this scene, you might want to paint a lathed table leg a metallic color or something. What I did requires a little more retouching to work. I modeled a metallic handle in Caligari's trueSpace (a 3D graphics program), sizing and making the angle of rotation the same as the plant stake.

So you're basically in business by copying the handle to the Lars.psd composition, and then masking away areas where Lars' fingers should be, around the handle:

Adding a Handle to the Sword

1. Open the Handle.psd image from the Examples/Chap09 folder on the Companion CD.

2. Click on the Lars Wuhdqax title on the Layers palette, and then with the Move tool, drag the handle image into the Lars.psd window, as shown in figure 9.37. Close the Handle.psd image without saving now.

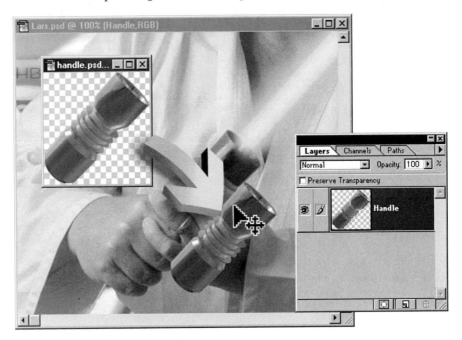

FIGURE 9.37   *Pick the layer on which you want the new layer to land, and then use the Move tool to drag it there.*

3. Zoom to 200% on the image. Position the handle so that its outside edge is behind the end of the laser light. Basically, you're placing the modeled handle over the flashlight. Click on the Layer Mask icon at the bottom of the Layers palette.

4. Choose a hard-edge (top row) Brushes palette tip (choose the third tip from the left and see how you feel about it). Choose the Paintbrush tool, and press 0 on the keypad to make the Paintbrush 100% opaque. Carefully stroke around the edges of Lars' fingers to hide the unwanted part of the handle, as shown in figure 9.38.

FIGURE 9.38   *In Layer Mask mode, foreground black hides image areas, and white restores hidden areas.*

5. If you stray into Lars' fingers, press X (swap foreground/background color selection boxes) and then paint to restore the parts of the fingers. Then press X again, and conclude your retouching work. Then, drag the Layer Mask thumbnail into the trash icon, and when the query box comes up, click on Apply.

6. Press Ctrl(⌘)+S; keep the file open.

One last element in the composition needs refining. As you can see, the handle I provided for Lars is not wide enough to cover the plastic flashlight top in the image. This is easy enough to fix if you read chapter 7.

Adding Texture to the Outfit using the Rubber Stamp tool

The flashlight top is so close to a monochrome karate outfit that you can easily paint karate outfit texture over the flashlight head. Here's how to finish our episode with Lars Wuhdqax, Alien Hunter:

Cloning Over the Flashlight

1. Click on the Lars Wuhdqax layer title on the Layers palette to make this the active editing layer. Choose the Rubber Stamp tool, and make sure Use All Layers is *not* checked on the Options palette.

2. On the Brushes palette, choose the second-from-last tip in the second row.

3. Alt(Opt)+click a sampling point near, but not too close to, the flashlight head in the image. Then make some strokes over the flashlight head to replace it with karate outfit texture, as shown in figure 9.39.

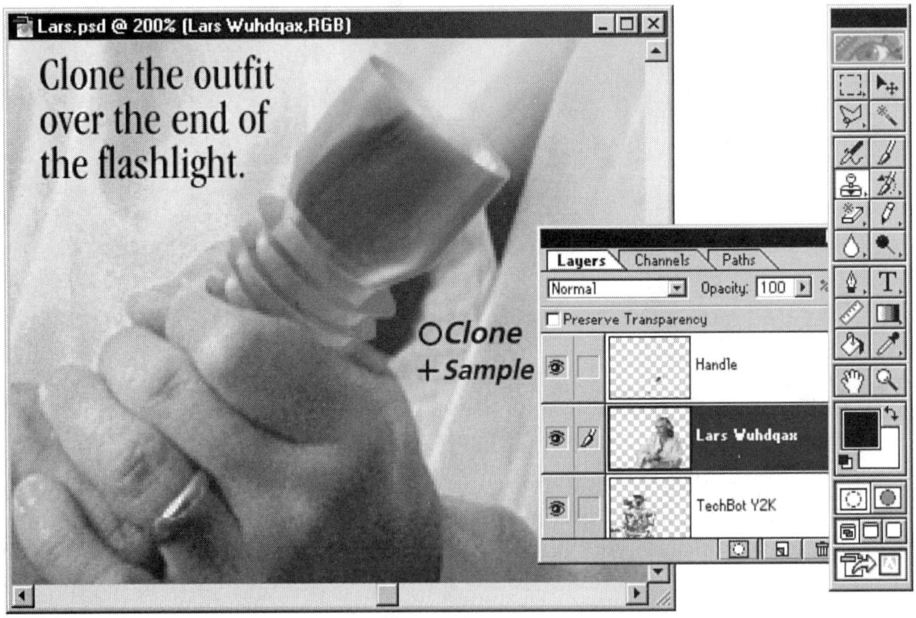

FIGURE 9.39   *Keep resampling in different clothing areas, and keep painting over the edge of the flashlight until you can no longer see it.*

4. Repeat step 3 as many times as necessary (two or three applications of the Rubber Stamp tool should do it).

5. Press Ctrl(⌘)+S. Keep the file open.

What I'd recommend at this point is that you do one or more of the following with the composition and Photoshop:

- Choose Edit, Purge, and then choose All. This releases resources held on the Clipboard and in RAM for multiple undos in Photoshop. Your system will stop creaking and swearing at you now. As held in memory, this layered image is 11MB.

- Press Ctrl(⌘)+Alt(Opt)+S. This is the shortcut for Save a Copy, and it's a good shortcut to add to your list. In the Save a Copy dialog box, name the file, pick a location for the file, choose the TIFF file format for the saved copy (this automatically merges layers in the copy, because the TIFF format cannot hold layers), and check Exclude non-image data (which means your copy won't have paths in it). Then close your working copy, Lars.psd.

- Choose Flatten Image from the Layers palette's flyout menu. Now, you can save the image in any format, but you can no longer access the power of editing the individual layers.

If you now want to put icing on the cake, follow these steps to add a title to the piece:

Adding a Title

1. Open the Title.psd file from the Examples/Chap09 folder on the Companion CD.
2. With the Move tool, drag the layer into the image.
3. Position the title so it's in a location similar to that seen in figure 9.40.
4. That's it! Go out for some popcorn and those tiny drops of candy that instantly remove fillings.

Okay, this is the end of the chapter, and if you feel tired and inspired simultaneously, this is not a bad thing. You've had quite a workout in what you might have thought was a "beginner's book." But if you think about it, did we ever do anything that wasn't covered in earlier chapters? It's how you *integrated* different techniques that led to the successful completion of some pretty handsome stuff.

A "fundamentals" book *doesn't* have to dwell 49 times on the same technique! You learn the foundation items, and then work your way up from there.

And there's still room for "fun" in "fundamentals"!

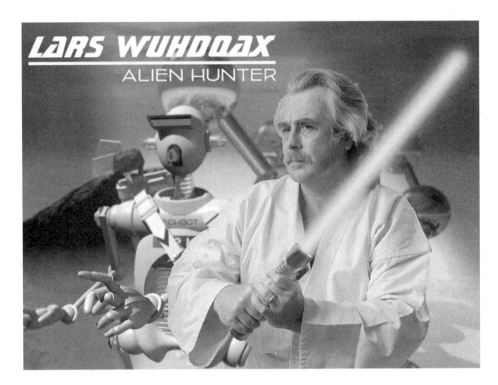

FIGURE 9.40 *Science fiction is simply another avenue that leads to all sorts of other photo-fiction when you have experience with Photoshop.*

Summary

There is a definite direction in your tutelage from this book. The direction is *up;* you're becoming more experienced because you already know a wide base platform of tricks and steps that lead to results in Photoshop. I'm reminded of the house metaphor—you build a decent foundation, and the rest will come quickly with the assurance of stability. Hopefully, this is what you've discovered in this book. And you can apply this learning technique to *other* books.

With luck, a few of them will be *my* other books.

In Chapter 10, you'll see how to allow your artwork to step outside the hard drive and land in other people's mailboxes, hands, and picture frames. We're going to take a lesson on how to print your Photoshop work so that it looks as beautiful on *this* side of the cathode tube as it does on the other.

Output Essentials

What I've written here is a lecture cleverly disguised as a reference guide, which is cleverly disguised as a chapter—specifically, as a chapter on output. We tend to use the term "output" these days because hard copy isn't necessarily rendered to paper. You can print to film, to glossy paper, T-shirt transfers—there are oodles of ways you can get an image off your monitor and onto something in the physical world.

Throughout this chapter I'm going to hand you tools in the guise of math formulas and nuggets of information that will

- Give you the confidence that your printing skills are top-notch.
- Give you the straight story on many of the parameters surrounding the action of output, rather than some of the myths that give you headaches and cause your work to look crummy.

Let's begin with a simple term that you will hear more and more often as you gain experience not only with personal printing, but also with commercial printing. The term is "interpolation."

Interpolation Means "Interpretation"

"Interpolation" is such a neat-sounding word, isn't it? Many of us have a vague notion (within context) of what interpolation means, but you need to understand *precisely* what it means when the action is performed on your work.

Interpolation, in computer graphics is an application's *interpretation* of what something should look like, especially when the software does not have sufficient data to carry our your request. Interpolation is always an *averaging* process of some kind. Say, for example, that you have a color image that is 4 pixels wide and 4 pixels high, and you want the image to be four times this size: 8 pixels by 8 pixels.

There isn't a program on earth that can create the new image with the sensitivity and talent of an artist. The reason is obvious: computers have neither talent nor intuition—these are human qualities. This is why you run the computer, and not the other way around!

When you want to resize an image up or down, Photoshop searches for data to help support the application's decision about what the resized image will look like. It is you who determines how extensively Photoshop uses interpretation—how much Photoshop searches to come up with new data for the image.

Bicubic Interpolation

Bicubic interpolation is the most sophisticated and elegant of Photoshop's resizing methods. It also requires the most processing power. In the year 2000, however, you probably would not notice even the slightest lag while Photoshop interpolates because our computers are so powerful. The image shown in figure 10.1 is 4 pixels high and 4 pixels wide (outstanding art it's not), with two horizontal and two vertical pixels that contain a color. I've drawn imaginary grids on the right side of figures 10.1 and 10.2 to help you visualize what's going on here.

The images at the bottom of figure 10.1 show what you can expect from Photoshop when you command it to use bicubic interpolation (the default interpolation method) to make this artwork 8 pixels wide by 8 pixels high.

By looking at figure 10.1 you can draw two conclusions about bicubic interpolation:

- The resizing of the art makes the component pixels in the new image show the visual content as being a tad fuzzy.
- Photoshop makes a smooth transition between background color and foreground color in this example. This effect is particularly important when you work with images whose *pixel count* (the number of pixels in the image) is far greater than the pathetic 16-pixel total we are looking at here.

Okay, so how did Photoshop come up with the intermediate pixels and pixel colors to fill in the gap caused by resizing the neighboring pixels? The term *bicubic* here means that Photoshop looked in all directions—horizontal, vertical, and diagonal—beginning with each pixel and then scouting outward. The new pixels are an *average* of the original pixel color, and the original pixel's *neighboring* pixel color. Photoshop performs a weighted average of the pixel and its neighbors along three directions and fits the new pixel between the original pixel and its neighbor.

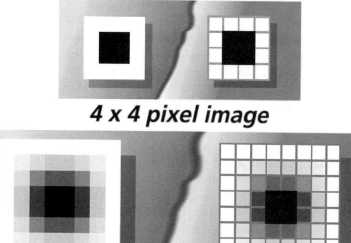

4 x 4 pixel image

bicubic interpolation to 8 x 8

FIGURE 10.1   *By default, Photoshop uses bicubic interpolation to resize an image or an image area.*

Artistically speaking, you probably want to use bicubic interpolation all the time, whether you're increasing or decreasing an entire image or just a selection. When an image is resized so that it's smaller—for display on a Web page, perhaps—bicubic interpolation also makes the new image somewhat fuzzy. This happens because you're commanding Photoshop to toss away pixels from the original artwork, and Photoshop must reassign the remaining pixels an average of the original colors at any given point. And this ain't easy because, again, machines and applications are poor at guessing. They do the next best thing, which is called *averaging <g>*!

Bilinear Interpolation

Bilinear interpolation, in contrast to Bicubic, only scouts across the horizontal and the vertical grid of a pixel painting to arrive at new colors, and although Bilinear interpolation performs averaging, it is not what math-type folks call *weighted* averaging, and the results (or lack of results) are visible.

Bilinear interpolation can be conducted on Photoshop images that you want to make larger or smaller. I would not recommend this process, however, unless you own a Mac Centra or a 386-class PC running on 16MB of RAM! Seriously, bilinear interpolation is less processor-intensive than bicubic because it does less examination of all the pixels in an image before it creates or deletes pixels as a result of averaging calculations.

The result of bilinear averaging (as shown in fig. 10.2—peek ahead) might not be obvious with very small images, as my famous 8-by-8-pixel artwork demonstrates. The new pixels and/or new pixel colors in an image on which you've used bilinear interpolation will not be as faithful to the original image as if the Bicubic method was used, however, because you commanded Photoshop to perform a decent but not thorough investigation to come up with data to be averaged.

Qualitatively, you have no reason to change this interpolation preference in the General Preferences dialog box. Many applications do not even offer the option of bicubic interpolation.

Nearest Neighbor Interpolation

Nearest Neighbor interpolation is the crudest, quickest way to shrink or enlarge an image. When you apply this method to an image, it rightfully earns the name "*no* interpolation" because the visual results are so wildly inaccurate. Nearest Neighbor interpolation might only be of some use when you are increasing the size of an image by an exact, whole amount such as 4 times or 16 times an original's size. Because pixels are square, when you increase the height of an image by 2, you are also increasing the height by 2, and therefore twice the resolution of an image file means 4 times its original size.

Can you see now that the Nearest Neighbor method performs no calculations or averaging, but merely repeats the pixel color at the edge of the original? This can lead to really ugly and inaccurate work, especially if you are increasing the size of an

PROFOUND WISDOM #19:

Whenever there is blurring going on, you should use sharpening to correct any fuzziness.

Okay, so this Wisdom is not all that profound, but you should make it standard operating procedure (SOP) that whenever you make a dramatic change in the number of pixels in an image, a trip to Photoshop's Sharpen filters is the smartest course of action. You can use a Sharpen command not only to fake restoring the focus of a large image made smaller through interpolation, but also to repair some of the focus to a small image that has been made much larger.

I recommend the Unsharp Mask filter at all times, except when you're creating a button or an icon for a Web page— when a 400-by-400–pixel image, for example, is reduced to 32 by 32 pixels. In this case, the Filter, Sharpen, Sharpen command produces an image that's a little exaggerated around the edges but that effectively communicates your artwork at a very small size.

image by a fractional amount or an amount that lies between two whole integers. In figure 10.2, I increased the size of my famous 16-pixel artwork from 4 by 4 pixels to 6 by 6. As you can see, the deck was stacked: There is a 100% chance that Nearest Neighbor resampling will return an image area that is incorrect in size when a number such as 150% the original size is applied to the image. The "magic numbers" to use with Nearest Neighbor resampling are 4x, 16x, and multiples thereof.

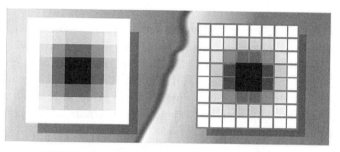

bilinear interpolation to 8 x 8

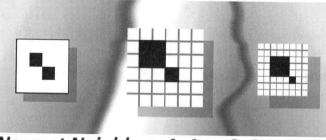

Nearest Neighbor: 4x4 to 6x6 to 8x8

FIGURE 10.2   *Nearest Neighbor evaluation of an image to be shrunk or enlarged will usually create uneven, inaccurate image areas.*

I've spent a good deal of time running down the types of interpolation Photoshop offers, not because I want you to change your preferences, but because I want you to understand the visual results of interpolation. Photoshop is not the only thing on earth that uses interpolation—imagesetting devices (printers) and film recorders use averaging processes, too, and your hard copy of an image can be nicely or ineptly rendered. Now that you understand the difference between methods, you have an important question to ask a service bureau (or tech support) that you did *not* have when you began this chapter.

Going from Continuous Tones to Halftones

Contrary to what the name might suggest, a halftone is *not* 50% of a tone! Halftones are the life blood of commercial printers, and are the only way you can get a continuous tone representation on paper. Continuous tones versus halftones merit a brief explanation, and then this section will get into the types of halftones that are at the designer's disposal.

What's the Difference Between Continuous Tones and Halftones?

When you look at the world, and there's a sunset with a rock in the vicinity, you'll see a subtle, *continuous*, falloff of light on the rock. There's no sudden, jarring area of tone missing, as the light gradually changes on the rock's surface. This is a continuous tone image, because Nature has every color with which to display images as the sun emits a spectrum, and as your eyes are equipped to receive the parts of the spectrum that depict the rock's tones.

On the other hand, a *halftone* consists of precisely *two* colors—not exactly our sunset scene! A halftone consists of an arrangement of dots (the foreground color, usually made up of black toner), against the paper (background) color. So how do you capture photographic qualities when your output is to a laser printer? You *simulate* continuous tones, which is done by the software instructing the printer to place dots of toner at different spatial intervals on the paper.

In figure 10.3 I've created an exaggerated example so you can see what a halftone sample looks like compared to a continuous tone that traverses the page from black to white.

The pattern you see in the halftone in figure 10.3 is an exaggeration of what anyone would expect from a laser printer. I think the resolution of the halftone is something like 15 lines per inch—a resolution so coarse you could drive your new car through there and not touch the paint.

We'll get into the mystical term "resolution" shortly, and demystify it. Next, though, let's take a look at how digital halftone cells help the accuracy with which a halftone image represents reality.

note

Please don't get on my case over the reality that this book is printed using dots on paper, and therefore could not possibly truly represent a continuous tone. This book is printed at 2,540 dots per inch, you can't even see the dots without a magnifying glass, and there's really no better workaround for showing you the principles of halftoning.

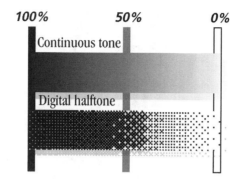

FIGURE 10.3   *A continuous tone image makes seamless transitions between light and dark. Halftone images must rely on the density of toner dots at any given area to simulate a continuous tone.*

The Digital Halftone Cell

When you learn about halftoning, it is helpful to imagine a grid placed above your original, continuous tone work. This imaginary grid helps define every inch of the image in terms of density. Suppose, for example, that you have a photo of an ice-cream cone against a white background. Slip a screen from a window or a door on top of the photo, and you will see something interesting happen. Pick a cell in the screen; pick it anywhere. Then take a look at the tone of the photo that is framed by the cell in the screen window.

If the tone is 50% black, what Photoshop and your printer would do is fill half an invisible, corresponding, digital screen on top of the printed page with toner that occupies 50% of the cell.

Now here's where it gets weird for a moment. In traditional printing, commercial printers have historically put a physical film screen over a photograph to make a halftoned copy. The halftones are round (usually) and each halftone dot is confined to a predetermined cell in a line of halftone dots. In figure 10.4 you can see a digital halftone cell compared to a traditional halftone. Digital halftone cells contain square (or rectangular) dots of toner, but in this figure you can see, in principle, how digital halftone cells closely mimic traditional coverage on a piece of paper or film. At the bottom of this figure you can see the specific coverage amounts.

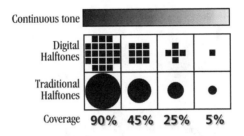

FIGURE 10.4   *Digital halftone cells are filled with a given number of dots that, viewed together (from a distance!), represent a specific tone.*

In the following section, we'll get into PostScript technology and how it affects printing. The reason for the excursion into the PostScript world is that, among other things:

- PostScript technology is the only real method of organizing toner dots (or emulsion on film) so that they truly mimic traditional, physical halftone screens.

- Because PostScript technology extends beyond merely organizing dots and into pre-press, there are math formulas that you really should know about (I'll do the pencil work for you in this chapter) and refer to if you ever want to make your own camera-ready art from a personal printer for commercial, ink-on-paper printing.

PostScript and Image Resolution

It's almost impossible to talk about PostScript rendering of images without talking about image resolution. Many readers have written to me in past years asking me what the input should be for a particular image, and I always have to respond with a question: What is your intended *output* for the file? It makes very little sense to choose an input resolution without first knowing whether the image is going to press, going up on the fridge, or going across the World Wide Web. Let's take a brief look at PostScript technology, and then get involved with *resolution*—both its meaning and how to calculate it.

PostScript as a Halftone Dot Shaper

What you can expect when you use PostScript to render a continuous tone image is the most faithful halftone renderings possible today. Other printing technologies put different-sized dots on a page, but those dots are not organized in screen lines that pressmen use. In figure 10.5, the image on the left is a (nearly <g>) continuous tone image of a duck. On the right is a PostScript halftone rendering of the same image. I've only used 30 dots per inch on the PostScript duck, which is a foolishly low resolution, but it helps display the individual dots better. Can you see how every tone on the duck on the left has a corresponding-size dot, and that, together, these dots represent the continuous tones?

Continuous tone duck   **PostScript™ halftoned duck**

FIGURE 10.5   *A continuous tone image compared to a PostScript rendition of the same image.*

It was not long after the invention of the traditional, physical halftone screen that the publishing world yearned for a little more flexibility in *how* a halftone is rendered. Does a single halftone always have to be circular? When a screen is applied to a continuous tone image at an angle other than right angles, what do you wind up with?

To answer these questions, take a look at figure 10.6. Elliptical dots are being used to fill the digital halftone cells, and the screen created by Photoshop is at a 45° angle.

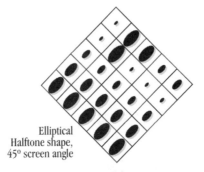

Elliptical
Halftone shape,
45° screen angle

FIGURE 10.6   *Photoshop offers six different shaped halftone dots, one of which is elliptical, plus a custom function, plus any angle for the screen you choose.*

It would help to squint at figure 10.6 to get a better idea of how stylized a halftone print can be when you use halftone dots that are not circular. We'll be getting into Photoshop's print options later in this chapter. There are many interrelated factors that determine the best halftone print of your work. I'll try to cover them all in the least confusing way.

The first factor in image rendering is called *resolution*. Resolution determines how much detail is visible in your print, and also can tell you how many samples per inch you should set your scanner for.

Image Resolution is a Fraction

Several accurate analogies can help you understand the term "resolution" as it applies to computer graphics. I've chosen speed, specifically the speed of a car, as an analogy.

When you measure the speed of a car, it is conveyed in one set of units over a *different* set of units, such as 55 miles (a unit of distance) per hour (a unit of time). Image resolution is expressed similarly: Resolution can be defined as units of data over units of distance. When someone tells you that an image is 2" by 2" at 150 pixels/inch, they are expressing the number of pixels in an inch; this is the resolution of the image.

PROFOUND WISDOM #20:

Image dimensions are inversely proportional to image resolution.

Because a pixel is the unit of measurement for the numerator of the resolution fraction (example: 65 pixels/inch), and because a pixel is only a placeholder, you have the flexibility of changing the size of an image by changing the resolution. The visual information in the image will not change at all. For example, a 10"-by-10" image at 100 pixels/inch can also be displayed as a 5-by-5 image at 200 pixels per inch.

You can tell that no image detail has changed when you change resolution, because the size of the image file remains the same. Keep this Profound Wisdom handy when you lay out printed work, and you always will accomplish the assignment 100% correctly.

On the other hand, and unfortunately this happens all too frequently, if someone tells you that an image is 200 pixels by 200 pixels, they have not told you the resolution of the image at all! How many pixels per inch is this 200-pixel by 200-pixel artwork? A *pixel* (short for *pic*ture *el*ement) is merely a place-holder, an entity of no fixed size that holds a color value. For example, red: 128, green: 214, and blue: 78 is the best description of a pixel that anyone could come up with. Resolution is the expression of how *many* pixels you want per inch.

If someone tells you that an image is supposed to be 2" by 2", you need to ask them what the resolution is, to create such an image. Conversely, if you are told that the resolution of an image is 300 ppi, you'd best ask this person for the physical dimensions of the image, as expressed in inches, picas, cm, and so on.

Let's take a stroll through the interface of a scanner and put all these nuggets of advice in order!

PROFOUND WISDOM #21:

An image expressed only in the number of pixels it contains is an absolute amount.

You learned in the preceding Profound Wisdom that resolution is somewhat flexible—you can decrease dimensions, increase resolution, and the number of pixels will remain the same. A good way to measure images destined for the Web or other screen presentations is by the number of pixels in the image. For example, a 640×480 screen capture will always contain 307,200 pixels, regardless of which monitor it is displayed on.

Scanning to the Right Size

I have a fictitious assignment here that involves scanning a piece of wood to 8½" by 11" with ¼" trim around each side (so I need 9" by 11½" scanned). As I mentioned in the previous section, a pixel is a placeholder that only takes up space after you have entered it as the numerator of the resolution fraction. Now here's a key that will unlock many graphics doors for you:

I'll explain the highlighted numbers in figure 10.7 shortly. What you're looking at is the TWAIN interface (a "corridor" between scanning hardware and imaging software—Photoshop) with a piece of wood imaged in the figure as a preview of what I'm going to scan.

Let's begin examining this scanner interface based on my need for a 9" by 11½" scan of some wood. First question, right? "At what resolution do you need the scan?"

I need the scan to be at 200 pixels per inch because my inkjet printer's resolution is 600 dots of ink per inch, and the guy at Epson told me that I should scan at one-third the final output resolution. This number is not carved in stone, but typically, for non-PostScript inkjet printers that use error diffusion as a rendering technique (which is impossible to quantify, since the dots of ink are not arranged in rows), one-third the output should be your scanning input.

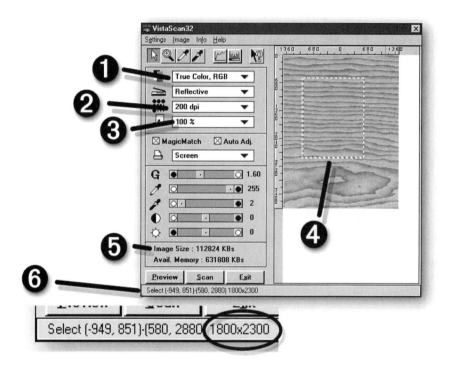

FIGURE 10.7   *Your scanner's interface might not look like this one, but you will find the same options on most models.*

Now for those explanations of the highlighted numbers in figure 10.7:

1. **Color Mode.** This should seem familiar; you see a Mode drop-down list every time you press Ctrl(⌘)+N in Photoshop. I've chosen RGB color here; however, there will be times when you want to scan in Grayscale, and most scanners offer this option.

2. **Resolution.** I want to get into a quarrel with scanner manufacturers, because they label the resolution in *dpi* (dots per inch). And scanners are actually scanning *samples* per inch (or *pixels* per inch). A dot is *not* a pixel. I've set the resolution to 200 because my final output to my ancient inkjet printer is 600 dpi.

3. **Scale.** Most scanners will allow you to zoom in on whatever is on the scanner's platen. Because I have a large sample of wood here, I

PROFOUND WISDOM #22:

Grayscale mode images are 1/3 the saved file size of RGB images.

The reason for this is that RGB images have three channels of image information, whereas grayscale images only have one channel (brightness).

want the scan to be only 1 to 1 (100%). But if, for example, you wanted to scan a postage stamp and print it at 8½" by 11", you'd use the scale option to really zoom into the stamp. Scaling does affect resolution. If you scale a scan at 200%, for example, you are scanning four times the information you'd be scanning at 100% (twice the width, twice the height).

4. **The cropping area.** Scanners enable you to pick only the portion of the sampled object you want. My scanner (this is *not* shown in the figure) will tell me in pixels or in inches how large my crop box is. Generally, you choose the interface's cropping tool, and then drag to select the part of the image you want scanned. Most scanners also come with rulers in the preview window, so guesswork is not necessary.

5. **Image Size.** This feature tells you how much RAM will be required to hold and acquire the image, and is also a good indicator of the saved file size. You'll note in this figure that the image size is about 11MB. This means that to scan from within Photoshop, I must have at least this amount (ideally about three times the amount) of RAM available and an equal amount of scratch disk space. Do *not* start a scanning session if your system resources are low—both the Mac and Windows have resource meters that keep you posted on such matters. Scanning is so processor-intensive, it makes downloading files look like a picnic.

6. **Absolute measurement.** As described earlier, the height and width of an image as measured in pixels is an incomplete description. I've got 1,800 pixels in width by 2,300 pixels in height marqueed in the preview window. What makes these numbers meaningful is that I'm scanning at 200 samples/inch. And 1,800/200 = 9 (inches), and 2,300/200 = 11.5 (inches).

End of story! You hit the scan button, and in moments you can save the image, which is perfectly proportioned, to hard disk and then print it later.

There are a few scanning issues I've overlooked in this section, such as interface options for contrast gamma control, saturation, and so on. My belief is to always "get it right in the camera" so your Photoshop correction work is not prolonged, but I've honestly never seen a scanner preview that was good enough to evaluate corrections you might make, using the interface controls. If an image looks halfway decent in preview, I scan, and then use Photoshop's features to make the image perfect.

We need to put the world of resolution and the world of PostScript together now, so you have some sort of guide to refer to when your scanner isn't my scanner, and your output device is not mine, either!

The Input/Output Chart

I've put together in figure 10.8 a table that includes a short list of scanning resolutions, the resolution of the printed work, and the expected file size of an acquired image. All these values presume that you are using PostScript technology—non-PostScript rendering technology is very difficult to measure, because non-PostScript printing does not follow any of the rules of traditional screening.

Various Output and Input Resolutions

For a 4" by 6" image at 1:1 sampling versus printing resolution

Resolution of Printed Work	Lines per Inch Output Device Uses	Recommended Scanning Resolution	File Size
300 dpi	45 lpi	90 to100 samples/inch	570 KB
600 dpi	85 lpi	170 samples/inch	1.99 MB
1200 dpi	125 lpi	225 samples/inch	3.48 MB
2450 dpi	133 lpi	266 samples/inch	4.86 MB

FIGURE 10.8   *Choose the printer resolution that most closely matches your printer, and you can see how large you should scan, and what the line screen frequency is.*

When rules in science are followed, the results are totally predictable. The same is true of PostScript technology—there are rules, and the next section presents you with the math you need to create the best camera-ready prints.

A Whole Bunch of Printing Math

Before you even consider making your own camera-ready prints, you should pay a call to the fellows who are going to make the printing plates, and ask the following questions:

- What is the line screen frequency and angle?
- What are the topmost and bottommost tones your presses can hold?

In figure 10.9 you can see the "times 2" rule. Commercial press houses do not measure the resolution of a halftoned image in dots. Images are measured in *lines* of dots, and the expression *lpi* (lines per inch) is relevant to your work.

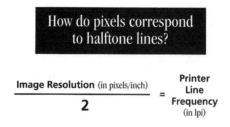

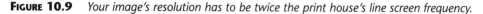

FIGURE 10.9   *Your image's resolution has to be twice the print house's line screen frequency.*

If a press house tells you that its line screen frequency is 100 lpi, then according to the formula in figure 10.9, you need to scan an image (or modify the resolution, using Photoshop's Image, Image Size command) at 200 samples (pixels) per inch. When you do this, your halftoned image will be optimal.

Now, toner dots from a laser printer are fused to the paper; the page is instantly dry. Such is not the case with offset printing, where *ink* is rolled onto paper. Ink bleeds, and very few press houses can hold a screen that contains 100% black. The area on the printed page would be a puddle of ink. On the bright side, there is a screen limit to the lowest density of the screen (the white point). Because 100% white has to meet the next darker value, the closer you keep the white point to your second brightest tone, the more even the print will look. Which leads us to figure 10.10.

FIGURE 10.10   *Print presses are wet, and laser prints are dry. Somehow, you need to change the tonal scheme of a print so that the print house's presses don't lay a puddle of ink on your work.*

When you've got your image balanced to your liking, make a copy of it, and perform some tone reduction so the press house can make plates from your work. Let's say that the pressman tells you that the presses can hold 10% (90% black) and 97% (3% white) on the top end of the tonal range.

Let's plug these values into the equation in figure 10.10:

$$256 - [90\times2.56] = 230.4 = \mathbf{25.6}$$

Great. What are you going to do with this 25.6 number? First, you're going to press Ctrl(⌘)+L in Photoshop to display the Levels command. Now, do you see the Output Levels area at the bottom? You type **25.6** in the left field.

Similarly:

$$256 - [3\times2.56] = 7.68 = \mathbf{248.32}$$

This is the number you type in the right Output Levels field. Click on OK, save the image, print a copy, and cart it off to the print house.

Now, there is a trade-off between the number of shades of gray that a laser printer can simulate and the line frequency of the print. This equation might not be of value in your work with a commercial printer, but it does serve as an introduction for personal printing—how to optimize that image you're going to send to your folks.

Lines/Inch versus Shades of Black

This section header sounds like a weird football game, doesn't it? Actually, you can do some fun stuff, and bring certain images up to print house specs if you understand the relationship between line screen frequency and the number of tones a printer can simulate, using digital halftone cells.

In figure 10.11 you can see the equation for determining shades of black at a given line screen frequency. We'll plug some numbers into the equation shortly.

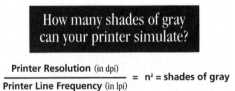

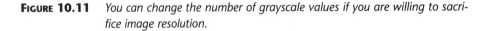

$$\frac{\text{Printer Resolution (in dpi)}}{\text{Printer Line Frequency (in lpi)}} = n^2 = \text{shades of gray}$$

Figure 10.11   *You can change the number of grayscale values if you are willing to sacrifice image resolution.*

Sometimes, you might want a special effect to enhance the visual content of a print. If you reduce the lines per inch the printer produces, you not only can get this effect, but also increase the number of shades the printer is capable of producing. You're not changing the resolution of the printer; you're simply playing with the input.

Let's say your printer is capable of 600 dpi; a PostScript printer will output about 85 lines per inch. So let's plug these numbers into the equation:

600 (dpi)/85 (lpi) = 7.06 (squared) = 49 unique shades

Now, 49 unique shades of black will probably not get you where you're going. Most grayscale images have almost 200 unique tones. Let's try lowering the line screen to 45 lpi (not a very high lpi resolution, but it's generally acceptable):

600 (dpi)/45 (lpi) = 13.33 (squared) = **196**

Whoa! Not bad! There will be practically no banding when you represent a continuous tone image at 45 lines per inch.

Hey, how else can you make personal "tack 'em on the corkboard" prints look super-special with limited resolution and money?

PCL Printing and Error Diffusion

Although the demands of PostScript printing are higher than those of non-PostScript printing, it would be nuts to ignore the alternatives to PostScript printing.

Hewlett-Packard has a very decent Resolution Enhancement Technology that belongs to the PCL (Printer Command Language) family of rendering methods. Every printer manufacturer has a different technology, but HP seems to hold the lead on high-fidelity, non-PostScript rendering.

In figure 10.12, the duck on the left was done using HP printing technology at 30 dpi, just to make the rendering technique visible to the eye. The results of the technology are not as elegant as PostScript printing, but the duck definitely has halftone shades across its body. The halftones are not really good enough to make a press screen from, but again, these prints are for you and your family and not for the world.

On the right of figure 10.12 is a duck rendered by using error-diffusion printing. Error-diffusion printing can be done from several applications other than Photoshop, or you can turn an image into an error-diffusion print by using Photoshop's Image, Mode, Bitmap—and then printing it as a normal image. Error-diffusion printing makes a soft, pleasing image using non-PostScript technology, but you absolutely *cannot* take one of these prints to a press house without getting laughed out the door! Error-diffusion prints are not rendered in lines, and they have no regard for digital halftone cells.

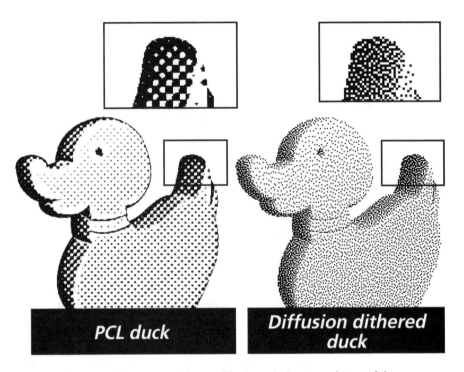

FIGURE 10.12   *Printer Command Language and error-diffusion printing are only two of the non-PostScript methods for making an interesting personal print.*

Mezzotints

A line of digital halftone cells is not the only way to represent continuous tones. Mezzotinting is not as refined a printing process as PostScript, and a mezzotint image is usually highly stylized—your attention can be torn between the visual content of the image and the way the print is executed, using lines, dots, and "worms" (more on this in a moment).

There's one newspaper in America that refuses to use halftoned photographs of anyone—pictures of financial moguls are done by using a mezzotint screen. Figure 10.13 is a cold-hearted parody of the newspaper, using a line-type mezzotint. As you can see, the screening process is quite visible, but you can make out the face of the gentleman, and the combination of the mezzotint and the visual content is quite aesthetically pleasing.

FIGURE 10.13   *Inflation actually has a positive effect on most pool toys.*

Stochastic (random) screening produces tiny shapes that look like worms, and the patterns are actually measured in worms per inch. Figure 10.14 shows a stochastic print. Stochastic printing is all computer-generated—print houses cannot duplicate a pattern that shifts according to the input brightness of an image at any given point. To the right of the stochastic duck is a line screen mezzotint that shows highlights going at one cut angle, with the deeper shades having a different line direction.

After this glowing review of other screening types, particularly mezzotints, I've got some good news and some bad news. The bad news is that Photoshop's Mezzotint filter (found under Filter, Pixelate) is miles from the quality effects and options Adobe's products are known for. You could not use Photoshop's Mezzotint filter to create the mezzotint effects shown in figures 10.13 and 10.14.

Figure 10.14   *If you do not mind a pattern competing for the visual content of an image, mezzotinting could be your ticket.*

The good news is that Andromeda Software offers a comprehensive assortment of mezzotint screens, over which you have complete control with respect to line frequency, angle, and so on. The Screens filters are available in demo format on the Companion CD (you can view, but not render, the mezzotints). They are available online for download at http://www.andromeda.com—all you need is a credit card and a fast Internet connection.

So far, we've spent a good amount of time on the fine points of printing, without much explanation of how to print from Photoshop. Allow me to correct this oversight...

Printing Options in Photoshop

There are two categories of output I'd like to cover—business output and commercial art—both of them under Photoshop's roof. First, printing from Photoshop is not as effortless as, say, printing from MS-Word. But then again, you're printing *art* from Photoshop, whereas you're printing formatted text from MS-Word—there's a chasm of sophistication you'd need to ford to bring the two applications' printing engines even remotely closer together.

Let's first look at the way Photoshop lets you know when the resolution of a file you want to print needs tuning.

The Image Size Command: A Career-Saver

Remember the "image dimensions decrease as resolution increases" line a few pages back? Well, Photoshop is a strict enforcer of correct image dimensions; it's a waste of paper to allow an image to be printed with clipping, all because the dimensions were not set up correctly.

In figure 10.15 you can see an image I want to print. Before printing it, however, I clicked on the Document Sizes area in the workspace, and a frame popped up to tell me that this image is going to print right off the edges of my paper.

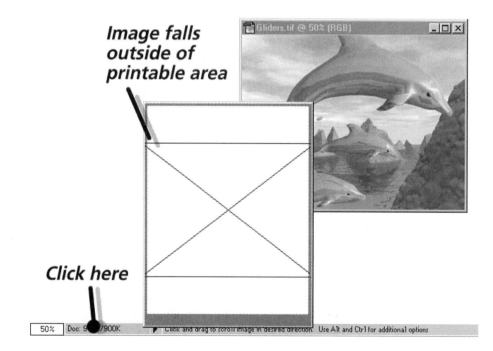

FIGURE 10.15   *Before printing, try to make it a practice to check the image frame. The large "x" shows the extent of the image, when printed at the current dimensions and resolution.*

In figure 10.16, I pressed Ctrl(⌘)+P—and to my surprise, I got my wrist slapped! Photoshop pops up a warning every time you try to print something that will run off the page.

Figure 10.16   *Choose to cancel printing if you get this warning.*

Now, there's a very easy solution to making this dolphin picture print, without your changing a pixel of the visual content. Photoshop is capable of resizing an image, but this means that you change the number of pixels, interpolation takes place, and you print a fuzzy image.

The solution lies in the first math formula in this chapter: If you increase the resolution of the image, you decrease the physical dimensions. Choose Image, Image Size to access the options for changing the resolution of the image.

What happens when you pour a quart of water into a 12-ounce glass? You get a spill, and this is sort of what happens when you decrease the dimensions of the image to the extent that the resolution is now far higher than your printer can print.

This is *okay*, though—the excess printing information is simply discarded during printing time, and you lose perhaps 15 seconds on a print job by doing this. But I feel it's better to waste a little print spooling time than to change the visual content of the image forever. Check out figure 10.17. Notice that I've decreased the dimensions so that the image will print to an 8½" by 11" page. And do *not* check the Resample Image box in the Image Size command.

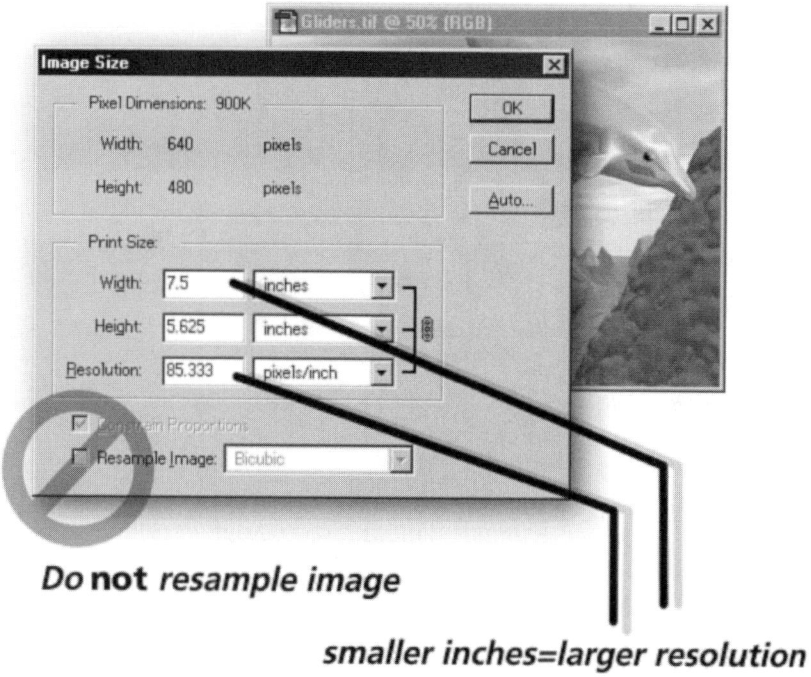

Do **not** *resample image*

smaller inches=larger resolution

FIGURE 10.17   *Increase the resolution so that the physical dimensions of the artwork will fit on a page.*

If you're printing to a PostScript device, you will want to choose File, Page Setup before you start printing. This is a fundamentals book, and therefore I can't go into every printing option—but how about the two most important ones?

In figure 10.18, you can see the Page Setup dialog box. You probably want to click on Screens after all of this chapter's talk about screening. It is from Screen that you get to pick the line frequency and angle, as well as the shape of the dots on the page. Also, you might want to enable Corner Crop Marks, because your art might not take up the whole page, and you might want to frame your work (so that it is centered in the frame).

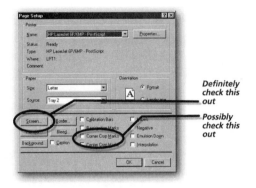

FIGURE 10.18 *You really might want to set only two options, unless you're an experienced imaging-type person.*

Let's take a look at what you'll see when you click on the Screen button. In figure 10.19, I make my recommendations for a 600 dpi PostScript printer. Eighty-five (85) lpi is correct for a 600 dpi printer, and the use of diagonal screens (such as 45°) has been a long-standing tradition among physical plate-making experts. It seems that when you run a diagonal screen, folks notice the individual dots of ink less. Try running a 90° screen on a print, and you'll see what I mean.

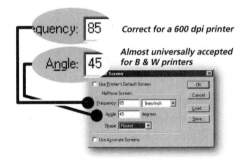

FIGURE 10.19 *The recommended settings for a 600 dip printer.*

Ah, at last we arrive at my favorite part of Photoshop imaging. It's called *film recording,* and might or might not even involve Photoshop, unless the service bureau you use owns Photoshop. Film recording is sort of the opposite process to scanning. With film recording, you're turning a digital image into a 35mm slide (or other film format). The results are breathtaking, and the steps you'll need to know are just around the corner.

Film Recording

Film recording from digital media is not a new process. If you hear a lot about it these days, that's simply because the price of film recorders has come down so much that if you've got two grand in your pocket, you could own a decent film recorder. Film recording has been fed by PowerPoint users for the past decade, but increasingly, fine artists have taken to putting images on a slide—the medium is eminently portable, and the colors are usually to die for!

Steps to Film Recording

Pick up the telephone book (or check out the Graphics Masters ad in the back of this book) and find a *slide service bureau*. Regular service bureaus do imagesetting work, set type, and do layouts, but the slide service bureau owns the expensive machinery that will turn your Photoshop work into a pocket-sized wonder. You can expect to pay around $8 per slide, and if you've got a lot of work, you might negotiate a discount. These service bureaus are also happy to take film negatives and write the info to film.

The first step to film recording your work is to make certain that the image has the correct *aspect ratio*. Fine; what's an aspect ratio? It's a proportion expressed by the relationship of one dimension of something compared to the other dimension—Width:Height is an aspect ratio. Your image is going from data on a disk to a 35mm slide, let's say. Chances are pretty good that your image does not have the 3:2 aspect ratio that belongs to a 35mm slide. And a service bureau is not responsible for adding a background or creatively cropping your image. You don't want anybody but you cropping your work, the service bureau doesn't exactly welcome a request for clairvoyance, and it's really very simple to whip your image into the proper aspect ratio.

To give you an example of the best way to discover how far off you are with the image, press Alt(Opt)+click on the Document Sizes area of the workspace, as shown in figure 10.20. My wind-up toy picture isn't even close to having a 3:2 aspect ratio.

In my opinion, the easiest way to get an image properly formatted is to add a background to both the horizontal and vertical aspects of the image. In figure 10.21, you can see the fail-safe method for picking out a background color that will not clash with the image. You press Alt(Opt) and click with the Eyedropper tool to pick up a background color that already exists in the image. Can you get more harmonious?

FIGURE 10.20   *It's your call as to how your image is turned into film. Try to make it easy on the service bureau by investing some time in getting the proportion the same as that on 35mm film.*

FIGURE 10.21   *Alt(Opt)+click over a neutral area of the image to set the background you'll soon create.*

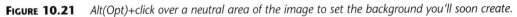

Let's pay another trip to the Image Size dialog box. This time, we are deliberately going to change the dimensions with absolutely no regard to the resulting resolution of the file. Why? Because film recorders don't care about image resolution—all that matters is image size, as measured in MB.

In figure 10.22, the Resample image box is unchecked, I've typed 1.7 (inches) in the Height field, and the Width field has changed to 2.2 (inches). This is good—it means that we can stop by the Canvas Size command and add to both the vertical and horizontal measurements of the image.

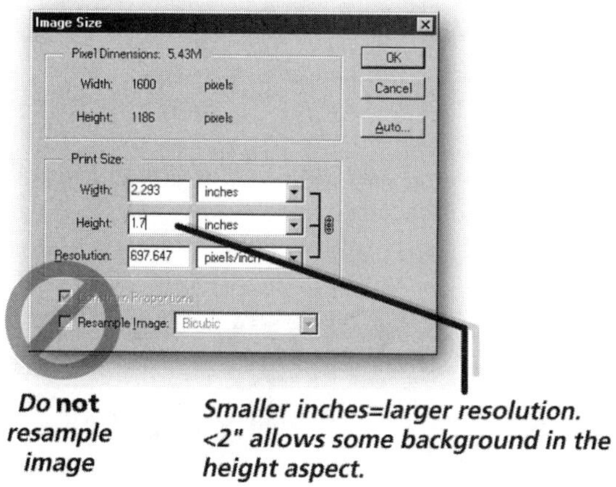

Do not resample image

Smaller inches=larger resolution. <2" allows some background in the height aspect.

Figure 10.22   *Keep the Width under 3 and the Height under 2, and then you can add background color to both aspects of the image.*

Now, choose Image, Canvas Size, and type **3** in the Width field and **2** in the Height field (see fig. 10.23). You've got a 3:2 image now! Click on OK.

In figure 10.24, you can see that I've add a little texture to the background areas of the image. You can do this, too, by filling the background area with a texture (you click with the Magic Wand tool, set to a Tolerance of 1 with no anti-aliasing, and then fill the area with a pattern—there are plenty of pattern tiles in the BOUTONS folder on the Companion CD).

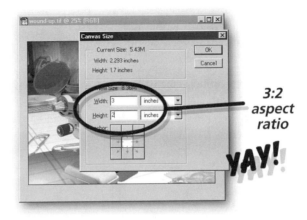

FIGURE 10.23   *The aspect of the image is now ideal for film recording, simply because you added background to the image.*

FIGURE 10.24   *Get the image onto a Zip disk and truck it on over to your slide service bureau.*

I never really mentioned what size is a good image size for film recording. I've had 900KB images written to slides, and the subject matter was simple enough that you never noticed the lack of image information. After experimenting for around a year with my slide service bureau, I've found that a 4.5MB image renders pretty well to film.

Here's a secret: Most RIPs (raster image processors— the software that enables a film recorder to render to film) will *interpolate* an image that is smaller than 18MB or so. This means that unless your image is 18MB, do *not* perform any interpolation yourself with Photoshop. Interpolation once is bad enough, but if it happens twice to your image before it's recorded, you might notice a resulting fuzzy 35mm slide.

PROFOUND WISDOM #23:

Aspect ratio follows an order: the first number is the width of the image, and the second is its height.

Perhaps I've been a little brisk with my explanations in this chapter about a few concrete measurements and proportions. Clearly, a 2:3 aspect ratio is not the same as a 3:2 ratio. And most service bureaus prefer that you give them a wider-than-tall image, because the film recorder that's writing the film, line by line, has fewer transverses to make if the image is wide.

Summary

Hopefully, you now know why I didn't call this chapter "Printing Essentials." There are more ways to get your data onto hard copy than you can shake a stick at. This chapter covered three methods: camera-ready for commercial printing, personal printing, and film recording. I'm sure that by the time this book comes out there will be a score of other output devices that'll make your work take its rightful place as art in the many fields that require graphics.

This chapter concludes the discussion of Photoshop as a lone entity. The rest of this book tells you about ImageReady, which ships with Photoshop version 5.5. If you have even the slightest interest in creating Web sites (is this like saying you have an interest in oxygen?), you're in for the lowdown on how to make Web pages sparkle.

PART IV

Introducing ImageReady

CHAPTER 11

Photoshop, Meet ImageReady—Click!

Photoshop has matured over the years from the world's favorite retouching application to the world's favorite design, retouching, and commercial pre-press software. And it's made this growth without sacrificing speed or ease of use—in fact, the program is easier to use than when it was a humble, four-disk installation program.

So what has happened in the past few years is that the World Wide Web has become a vacuum for artwork—everyone on Earth wants to see images, and those who don't are the *creators* of the images! And once again, Photoshop is the choice for designers who want the highest quality from the smallest dimensions and smallest number of colors in a picture.

Enter ImageReady

Today's WWW is more than images. It's interactive, it has spawned new media, such as animated GIFs, it has offered content creators truly slick interface conventions such as image maps and JavaScripts. It's replaced the corner coffee shop as the place to hang out! And Adobe realized that to make Photoshop ideal for the Web meant somehow adding a variety of media creation tools, but without estranging the installed base of users with a bloated version of Photoshop that tried to be everything to everyone. This folly can presently be seen with operating systems and a word processor with which I'm familiar <g>!

Nope, instead of trying to cobble monolithic plug-ins to extend Photoshop's capabilities, or adding more than a few lines of code, Photoshop is "Web Ready" through a sister program, ImageReady. ImageReady is the program I'll be discussing in the remainder of the book. To have an application geared for creating Web doodads is the best solution to keeping Photoshop fresh. Plus, you don't even have to use ImageReady, or conversely, you need not ever click on Photoshop's icon, because there is a lot of overlap between program features. Do you want to retouch a picture? Fine—launch Photoshop. But if you want to design navigation buttons and generate HTML code so that the buttons link to other documents on the Web—come a'clicking on ImageReady's door.

Profound Wisdom #24:

Cutting-edge technology displaces current technology, but current technology refuses to become legacy technology.

So the easiest thing for a programmer to do is to add code to applications—to make the software run slower, take up more hard disk space, and contain cutting-edge technology.

File Formats of the New Media

One of the slowest-growing segments of all this WWW jazz has been the types of files that are universally understood. Netscape (AOL) Navigator/Communicator and Microsoft Internet Explorer probably account for 98 percent of the browsing software that Internet surfers use. And yet, these browsers, going into a new millennium, still confine native graphics support to GIF and JPEG format images. The Portable Network Graphics (PNG) format is clearly a superior technology (no visual fidelity lost by copying, say, a TIFF image to this format) but is not yet supported by the two major browsers.

A big-time licensing disagreement between the holders of the GIF format's code and software vendors led to the creation of the PNG format—PNG is and always will be a royalty-free technology. In fact, Adobe, waiting for the day when Web browsers natively support PNG, currently offers PNG as a file format in ImageReady. But ImageReady is more ready than the browsers, I'm sad to say. Anything that is special—meaning something other than JPEG and GIF images—must be browsed by using a helper application for your browser, and it's inconvenient and takes up hard disk space when you get geared, for example, for a ShockWave piece of media you might encounter.

Actually, I see it as a challenge more than a hurdle to create Web pages that are interesting and small in download size. That's the name of the game: How small can you make the contents of your Web page (so visitors don't have to wait for your page to download) and still produce gems that everyone wants to see on the Web?

GIF and JPEG deserve more than a comparative list here; you're going to learn foresight while learning what it takes to be a Web designer in this chapter. We're going to begin slowly in this chapter, and merely concentrate on how to make small, beautiful images—*optimizing* an image, it's called—and we'll tackle the who, what, and where of the JPEG and GIF file formats in separate sections.

JPEG Optimized Images

Early on in the history of computer graphics, the Joint Photographers Experts Group (JPEG) saw the need for a way to show an image that would open or download with incredible speed, and yet be fairly large and very colorful. JPEG compression is called *lossy* compression, because some of the original image detail is lost when you save an image to the JPEG format. But the creators of JPEG technology are betting you won't really *notice* the information that is missing. JPEG performs its magic compression by averaging the hues in an image, while leaving the tones alone. The human eye is very sensitive to changes in tones, but is relatively insensitive to a 2 or 3 percent hue averaging, which in turn could offer a 10:1 compression ratio.

The JPEG file format's capability is 24-bit color (millions of colors), which is why a JPEG, when compared to an equivalent GIF file, looks much more realistic. There are pros and cons for both GIF and JPEG file formats. The following list describes the rewards and the caveats of the JPEG file format:

- **You can decide on the amount of compression used on a JPEG image.** Photoshop and ImageReady offer Low, Medium, and High quality (corresponding to high, medium, and low amounts of compression). ImageReady also offers a slider, from 1 to 100, so you can set exactly the amount of compression you want to use *on a copy* of your original image (don't *ever* save an original as a JPEG—you'll lose color information you'll never get back again). So, with status lines in ImageReady telling you the proposed saved size of a file, you can tweak the amount of compression to arrive at an ideal trade-off between quality and size. Most of my friends are using 28.8Kbps Internet speed, and I've found I can amply supply friends with all the visual information they need by sending a 50K e-mail attachment that takes five seconds to completely download.

- **There are JPEG bells and whistles that accompany the compression.** There are three different subformats to JPEG compression: Standard, Standard Optimized, and Progressive. Progressive is an interesting setting because a visitor to your site could immediately see the JPEG image in a crude state onscreen, and the JPEG image continues to build itself until it's finished. The only problem with progressive JPEGs is that if you save them, not all imaging applications are aware of the file structure, and will not open them. The difference between Standard and Optimized is that you achieve a little better compression and quality with Optimized, yet all of today's modern applications and today's Web browsers can read an Optimized image.

- **JPEG is very good at handling tons of different colors, and really rotten at handling the transition between colors**. Images are often referred to as high-frequency or low-frequency. The distinction lies in how steep a color transition there is between pixel and neighboring pixel. A photo of confetti being tossed would fall into the high-frequency category, and JPEG images, because they average unique tones, are utterly unsuited to handle the visual complexity of such a scene. However, when you take a picture of a beautiful sunset, with shades of gold flowing into each other and silhouettes of trees in the foreground—JPEG is your ticket to the best compression, because although there are many unique hues, the hues are within a small range of one another.

- **JPEGs cannot perform animation.** If you're looking for the famous GIF89a animation property, you will find it only in the GIF file format. JPEGs do not animate—it has to do with the interaction between the Web browser and a GIF image that contains multiple images. But you can certainly use JPEGs as JavaScript rollovers, which can appear to change in response to the user's cursor movements. JPEGs can also be used in Java applets (which are *nothing* like JavaScripting, and ImageReady does not perform Java applet construction), and as the background to a Web page.

Let's pick apart the GIF file format now.

GIF: Indexed Color and a Great User Challenge

First, I need to admit that I have this love-hate thing with GIF images. Why? Because they belong to a file format entirely different from TIFF, Targa, PSD (Photoshop's native format), and JPEGs. GIFs are indexed color images, which means that the largest number of individual colors you can pump into a GIF image is 256, as compared to the thousands if not millions of colors contained in other formats. So you really have to play a lot of tricks when you optimize an image to GIF indexed-color format to make the image look halfway decent.

The "love" part of my professional equation here is that you can create animations, using the GIF format. Let me run down the specific triumphs and shortcomings of working with GIF:

- **The GIF89a format is capable of animation in most Web browsers.** The GIF file format is not news; in fact, due to the beautiful color you could find nowhere else on a computer, this was the format of choice for pictures posted to BBSes in the early 1990s. The 89a subformat is more of a specification than a unique subformat—it's just that there have been many upgrades and modifications to the format by CompuServe over the years, and "89a" means it's both the most current version, and that it can contain multiple images in one single file.

Animation is achieved by creating individual images, and then using a compiler to create a single GIF89a file. The file will only animate in a Web browser, so don't go building these in ImageReady for desktop amusement! You'll learn how to create animations in chapter 12.

- **GIF images are small in file size**. From 256 colors down to 2, you can specify how many colors are contained in a GIF image. The smaller the number of colors, the more original image information is lost, but the faster the transmission time on the Web.

- **The Indexed File format for GIF images is designed for compactness.** Unlike "full color" (16.7 million, 24-bit color) images, GIFs use an index in the header of the file to shorthand which colors are located at which pixel. For example, if I told you that I want you to use the color Red: 233, Green: 125, and Blue: 11 every time you use this color, I'd say, "Use 14." I've saved a lot of words. A header in a GIF file contains the color palette for the image (often called a *color table* or a *lookup table*) that is a shorthand reference of every color in the image. The application that is reading the image into memory has to understand only that a specific color is tagged with a unique number once, and then the software can very quickly build the image. Figure 11.1 is an illustration of what the top of a GIF file would look like if it were a visual thing.

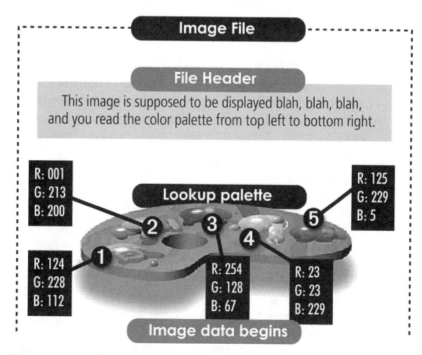

FIGURE 11.1   *Colors are not explicitly spelled out when software reads a GIF file. Instead, the software reads the color palette, and then "colors by the numbers."*

- **GIF optimization handles high-frequency images well and low-frequency images poorly.** GIF images simply do not have the color capacity to capture the true colors of confetti being thrown in the air, to use the JPEG example here. GIF images are good for handling sharp changes in color in an image, though, like a bunch of balloons in five different colors. GIF is also a poor choice for handling gradients, because gradients contain a smooth transition between two or more colors, and GIFs can't contain as many colors as are needed.

- **GIF images can contain one drop-out color.** We often refer to a GIF image that has one blank entry in its color palette as a *transparent GIF*. Transparent GIFs are useful when you want to place an image over a background that has many different colors. Buttons, especially round ones, are good candidates for the Transparency option in ImageReady.

- **GIF images can have three types of dithering applied to them to simulate the colors that are missing in the file.** *Dithering* means putting pixels or printer dots of different colors next to each other to visually simulate a missing color, when the image is seen from a distance of about 1.5 feet or more (about the distance between you and the monitor). ImageReady offers pattern, diffusion, and noise dithering to help the visual content of the image retain some of the original image's details. Additionally, ImageReady and Photoshop have a new plug-in called the Dither Box, where you can design your own dithering pattern and apply it to different selected areas in an image.

As I mentioned earlier, the only thing we'll pursue in this chapter is how to optimize an image for electronic transmission and viewing. Think of this chapter as how to make the best image of your first grandchild (or child) and send it to relatives all over the world as an e-mail attachment. Once in a while, I'll discuss Web implementations of features, but this chapter is all about "small is beautiful."

Let's begin in Photoshop, chanting the "detect before you correct" mantra. In other words, let's take a look at the visual content of the image before deciding on a file format, a compression ratio, a dithering type, or who we're going to e-mail this to.

note

You'll find the Dither Box under Filter, Other. I'm not going to get into how the Dither Box works because you already have enough options for dithering an image so that it looks nice. You have more important things to learn, and besides—Adobe's documentation on the Dither Box is fine.

Optimizing ImageReady

Like any new software, you're going to run into features that seem immediately useful, and others that you use only on April 17th. When you first bop into ImageReady, all 16 of the palettes are neatly arranged in front of you, and if you're running 640 by 480 monitor resolution, you will feel as though you'd be hard pressed to design a postage stamp in the area available for designing!

So we'll clear away those palettes that are not of immediate value, and then bring the image into ImageReady.

tip

To minimize a palette, double-click on its title bar. You can "roll down" the palette to its fun and functional size by double-clicking a second time.

Fine-Tuning ImageReady for E-mail Attachments

1. Launch Photoshop, and then open the Fall.tif image from the Examples/Chap11 folder on the Companion CD.

2. Click on the bottom, right icon on Photoshop's toolbox, as shown in figure 11.2. This launches ImageReady from within Photoshop. If you feel you want to conserve resources, in the future you might want to simply double-click on the ImageReady executable icon in the Photoshop 5 folder on your hard drive. Make no mistake; you now have two power-hungry applications loaded!

FIGURE 11.2 *ImageReady can be launched from Photoshop by clicking on the ImageReady icon or by pressing Ctrl(⌘)+Shift+M (in case your toolbox is underneath a palette or something).*

3. In ImageReady, you'll see the image you began with in Photoshop, and a bunch of grouped palettes, as shown if figure 11.3. My advise is to close the animation palette, the Layers palette, and the Color palette, and then stack your palettes to the right of the workspace.

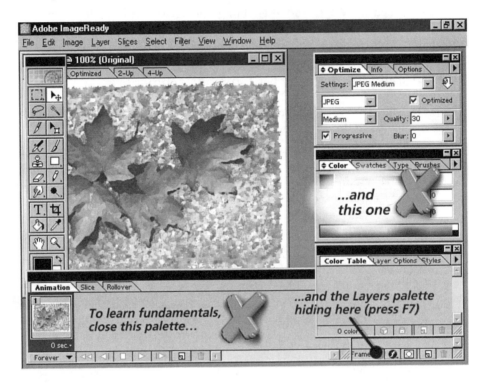

Figure 11.3 *You don't need animation to make an optimized e-mail attachment. You also don't need the Layers option, or a Color palette. All you need at your fingertips are palettes that contain optimizing features.*

4. There are five label callouts in figure 11.4. After each letter in the following list is an explanation of the purpose of what you did, or why something exists onscreen.

   a. **The 2-Up** view of the image in the window. I've found this view to be the most useful because I can see how changing color depth, compression, and so on affects the finished image and compares it to the original. You can use the Hand tool (or hold the Spacebar) in either of the panes to scroll the image view, and you can edit (use paint, make selections) in the Original window only. So click on the 2-Up tab now.

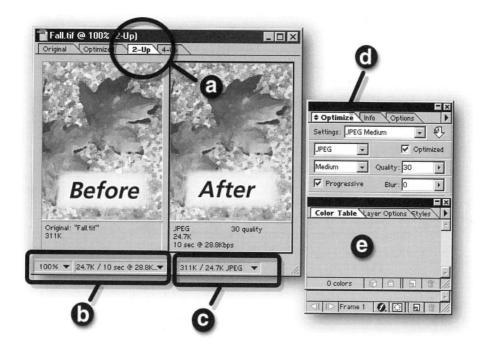

FIGURE 11.4 *Follow the callouts and you will be home free, as far as optimization goes.*

b. **The Document Sizes** areas on the image window can tell you two things at once when you are using a 2-Up view. I've dragged on the drop-down list you see highlighted, and I've chosen Optimized file size over how long it will take to download the image at 28.8Kbps. You are free to choose from the other options on the drop-down list.

c. **The Document Sizes** area called out here is the second info area, which you can set to an entirely new set of parameters. For example, here I've chosen to show the original size of the document compared to the compressed size.

d. **The Optimize palette** enables you to choose the file format for a saved copy of your work. Besides file type, there are compression amounts, dithering options, and every field you need to have total control over the optimization process. Choose JPEG Medium from the Settings drop-down list now, and take a look at the Optimized pane in the image window. It doesn't look too bad, does it? This is because the JPEG format is very good at displaying a lot of different colors whose hue is not dramatically different from the next hue—which is sort of what the pavement behind the leaves suggests.

e. **The Color Table palette** is simply a point of interest on your tour here. If you were making a GIF image, the Color Table would list all the colors in the optimized image in the form of a color swatch. But because JPEG is not a color table–format image type, the Color Table palette is currently blank.

5. Close the image without saving it in ImageReady. Use Finder (Macintosh) to display Photoshop and close it without saving the image. Windows users can cool switch (Alt+Tab) to Photoshop and press Ctrl+F4 without saving changes to Fall.tif. There's no point in having Photoshop running and gobbling up resources when our concentration is on ImageReady. Keep ImageReady open.

Because you'll be doing so much palette switching as you proceed, here's a cheat sheet of what the F keys do in ImageReady. Many of the palettes the F keys display are consistent between Photoshop and Image Ready.

note

Always watch the screen as you use the toolbox button to toggle from Photoshop to ImageReady and back again. If you want changes saved, click on the appropriate button in the dialog box. You see, both programs are accessing the same image file data, but only one at a time is writing saved changes from memory to disk.

And it would be bad if you wrote to disk from one application without saving changes from the other program, which is holding the image in memory (RAM).

Key	Function in ImageReady
F1	Help
F2	Open
F3	Open
F4	Open
F5	Brushes palette (same as in Photoshop)
F6	Color palette (same as in Photoshop)
F7	Layers palette (same as in Photoshop)
F8	Info Palette (same as in Photoshop)
F9	Actions palette (same as in Photoshop)
F10	Optimize palette (an important shortcut)
F11	Animation
F12	Open

Exploring the Optimize Palette

The Optimize palette is about as important in ImageReady as the Layers palette or Levels command are in Photoshop. You'll find that you access the Optimize palette frequently. So I thought we'd fine-tooth comb the palette in both JPEG and GIF modes to come to an understanding of what all the fields do. Believe me, if you understand this stuff, you have enormous imaging power behind you. And believe me, at first I, too, was intimidated when I looked at the palette—it looked like a 747 cockpit or something!

Figure 11.5 shows the same palette in two different modes. The color palette you see in this figure pops up whenever you click on the down arrow to the right of the Matte field.

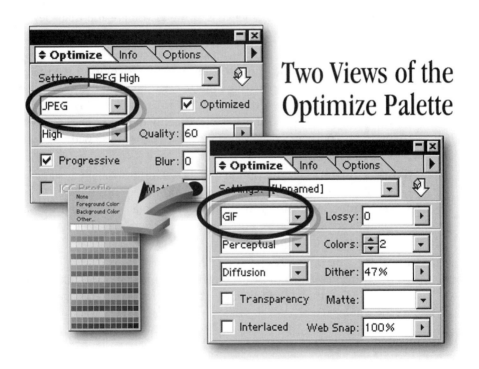

FIGURE 11.5 *Let's cover the options on the Optimize palette.*

Let's tackle the Optimize palette's JPEG mode first—it has fewer options:

- **The Settings drop-down list** enables you to choose High, Medium, or Low JPEG compression for the current image. You can manually tune the amount of compression, using the Quality field and slider. When you do this, the JPEG

Settings field turns to [unnamed]. You can save the current setting by naming it. To do this, you click on the flyout triangle (at the top right of the palette), and choose Save Setting from the menu.

- **The Optimized check box** determines whether the resulting JPEG file is as small as it can be, with the highest quality. In other software applications, the opposite of Optimized is usually called Standard. I think you want this box checked every time you create a JPEG image.

- **The Progressive check box** should only be used if your audience is hip to the latest enhancement for Web-destined images. A Progressive JPEG begins downloading immediately to a Web visitor's monitor, and gradually completes itself. This behavior of downloading first components first and gradually building to completion is often called *streaming data*. Only use the Progressive option if you know that your audience is as hip as you are and that they own equally hip, cutting-edge viewing software.

- **The Blur field** can blur an image as it is converted to JPEG. You see, JPEG images sometimes have *artifacts* (unwanted pixel colors in the image), especially where edges of objects in the image exist. Blurring the image solves the artifact problem, but then it causes a blurring problem. My advice? Use higher compression amounts. The JPEG file is going to be a little larger than necessary, but then you won't need blurring at all. High-quality settings equal very few image artifacts.

- **ICC Profile.** Leave this option unchecked, unless you understand what an ICC profile is. (And I have not covered ICC profiles in this book.) ICC profiles are a standardization method to ensure color accuracy from device to device—and chances are good that you do not yet need to collect different profiles from service bureaus and print shops.

- **Matte.** This option is a pop-up of Web colors (colors that do not display dithering when viewed in Netscape or Microsoft browsers) and other colors that will surround your image if the image is on a layer, and the image does not take up the whole layer.

It's time to take a look at the GIF palette now.

The GIF Optimize Palette

Like the JPEG optimization options, the GIF options give you many ways to produce dramatic changes when you create a GIF copy of your artwork. Here are the options on the Optimize palette:

- The **Settings** drop-down list offers a number of maximum colors for the artwork at hand, and offers the colors in a dithered or nondithered arrangement.

Hint: Don't create GIF artwork without dithering the visual information. You'll see hard edges and banding all over your creation. Like the JPEG options, you can save a specific set of options you choose on the palette by accessing the fly-out menu, choosing Save Settings, and then naming your custom blend.

- The **Lossy field** is offered to enable you to control the amount of dithering that takes place in an image. This is a truly nice feature because up until 1999, we designers had only a dither/no dither option with GIFs. You can pick a little or a lot of dithering with this control.

- **Perceptual, Selective, Adaptive, Web, et al.** When an image is dithered down to 256 colors or less, you sort of have to decide which colors go, which colors are changed to simulate a broader palette in the image, and which colors are cast away. This drop-down contains seven options, four of which I will cover. I see no need for you to dither to a system palette or a custom palette (since no one has made this request of you <g>)!

A **Perceptual palette** is created from colors that the human eye can detect most readily. In other words, the human eye is very sensitive to greens and the least discriminating about hues of red. Therefore, when an image is dithered using the Perceptual mode, you're going to see more pure shades of green, and more dithered shades of red and magenta in the image. A picture of outdoors is ideal for Perceptual dithering, while this mode would be dreadful to show off a lipstick collection in a photo.

Selective palette is the default mode for dithering GIF images. It is similar to the Perceptual palette in that it retains color fidelity in image areas where there are colors to which the eye is most sensitive. But at every opportunity, Selective mode will change existing colors to Web colors (see following explanation), so dithering is minimized. Web colors do not dither.

Adaptive palette creates a color palette that is most in synch with the frequency of specific colors in the image. For example, a picture of a blue sky with clouds would be dithered down to an adaptive palette primarily consisting of blues, whites, and neutral tones. There would be no greens, reds, or other colors not found in the image in this palette.

The **Web palette** is a collection of 216 predefined colors that are common to Windows, the Mac OS, and UNIX operating systems. You might not have a need for this palette when you already have a photograph to be dithered. The reason? Unlike the other methods of dithering, the Web palette is always *fixed*—you can't add custom colors like those offered by the other color palettes. And that means more dithering than you might need. The only good thing about the Web palette is that if you use it while painting an image, your audience out there that is running only 256 colors on their monitors will see no dithering. This is more important than it might sound at first. A lot of government agencies and enterprises don't just pass out 12MB video cards! You might miss your target if your image is not optimized for 256 colors using the Web palette's 216 colors (40 colors are reserved in the Web palette to be used by the Web browser's interface—you can't use them).

- **Dithering.** There are three types of dithering (plus a no dither option) when you build a GIF image. **Diffusion dithering** is also called *error diffusion* in the trade. Colors are shifted to neighboring "slots" in the weave of your pixel image until the error of the color versus the original color is less than 50%. It's sort of a musical chairs type of dithering, and the result is a soft, diffuse image that occasionally has erroneous pixels rendered outside of objects in the image. **Pattern dithering** can come in handy when you're using a minimum of colors in the image's palette, but this type of dithering is less than wonderful when it's applied to images with small dimensions, because the pattern graphically overwhelms the visual content of the image. Again, we'll run an example a little later that involves pattern dithering. **Noise dithering** is something new to Adobe offerings. Noise dithering scatters pixel colors around like diffusion dithering does, but it produces a cleaner image than diffusion, for some reason.

- **Lossy**. This control determines how many original colors are knocked out of the GIF image. At high settings, there will be fewer original colors in the image, but the image will be very small in saved file size.

- **Colors.** Pick a number between 2 and 256, and watch as the right panel in the image window displays a picture using the requested number of colors. The more colors you allow, the larger the file size of the image will be.

- **Dither**. This is where you get to pick the amount of dithering that is applied to the image. There is a relationship between number of colors, type of dithering, and amount of dithering. For the best images, use higher amounts of dithering when an image has a broad spectrum of colors (or better yet, use the JPEG setting), and a smaller amount of dithering when you have a monochrome-type image, such as a sunset.

- **Transparency.** This check box is relevant only when the image in ImageReady is on a layer, and some of the layer is clear. If this is the case, ImageReady will assign a color to the transparency that Web browsers will read as, "No content here. It's blank, transparent."

- **Interlace.** I'd leave this option on always. Interlacing is the GIF file format's method of sending streaming data. The interlaced image begins to appear immediately in a Web browser, and eventually completes itself, given time.

- **Web Snap.** This option "snaps" colors that are in the dithered GIF image to the closest colors it can find that match the Web palette. This can be a useful option when you want to accommodate visitors who are running 24-bit color (millions of colors), as well as those who can only receive 8-bit, 256 colors. You decide how aggressively you want the colors in your image to snap to their closest mates on the Web palette by increasing the percentage in the Web Snap field.

Whew! I think we've covered the most important palette in ImageReady fairly thoroughly, and this means we can now have *fun* with what you've learned. Next section, please!

The Best and the Worst GIF Images

The steps that follow aren't really leading to a finished masterpiece. All we are doing in this chapter is experimenting, and seeing qualitative differences that result from applying different options to an image. Our goal is to seek out and use the options that will make the Fall.tif image look its best at its smallest file size in a different file format. In the following steps, you'll be guided to the best image quality/file size image, and also to a very poor choice of options (and image) when one doesn't play detective with an image before modifying it.

Here's how to put what you've learned so far to good—and bad—use:

Fine-Tuning a GIF Image

1. With the Fall.tif image in ImageReady's workspace, choose GIF 128 dithered from the Settings drop-down list on the Optimize palette. Make sure that you are in 2-Up view of the image, and that file size and download time are the Document Sizes options.

2. Hmmm. The image is composed of mostly peach-colored stone behind green leaves (which have some minor hue variation). Choose Selective from the drop-down list, and take a look at the before and after panes in the image window. There should not be a perceptual difference in the two views at this point.

3. Choose Noise as the dither type, and wait while the preview side of the image window updates the image. Harsh areas seem to be removed, and I believe that we can now be a little more adventurous concerning the number of colors in this image.

4. Choose 64 from the Colors drop-down list. I believe you will begin to see harsh areas appear in the GIF version of the image. So turn up the dithering to about 90%, as shown in figure 11.6. Note that what is a 311K image in its original state can now be a 54K image (a very nice size for an e-mail attachment), while the GIF still represents the original image with really nice fidelity.

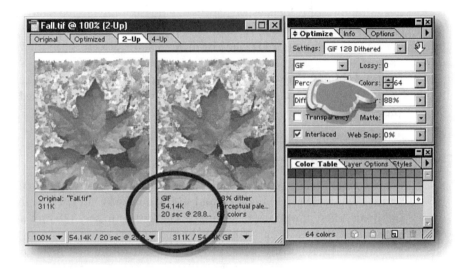

FIGURE 11.6   *A GIF image can be tuned so that its contents closely mimic the original detail of the scene.*

5. Keep the image open. We're going to try the dumb and futile way of optimizing the same image next.

The Web Palette's Inadequacy

I realize that it was a tough call to make when Netscape originally designed the "Web-safe" (no dithering at an 8-bit, 256 color view) palette. To create such a palette is sort of like trying to be everything to everyone. The Web palette is optimized for warm colors, actually, with an emphasis on flesh tones (so photos of people don't look disgusting).

There will be a time when you will have to make the decision, "Do I go with a lot of dithering and the Web palette, or remain quite faithful to the original image's colors by creating a custom palette, such as the Adaptive, Selective, and Perceptual modes offer?"

Here's a real quick example of swimming uphill, just so you can avoid the hard way around things in the future:

Creating a Web Palette Image, Using the Wrong Type of Image

1. Choose GIF Web Palette from the Settings drop-down list. You'll notice that there is severe inaccuracy in the proposed GIF image in the right 2-Up pane in the image window. But ImageReady did choose 32 of the closest matches from the image, based on a Web palette. The dot in the center of a color swatch indicates that the swatch is a Web color.

2. Let's try to soften the image. The default setting for dithering when GIF Web Palette is chosen is None—go figure. Choose Noise, as shown in figure 11.7, and see if this doesn't help the image. As you can see, it does—but not by much. The Web palette simply doesn't have many colors in common with the image, and this is one of the problems with a fixed palette. Your operating system's system colors and the Web palette are all fixed palettes.

FIGURE 11.7 *The Web palette can be useful when you're defining colors, but the Web colors don't always come close to existing colors in an image.*

3. You can close this image at any time now without saving it.

You also should know that one option you did not play with in the vain attempt to rescue this image from the Web palette would not have worked. The Web Snap slider is completely dysfunctional when the Web palette has been chosen because ImageReady presumes that all colors are already Web colors, and no snapping is required. Use the Web Snap option when you're using a flexible palette, such as Adaptive, Selective, and Perceptual.

Experimenting with Low-Frequency Images

We've been working with a high-frequency image here for so long, that I've forgotten about low-frequency images! You most certainly will encounter or produce low-frequency images if you decide to have a career in Web building. Why? Because all those 3D buttons out there on the Web are low-frequency images—the metallic or plastic sheen on these illustrations make gradual transitions between tones (which suggests already that JPEG might be a good format for buttons).

In the Examples\Chap11 folder on the Companion CD is the file Button.tif. To keep the experiments here simple, there are no predominant colors in the image, although the image is in RGB Color mode—only tones of black make up this button.

Let's use our guesstimation powers and simply experiment to see what the best settings for a monochrome, low-frequency image might be:

Using Different Palettes on an Image

1. Open the Button.tif image from the Examples/Chap11 folder on the Companion CD, and make sure you have the 2-Up view of the image window.

2. Choose JPEG High from the Settings drop-down list, and take a look at the optimized image, as shown in figure 11.8. You've done nothing to manually optimize the image, and yet it looks essentially the same as a 3K JPEG image as it does as a 28K original image.

3. Now let's see how the GIF format can handle the Button.tif image. Choose GIF 64 No Dithering from the Settings drop-down list. The button looks okay because the human eye has a tough time distinguishing between 64 different shades of black. But then again, this image is 1K larger than the JPEG. Try typing 16 in the Colors field, press Enter (Return), and see what happens. The saved file size is smaller than the JPEG equivalent, but who would want to save this image? Clearly, as you can see in figure 11.9, the eye can distinguish between 16 shades, because an effect called banding is obvious.

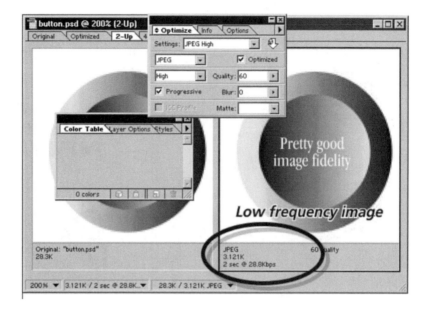

FIGURE 11.8   *Low-frequency images reproduce fairly well as JPEG equivalents.*

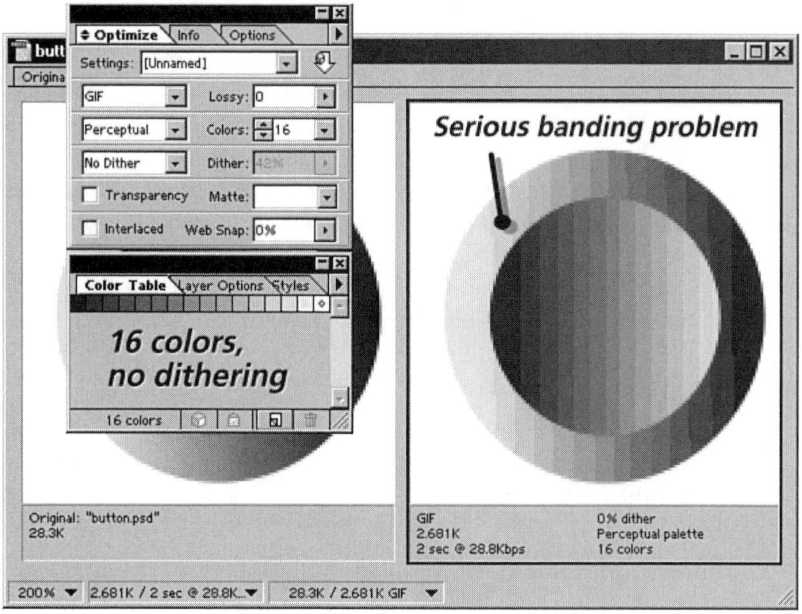

FIGURE 11.9   *Banding is the result of failing to dither an image, when the color sampling is very small for the image.*

4. Choose GIF Web Palette from the Settings list, and choose Diffusion dithering. As
    you can see in figure 11.10, diffusion dithering has virtually no effect on the
    harsh banding that is caused by using a fixed palette on a continuous-tone image.

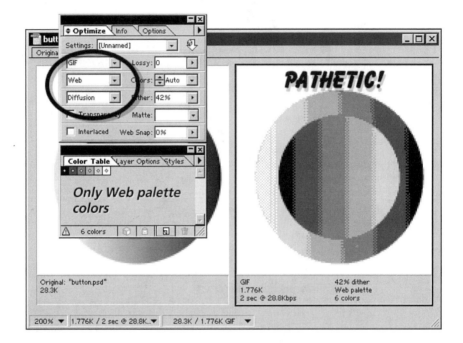

FIGURE 11.10 *The Web palette has a very limited facility for providing shades of neutral
color to an image. As you can see, there are only six color matches, and the
button looks hideous because of the inability to match the tones.*

5. Try Pattern as the dither type, as shown in figure 11.11. You'll see a dramatic
    improvement, as ImageReady is able to weave an acceptable but not totally pro-
    fessional simulation of a gradient fill, using only six colors. Yeesh—my first box
    of Crayolas was more robust!

6. Try out the Noise option and hold onto your seat. As you can see in figure 11.12,
    there is a dramatic difference in image quality when you allow ImageReady to
    dither the button image using noise. And to top it off, the image is 1.5K smaller
    than the JPEG image.

    I'll share something with you here. You could go back and decrease the quality
    of the JPEG image so it would be smaller than this noisy button right now. But
    the JPEG version would start to show artifacts around the edges, where differ-
    ent tones meet, and the resulting button would look as though file corruption

had happened. It's your choice as to whether you want a corrupted-looking image, or one that has kind of pleasant-looking noise going on. All image optimization is a trade-off between "How low can you go?" in saved file size, and how good the image looks. Me? I don't spend a lot of time looking at the design of buttons on the Web, so a noisy button might just sneak past me. And you. And your audience.

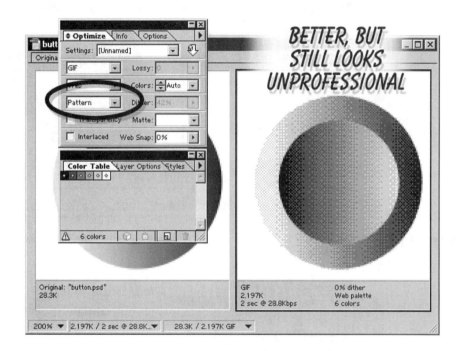

FIGURE 11.11 *Pattern dithering can sometimes provide the simulation of a lot more colors than actually exist in a palette. You simply have to pick an image whose visual content is very simple and can be overrun by the pattern's strong visual effect.*

7. Just for kicks, type 16 in the Colors field, and use Perceptual as the palette type here. You'll see, as shown in figure 11.13, that the combination of 16 specially sought-out colors in combination with the Noise dithering offers an image that is the same file size as the JPEG we started with, but is in many ways smoother and more pleasing to look at.

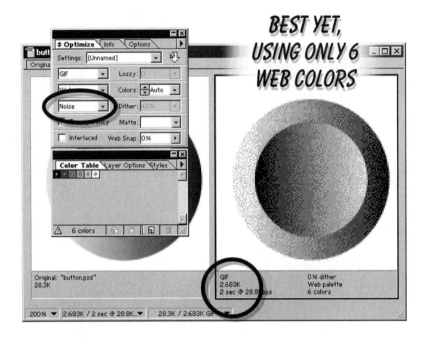

FIGURE 11.12 *Using six colors and noise presents a fairly decent interpretation of the original button file.*

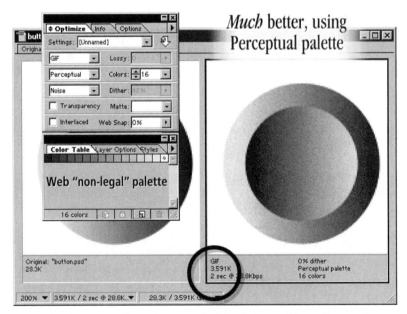

FIGURE 11.13 *Limited colors can still produce wonderful minimasterpieces if you allow ImageReady to select the right colors for you.*

8. You can close the image now without saving it.

What I've attempted to show you here is that, through experimentation, you can be happily surprised by how small an image you can make that still has a semblance of the original image. And that's the goal on the Web.

In the following section, I'll show you how "minimalist art," when done with a computer, can carve a niche on a Web site.

Bitmap Color Mode and ImageReady

Adobe has given the term *bitmap* to a color mode within the program—at any given pixel, the light's turned on (white) or it's turned off (black). Technically, Adobe is correct in this nomenclature—a bitmap, strictly defined, is a map of bits of information. But we use the term *bitmap* to describe *all sorts* of pixel-based images, so things can get a little confusing here. For the following discussions, when I use the term bitmap, I mean an image with a color capacity of exactly two unique colors.

Do you think nothing creative can be done by using only two colors? How about a pencil or ink sketch? Better yet, how about the error diffusion and the pattern diffusion images in figure 11.14? Don't they simulate the tones of the original image (at left) pretty well?

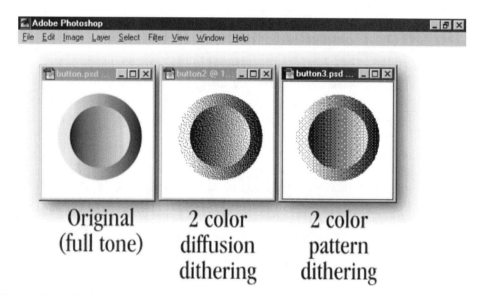

FIGURE 11.14   *Limited colors don't equal limited design possibilities. It's all in where you place those pixels!*

Creating a Two-Tone Pawn

A friend of mine (whom I've already mentioned in this book, so I need not bother a second time <g>) is one of the best hosts on the Web. His site is tuned so tightly for speed that it almost squeaks. One of the things he likes to do is reduce images to two colors: the background color of the site (so all images appear to float against the background) and a harmonious foreground color with which images are written through dithering filters.

Pawn.tif is in the Examples/Chap11 folder on the Companion CD, and it's a very pretty rendered model of a gold chess piece. Now, if I were to ask you which is more important about the image: the coloration and surface texture of the pawn, or the outline of the pawn, I think you'd agree that the *outline,* the profile of the pawn, is what makes it distinguishable as a chess piece, and that the shading is of secondary importance.

Perfect!

We have an image whose content can be reduced (color-wise) to the bare minimum, and we can still convey the artistic message of a pawn sitting on a lonely square perch.

Here's how to dive right into the action with what you've learned so far, and create a *reallllllly* small image file of the pawn:

Forget About Colors and Concentrate on the Shape

1. Open the Pawn.tif image from the Examples/Chap11 folder on the Companion CD, and make sure you have the 2-Up view going on with the image window.

2. On the Optimize palette, choose GIF as the file format, choose Selective as the palette type, type 2 in the Colors field, and choose Pattern as the dither type. What you'll see in a moment is a fairly ugly brown pawn, dithered against a white background, as hinted at in figure 11.15. The ugly shoe-brown of the pawn can be changed—what you've witnessed is how intelligently ImageReady boiled the 7,000 (yes, 7,000) different shades of gold down to one, and left the white background as white (which we'll change, too).

> **note**
>
> The Color Table palette has two colors on it, as shown in figure 11.15. The white has a diamond in its center because it is a "legal" Web color, whereas the custom brown color does not have the Web seal of approval.

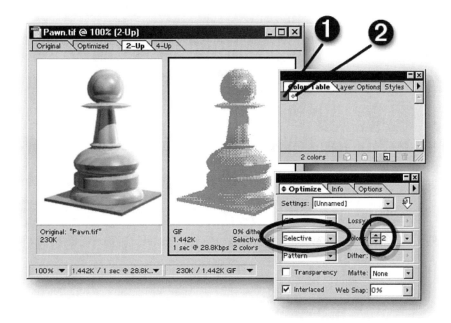

FIGURE 11.15 *The pawn still gives the immediately recognizable shape of a pawn, but you've gone from 230K to less than 1.5K by choosing the right number of colors and the right palette.*

3. Double-click on the brown swatch on the Color Table palette. This displays the Color Picker. Now click on the Use Web Colors checkbox. The Color Picker will display a smaller number of colors, all delimited with a hard edge.

4. Click on the orange sliver on the hue strip in the Color Picker, and then click on a warm brown. As you can see in figure 11.16, I've chosen 663300 (this is the hexadecimal name for the Web color, and it's used in HTML language to specify a color on the Web). You can type this number in the number field if you like (saving a little searching on the Color Picker) and then press Tab and click on OK to return to a new brown-shaded pawn against white.

5. Double-click on the white swatch on the Color Table palette, as shown in figure 11.17, and then pick a pale cream color (FFFF99 is good) for the background color. Select it, and then click on OK to return to the artwork.

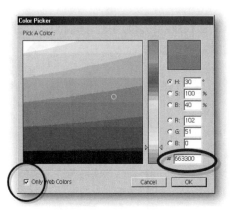

Figure 11.16   *Pick a background color other than the default white. But make it a light shade that will not fight with the existing brown foreground color.*

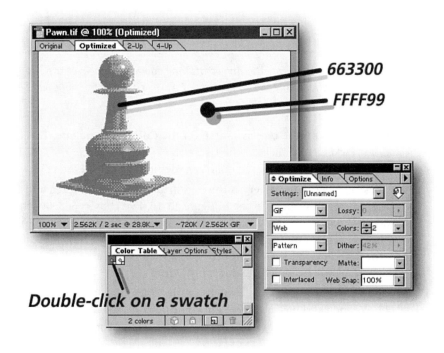

Figure 11.17   *Choose new colors for existing ones in your image by double-clicking on the Color Table palette's swatches.*

6. Choose File, Save Optimized As, and then save the optimized image as Pawn.gif (GIF is the only file format available in the Save dialog box) in a location where you can immediately retrieve it.

7. Close the original Pawn.tif image without saving changes, and load Pawn.gif into ImageReady's workspace. I'm going to show you something.

Here's something that ought to be a Profound Wisdom: Once you start changing colors and color modes, it's next to impossible to return to a previously saved state (after the file is closed) because pixel-based images have change created upon change upon change, and there's no real path back home. It's like shuffling cards twice. Do you think the chances are good that the cards will return to their original order if you shuffle them twice more? If you do, I'd *really* like to play cards with you.

Nope. It's usually best to go back to an original picture, add or subtract whatever elements you need to complete the picture, and then optimize the image again. But—and this is a huge "but"—I'm going to show you how to use ImageReady's powers to add text to that pawn image you saved without introducing extra colors, forcing anti-aliasing, or anything. It's not so much a trick as it is the power of an extremely flexible application.

Adding Text to a Two-Tone Image

I've got a headline waiting for this pawn graphic. The only problem is that the text is in RGB color mode, and it's black on white, so it won't really blend into the Pawn.gif graphic.

Wait a second. You can do anything you *want* with ImageReady! Here are the steps to prove it!

Adding an Element to an Indexed Color Image

1. Open the PawnText.tif image from the Examples/Chap11 folder on the Companion CD. There's a good reason this text is not anti-aliased. We want to add it to a different image without changing the number of colors in the image. Anti-aliased text is actually made up of a number of different shades of color.

2. Press F7 to bring the Layers palette to the screen. Tip: ImageReady sees an image as a layered image whether it was saved that way in Photoshop or not. In other words, the Background layer in images is not acknowledged by ImageReady. So don't panic.

3. Click on the Pawn.gif title bar to make it the current image, then click on the Original tab. Click on the PawnText.tif image's title bar, and then drag Layer 1 title on the Layers palette into the Pawn.gif Original image window.

4. Choose Multiply as the Layers palette's mode for the new layer. Now you've got black text against the pale background color in the image. With the Move tool, move the text into position, as shown in figure 11.18, and then click on the Optimized tab to see what the text will look like against the pawn image.

FIGURE 11.18   *You can't edit in the Optimized window pane, but you can do everything you do in Photoshop in ImageReady's Original pane.*

5. The Optimize palette has been traumatized by our swift editing, and you need to respecify some of the settings. The palette should be Selective, the number of colors should be 2, and the type of dithering should be Pattern. Make these changes and then save the file as Pawn.gif, overwriting the original image. You can close the image, and close PawnText.tif, too, at any time now.

You've probably noticed that working with only one palette, the Optimize palette, you have a lot of features, and also a lot to remember about what you've done to a copy of an image. Want to simplify your life? That's what computers were intended for, and what the next section is all about.

What Was That? A Droplet?

Playing off the popularity of Photoshop's Actions palette comes ImageReady's Droplets. Droplets are easy to use and easy to save. A *droplet* is a group of optimization settings you've made, bundled into an executable file. When you have a dozen images that need optimizing in the same way, you don't have to take notes beforehand; you merely save the settings as a droplet, and then drag and drop the images on top of the droplet.

Here's how it works:

Drag and Dropletting

1. Open the G-Clef.tif image from the Examples/Chap11 folder on the Companion CD.

2. Now, perform a simple modification to the image. Converting it to medium-quality JPEG is enough for this example.

3. Windows users: You're going to have to click on the Restore/Maximize button so you can see the desktop. Macintosh users don't have an ImageReady workspace background, so you don't need to pay attention to the preceding. Click on the Droplet creation icon, and then drag onto the desktop, as shown in figure 11.19.

4. Pick a file, any file, from your hard disk, and drop it onto the droplet, as shown in figure 11.20.

5. ImageReady launches, and a processing status line appears, as shown in figure 11.21. When the image(s) have been processed, ImageReady (unfortunately) does not close, so you need to close it when you're finished. Better yet, launch ImageReady, minimize it, drop a ton on images on your droplet, and then simply close the minimized ImageReady when you're finished.

Because both the Mac OS and Windows 95/98/2000/etc. support long file names, Adobe engineers have ingeniously created long name labels for the droplet icons. There's not much chance of accidentally dropping an image on the wrong droplet. And if you do, it's no big deal because droplets perform changes on *copies* of your work, and never on the originals.

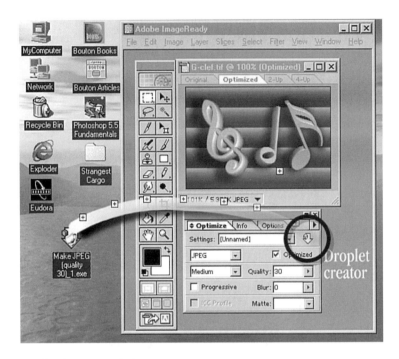

FIGURE 11.19   *Drag a droplet to your desktop.*

Drag and drop an image from the desktop or a folder to the droplet

FIGURE 11.20   *You can drag a file onto the droplet on your desktop, or even move or copy the droplet to a folder and use it from there.*

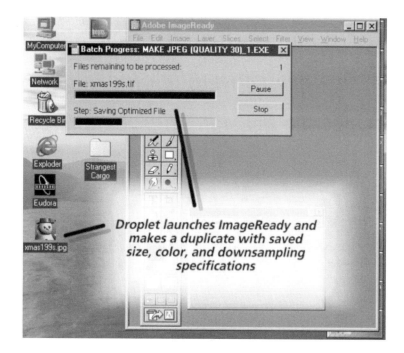

FIGURE 11.21 *When ImageReady launches, the Batch Progress dialog box shows the status of the images being processed.*

Summary

I kid around a lot (not obvious, huh?) but I have to truthfully say that I'm excited about ImageReady. This program has many of the features of Photoshop, but more important, it has features Photoshop lacks, and it does these tasks so well it's almost disgusting. You've just been introduced to a fraction of ImageReady, but it's the fraction that'll make the rest of the stuff make sense. In chapter 12, we're going to dive right into GIF animation; how it's done, what your options are, and how the Actions palette in ImageReady can guide you on your way to becoming Master Animated GIF Creator!

CHAPTER 12

Creating GIF Animations

A discovery that surprised everyone a few years ago was that the combination of Netscape Navigator 2.0 and a GIF file that contained multiple images would play an animation when loaded in the browser. Microsoft (which is no one's fool) quickly emulated the technology, and it wasn't long before GIF animation kits were being offered all over the Internet.

The Technology Shouldn't Be More Sophisticated Than Your Idea

One of the perks to owning ImageReady as a sidekick to your Photoshop purchase is that Adobe makes it simple to create GIF animations. And at the same time, you have more control and options for the animated GIF than you will probably ever need. I'll point out all the features of ImageReady's Animation palette, but because a lot of the palette is self-explanatory, my primary emphasis will be on *concept*—the idea behind the animation. It's all too easy to use Adobe's wonderful technology to produce an uninspiring piece.

You'll create four different types of animations in this chapter, each with its own reason for being. To a certain extent, all animations on the Web, especially banners, have but one purpose—to catch your eye. But you need to follow through! Once my attention is there, what are you going to tell me? Now *that's* a working framework of a concept.

Three Different Approaches to GIF Animation

Here's a working list of some of the qualities you *do* want to include in your animation:

- **The animation has to be short in time, small in dimensions, and contain a minimum of colors.** There's nothing more depressing for the creator, and nothing quite as irritating for the viewer, as an animation that takes more than five seconds to load and animate. This is the Internet, and we're all surfing on Internet Time (I think it's about one traditional year equals five Internet minutes). Speed is your friend because you're using immediate thrills to introduce visitors to your site. If you catch your audience by surprise (for example, by having a page that downloads in five seconds), they will come back because you're a good showman.

- **The story line of a GIF animation has to be simple, and it should end where it begins.** This is called *looping,* and you get more play out of your work when the animation repeats nonstop. There are three different types of scenes that I can think of that you can follow:

  1. The camera or the object moves. You are constrained to left, right, up, and down, because you cannot rotate around a 2D object. (There are 3D animation packages, such as XARA 3D, that can animate in 3D.)

     An example of this type of scene is a logo that flies on and then off screen, from left to right. I'll show you how to do an animated object in this chapter.

  2. The object's outline changes shape. You might morph one object into another (for example, changing a company's logo into the product the company makes), or the object might simply wiggle, changing the contour of its shape. In this chapter I'll show you how to create a bouncing ball that changes shape as it hits the ground.

  3. The object's texture changes. A good example of this is what MTV used to do with their logo; the logo remained the same shape, but colors and textures changed within the logo. We have an example of texture-changing coming up that is eye-soothing (you're supposed to do this on the Web?), and easy to create.

I'm sure that right now you can think of at least 50 examples of animations that fit into these categories. We'll start with my own examples, but they only exist to show you the features for animation in ImageReady, and what each option does.

Using an Action and Your Own Art

The Actions palette in ImageReady more or less serves the same purpose as the one in Photoshop, except that ImageReady's presets can give you a leg up on animating stuff. There are Actions on the Actions palette that create zoom-ins and outs, and Actions that rotate your artwork.

In the steps to follow, you actually get your hands right on the controls, and I'll just sit in the back seat here and call out the instructions for creating an animation with the camera zoom, supplied by an ImageReady script provided on the Actions palette, and any art you might care to use:

A Little Adobe and a Little of Your Own Inspiration

1. Launch ImageReady. It would be a good idea to put ImageReady's icon on the desktop as a shortcut (alias) so that when you don't want to load Photoshop to get to ImageReady, you're all set.

2. Open the Hi.psd image from the Examples/Chap12 folder of the Companion CD. I added an unnecessary layer to the background of this image because I wanted to check for anti-aliasing after the file was created. One of your first moves is to drag the Layer 1 title on the Layers palette (press F7, and you will be using the Layers palette that displays often in animations) into the trash icon. Then, as shown in figure 12.1, press F11 to display the Animation palette. You will also need the Optimize and Color Table palettes for animation, but these can be minimized by double-clicking on the title bar at the top of the palette, and then stowed in a corner of the workspace.

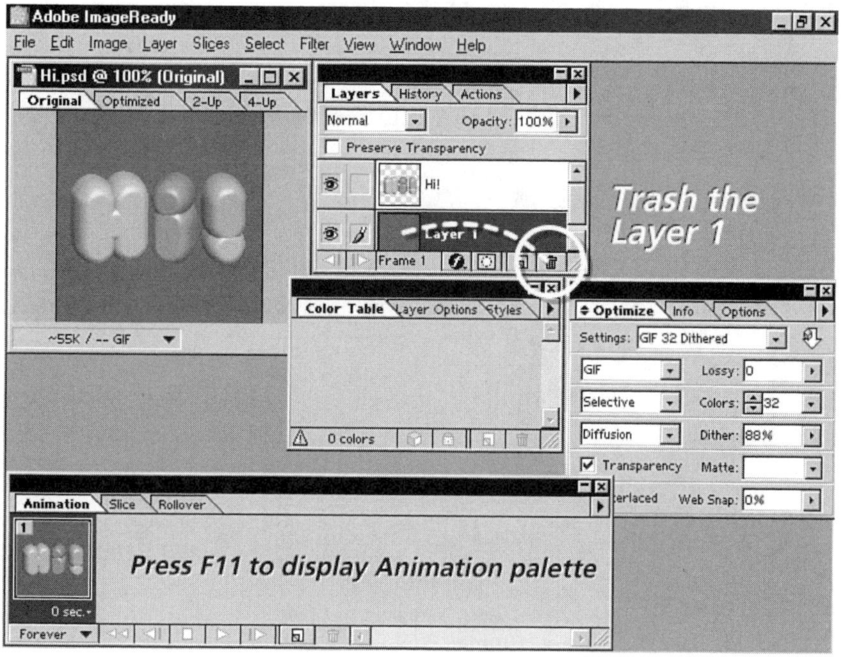

FIGURE 12.1   *F11 is the keyboard shortcut to Window, Show Animation.*

3. Now, when you tell ImageReady to duplicate a frame, you are also duplicating the length of time that the image is onscreen. By default, all new frames are created to display for zero seconds (I know, this is impossible—what Adobe means is that there is no delay in loading a frame). So the first thing you want to do is set a time of .1 seconds for the first frame. This is done by holding on the time area to the lower right of the thumbnail preview on the Animation palette to make a menu pop up, and then you choose .1 seconds (a good choice for the speed of the animation, considering that every class of machine on earth is plugged into the Web), as shown in figure 12.2.

A tenth of a second might seem too fast when it's played back on your machine, but when it's up on the Web, the animation will probably please most visitors. Some will see it too fast (they have a processor and RAM greater than yours) and some will see it a little too slowly (they have a processor and RAM that's less than yours—like an Intel XT or a toaster or something).

Once you've set the time, click on the Spinning Zoom In title on the Actions palette, and then click on the forward button, also shown in figure 12.2.

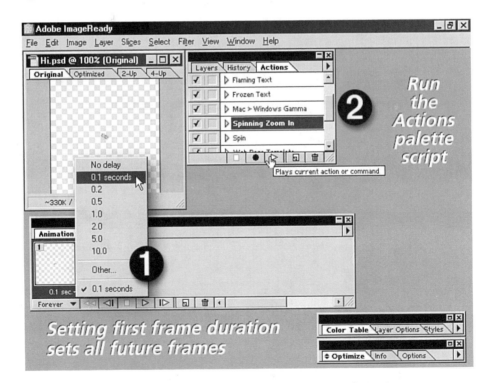

Figure 12.2   *Set the length of each frame before you allow the Actions palette to auto-matically animate your image by copying and then editing the first frame.*

4. On the Animation palette, scroll to the last frame (frame 12), click on the time area, and then choose 2 seconds, as shown in figure 12.3. This is called *timing*. If you let the last frame linger, the message will make a more lasting impression on the viewer and on the phosphors of the monitor.

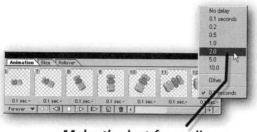

Make the last frame linger

FIGURE 12.3   *Once the object has ceased spinning, it would be nice to let the audience gaze at the message before the animation begins to repeat.*

5. Click on the Optimized tab on the image window, and extend the Color Table and Optimize palettes.

6. On the Optimize palette, choose GIF 32 Dithered. The next field is automatically set to GIF when you're creating an animation. The reason you want the Color Table extended is to make sure the colors you specify are the colors you get—the Optimize palette gets confused occasionally.

7. I've played with the scenarios for dithering and have found that Selective and Diffusion create the best-looking frame with the available colors. But experiment here and see if you can't outdo me.

8. As you can see in figure 12.4, I've decreased the number of unique colors for the animation to 25, lost a K (kilobyte) or two for the animation by doing this, and the still frames that comprise the animation look pretty decent. Also, notice in figure 12.4 that the saved size of the animation is a wonderfully small 15K. The gum on the bottom of your shoe is bigger than 15K!

9. Because we want the background of this file to be transparent, you must choose a Matte color. It would be a good idea, right now (if this were a paying assignment), to get on the Marconi and ask the guys who are designing the Web page what the

PROFOUND WISDOM #25:

You can get away with a minimum of colors in an animation, because the frames are changing all the time.

Unlike static images that are subject to scrutiny for indefinite periods of time, an animated GIF keeps changing its appearance. And if the dithering on each frame is a little excessive, who's going to notice when the frame only lasts onscreen for a fraction of a second?

background color is. Ask them to express it in both hexadecimal and in RGB color (in increments from 0 to 255, *not* in percentages). Pretend I'm the guy designing the pages: "Sir, the background color is CC33FF in hexadecimal." End of conversation. Click on the background color selection box on the toolbox. In the Color Picker, check the Only Web Colors box, and then type **CC33FF** in the # field, as shown in figure 12.5. Press Tab to make the entry, and then click on OK to exit the Color Picker.

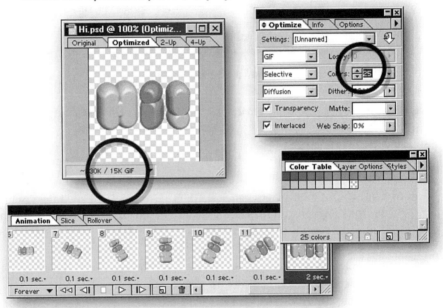

FIGURE 12.4   *Experiment with number of colors and type of diffusion, and then check out the saved file size of the animation.*

10. Although this is an indexed color animation, there needs to be some fringing, especially around the edges of the flying object, so that the animation is placed on the Web page (of identical color to the fringing) and the Web page seamlessly comes together. Click on the Matte field's down-arrow button, and then choose Background color, as shown in figure 12.6.

FIGURE 12.5   *Pick a color background against which the transparent GIF animation can anti-alias.*

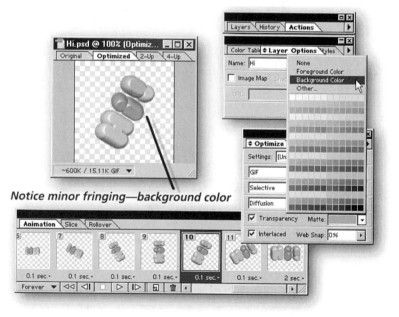

FIGURE 12.6   *To avoid fringing around the animated object, choose the Web page's color as the background color.*

11. Choose File, Save Optimized As, and then call the
animation Hi.GIF. You can preview the animation
at any time by clicking on the Animation palette's
Play button (and stopping the animation with the
Stop button—they're just like VCR controls except
they never flash 12 after a power outage).

12. Save the animation in the workspace as Hi.psd in
Photoshop's native file format (your only option
for layered images). You can close ImageReady to
decrease the burden on system resources, and take
a gander at your work on "the Big Screen"—
Internet Explorer. You can drag and drop the GIF file from a folder onto the
Explorer icon, or if you want to see this animation in context, look on the
Companion CD in the Examples/Chap12 folder for a file called Index.html.
Double-click on it, and you'll see a whole composed page with the animation, as
shown in figure 12.7. Or you can twirl this book around to make this page look
animated.

tip

If you click on the field instead
of the Matte down arrow on
the Optimize palette, you'll be
taken to the Color Picker,
where, if you like, you can
specify the color. I simply think
clicking on the arrow to get
the pop-up is quicker and
easier.

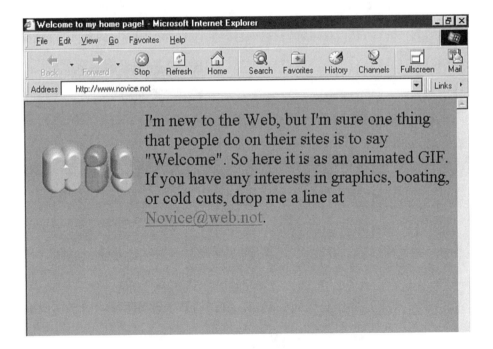

FIGURE 12.7   *It adds a touch of class when your animation blends seamlessly with the
background of the document.*

In the next section, you will work without the animation assistance of the Actions palette. Yup, you're going to handcraft a short animation.

It's All Done with Layers

You'll find in the upcoming example that in animation by hand you use a combination of the Animation palette and the Layers palette. When you click on that tiny page icon on the Animation palette that creates a new frame, it does so by using the currently highlighted frame as the target, the last frame as the destination for the new frame, and it also copies all layers, intact, to the new frame position. What this means, in a nutshell, is that you have the same elements to play with on any given duplicate frame that you have with the original. Actually, nutshells aren't contingent upon anything here. You can add to the current frame—edit objects or create new layers—and all the work is reflected in a duplicate frame of your work.

The assignment to follow, quite literally, is *fun*. I've provided you with a PSD file on the Companion CD that has the word "fun" floating on top of a cartoonish background. Your assignment is to make the word bulge out at the visitor (the object's outline changes shape—example #2 in the list of animation possibilities earlier in the chapter), and eventually come full circle and assume its default shape. All the special-effects equipment you need is a single Filter, Distort, Pinch command. Here's how to get animating:

Animating by Hand

1. Open the Fun.psd file in ImageReady from the Examples/Chap12 folder on the Companion CD. Make sure you have the Layers palette out (press F7 if it's not).

2. On the Animation palette you will see one frame. Click on the time area and choose .1 seconds.

3. On the Layers palette, drag the Fun! title into the Create new layer icon, as shown in figure 12.8. A new Layer, Fun! Copy, appears; it is the current editing layer.

4. On the Animation palette, click on the Duplicates current frame button; you now have a frame 2 that contains all the layers in the original image, as you have specified.

5. Choose Filter, Distort, Pinch. Drag the slider to the left until it reads –38 or so. You're really punching, not pinching the image, as you can see in figure 12.9. Click on OK to apply the change to the new layer.

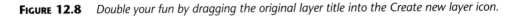

Drag layer title into
Create new layer
icon to duplicate
the layer

FIGURE 12.8   *Double your fun by dragging the original layer title into the Create new layer icon.*

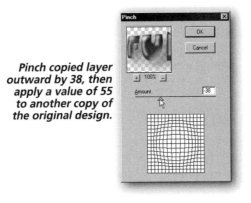

Pinch copied layer
outward by 38, then
apply a value of 55
to another copy of
the original design.

FIGURE 12.9   *The Pinch filter can bow a selection either inward or outward.*

6. Using the first, original, undistorted frame, repeat steps 3–5 so you have a Fun! Copy 2 layer at the top of the stack, and then apply the Pinch filter, but at 55 rather than at 38, so the Fun! Text looks really bloated. You should have 3 frames at this point, as shown if figure 12.10.

7. Click on frame 2 on the Animation palette. Hide the Fun! layer, and unhide the Fun! copy layer on the Layers palette.

8. With frame 2 highlighted, click on the Duplicate current frame icon on the Animation palette, so frame 2 and frame 4 in this animation are the same. The word inflates, then the word deflates.

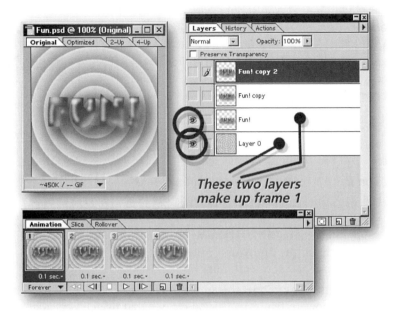

These two layers
make up frame 1

FIGURE 12.10   *The layers that are visible at any given frame are the ones that will be written as part of the GIF animation.*

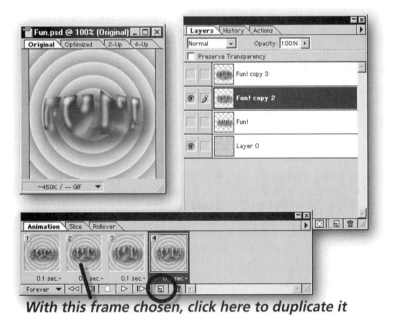

With this frame chosen, click here to duplicate it

FIGURE 12.11   *Duplicate frame 2 to frame 4 so that in the animation, the Fun! lettering will appear to deflate to its original size back at frame 1 again.*

9. It's layer editing time. You should not remove a layer that you want invisible at any frame because removing a layer from one frame removes the layer from *all* frames. Instead, you will hide the layers you do not want visible at any given frame. For example, click on frame 1, and then uncheck the eye icons for the Fun! Copy and Fun! Copy 2 layers on the Layers palette. Frame 2 and frame 4 use only the Fun! Copy layer, so hide the other layers when these frames are selected.

10. Click on frame 3 on the Animation palette. Hide the Fun! and Fun! Copy layer, and unhide the Fun! Copy 2 layer on the Layers palette.

11. Play your animation in ImageReady by clicking on the play button on the Animation palette, and look at the image window. Fun, huh?

tip

If you want to move a frame to any location, click and hold on the thumbnail on the Animation palette, firmly drag to the left or right, and then drop the frame where you want it to go. By the way, the frame assumes the correct number in sequence, so if you dragged frame 3 over to the right of frame 8, frame 3 would be titled frame 8.

Oh, yeah: If the thumbnails are too teensy for you to see a subtle change in frames, click on a frame and then look at the image window.

12. Use your judgment as to how the animation must be optimized now. In figure 12.12, you can see that I've chosen Adaptive dithering, Pattern-type dithering, and 32 colors. The file is still a fairly large 38K, as you can see in the Document Sizes area, but there's a reason or two for this. First, there are lots of colors in the image—17 more than in the Hi! Animation— there's a background where HI! had none, and the dimensions of the image are huge as animations for the Web go. If you really want to post this Fun! sign on the Web, I'd suggest shrinking and sharpening the frames—60 percent of the original size will still bear some fun.

13. Choose File, Save Optimized As, and call the animation Fun.gif.

14. Save the animation in the workspace as Fun.psd, in Photoshop's native file format. You can close the file at any time now.

I've got the animation placed on an HTML page called Fun.html, and it resides in the Gallery folder within the Chap12 folder on the Companion CD. Double-click on the HTML file name, and see what I've *added* to the page; it's a small animation I did using The VALIS Group's Flo' and ImageReady.

We've covered all the options you need to know to make an animated GIF. But I'd like to leave you with an idea or two on which you can create a plethora (okay, not a plethora...a miasma) of variations.

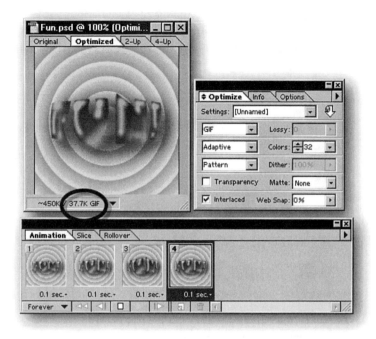

Figure 12.12   *The file is a little large, but it's a lot of fun.*

Blueprints for Future Animations

I'm sure your head is filling up with ideas faster than the Boardwalk at high tide, but please allow me to kibitz for a moment. I've got two animations you can try out, and they are way cool.

The Bouncing Ball

This animation is only five frames, but you'll be surprised at how terrific it looks on a Web page at any size. Part of the reason it looks so, well…animated, is that I observed one of the rules for animation set forth by Disney and carried on today by PIXAR's John Lasseter. It's called "stretch and squish"—an object, specifically one that bounces up and down, must observe conservation of mass. So when the ball hits the ground, it flattens but also becomes wider. And when it bounces back up, to exaggerate the motion, I make the ball lean and tall. In the last frame, the ball pretty much resumes its first position and shape.

So two things are going on here: Change of placement in space, and change of shape. How can you lose? Notice the size of the shadow I created for the ball in figure 12.13, and simply design these frames in ImageReady, using the techniques you already know.

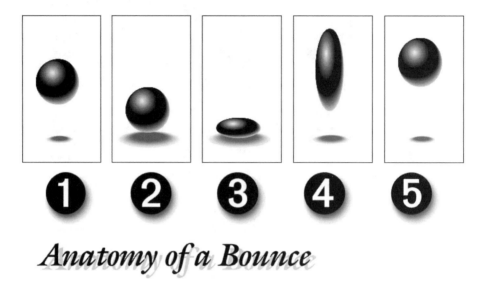

FIGURE 12.13   *Here's the blueprint for a very jelly-like bouncing ball.*

Check out the Bouncer.html document in your browser. The file's in the Chap12/Gallery folder.

The Subtle Elevator Effect

You can keep an image's shape and location stationary, and still add animation by changing the colors or textures inside the shape of the hero of the GIF animation. Although you can't see it too well, because the book's in black and white, I've got an elevator effect going on in figure 12.14. A light green travels vertically down the lettering and is gradually replaced with black. Then the cycle starts again. If you want to see this in color, moving, check out Chap12, Gallery, download.gif in your Web browser.

Here are the blueprints:

note

As an extra bonus, you can open and use the PSD files in the Gallery folder to create animations in ImageReady. These are the files I used to create the tutorials, and although I'd like you to build all these animations completely unassisted (okay, this book is, technically, "assistance"), I'm going to delete the files eventually. So it's better to loan than to throw out.

FIGURE 12.14   *Follow these illustrations to make a four-frame color-shifting animation.*

I've seen all types of animated GIFs on the Web, and even seen deals such as "100,000 GIF animations for $12." But I feel it's much more personal to provide things you yourself have created for your Web site—and you wouldn't be reading this book if you didn't want to become a Content Creator.

Summary

Frame 1: The author tells you about the three different types of animation, and how you can use ImageReady to create them.

Frame 2: You get your feet wet with a graphic the author provides, and an animation action from the Actions palette.

Frame 3: You slowly develop an interest in GIF animation, and you now create your own animation, using only the sketchiest of details from the author.

Frame 4: You realize that you don't need the author anymore, you create a two-hour GIF movie that's only 38KB, and you head for Hollywood.

Frame 5: Fade to black; roll credits.

Hey, it's a little piece of the Web that's like Hollywood. Anything can happen.

In chapter 13, you'll earn your degree in image *mapology*—the science (some call it an art) of making a single graphic that has several different hot spots that you can assign to any URL. C'mon, your site probably needs directory buttons. Let's move onward and upward!

CHAPTER 13

Creating Image Maps

To get through this chapter with the most rewarding results and the least confusion, it helps to break the term *image map* into two parts. The *image* part is a single GIF or JPEG image that has no special properties at all—it doesn't link to sites, it doesn't take out the trash—nada. The second part of the term, *map,* makes image maps possible. The map is written to an HTML file that specifies coordinates on the image; if you click within a zone that connects to an URL, then you've just experienced the thrill of using an image map.

This chapter takes you through image map creation, how to specify local and off-site links, the method for beginning with an image map and winding up with a site, and more. So roll up your sleeves for a challenge that many digital designers before you have met and conquered.

Making Standard, but Professional-looking, Buttons

One of the most popular uses for image maps is to create buttons that, when clicked on, take the audience to a different page. Sure, you could draw a figure of the human anatomy and have each body part when clicked on, lead to a comprehensive document about that body part, but mostly, image maps on the Web are shaped like your garden-variety buttons, usually rectangular or circular. You will often need to make buttons that *look* like buttons, so that is where we will begin.

Really Polished-looking Buttons from ImageReady

The Styles palette in ImageReady has 16 preset button textures, and adding them to an area in your image is as easy as:

1. Filling an area on a layer with opaque color (it doesn't matter whether there's an active marquee around the area).

2. Dragging and dropping a Style thumbnail into the opaque area on the layer. Alternatively, you can double-click on a thumbnail to fill the currently active image layer.

Let's create a button now:

Creating an ImageReady Button

1. Press Ctrl(⌘)+N and in the New dialog box, type **300** in the Width field, type **300** in the Height field, and in the Contents area, click on Transparent. In the name field, call the image **StringBean.psd**, and then click on OK to open the new image. Don't worry that the document size is sort of large; you need some elbow room in order to create the buttons.

2. Press Alt(Opt)+click on the Create new layer button on the Layers palette (press F7 if the palette's not in view). In the dialog box, type Welcome in the name field and then press Enter (Return).

3. With the Rectangular Marquee tool, drag a button shape that's about 140 pixels wide and 48 pixels high. Okay, Gary, how can you tell when the marquee is sized correctly? Press F8 to display the Info palette, and quit dragging when the W(idth) coordinate field says 140 and the H(eight) field says 48.

4. Press Alt(Opt)+Delete (Backspace) to fill the marquee with foreground color. It makes no difference what the color is.

5. Choose Window, Show Styles, and then double-click on a preset Style that appeals to you on the palette. (Hint: choose the first row, second-from-left to make this assignment go easier.) As you can see in figure 13.1, I'm choosing the second button in the top row (but I'm going to change the color shortly. And so are you).

tip

If you want to make your own presets and add them to the Styles palette, click on the Effects right triangle directly below the layer title on the Layers palette. Then, change a parameter—change the color, the texture, the direction of a color gradient—anything you like. All your changes are reflected in the image window to which you applied a style. To save your new style, click on the menu flyout button on the Styles palette, and then choose New Style. Give the Style a name in the dialog box, click on OK, and you have another style to use in the future.

note

An area that you want filled with a style can be any shape you want. Try this: Draw a squiggle with the Lasso tool and then fill it. Then apply a style to it. Instant weirdness!

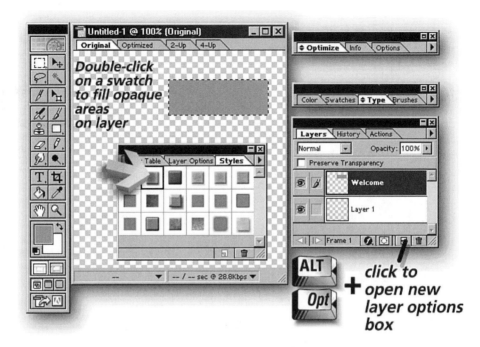

Figure 13.1   *Create an opaque area on a layer, and then double-click on a Style thumb-nail to make the opaque area into a button. You can also drag and drop an icon onto an opaque area.*

6. On the Layers palette, click on the arrow to the left of the word Effects, and after the Effects title has dropped down, double-click on the Color Fill title. A Color Fill palette appears.

7. Click on the Color box down arrow to access a Web palette pop-up, and then choose a pale, medium green (69966 is a good Web color for the foreground color), as shown in figure 13.2. The button immediately takes on the chosen color, with the other effects that make up the button left intact. Double-click on the layer title on the Layers palette; in the dialog box, type **Welcome** as the name, and then press Enter (Return). It will become critical, can we say something like: "It is critical that you name layers as soon as you create them in this assign-ment." (Trust me—soon you'll understand why!)

8. Choose File, Save, and then save the file as Stringbn.psd (for *StringBean LeisureWare,* your fictitious client). You have no other format choices because this image has a layer.

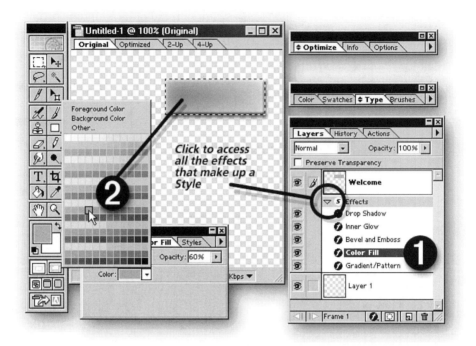

FIGURE 13.2 *Change one or more of the components of a preset button by accessing the drop-down list from the Effects title on the Layers palette.*

9. Press Ctrl(⌘)+S; keep the file open.

This button you've created is a little large, as buttons go. The reasoning for the size is that the button's title will be clearly legible, thus eliminating the need to support the graphic on the Web page with additional text.

So this means our next stop is the Type tool, and an effect you'll apply to the button.

ImageReady and Embossed Text

The Type tool in ImageReady does not work like the Type tool in Photoshop. Everything is done "live," so to speak. You click an insertion point right in the document, start typing, and text appears instantly. Now, in this example you'll be creating 3D text. The

> **note**
>
> It's best for Windows users and Macintosh users alike to abide by the eight-character name, with a three-character extension, just as a good practice. UNIX servers out there on the Net need file extensions, and some machines accessing the Net can't read longer file names than eight characters.

best choice for text that's embossed is a simple, bold, clean font. It would also be nice if the text had the same color as the button, so click on the foreground color selection box right now, and choose 669966 as the foreground color.

I'm using a heavy weight of Kabel in the following steps. If you have no font that's clean and heavy, use Kibbutz KnockOutLine in the Boutons folder on the Companion CD.

Here's how to add text:

Adding Text; Embossing for an Effect

Because no two fonts are created at exactly the same size, I'm going with a font height of 30 pixels to fit in a button that is 48 pixels high. My reasoning? When I create an embossed version of the text, it will take up just enough vertical space to make it float nicely inside the button.

1. Double-click on the Type tool to access the Type palette, choose your font from the drop-down list, and then type **30** in the field directly below the font name field, as shown in figure 13.3. Also, choose center alignment. Click in the center of the button, and then type **Welcome**. You will be copying and modifying the text, and if it's centered now, then copies of the text will also be centered in the button. When you've typed your message, click in an empty area of the image then hold Ctrl(⌘) and move the text so it looks centered in the button.

2. Right-click (Macintosh: hold Ctrl and click) on the text layer (it says Welcome and has a T—for "Type you still edit"—in the layer title). A pop-up appears with Layer Effects options. Choose Bevel and Emboss from the list, and the Bevel and Emboss palette shown in figure 13.4 immediately appears. Alternatively, you can click on the *f*-in-a-circle icon at the bottom of the Layers palette to apply a drop-down list of effects to the chosen layer.

3. Choose Pillow Emboss from the first drop-down field on the Bevel and Emboss palette, and accept the other values at their default.

4. Press Ctrl(⌘)+S; keep the file open. Now that you have one button created (using two layers), it'll be easy to create three other buttons.

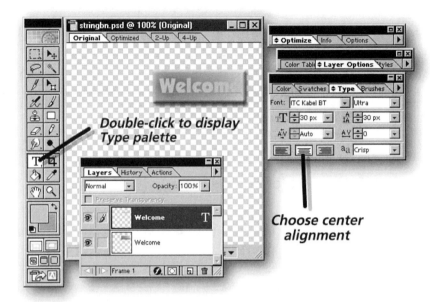

FIGURE 13.3   *Choose the right font, center alignment, and a color for the text that is harmonious with the color of the button.*

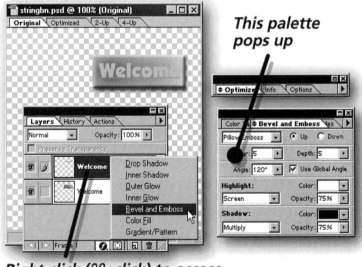

FIGURE 13.4   *You can add an effect to text by simply right-clicking (Macintosh: holding Ctrl and clicking) on the text layer title.*

There's absolutely no reason to *create* other buttons, or to use Layer Effects on other text, now that you have a perfectly good button and some pillow-embossed text. In the following section, you'll create the other navigation buttons for the StringBean LeisureWare page.

Copying the First Button

1. Drag the Welcome button (*not* the Welcome type title) title on the Layers palette into the Create new layer icon at the bottom of the Layers palette. A new button appears above the Welcome button, and its title on the Layers palette is "Welcome copy." Double-click on the title to access the Layer Options box, name the layer **History**, and then click on OK to leave the dialog box.

2. Press V (for Move tool), Hold Shift, and then press the down-arrow key six times to move the new History button, as shown in figure 13.5. You have just done your first *power nudging,* which is what we call holding the Shift key, with the right layer selected, while you press the arrow keys. This action moves the contents of the layer by 10 pixels.

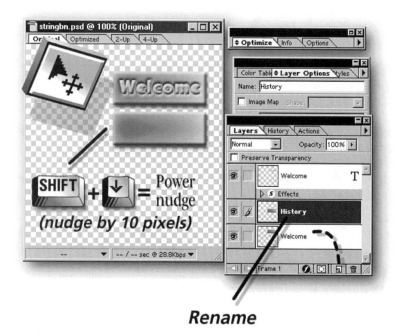

FIGURE 13.5   *Power nudge the new, blank button down beneath the original.*

3. Duplicate the Welcome type on the Welcome (type) layer by dragging its layer title into the Create new layer icon at the bottom of the Layers palette. With the Type tool, highlight the Welcome type, and then type **History**. Then double-click on this new layer title, and type **History** in the dialog box; click on OK to close the box. These actions are shown in figure 13.6.

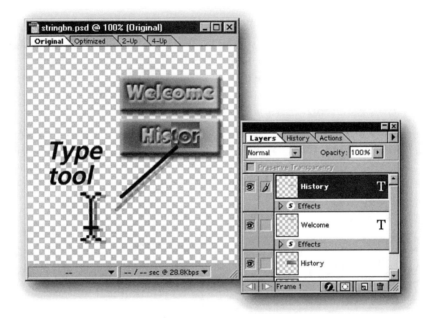

FIGURE 13.6   *Duplicate the editable text, and then change the text by simply highlighting and typing over the text.*

4. With the Move tool chosen, press Shift+down-arrow key six times to get the text on top of the second button.

5. Take a moment to organize the layers. From top to bottom on the palette you should have History (text), History (button), Welcome (text), and finally Welcome (button). The way to arrange these guys is by dragging and dropping their titles into different positions on the Layers palette.

6. Press Ctrl(⌘)+S; keep the file open.

You don't need any new steps to complete a four-button navigation image. A "Contact" button should be part of StringBean LeisureWare's Web page, as should "Products," which in theory should lead to a Web catalog of products. Create the Contact and Products buttons, and then drag the layer titles on the Layers palette so the palette looks like the one shown in figure 13.7. You should have a text layer above every button layer.

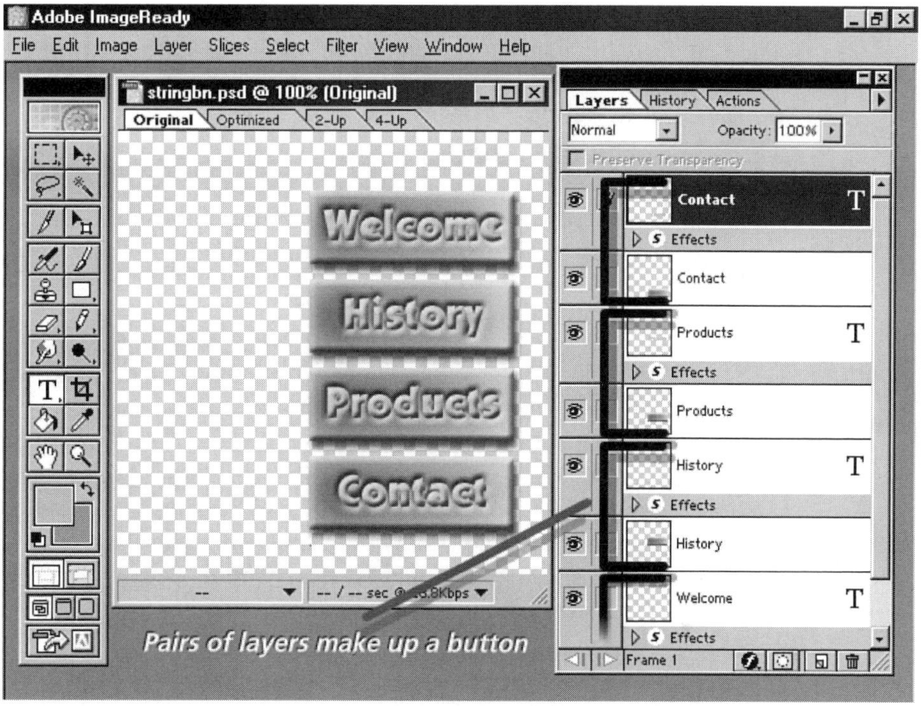

FIGURE 13.7   *If your layers are in the order shown here, you're all set to start merging layers.*

Finalizing the StringBean Navigation Buttons

Actually, you're going to learn 1½ things in the steps to follow, if you've been reading this book sequentially. First (this is the ½ part), you are going to merge each text layer with the corresponding button layer. This means you will wind up with four layers (and the original image Layer 1 at the bottom, which you'll trash), and four layers equals four image-map regions that the reader can click on.

Now, you might ask, "What am I going to link my buttons to?" Good question. I've provided the answer in the Chap13/Gallery folder on the Companion CD. If you copy the Stringbn folder to your hard disk (make real sure you remember where you've copied it!), call the folder **beanpage**, and then delete the stringbn.jpg and stringbn.html files from this folder, you can write your own JPEG and corresponding HTML files to this folder, and you will have a completely linking, functional system. That is the second thing you'll learn in this chapter.

The only catch is that you must type specific link names in ImageReady. I'll repeat this section when we get to the individual steps, but here's what the links are going to be

- The Welcome button = bluepage.html
- The History button = grenpage.html
- The Products button = redpage.html
- The Contact button = orngpage.html

Let's polish off the Web work so you can see the results and the possibilities:

Merging Layers and Linking Links

1. Drag the Layers palette's edges far enough away from the center so that you can see every layer. Drag the Layer 1 title into the trash icon.

2. Click on the top layer title (Contact, the type layer), and then press Ctrl(⌘)+E. It is *very* important that you use only the Ctrl(⌘) and the E keys, because *other* modifier keys will do something unexpected and unwanted here. What you've done is to perform the Merge Down command, using a shortcut. The Contact Text layer merged into the underlying Contact button layer, and as you can see in figure 13.8, now there's only one Contact layer.

Figure 13.8   *Ctrl(⌘)+E merges the selected layer into the layer lying directly beneath it.*

3. Perform step 2 on the other three sets of layers until you have only four layers, titled correctly.

4. Click on the Welcome layer title, and then click on the Layer Options tab on the Layer Options palette (if you closed the palette, choose Window, Show Layer Options Effects.

5. Click on the Image Map check box; then, in the URL field, type **bluepage.html**, and then press Tab. As you can see in figure 13.9, the URL appears beneath the layer title on the Layers palette.

6. Perform step 5 with the other three layers. I've already given you the URLs—simply enter them, and we'll move on here.

7. On the Optimize palette (F8), click on the Matte swatch, shown in figure 13.10, and then choose CCFFCC in the Color Picker, and press Enter (Return). This color will be the background of the Web page; it's sort of string-bean-colored and works well with the button colors.

> **tip**
>
> You can access an Options dialog box instead of the Layer Options palette at any time and perform the same feats you're performing here. All you do is double-click on the layer title on the Layers palette to display the Layer Options dialog box.
>
> When you use the dialog box, however, it's a hassle to name URLs when you've got more than one or two of them to tag.

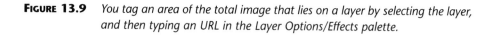

FIGURE 13.9   *You tag an area of the total image that lies on a layer by selecting the layer, and then typing an URL in the Layer Options/Effects palette.*

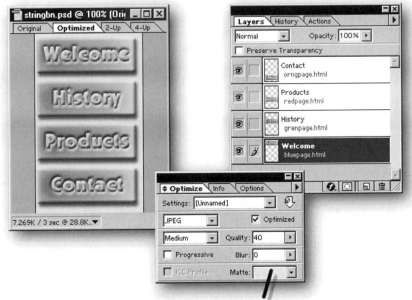

Click here to display Color Picker

FIGURE 13.10   *Choose a background color for the buttons and the Web page. The color is not added to the image, but instead it is written to an HTML file—ImageReady is merely showing you how it will look in the Optimized view of the image window.*

8. Choose JPEG Medium from the Optimize palette's top settings drop-down list. Then, click on the Optimized tab of the image window. The image looks pretty decent and it will be saved to a small file size.

9. Choose File, Save Optimized As, and then find the beanpage folder on your hard disk in the directory box. Once you're there, save the image as stringbn.jpg. (It is *very* important to match the case of what I've written here—no caps, or the page won't be able to find the graphic. On the Web, UNIX rules, and UNIX is case-sensitive). Make sure that both the Save HTML file and Save Images check boxes are checked (see fig. 13.11).

10. Click on OK, save everything in ImageReady, and you can close ImageReady for a moment or two.

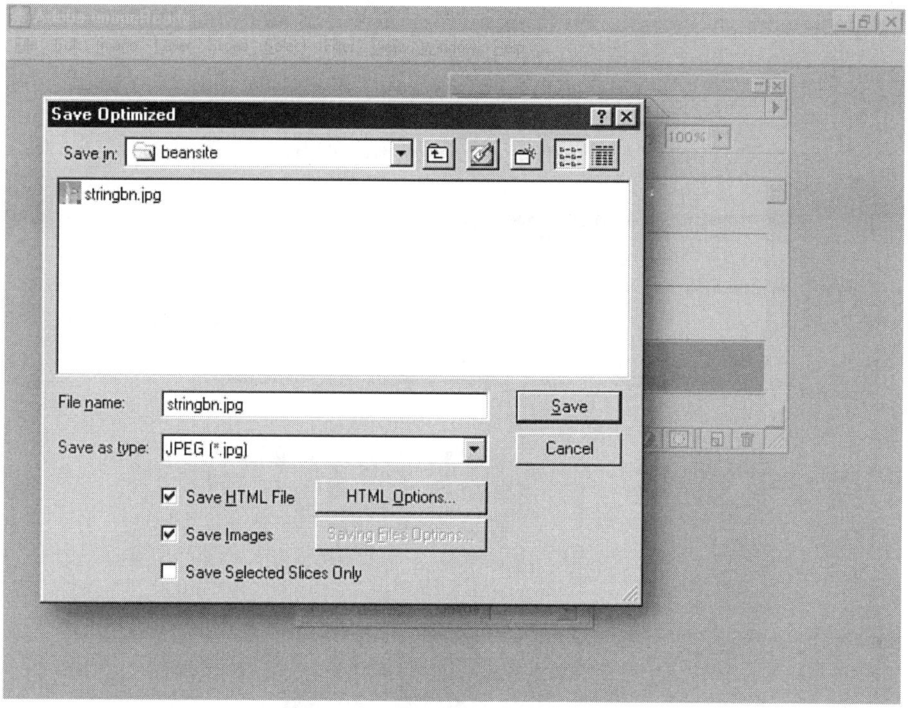

FIGURE 13.11   *Your Save Optimized directory box should look like this.*

In the beansite folder, double-click on the stringbn. html document (ImageReady wrote this file for you). This should cause your Web browser to launch, and because I've added code to this folder as well as images, you'll not only see your completely functional image map artwork (see fig. 13.12), but also a logo and some text. Click on one of the link buttons and see what the Blue page and the Orange page look like, and how you can navigate back home using the home buttons on these pages.

All About URLs

An URL, alternatively known as a *Uniform* or *Universal Resource Locator* (depending on who you're talking to), is not limited to Web links. In the preceding example, all the links were internal and easy to fill in because the targets for the links you created all resided in the same folder.

note

Even though the art for the logo of StringBean Leisure-Ware is in the beanpage folder, you will not be able to re-create the HTML document that organizes the text and images without the use of an *HTML editor.* This type of program (I used Adobe's GoLive!) enables you to place text or graphics in tables and/or align things, specify link color for text, and many more niceties you've seen on other Web pages. ImageReady is a little more than half the solution to creating a Web page. It can generate HTML code for graphics that you want to be dynamic, but ImageReady is not designed to compile a Web page.

As we get into the following section, however, you will be using *absolute links*. This has nothing to do with vodka—a complete, absolute link would be something like http://www.adobe.com. You type this absolute link into the URL field in the Layer Options palette, and a browser will take the visitor there, regardless of browser type, machine type, or what type of person the visitor is.

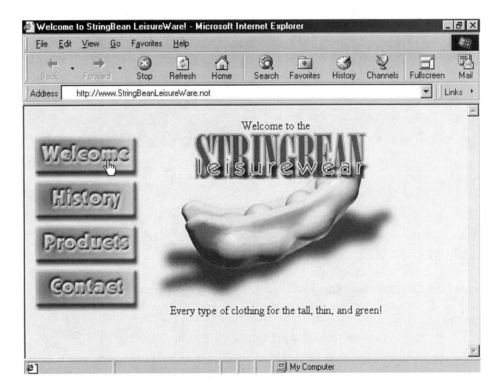

FIGURE 13.12   *An image map makes it easy for viewers of your site to find precisely the information they are after.*

Also, it's worth mentioning that you can create a link that will trigger the visitor's e-mail program to load, so the visitor can write to you. It's called the "Mailto:" protocol. If I wanted a button on a page to launch a mail browser, and the destination was my mailbox, I'd type **Mailto:Gary@TheBoutons.com**. Exactly like that, no spaces (and no period at the end). So links aren't necessarily to http protocols.

Shaped Links and Absolute URLs

The following exercise is like the StringBean exercise only in the sense that you are designing image maps. We'll design circular, not rectangular, hot spots in the image, and you'll type in absolute URLs that actually lead to the sites of some of my fellow artists.

Let's start slowly, and I'll explain to you the design and the concept of the page.

A Telephone Image Map

The stylized image of a telephone with seven press buttons seems like an appropriate graphic for "dialing" up art professionals. Creating the graphic for this was the easy part. If you have a telephone on your site, you'd better have a directory, too. The directory part of the assignment you cannot complete yourself without an HTML editor, but as with the StringBean assignment, I've got the missing parts stashed on the Companion CD.

Before we begin, copy the Artists folder in the Chap13/Gallery folder to a place on your hard disk where you can easily locate it.

Okay, now let's link the telephone numbers to specific URLs.

Using Different Shapes for URL Hot Spots

1. Open the Phone.psd image from the Examples/Chap13 folder on the Companion CD, and then save it to your hard disk as Phone.psd (because it's a picture of a phone).

2. Press Ctrl(⌘)+ the keypad's plus key until you have a 400% viewing resolution of the image.

3. Press Ctrl(⌘)+R to display the rulers, drag a horizontal ruler to the top of the "1" button on the phone in the image, and then drag a vertical ruler to the left of the number "1" in the image. With the Elliptical Marquee tool drag from the intersection of the two guidelines to the right and down until you've encompassed the number 1 button in the image.

4. Right-click (Macintosh: hold Ctrl and click) and then choose Layer Via Copy from the context menu, as shown in figure 13.13.

5. Double-click on the new layer title on the Layers palette, type **1** in the Name field, and press Enter (Return). On the Layer Options palette, click on the Image Map check box, and choose Circle from the Shape drop-down list, as shown in figure 13.14.

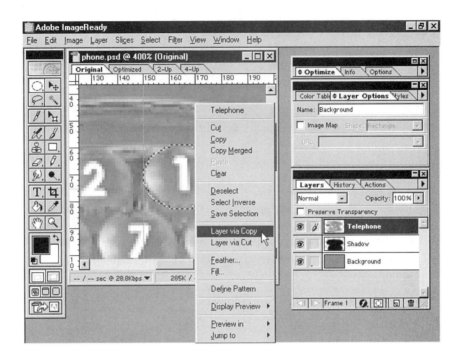

FIGURE 13.13   *Give yourself some guides if you are not confident with making selections freehand.*

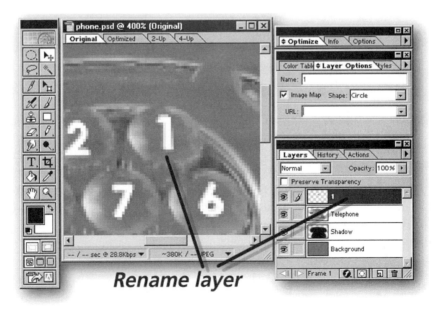

FIGURE 13.14   *Rename the new layer and choose the circle shape for the image map coordinates for this part of the image.*

6. Launch Acrobat Reader 4. If you have not installed this program from the Companion CD (or Photoshop's CD), do so now, and then load the URL.pdf file that is in the Examples/Chap13 folder.

7. Your first URL (number 1 on the phone) will be Daniel Will-Harris. Click on the Text tool, highlight the URL (see fig. 13.15), and then press Ctrl(⌘)+C to copy the URL to the Clipboard. You might as well leave Acrobat Reader open; there are more URLs to come.

8. Switch back to ImageReady, insert your cursor into the URL field on the Layer Options palette (be sure Image Map is checked), and then press Ctrl(⌘)+V, as shown in figure 13.16. Then press Tab to make the entry permanent. You should see the URL listed a second time, on the 1 layer title on the Layers palette.

note

Not every program that can create image maps does so by requiring that a layer contain a copy of the underlying image. Do not make the mistake of assuming that ImageReady is going to export five or six images, for example, simply because you have defined these areas on layers.

In the end, ImageReady makes a single GIF or JPEG image, and generates text code telling the coordinates for the hot spots, based on the layer information.

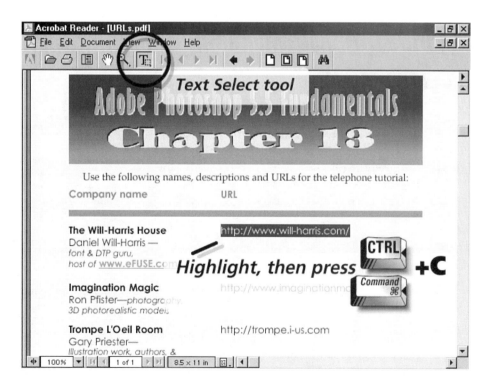

Figure 13.15   *Copy the URL from the Acrobat page to the Clipboard.*

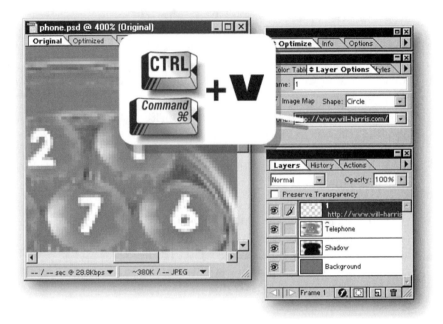

FIGURE 13.16 *Paste the URL you copied from the Acrobat document into the URL field on the Layer Options palette.*

9. I'm afraid that completing the telephone image map requires no special steps from me. You copy the steps here, from 3–8, increasing the number of each new layer to correspond to the button to which you're linking. You might find that you do not need the rulers or the guides to make further circular selections. If this is the case, choose View, Clear Guides, and then press Ctrl(⌘)+R to hide the rulers.

10. Once you've got all seven buttons on different layers and the URLs copied to the corresponding button, there's no reason you can't treat yourself right now to a fully working composition-in-the-works <g>. Start your machine's Internet connection, and then, as shown in figure 13.17, choose File, Preview in, and choose the browser you own. If ImageReady cannot find your Web browser, it will display an attention box, and you can then browse your drive for the Web browser you use.

note

It might not have been obvious, but I wanted to give you, the designer, complete control over the appearance of the image map, which is why the phone, the shadow, and a medium-black background are all on separate layers. If you want to exclude the background or change its color, fine. If you want no shadow, that's possible, too. If you want to merge these layers at any time, click on the Telephone layer, press Ctrl(⌘)+E, and then click on the resulting layer (the one above the background layer) and press Ctrl(⌘)+E again.

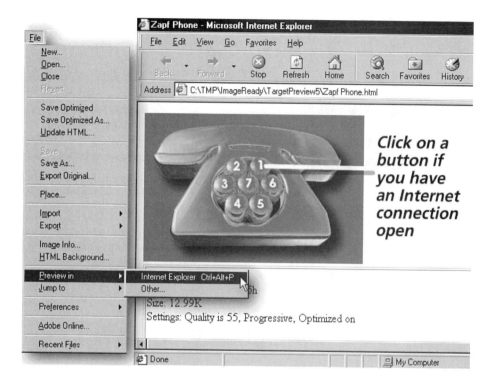

FIGURE 13.17   *Preview your work in your Web browser.*
Click on number 1, for example.

11. I clicked on number 1, and wouldn't you know it?—Daniel Will-Harris's site pops up, as shown in figure 13.18. To return to your composition, click on the Back button in your browser.

12. Close the browser, and return to ImageReady. Press Ctrl(⌘)+S; keep the file open.

note

You might be asking, "Why did we create circle hot spots to define URLs in this image map?" Why wouldn't rectangles work equally well?

The name of the game is to place two hot spots close to one another without their overlapping. If you used rectangles, the hot spots might have been too small to hit accurately with the cursor, or the rectangles might have overlapped, in which case the browser would get confused.

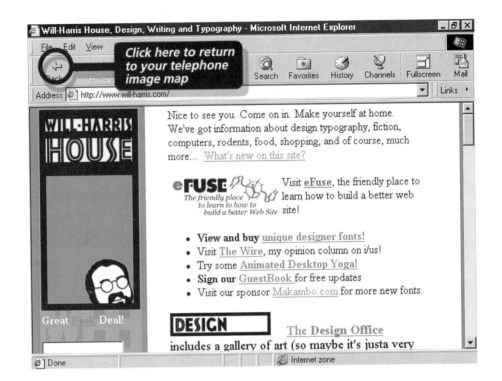

FIGURE 13.18   *Your image map does not need a complete HTML page to function. See how you can preview your work, using the Internet, at any time during your work?*

There's one last thing you need to do with the image before you save an optimized version with a corresponding HTML file—you need to optimize the image. You do this by opening the 2-Up view of the image window, and then comparing, side by side, whether GIF is going to reproduce the image adequately at a small size, or whether the JPEG format shows off the image better.

In figure 13.19, I've run several different amounts of compression and data loss in both GIF and JPEG format for the telephone image, and JPEG is the clear winner. Do you know why? Because the telephone is a low-frequency image—there are no sharp color shifts (okay, there are very few) and I mentioned earlier in this book, JPEGs work most successfully with slow-transition (low-frequency) images.

note

For both JPEG and GIF exports, it might be a good idea to (needlessly, from a visual standpoint) sharpen the image before exporting it. Why? Because both GIF and JPEG exports soften the focus of an image ever so slightly, and more so when the image is small in size. So you sharpen, allow the saving process to blur the piece a little, and you net-out even.

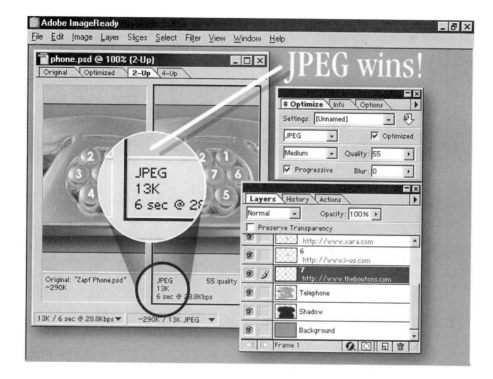

FIGURE 13.19   *Play with the Optimize palette before you commit to saving a copy in a certain format. Sometimes GIF works best for an image, while JPEG is the clear winner with other types of images.*

In figure 13.20, I've brought the telephone and the HTML code into Go Live!, and created a directory that surrounds the telephone. Each number tells who the artist is by name and by specialty, and in the text the numbers themselves actually are links out to the various sites. You can do this kinda stuff in an HTML editor.

Figure 13.21 shows the completed Web page, viewed through Explorer. By the way, the Examples/Chap13/Gallery/Artists folder has an HTML file, called artists.html, that will launch the page you see here in your Web browser.

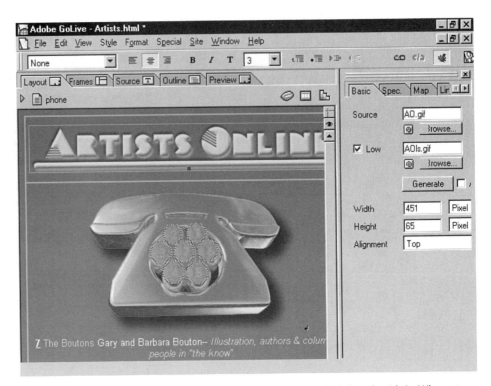

Figure 13.20   *The telephone image map is beautiful, and you did wonderful work with it. Why not invest now in an HTML editor, or find an HTML whiz, and pair up with them to offer a complete Internet Website solution?*

A Parting Polygonal Image Map Picture

As I mentioned earlier, image map hot spots can come in three flavors: the default rectangle (which will not confuse earlier Web browsers, such as version 2 of anything from Netscape or Microsoft), circle, and polygon. I encountered a self-imposed design dilemma (don't you hate it when you out-design yourself?) in figure 13.22: The vegetables and flowers all link to a different page that goes into detail about how to grow such things, but boy, are those pictures crowded together! The solution? Trim carefully around them, using the Polygonal Lasso tool (it's next to the regular Lasso tool, as a flyout on the toolbox), copy the image to a layer, and then on the Layer Options palette, define this image map hot spot shape as a Polygon.

In the real site (called "Garden" in the Gallery folder on the CD), you will not see the outlines of the hot spots. I've outlined one in figure 13.22, however, so you can see how intricate you can get with tightly spaced objects that need URLs but don't need overlapping hot-spot borders!

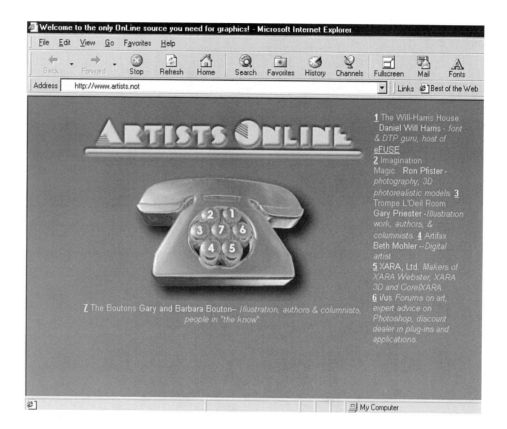

FIGURE 13.21   *It's clean and novel-looking. Making an image map that is easy to access should be a priority whenever you design one.*

And I'll bet you thought that the Hard Rock Café was the only hot spot you'd encounter in your life!

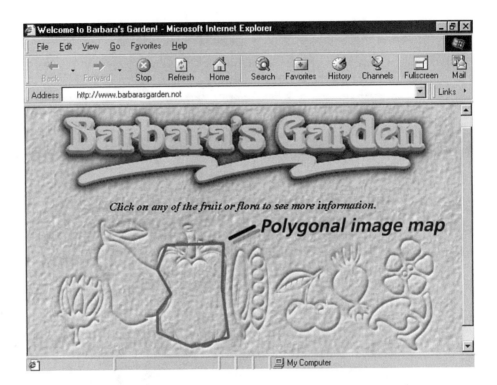

FIGURE 13.22   *Polygon hot spots in an image enable you to make a very fine distinction between hot-spot areas and areas that have no links.*

Summary

In this chapter you've seen how local links, http protocol links, and even a brief note on Mailto: links, can all be written as HTML coordinates that work with the image you prepared as an image map. You've seen that there's nothing special about the image; but if you look at the HTML text in a plain text editor, you'll find exactly how your graphical commands were translated by ImageReady into text coordinates. An HTML editor would be a welcome addition to your toolbox, so you can finish what you start. But you can still do what other business folks can't, when you create image maps and let someone else do the Web page integration.

In chapter 14, we will get into two additional ImageReady talents that you positively will want to use. Image slicing can become image mapping or simply a device to make images load faster, and JavaScript can make the buttons on your page change color and shape when the visitor hovers the cursor over them. This is the *really* cool stuff! Let's forge on!

CHAPTER 14

Image Slicing and Rollovers

There are yet two more special effects–type of Web page elements, and ImageReady makes their creation a nearly effortless task. If you thought that GIF animation was the end-all-be-all of Web elements, hold on tight here!

Image slicing is a little like creating image maps, except a copy of your file is actually sliced into several partial images, only to be assembled by the audience's browser. Why would you want to do this? I have some compelling reasons, as you'll discover a few pages from now. And a *rollover* belongs to the Web element class of JavaScripts. Rollovers are multiple images appearing at different times in the same location on a Web page, and the specific graphic displayed is up to the visitor by hovering or clicking over the image area. In case you don't know what a JavaScript is, it has nothing to do with Java programming, and is most closely related to other scripting languages, such as Apple Script, or a batch file that executes commands depending on user input.

Let's look first at the possibilities held by slicing, as it might find a home in some of your work.

Image Slicing: A Tight Table that Holds Graphics

If you've ever worked with an HTML editor, you're already aware that it's next to impossible to get images butted against one another, particularly if the images are in neighboring table cells. You can't plunk images in a table and expect them to be seamless because there are many supporting

HTML tags you might not be familiar with (either by name or in context) that enable you to perform this feat. The image slicer in ImageReady, fortunately, creates elegant commands in HTML that fit the sliced image together.

As I mentioned, slicing can land you an opportunity to attach an URL tag to every sliced image, or it can simply help you speed up the download of large graphics (one large graphic takes longer to completely load than several smaller files).

In the following section, I'm going to show you an excellent use for slicing—to selectively optimize each part of the image, so there are different compression amounts, and yet the image appears whole to the audience.

Image Slicing the Right Type of Image

The sky's the limit when you have a powerful tool such as ImageReady, with all its features, to help you. I'm going to show you first a modest, practical use for image slicing—image optimization—and then a special effect you can do with the sliced image.

First—have you ever considered that any given photograph might have an intense area of attraction, while the other areas are sort of static, and although they support the whole image, these background areas are totally subordinate to the main attraction in the image. I've created just such an image, using RayFlect's Four Seasons sky creation software (http://www.rayflect.com/web/home/index.htm), and some brushwork over it, using Right Hemisphere's Deep Paint. If I use JPEG Medium compression, and do not use the Progressive option (which messes up the view from several image viewing programs), my 400-by-300-pixel masterpiece can be pretty faithfully optimized from its native 354KB to a small 10KB, as shown in figure 14.1.

The objective in the steps that follow is to isolate the area in the image that has high-frequency content (a lot of colors changing from pixel to pixel), to allow this area to have less compression than the other slices of the image, and then to really see how low we can go with areas (slices) of the image that have very slow transitions in color and very few distinct colors.

Let's get out a new tool, the Slice tool, right now:

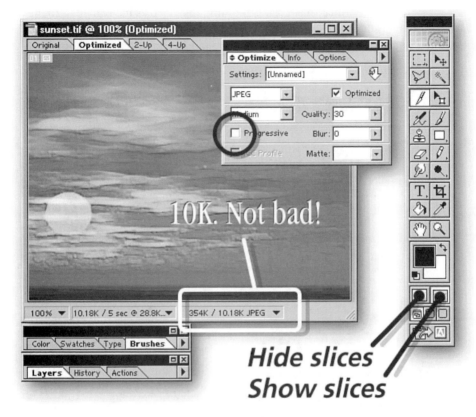

Hide slices
Show slices

Figure 14.1   *JPEG works best when an image does not have many color transitions.*

Slicing According to Image Area Importance

1. Open the sunset.tif image from the Examples/Chap14 folder on the Companion CD. As you can see, there is only one area of interest in the image—the sun as it hits a few clouds. On the Optimize palette, choose JPEG Medium, and then uncheck the Progressive check box.

2. Click on the View Slices mode button, toward the bottom of the toolbox (see fig. 14.1).

3. Click on the Optimized tab at the top of the image window, choose the Slice tool, and then draw a rectangle around the sunny part of the sunset, as shown in figure

14.2. You will notice that the surrounding image areas have divided themselves automatically into other slices. You will also see strange, tiny glyphs in the upper left of each image slice. I'll explain them, and you'll use them, shortly.

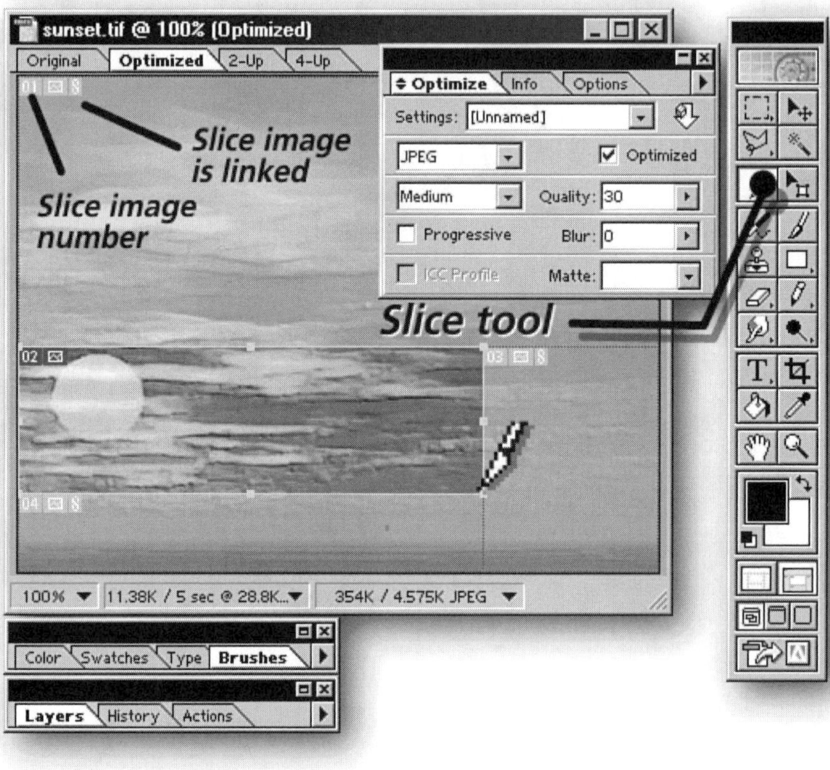

FIGURE 14.2   *There are tiny slice image link icons and number icons in the upper left of all the slices except the one you drew, which contains no link.*

4. The link icon (top left, far-right icon) in a slice means that if you change the compression settings for this slice when it's highlighted, all the other linked slices will take on the same compression. Useless, huh? Choose the Slice Select tool (see fig. 14.3), right-click (Macintosh: hold Ctrl and click) on the link icon you see on the top left slice. Then, from the context menu, choose Unlink Slice, as shown in figure 14.3, and then drag the Optimize palette's Quality slider down to about 17.

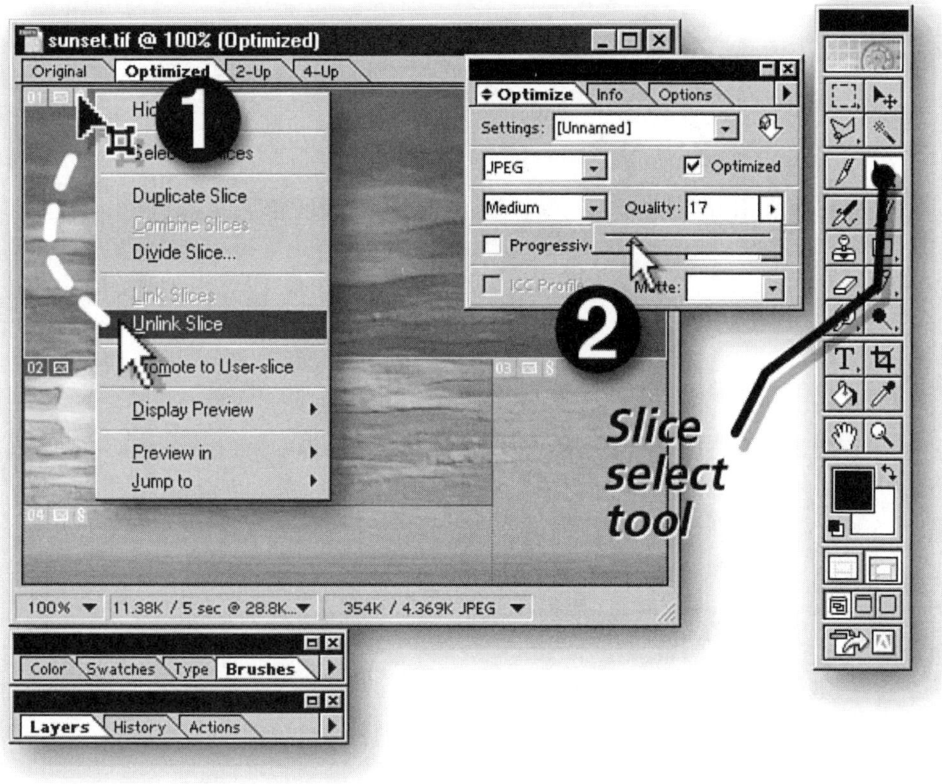

FIGURE 14.3   *You probably will not see the difference in quality between 30 and 17 for the top slice of image, but you will lose about 1KB of total saved file size by doing this.*

5. Perform step 4 with the other slices, except the one you drew.

6. Click the Hide Slices button, and then look at the Document Sizes field for this image. You went from 10K to 9K, as shown in figure 14.4 simply by optimizing areas that need optimizing.

7. Choose File, Save Image Optimized as, and then create a new folder called Sunset_GIF, and save both the images and the HTML code to this folder on your hard disk. I found that when I loaded the HTML document in my browser, the sliced image actually loaded faster than a 400-by-300-pixel, complete image, even when the image was optimized.

8. Close Sunset.tif without saving, and then open it again for the next section.

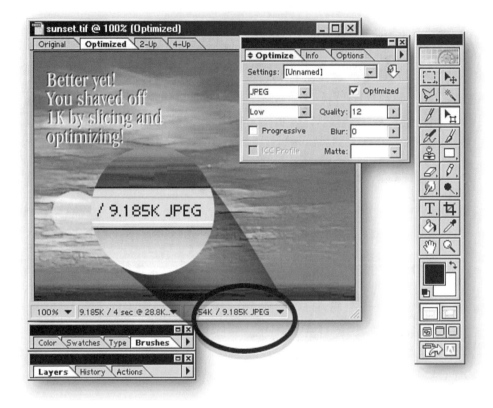

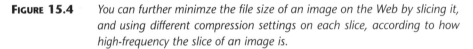

FIGURE 15.4 *You can further minimze the file size of an image on the Web by slicing it, and using different compression settings on each slice, according to how high-frequency the slice of an image is.*

Again, when you have an image sliced, you can select any of the slices, and then use the Layer Options palette to assign each slice an *URL* (a clickable area that contains a different address on the Web).

But I found something equally fun to do with image slices that, unlike image mapping, requires a tad of an explanation here!

Suppose you exported an image, sliced, in the GIF file format. And then suppose what would happen if you created an animation and replaced one of the slices with the animation. It works, trust me. Let's try it!

Grafting an Animated GIF into a Sliced Image

1. With the Sunset.tif image open in ImageReady's workspace, choose GIF 32 Dithered from the Settings drop-down menu on the Optimize palette. This is a good starting place for optimizing and slicing the image.

2. With the Slice tool, draw a tight rectangle around the sun in the image. The remaining areas become slices with links to each other.

3. Click on the Optimized tab at the top of the image window. As you did with the JPEG optimization of this same image, right-click (Macintosh: hold Ctrl and click) and then Unlink the slices, and assign them different numbers of colors. For example, the top of this image still looks pretty good and not too dithered using 16 colors, Selective evaluation of the area, and Diffusion dithering.

4. When you've finished optimizing all the other slices, optimize the sun area; then, from the main menu, choose Select, Create selection from slice, as shown in figure 14.5.

5. Press Ctrl(⌘)+C, press Ctrl(⌘)+N, click OK, and then press Ctrl(⌘)+V to copy the selection to a new image window. Click on the title bar to the sunset.tif image, and then look very carefully at the glyphs in the upper left of the sun slice area. We will check twice before overwriting a file, but it looks as though the animated part of this image will contain the number 3 in the name of the image. Choose File, Save Optimized As, and save the images and HTML code as Sunset_GIF to an easy-to-find location on your hard drive. Close the sunset image now without saving. You've got the pieces you need tucked away in a new folder.

6. Press F11 to display the Animation palette. Make the sun appear in the image for 1 second by clicking on the really small down triangle beneath the thumbnail on the Animation palette.

7. Click on the Duplicates current frame button on the Animation palette, and then on the Layers palette (press F7), drag the Layer 2 title (the image of the sun pasted into the image window) into the Creates new layer icon. Finally, click on the Layer 2 copy title on the Layers palette to make the duplicate the active layer; then, in the image window, paint a smiley face on the sun, as shown in figure 14.6.

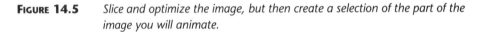

FIGURE 14.5   *Slice and optimize the image, but then create a selection of the part of the image you will animate.*

8. Choose File, Save Optimized (as a GIF) to your hard drive. You will be renaming the file soon, so keep the image in close proximity to your sliced GIF image folder.

9. Go to the folder where you placed all the GIF slices. In figure 14.7, I'm using a Windows utility called PicaView to preview the sunset_03.gif that ImageReady wrote to the Images folder. It appears on the shortcut menu when you right-click over an image file.

   Yup, this is the file that needs to be overwritten. (On the Macintosh, Graphics Converter, also shareware, can open images more quickly than Photoshop, because it is not burdened with all of Photoshop's features.) Rename your animation sunset_03.gif, and then delete sunset_03.gif in the Images folder. Then, drag the animated, newly renamed sunset_03.gif into the Images folder.

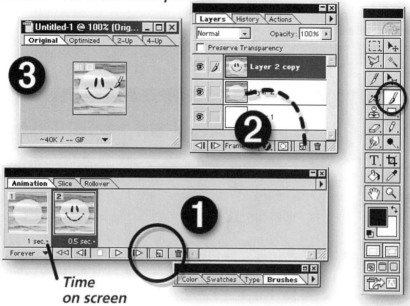

FIGURE 14.6   *Aww, why not?*

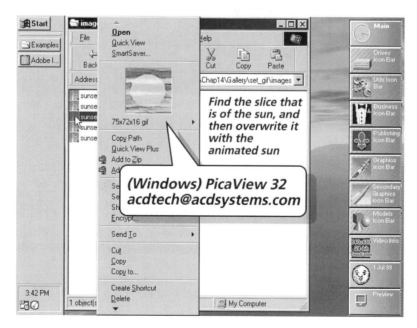

FIGURE 14.7   *It would be wise to receive visual confirmation that the file you are going to overwrite is the correct file!*

10. You can close the sunset image without saving, and then go to that folder you created, and drag and drop sunset.html into your browser. I think you'll be surprised and delighted that the sun in an image now animates, and FYI it only took one more kilobyte to make than a sliced GIF image without the animation. Check out figure 14.8.

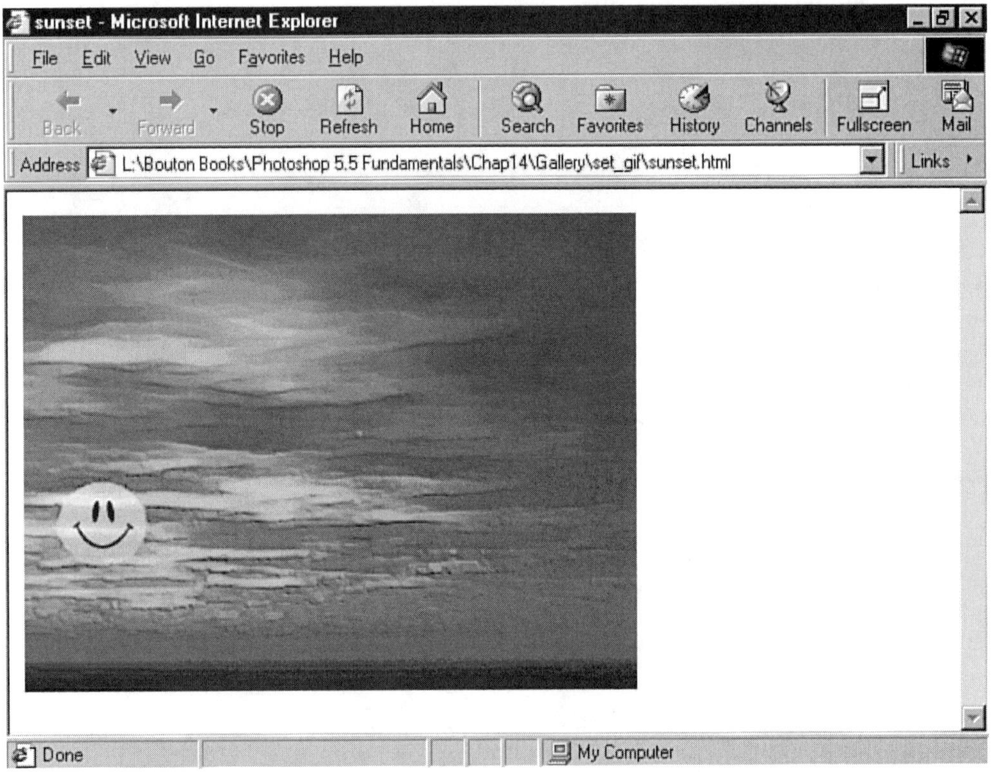

Figure 14.8 *Okay, this smiley is a dumb use of slicing technology, but think of the possibilities of this technique in your own work when you need an element to change?*

In the following section, you're going to learn more about states than you ever did in History class, as we explore the changing states of a JavaScript rollover Web element.

JavaScript Rollovers

Okay, first, JavaScript has nothing to do with Java programming language. It was originally called LiveScript by Netscape Communications, which later decided that LiveScript needed a sexier, yet very misleading new name.

I, myself, am a little guilty of practicing misleading nomenclature in this chapter, and by confessing right now, you'll get a better understanding of scripting language. JavaScript is scripting language, and scripting language is *not* code. We often call HTML "a few lines of code," but it's really "a few lines of scripting language," like *Lingo,* which is used to script Macromedia Director shows. *Engineers* write code; we artists can handle scripting—and you can do a lot of stuff with scripts.

A JavaScript is perhaps the most courteous way of displaying info that reacts to cursor movement while the visitor navigates your Web site. This is because JavaScripts are never downloaded to a visitor's computer (Java *applets*—actual Java programming of small utilities—need to assemble parts of themselves on the host's machine and doesn't that make you a little nervous, as in, "assemble virus here"?) Thankfully, Java*Scripts* cannot breach your machine.

Also, because JavaScripting is text commands, not code, you can read and copy anyone's script, and they in turn can read and copy yours. This isn't stealing, folks; in fact, a lot of sites that feature rollover buttons and slide shows actually tell you to download the script. Now *that's* called sharing, and that's the spirit of the Web—learning through imitation.

Although there are many different types of JavaScripts, ImageReady offers a graphical interface for creating only one of the JavaScripts out there—the really cool one—the rollover. A *rollover* is what makes a button or illustration change when you click on it, hover the cursor over it, release the cursor, and so on. Rollover navigation buttons can add a lot of polish to your Web page, so let's get going!

Creating the First State for the JavaScript Button

By default, when you enter a Web site, you aren't clicking on anything immediately, so the first *state*—the set of conditions by which the JavaScript knows which image to display—is called the *default state.* This state exists when you're not clicking on anything.

I think that "Knock here" is a slightly humorous message on a button in its default state, so the following steps show you how to accomplish this:

Preparing the Default Button

1. Press Ctrl(⌘)+N, and in the New dialog box specify that an image should be created that's 75 pixels tall by 200 pixels wide. This is, for sure, a large size for a button, but not if it's the only thing on the HTML page!

2. Fill the layer with foreground color, and then on the Styles palette, drag the deep purple–style thumbnail into the image window. Then, use the Type tool and a lighter shade of purple to type **Knock here**. I suggest a heavy font such as Kabel at 30 points for the type. The text is added to a new layer. Right-click (Macintosh: hold Ctrl and click) on the Type layer title on the Layers palette, and choose Bevel and Emboss, as shown in figure 14.9.

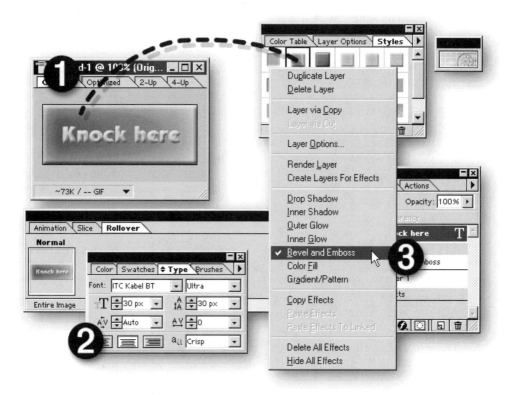

Figure 14.9   *Create a button, and then create the type for it on two separate layers.*

3. Choose Flatten Image from the Layers palette's menu flyout. You only have a Knock here layer on the palette and in the image now. Save the image to hard disk as Welcome.psd, in Photoshop's native format.

The second state for the button will be a Welcome! button when the audience hovers over the button with their cursors.

Creating a "Hover Over" State for the Button

Let's get a little more adventurous with the second button for the JavaScript rollover. You'll keep the button basically the same overall color, but you'll add banding to the shading (by learning a new technique) and make the coloring lighter than that of the Knock here button so the audience will see immediately that this is no mere image map button! Finally, you'll create new text so the button will appear to change its message.

Here's how to create a button that will appear when the *MouseOver* state is in effect (the visitor has the cursor over the button):

Creating Graphics for the MouseOver State

1. Create a second state for the graphic by clicking on the Creates new rollover state icon at the bottom of the Rollover palette. By default, the second button is called the Over button, which is what we want. If, in your own work, you wanted a different state, you could click on the down arrow next to the word Down, and choose from a list of other states.

2. Create a new layer in the graphic by clicking on the Create new layer icon at the bottom of the Layers palette. Then press Ctrl(⌘)+Delete (Backspace) to fill the layer. Drag the deep purple–style thumbnail into the image window to apply the style.

3. Click on the Effects triangle on the title directly beneath the Layer 1 title on the Layers palette. This causes all the effects that make up the layer to cascade down, and you can change any of the components.

4. Double-click on the Color Fill title. A Color Fill palette will pop into the workspace. Click on the Color field on this palette (marked with a 2 in fig. 14.10) to display the Color Picker. Choose a lighter shade of purple here, and then press Enter (Return) to return to the workspace.

5. Why we're at it, let's change the shading effect that lies over the Color Fill. Double-click on the Gradient/Pattern title; a Gradient/Pattern palette appears, and you should choose Copper from the drop-down list, as shown in figure 14.11. Does this turn the button to a copper color? Not at all; what you've done is "influence" the sum total of interacting effects units to display the banding—the tonal quality—of the button's appearance. It's still a light purple button...sort of <g>.

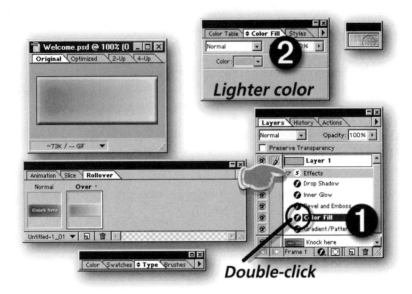

FIGURE 14.10   *Change any or all of the effects that make up a button on a layer by dropping down the Effects list and double-clicking on a title.*

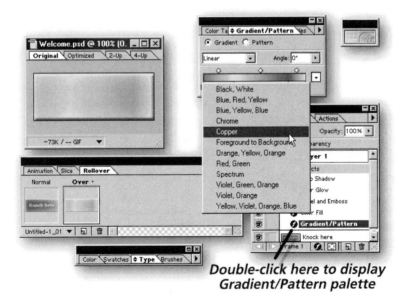

FIGURE 14.11   *Change the shading on the button from a Linear Gradient to a preset Copper color scheme.*

6. With the Type tool, click on the center of the button (remember, you left the alignment of the Type tool to centered), and then type **Welcome**, using the last-used font and font size. Now, the Type layer doesn't care at all about what the effects presets Color Fill was for the underlying button, so you must display the toolbox (you'll notice that I have it minimized a lot in these figures; double-clicking extends and retracts it), click on the foreground color selection box, and then choose a light purple. The type on the layer will immediately change to this color.

7. Add a pillow emboss effect by right-clicking (Macintosh: holding Ctrl and clicking) over the Type title on the Layers palette, and choosing Bevel and Emboss. A Bevel and Emboss tab appears on the Styles palette. To fine-tune the pillow emboss, click on the menu flyout on the palette to display the Show Options area, where you can change the angle of the shading and other things, as shown in figure 14.12. The type layer and the button layer together are going to represent the MouseOver state on the Rollover palette.

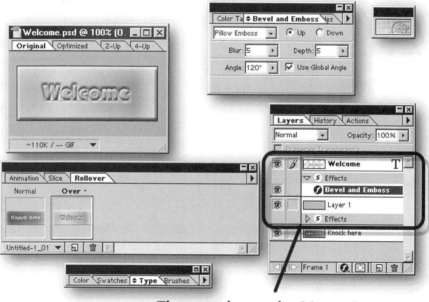

These make up the MouseOver state

FIGURE 14.12   *The second button exists on two layers right now, but we'll correct this.*

I don't know why merging down does not work with layers that have effects tagged to them, but you *cannot* use the Ctrl(⌘)+E command to make a single layer out of the type and the button.

8. Okay—hide the bottom, the Knock here layer, by clicking on the eye icon to the left of its title. Then, press Ctrl(⌘)+Shift+E to merge visible layers, as is elegantly illustrated in figure 14.13. Now, you have a first and second state image for the rollover button. Press Ctrl(⌘)+S; keep the file open. You should make the buttons visible again by clicking in the eye column to the left of the titles.

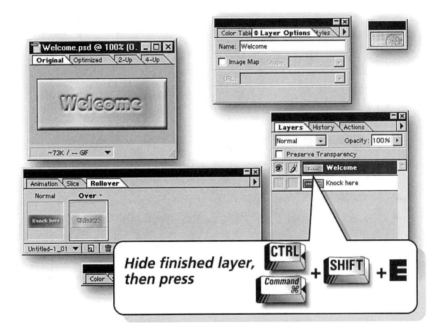

FIGURE 14.13   *Merge all the visible layers—this includes only the new type layer and its corresponding button.*

The next section should come as no surprise to you. You're going to create the MouseDown state for the button. This is what all visitors will see when they click on the button, and you'll want to attach an URL to this button. Come see for yourself!

Creating the Third State for the Button

Oh, I'm thinking that a button that's really deep in color will make a splendid "entrance" when folks click on your rollover button. So let's make it a nearly black button with gleaming green text that says "Loading" (as in, "Now I'm going to load the page you asked for").

We'll play around with an undiscovered feature or two, but basically, to do the third state for this Web object, you do this:

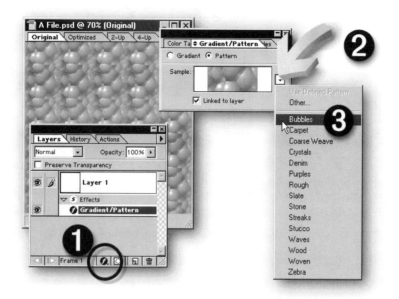

Figure 14.14   *ImageReady ships with over a dozen interesting patterns that can be effects components; or you can use them, undiluted, as an image background.*

Creating the MouseDown State for the Button

1. Click on the Create new layer icon at the bottom of the Layers palette, and then fill the layer. I suggest 4F4F4F, a deep shade of warm black.

2. Click on the Creates a new rollover state button on the Rollover palette. You can see that Down is the state assigned, by default, to the new entry.

3. Drag the fifth-from-left Style button into the image window. As you can see in figure 14.15, the button is a deep color, but you can still see the edges of the button—the highlights and shading.

tip

If truth be known, sometimes Tips pop up in this book when there's no other good place to put them! Seriously, did you notice that one of the effects shaders was called Gradient/Pattern? What patterns are available when you click on the Pattern button on the palette?

In figure 14.14, you can see that I've filled a new image window with the Bubbles pattern. You can use these patterns for anything you like; these patterns tile, but because they are so small, you can't use them on images larger than say, a button, before you begin to see the repeats in the tile.

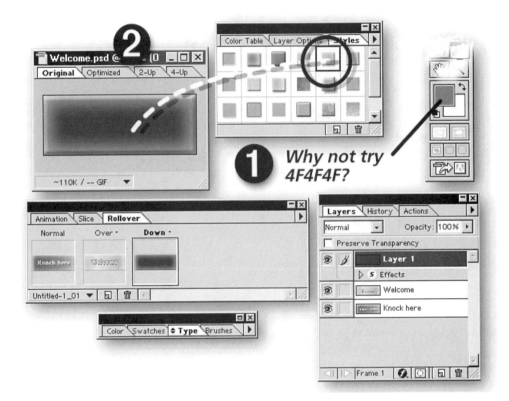

FIGURE 14.15   *Some of the buttons on the Styles palette require that you already have a dark or light color filling the current layer. This is one of those Styles palette buttons.*

4. Add the word **Loading** to a type layer on top of the button. Make it a bright green color and pillow emboss it, just as you've done twice before in this chapter.

5. Click on the triangle to the left of the Effects title, directly below the type layer, to expand the Effects list that makes up the type's shading. Double-click on the Bevel and Emboss title to display the Bevel and Emboss palette.

6. Now, click on the right-facing triangle directly to the right of the Angle field, and then drag the line in the circle down until the field reads about −57°. You'll notice in figure 14.16, that because Use Global Angle is checked, not only the type changes lighting direction, but so does the underlying button layer! You *want* this to happen, because now the button looks indented (as though you had physically pushed in the button with your cursor).

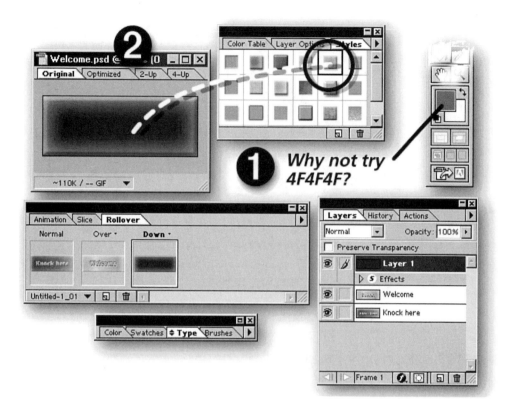

FIGURE 14.16   *Change any underlying layer that has effects applied to it by keeping the Use Global Angle check box checked.*

7. Extend the palette by choosing Show Options on the palette's menu flyout. You're going to make this text a little less hard on the eyes by softening the shadow areas. Click on the shadow color, as shown in figure 14.17; then, in the Color Picker, choose about a 70% black. Press Enter (Return) and return to the scene.

8. Hide the Knock here and Welcome layers, and then press Ctrl(⌘)+Shift+E to merge the Loading type with the button. Then, make every layer visible by clicking to make the eye icons visible in the eye column to the left of the titles.

9. Click on the Loading layer title to make it the current editing layer. In the Rollover palette, the third thumbnail (Loading) should be highlighted.

10. On the Optimize palette, choose JPEG High from the Settings field, and then uncheck the Progressive check box. This button is small and is the only element on the Web page, so you can splurge a little with JPEG quality.

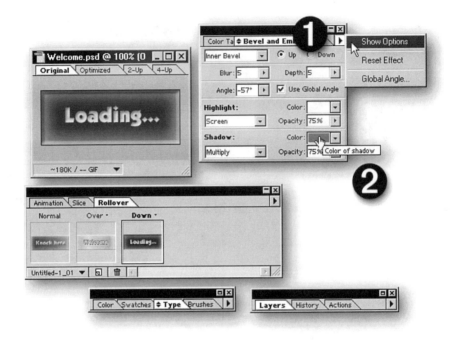

FIGURE 14.17   *You can make the highlight and shadow colors any color you want, and even increase or decrease the percentage of their presence in the type.*

11. Check the Image Map check box on the Layer Options palette (Window, Show Layer Options/Effects), and then in the URL field type any URL you please. In figure 14.18, I've typed Adobe's home page URL because their Webmaster likes to get a lot of hits.

12. Hey—basically, you're done! Choose File, Save Optimized As, and then find a good spot on your hard disk for both the HTML and the images that make up the rollover button. You can close ImageReady and the images at any time after you've pressed Ctrl(⌘)+S one last time (in this *chapter*—I don't mean you'll never press Ctrl+S again).

If you'd like to see this JavaScript rollover button in action as much as I would, simply find the Welcome.html document on your hard drive, and double-click on it, or toss it at the icon of your Web browser of choice. In figure 14.19, you can see what happens when I hover my cursor over the button. Neat, huh?

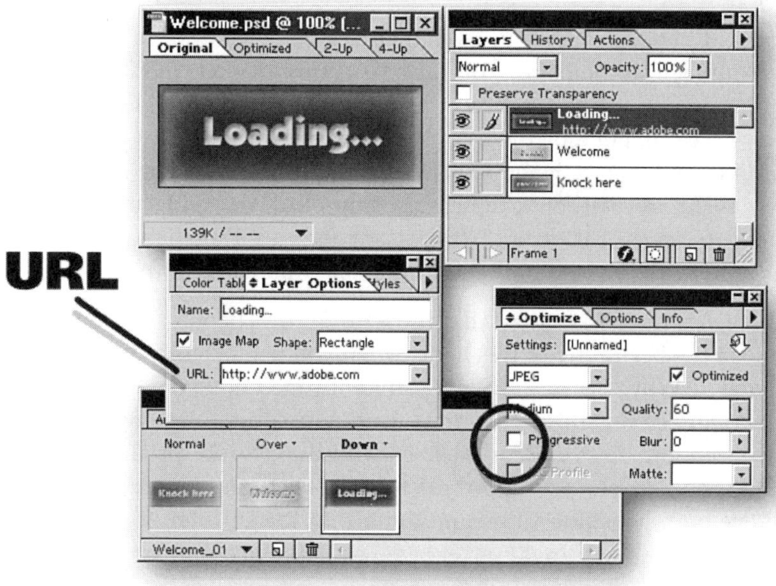

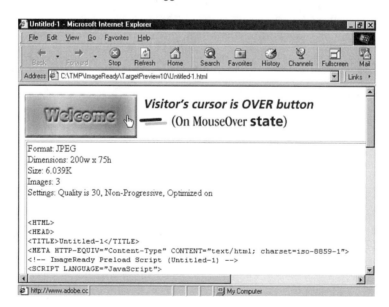

FIGURE 14.18   *Make the MouseDown state trigger a link to an URL.*

FIGURE 14.19   *Does a rollover button make your site interactive? Emmm, not really, but it adds pizzazz and keeps visitors to your site awake and active!*

Summary

I think (I hope) that I've uncovered all the tricks, or at least the keys to the tricks, that ImageReady holds for you—if not in this chapter, then in the three chapters before this one. Does that mean the party's over? Not in the least. There's a plethora (okay a wealth, not a plethora) of variations you can perform on this program's core features—and, naturally, on Photoshop. Oh, by the way, you might be interested to know that these past four chapters also improved your skill with Photoshop, whether you were aware of it or not. ImageReady uses a lot of the same key commands as Photoshop, and we certainly reinforced key commands in this chapter.

You might also have noticed that the steps in this chapter are about twice the size of those at the beginning of this book, when you first cracked the spine and dove into chapter 1. Why? Because if you're still with me here, you are capable of handling many more commands in the time it used to take you to press Ctrl(⌘)+N for New image window. You've become skilled with these Adobe products. A lot of my repetition in this chapter was done only to reinforce things you already know. You might say I've been polishing your suit of armor in this chapter, so you can better go out and slay those really tough pixel-based assignments. And you're pretty handy with Web media now, to boot, huh?

In the next chapter, we're going to run a steroid-driven, lightning-paced race from chapter 1 or 2, to this chapter. Remember selections? Remember how to use type? I'm going to let you brush up on everything we've covered in this book, but I'm also doing it to show you how Photoshop and ImageReady integrate.

Ready for the ride of your life?

PART V

Integrating the Whole Enchilada

CHAPTER 15

If You Read Only One Chapter...

I've always liked that selling phrase, commonly overused in the motion picture industry, like, "If you see only one film this summer, see *Blah-Blah Blah, the Sequel.*"

But I'm not trying to sell you something in this chapter; okay, if ideas always come with a price tag, then I'm trying to sell you a little here. Chapter 15 is a potpourri of all the other chapters in this book. Remember how you learned about selections, graduated to the Rubber Stamp tool, and then layers? And then ImageReady? This chapter takes you through all the key techniques found in earlier chapters—you create a selection, you use color controls to recolor the selection, you make a brush tip from it, and so on. So if you've read the book already, this is the best refresher course I could leave you with. And if this is the first chapter you've dived into, read it—and you might just be motivated to check out the rest of the book's info.

Creating an eFlorist's Site

You can order flowers over the Web, you know? Me, I'm waiting until you can order *gardeners* over the Web. The concept in this chapter is that the fictitious Susan, who is partial to black-eyed Susans, comes to you with a request to make some top page Web site art for her company, Susan's Susans. This involves generating some art, some text, some optimizing in ImageReady—hoo, boy, is she going to get a bill!

The place to start is with a photo of a black-eyed Susan.

Modifying Existing Art to Serve a Composition Need

Now, I could have snapped a picture of a black-eyed Susan right in my back yard, but I thought, "Nah—not enough of a challenge." If you think about it, a daisy looks very much like a black-eyed Susan, except for the coloration. So I've provided you with a bunch of daisies in Daisy.tif on the Companion CD, and what you're going to do is select the best daisy from the herd, and then recolor it.

In figure 15.1, I propose the two best methods for separating the daisy you'll use from the others. My very first attempt would be with the Pen tool, because the daisy has well-defined edges. And using the Pen tool, you could expect to take about half an hour creating a perfect path outline.

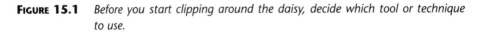

The Pen tool? The Layer mask mode?

FIGURE 15.1   *Before you start clipping around the daisy, decide which tool or technique to use.*

Now (imagine the word "Now" at 48pts.), one of the things I've been saying all along in this book is the mantra, "Detect before you correct." Have you done your inspection work with the image? If so, you will find an alpha channel in the image that perfectly describes the outline of the daisy you need; you just Ctrl(⌘)+click on its title to load it.

Was this whole set-up a cheap trick? Not in the least. I get images handed to me all the time where the creator has left paths, alpha channels, named the image in the wrong file format—you name it. The point is that it never hurts to spend two seconds browsing a file you've been handed to check for easier ways than usual to accomplish a task.

Don't get me wrong—it would please me to no end for you to use the Pen tool, or even Layer Mask mode, to create your own selection around the daisy. It would keep you in good practice with Photoshop. But if you're weary of selecting stuff and you want, this time only, to go with my selection, that's why I created the alpha channel.

Here's how to separate the daisy, and then recolor it so it looks like a black-eyed Susan:

Changing the Color of a Selection

1. In Photoshop, open the Daisy.tif image from the Examples/Chap15 folder on the Companion CD. 100% viewing resolution is good.

2. Press F7 if the Layers/Channels palette isn't in the workspace. Click on the Channels tab, and then Ctrl(⌘)+click on the Alpha 1 channel. A marquee selection will appear around the daisy.

3. On the Layers palette, Right-click (Macintosh: hold Ctrl and click) on the layer title (not the layer thumbnail picture) and then choose Layer Via Copy from the context menu, as shown in figure 15.2. Then, hide the base layer—the layer from which you copied the daisy; click on its eye icon.

4. Alt(Opt)+click if necessary on the icon, but get the Quick Mask tool in the mode where color indicates selected areas; the circle on the icon should be colored in. Then, using the top-row, far-right tip on the Brushes palette and the Paintbrush tool, paint over the center of the daisy so your brush strokes will become a selection area (see fig. 15.3). Press Q to return to Standard editing mode.

5. Press Ctrl(⌘)+U to display the Hue/Saturation dialog box, and then drag the Hue slider to –20 and the Saturation slider to –31. As you can see on your monitor (or in black-and-white in fig. 15.4) the center of the daisy is looking light brown, like a sienna wash. Click on OK, and we're off to further modifications on the piece.

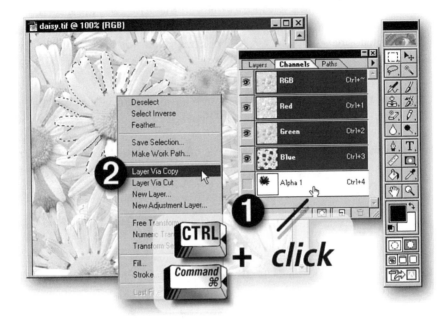

FIGURE 15.2   *Load the alpha channel as a selection, and then copy the contents of the selection to a new layer.*

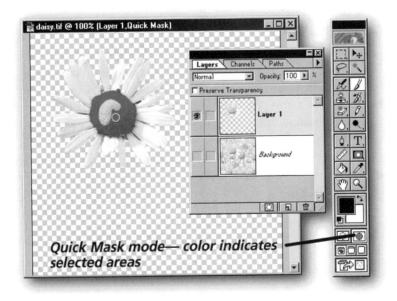

FIGURE 15.3   *Cover the area that you want selected, using Quick Mask overlay.*

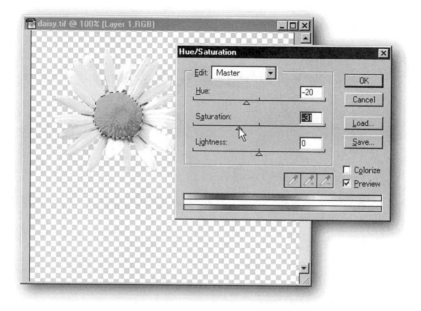

FIGURE 15.4   *The Hue/Saturation command is a very powerful tool. Adult supervision is recommended.*

6. This is not the nicest brown you can come up with using only the Hue/Saturation command. The area needs more contrast—then the brown shades will really stand out. Press Ctrl(⌘)+L to display the Levels command.

7. Drag the black point input slider to about 59. Doing this accentuates the darker tones in the center of the flower, and makes the brown stand out more. Also, as shown in figure 15.5, drag the white point output slider to about 221. This decreases the amount of white in the selection, making the center look an even richer brown. And use your eyes while doing this; my suggested values might not be exactly what you need, because your Photoshop gamma is not the same as mine, or you could have gone with a different hue earlier when you corrected the selection—whatever. Trust your eyes—when you see a rich brown (who *is* Rich Brown?) center to the flower, press Enter (Return).

8. Getting the petals to look yellow is a piece of cake. First, press Shift+F7 to invert the selection. Click on the Preserve Transparency check box on the Layers palette. Press Ctrl(⌘)+L; in the Levels dialog box, drag the white point output slider (the right slider at the bottom of the palette) to about 230. This (and this is an advanced trick) makes the petals a dirty shade of black. *But*—there's detail in the petals, and Photoshop's Color mode will only work with less than white pixels. Click on OK to leave the Levels box.

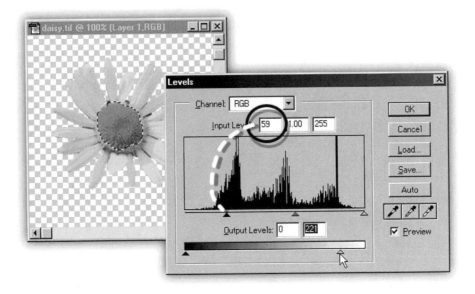

Figure 15.5   *Increase the density of the tones within the colored selection to make the selection look browner.*

9. Click on the foreground color selection box and choose a cheery lemon color for the black-eyed Susan petals. With the Paintbrush tool, set the modes drop-down selection on the Brushes palette to Color, and then stroke away. You'll see that the petals not only have color but also visual content from the darkened tone in them.

10. Choose File, Save As, and save the file as Daisy.psd. I know, I know—it's a black-eyed Susan now, but we will create a finished file later (that is not this file), called "Susan." Keep the document open, and press Ctrl(⌘)+D to deselect the current selection.

Pretty neat, huh? You changed a daisy into a black-eyed Susan, and you don't even know about horticulture or gene splicing.

Creating a Brush Tip and a Floral Background

Here's the game plan: You will use the black-eyed Susan later as the centerpiece of a bunch of smaller black-eyed Susans. To create a bunch of small Susans, you'll create a custom brush tip out of a smaller version of the Susan you just retouched. Then, you can sprinkle small, black-and-white copies all over a new image. And finally, you'll colorize the monochrome Susans.

Here's the first set of steps, creating the brush tip:

Making a Black-Eyed Susan Brush Tip

1. Drag the Layer 1 title into the Create new layer icon on the Layers palette. This creates a new layer, Layer 1 copy. Hide the other two layers, as you do not need them right now.

2. Press Ctrl(⌘)+T to place the Free Transform bounding box around the flower. Hold Shift (to constrain dragging to proportional resizing), and then drag on a corner handle (corner handles are for scaling and rotating objects) toward the center of the flower until the flower looks to be about ¼ the size of the original flower, as shown in figure 15.6. Double-click on the inside of the Free Transform box to finalize the transformation. After resizing image content, the Unsharp Mask is the best tool for eliminating the resulting fuzziness. Choose Filter, Sharpen, Unsharp Mask, and then use these settings: Amount 50%, Radius: 1 pixel, and Threshold: 1 level. Click on OK to apply the sharpening.

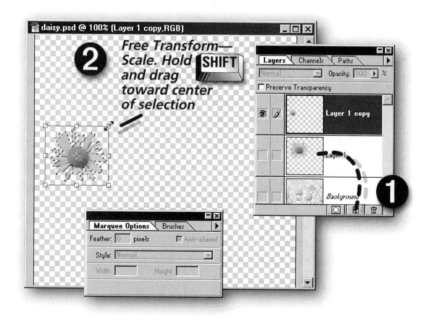

FIGURE 15.6 *Use the Scale Free Transform command by dragging on a corner handle.*

3. With the Rectangular Marquee tool, drag a very tight selection border around the flower. Then on the Brushes palette, click on the right-facing triangle toward the top right of the palette, and choose Define Brush from the menu flyout, as shown in figure 15.7. Immediately, a portion of the flower sample appears at the tail end of the Brushes palette.

Before we get to the point, I'd like to note that this capture of the black-eyed Susan design, when applied to a layer, will result in different degrees of opacity when any color is used to render the brush stroke. That is, the lighter area—the petals—will show more transparency than the much denser center. This property of the defined brush poses a problem when you try to add color to the design, but not if you first flatten the image, so the image is foreground color (black) against a white background.

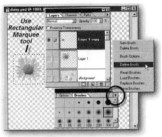

FIGURE 15.7

Only the Rectangular Marquee tool can be used to define a brush tip from an image.

4. Create a new image, specify that both the height and width are 400 pixels, specify RGB Color Mode, and specify that a transparent background makes up the image.

5. With black as your foreground color, start clicking in a random fashion, using the flower brush tip and black foreground color, as shown in figure 15.8.

Actually, you could have specified a white background, but I wanted you to see the transparency effect with the brush tip you built.

6. Choose Flatten Image from the menu flyout on the Layers palette, and then choose Select, Color Range. With the eyedropper, click on a petal in the image, and then drag the Fuzziness slider to the left or to the right until only the petals appear in white (they are selected), as shown in figure 15.9. Press Enter (Return) to apply the selection and return to the worksapce.

7. Press Ctrl(⌘)+U to display the Hue/Saturation dialog box. Click on the Colorize check box. Drag the Hue slider to 50, drag the Saturation slider to 78, and drag the Brightness slider down to about –8. Click on OK to apply this change to the picture.

8. Press Ctrl(⌘)+D to deselect the marquee. Choose Select, Color Range, and this time, click the eyedropper over the center of a flower. Press Enter (Return) to return to the workspace. Press Ctrl(⌘)+U to display the Hue/Saturation dialog box. Click on the Colorize check box. Drag the Hue slider to 36, and then drag the Saturation slider to 38, as shown in figure 15.10. The flowers are looking like a swarm of black-eyed Susans now, aren't they? Click on OK to return to the workspace.

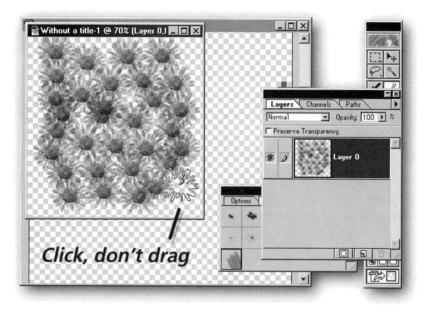

FIGURE 15.8 *Click, but do not drag, as you populate the image canvas with the flower brush tip you created.*

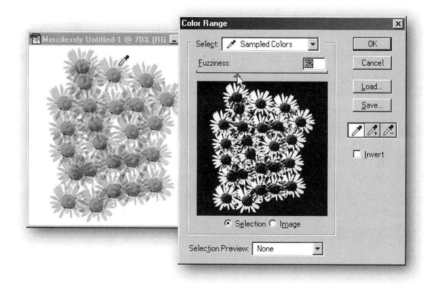

FIGURE 15.9 *Use the Color Range command to isolate a specific range of tones in the picture.*

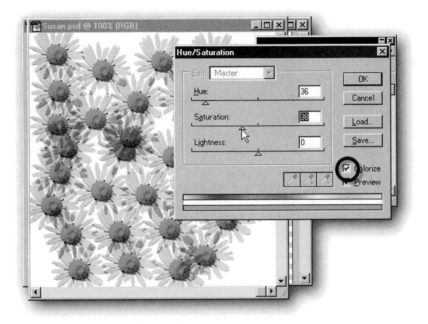

Figure 15.10   *Use the Colorize feature to convert tonal information to different bright-nesses of a single hue.*

9. Save the image as Susan.psd in Photoshop's native file format.

10. I think we need a different background than white for this composition. Choose the Magic Wand tool from the toolbox by double-clicking (this displays the Options box), type **5** in the Tolerance field, make sure the Contiguous check box is *not* checked, and then click on a white area of the design, as shown in figure 15.11.

11. Click on the foreground color selection box on the toolbox, check the Only Web Colors check box, and then pick out a color that complements the flowers. I went with a burnt orange, as shown in figure 15.12. You should probably use this color, too. Type **CC9900** in the # field, and then press Tab to move on but also to register your text entry. This is a good color not only because it's a nature color, but because it's a Web color. As you may recall from earlier chapters on ImageReady, the Web palette does not produce dithering when shown on a monitor with limited colors.

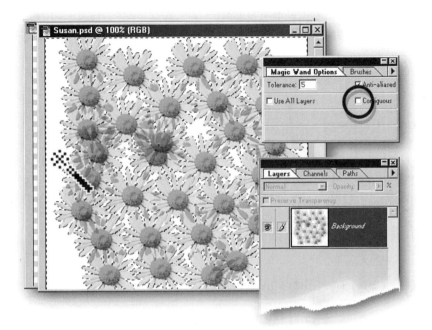

FIGURE 15.11   *Select the background only; no petals and no centers of the flowers.*

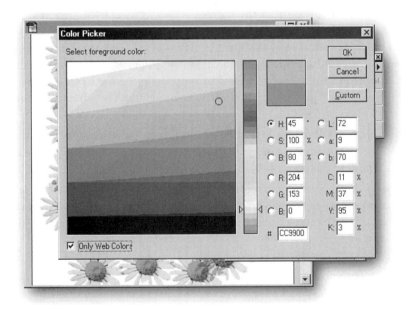

FIGURE 15.12   *Choose a color for the background of the image.*

12. Press Alt(Opt)+Delete (Backspace), and then press Ctrl(⌘)+D to deselect the marquee. Press Ctrl(⌘)+S; keep the file open.

The design is coming out fine, but don't you feel as though it needs a central focal element? We'll address this in the next section.

Adding a Centerpiece to the Design

A natural enough (and easy to get) centerpiece to the gathering of flowers would be the larger, original black-eyed Susan you created earlier. But it will not stand out if you simply add it to the piece. It needs shading, specifically the shading you learned in chapter 4's nuts and bolts assignment, to help the large Susan to stand out in the crowd.

Here's how to add this large central element:

Adding a Layer to the Design

1. Drag the image windows and palettes around until you find Daisy.tif buried there somewhere. On the Layers palette, make sure that Layer 1 is chosen and that the other layers are hidden (to prevent visual confusion).

2. Choose the Move tool from the toolbox (the following trick doesn't work with other tools). On the Layers palette, while holding Alt(Opt), drag the Layer 1 title into the Susan.psd image, as shown in figure 15.13. The Alt(Opt) modifier here drops a copy of the contents of the layer into the center of a new layer in the target image. You still might want to fuss with the placement, but only by a pixel or two, I think, and you can do this with the Move tool chosen and the arrow nudge keys.

3. Ctrl(⌘)+click on the new layer title on the Layers palette to load the silhouette of the flower to become a marquee selection. Choose Select, Modify, Expand, and then type **5** in the pixels field, and press Enter (Return).

4. Click on the Background layer title, and then click on the Create new layer icon. You should now have a Layer 2 below the large Susan you copied over in step 2. With black as the foreground color, press Alt(Opt)+Delete (Backspace), then press Ctrl+D to deselect the selection.

5. Choose Filter, Blur, Gaussian Blur. As shown in figure 15.14, you want about 4 pixels as the value.

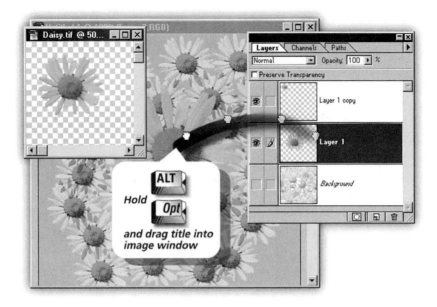

FIGURE 15.13   *Hold Alt(Opt) while you drag the Susan into the other image window to center it in the new image window.*

FIGURE 15.14   *Blur the black shape you created on Layer 2 by using the Gaussian blur filter.*

6. Click on OK to apply the filter's blurring. Now, with the Move tool, drag the drop shadow down and to the right ever-so-slightly, drag the Opacity slider (first you have to click and hold on the triangle on the Layers palette) to about 77%, and then choose Multiply as the layer mode, as shown in figure 15.15.

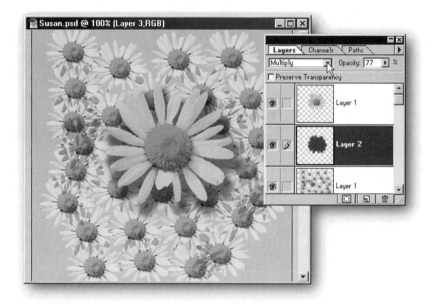

Figure 15.15   *It's hard to believe that you started with only a clipping of a daisy, huh?*

7. Choose File, Save a copy, and then save a flattened copy of your work as Susan.tif in the TIFF file format. You'll need this flat copy in a moment. Press Ctrl(⌘)+S; keep the file open.

In the next section, you'll need Illustrator (or a similar drawing package) to form text into an arc. If you don't own Illustrator, CorelDRAW, or CorelXARA, not to worry. At the appropriate step, I'll tell you to go to the CD and fetch an Illustrator file that fits the bill. Cool?

Adding Text to the Graphic

As you saw (hopefully) in chapter 8, sometimes the best text you can add to a Photoshop creation comes from an outside source. In this example, our fictitious client wants the lettering "Susan's Susans" to arc around the top of the large, center black-eyed Susan, and she wants "eFlorist" at the bottom of the flower—straight, no fancy arc.

Photoshop doesn't do text on an arc, but these days Illustrator, and indeed, most drawing programs do. The trick is to export to a format that Photoshop can read—and it makes sense that it's *Adobe* Illustrator's format.

If you've already found the fonts in the BOUTONS folder on the Companion CD, terrific. Load Beacon to your system as a Type 1 or TrueType font, and our next stop is your drawing program.

Here's how to create the text for the design:

Creating Custom Text

1. In Illustrator or another drawing program, import the Susan.tif image to the workspace, lock it on the current layer, and then add a new layer to the composition. This keeps the picture from accidentally being moved.

2. Create an arc around the top of the large black-eyed Susan, as shown in figure 15.16. All drawing programs have some sort of pen or pencil tool with which you create an arc by dragging and leaving anchor points wherever there are turns in direction of the arc.

3. In Illustrator, click the Type tool at the beginning of the arc, and start typing. In CorelDRAW and XARA, you type the phrase first, then select both the type and the arc, and use the Fit Text to Path/Curve command. In *any* program, click on the control that centers type—we want the type to be centered in the design. In figure 15.17, you can see that Beacon PS at 36 points highlights the design beautifully.

tip

If you do not know how to add a font to your system, that's cool. When I first started, I tried to pour fonts down the vents on the top of my monitor.

On the Macintosh, if you have Adobe Type Manager 3 or later installed, simply drag the fonts into your System, Fonts folder.

In Windows, if you want to add a Type 1 font to Adobe Type Manager, you launch Type Manager, click on the Add Fonts tab, and then direct the program to the path X:\Boutons\Fonts, where X is the drive letter of your CD. If you want to go TrueType, open Control Panel, Fonts, choose File, Install new font, and then direct the application to the path on the CD where the type is located (Boutons/Fonts).

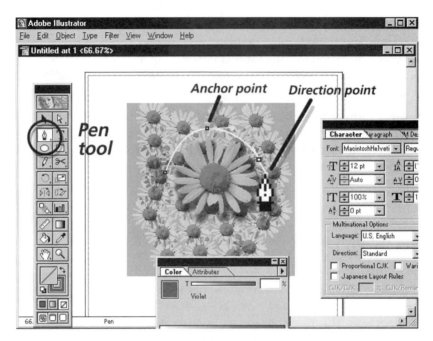

FIGURE 15.16   *Create an arc that will be used by your drawing program to fit text.*

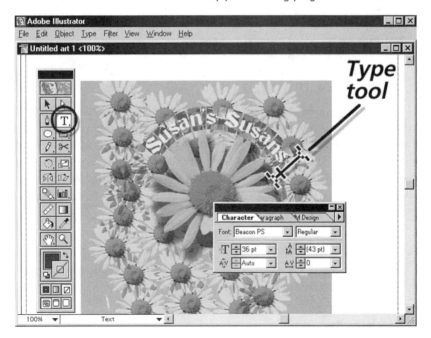

FIGURE 15.17   *Use an appropriate font and arc it so it fits like a cap on top of the main black-eyed Susan in the composition.*

4. Using the same font and font size, type **eFlorist** below the main black-eyed Susan. Drag it around, if need be, to make the lettering centered.

5. Delete the bottom layer with the picture, delete the arc you used as a guide for the text (or assign it a zero width), and then save the lettering as text.ai. Corel users need to use the Illustrator format for export (*ai, *eps).

6. Close your drawing program, and launch Photoshop (if you closed it).

There are two ways of getting Illustrator text into Photoshop; the first, by the Place command, which allows you to scale the objects and position them before finalizing their conversion between vector art and bitmap images. The second way is to open the Illustrator file, and then move a copy of the art into your target image window. Because Illustrator is PostScript by design, it uses a page-descriptor language in the header of the file, which tells Photoshop how large it should open. This means when you are presented with the Rasterize EPS dialog box, you can simply click on OK and use the values presented to you in this box. Why? Because you were scaling the text according to a TIFF copy of the black-eyed Susan work—the TIFF image is the same size as your target file.

Here's how to add text to the design:

Bringing an Illustrator File into Photoshop

1. Open Susan.tif from your hard disk. This is the flattened image you created to use with a drawing program. Hey, we were going to flatten the image eventually, anyway.

2. Choose File, Open, and then from the Examples/Chap15 folder on the Companion CD, choose Text.ai. The Rasterize Generic EPS File box will open—and you? You simply click on OK, and in a moment, black lettering will appear against a transparent background.

3. With the Move tool, hold Alt(Opt) and drag the Text.ai title on the Layers palette into the susan.tif image. It should be centered now; if it's not, drag on it a little using the Move tool (as shown in fig. 15.18), or use the arrow nudge keys.

4. Click on the Text.ai layer title to make it the target layer, check the Preserve Transparency box on the Layers palette, choose white as the foreground color from the Color Picker, and then press Alt(Opt)+Delete. Poof! Instant white text, which although it looks nicer, needs help to separate it from the background.

5. Uncheck the Preserve Transparency check box, and then choose Layer, Effects, Drop Shadow. Click on the Apply button, as shown in figure 15.19 (if Photoshop hasn't already done this for you), accept the default values (because you only need a little separation between text and background—the shadow is a device, not really an effect in this instance), and then press Enter (Return).

FIGURE 15.18   *The text looks nice, but black doesn't seem to be a very good choice of colors.*

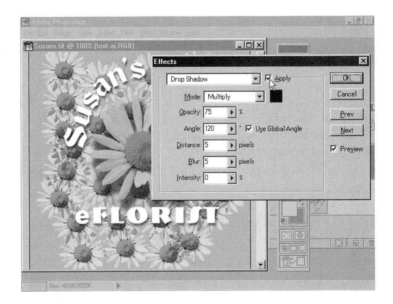

FIGURE 15.19   *Use the Layer Effects as a substitute for the manual Gaussian Blur technique when you don't need as much control over the outcome of a shadow.*

6. With the Type tool, click an insertion point in the center of the main flower, and in white type, Helvetica, 14 points, type **Click here**. You can use figure 15.20 as a guide for where to put the text and what it should look like. Later, you'll link this area to a page I've created for you in this assignment (so you don't have just a one-page site to work with).

FIGURE 15.20   *You need to tell your audience that the center of the main flower is a clickable region that'll send them off to a page with more information.*

7. From the main menu, choose Layer, Type, Render Layer. Press Ctrl(⌘)+Shift+E to merge all visible layers, and then save the image again. TIFF format images can't have layers, and you won't need layers in Photoshop from this point on. Why? Because you've finished your work in Photoshop and it's time to go to ImageReady.

We're moving right along, eh? I'll bet we've covered (um, briskly) 10 chapters up to now, and it's time for some ImageReady maneuvers (and chapter synopses).

ImageReady: Final Destination for Web Media Touch-Ups

As you've seen in previous chapters, ImageReady has many of the same key commands and features as Photoshop, so you really should feel more at home with the software than you did the first time we used it. From this point on, you can stop thinking of the Susan's Susans graphic as simply a bitmap image, and start thinking about how it can be optimized for the Web and loaded with a link area.

Moving the Design to ImageReady

I think it might have slipped out earlier that if you have both ImageReady and Photoshop open at the same time, you might be riding a system-memory roller coaster, straight down. So right now, if you've got 96 MB of RAM or more on your machine, go ahead and click on that lower-right icon at the bottom of Photoshop's toolbox to launch ImageReady with your image already in the workspace.

My system has plenty of RAM (the idea is, you buy large amounts when the RAM market is down), but I'm going to chicken out here, close Photoshop, and then launch ImageReady from a shortcut (alias) icon I placed on my desktop. Why? Because I have no idea how fragmented my machine's memory is at this point, and because I will not need Photoshop for the remainder of this assignment, and also because my dad once told me, "Better safe than sorry," which I didn't comprehend fully until I bought my first used car.

Using either scenario presented here, get Susan.tif into ImageReady, and get ready for review time as your image becomes bonafide Web media:

Creating an URL Hot Spot

1. With the Elliptical Marquee tool, drag a circle around the center of the main flower, where it says "Click here." As in Photoshop, you can reposition a selection by using a Marquee tool; it doesn't disturb the pixels on the underlying layer.

2. Right-click (Macintosh: hold Ctrl and click) inside the marquee and then choose Layer via Copy, as shown in figure 15.21. The circle shape becomes the contents of Layer 2, and we can now define it as a hot spot in the graphic.

Profound Wisdom #26:

A hot spot is simply a clickable area of a graphic.

When the graphic is loaded into a Web browser, and an Internet connection is active, a click on the hot spot takes you to the URL that has been defined for that clickable region. You don't need something that looks like a button in this clickable region, but it's a lot less confusing and irritating if you give some clue as to the hot spot(s) in a Web page.

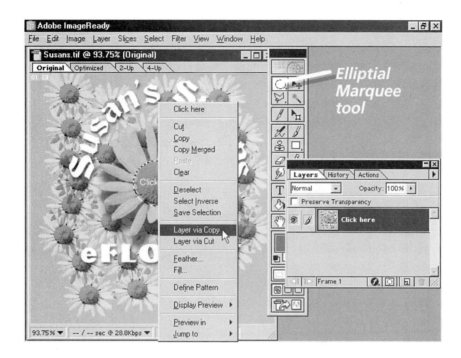

FIGURE 15.21   *The way ImageReady defines URL hot spots is by defining a shape on a layer.*

3. With the Background layer selected, choose Filter, Sharpen, Unsharp Mask. Apply about a 50% sharpening to the graphic, using the settings shown in figure 15.22. Why sharpen? Because both GIF and JPEG compression tend to blur images.

4. On the Optimize palette (F8), choose JPEG Medium as the compression method used, and uncheck the Progressive check box, because not all browsers and graphics browsers can *parlez* Progressive compression. As you can see in figure 15.23, the potential JPEG copy of the image comes in at about 14 seconds, using a 28.8 modem. This is not bad, really, using the time-honored rule of thumb for the Web, "No top page on a site should weigh in at more than 50 KB. This file is the only graphic on Susan's top page, and it's only 38 KB in file size, and life is good so far.

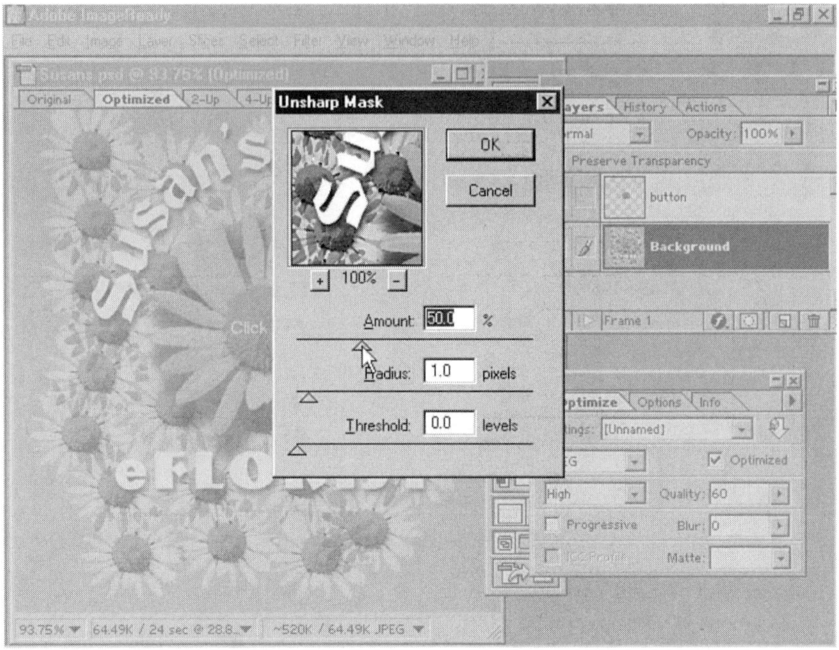

FIGURE 15.22   *Compensate for the reality that compression softens the focus of an image. Make your image super-sharp, and the compression process will even out the focus.*

5. Double-click on the Layer 2 title on the Layers palette. You will see a Layer Options box, where you can define the URL for the center (the pupil?) of the black-eyed Susan. Choose circle as the shape of the hot spot. Check the Use Layer As Image Map check box, and then, in the URL field, type **flowers.html**, exactly as it appears here (URLs are case-sensitive) and in figure 15.24.

6. Drop back to your system desktop and create a folder. Call it **Susan**, and if you're a guy, tell your mate that it's a tutorial from a terrific book, and not a collection of love e-mail.

7. Back in ImageReady, choose File, Save Optimized As, and then choose as the destination the Susan folder you created. Check both the Save HTML and the Save Images check boxes, name the file **Susans.jpeg**, and then click on OK. Close ImageReady without saving the susan.tif image.

8. Go to the Examples/Chap15/Gallery folder on the Companion CD, and then copy flowers.gif and flowers.html to your Susan folder on the desktop.

FIGURE 15.23   *The speed limit is unofficially 50 KB per page. Stay under it, and your audience will stay with you and not switch channels while their browser attempts to load the Rock of Gibraltar.*

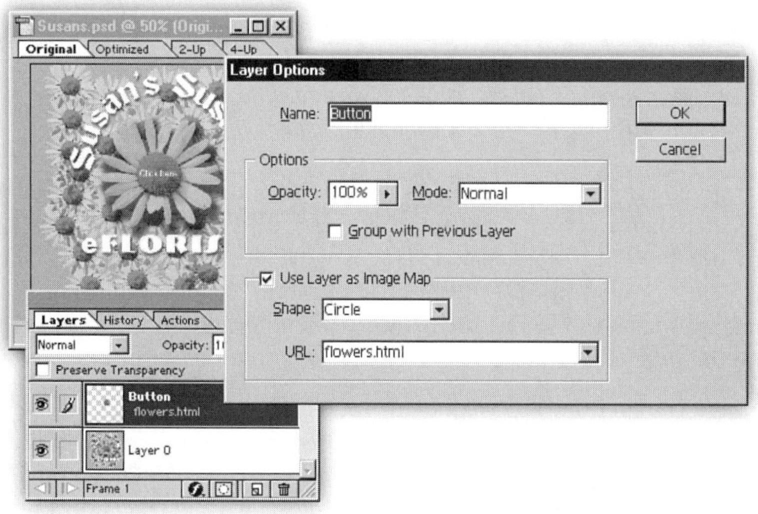

FIGURE 15.24   *Don't worry that you have no idea what the flowers.html URL means; it's a page I've created for you on the CD so you'd have a Web system, and not simply a Web page.*

Now for the fun part. Double-click on the Susan.html file in the Susan folder. The page you designed will appear in your Web browser. And, if you click on the hot spot, as shown in figure 15.25, off you go to the flowers.html page. Hopefully, this HTML linking stuff makes sense now <g>!

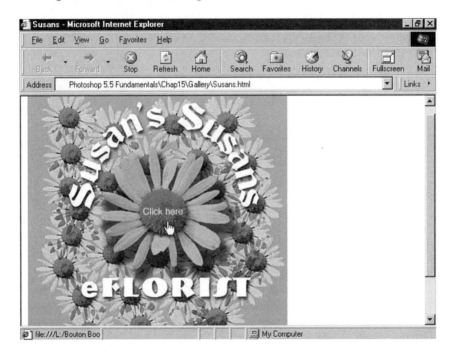

FIGURE 15.25 *View your dynamic linking page in your favorite browser. (Hey, after Netscape was sold, is there anything but Explorer?)*

Now that you are on the flowers page, shown in figure 15.26, you can see the potential for there being several links to other pages, and the Web system could in fact branch out to many, many pages. This is why your next purchase should be an HTML editor, so you can fill in the missing pieces, such as choice of background, placement of text, and so on. By the way, the center button on this page takes you back to the page you created.

Well, there you go now. You've done it! You've taken all the skills you've learned in previous chapters, integrated them, and created something you could not have created before. This is not only your reward for your hard work and studying, but it's also the *teacher's* reward, you know? For having such a capable and willing student.

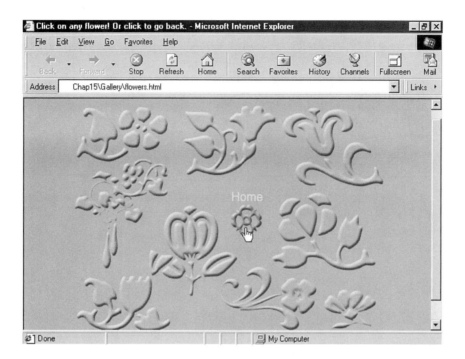

FIGURE 15.26   *The World Wide Web is often called "the largest single HTML document in the world" because just about every page out there links to a different page.*

Summary

The more ambitious your goal, the more puzzle pieces you are going to have to play with. If you completed this chapter, it demonstrates that you have a firm grasp on—let me do this as a list, okay (and I *hate* lists!)—the following:

- How to select areas of an image
- How to create a brush tip from an image
- How to recolor and how to colorize images
- How to use selection tools and create background colors
- How to use text like the pros

PROFOUND WISDOM #27:

If you are asked for a link from your Web site to someone else's, you make darned sure they provide a link to *your* page.

As you grow in experience and thrill to putting up your first personal Web site, you will start to receive e-mail asking you to put on your page a link to the e-mailer. Is it a pain to do this? Yeah, a little, just when you had everything humming, but "link swapping" is one of the best ways of getting yourself and your talents known. It's the new currency of the Web. I, personally, am trying to get Adobe to link to my site. (What's the difference between "slim chance" and "fat chance"?)

- How to optimize an image for the Web
- How to create a hot spot for an URL link

I'm sure there's more, but hey, you only had to read this chapter. I had to *write* it, so I need to gather my thoughts more completely someday.

Chapter 15½ is not about Photoshop, ImageReady, or anything you've previously read in this book. It's two things:

1. Where I show off my favorite Photoshop plug-ins. (And guess what? On the Companion CD there are trial versions of all of the plug-ins.)

2. My chance to stop chanting numbered lists, and really give you a one-on-one piece of advice or two on where you should go from here.

CHAPTER 15½

Is There Anything I Missed?

You know, at various times, an author has to keep the whole book in his or her head, to better organize what is sometimes a pretty hefty body of work. *Photoshop 5.5. Fundamentals with ImageReady* wasn't too hard for me—it only took up about 95 percent of my cranium. Reserved head areas were for walking, eating, and conducting conference calls.

I'd like to leave you with two more things that I thought, from the very beginning, were extremely important to include in this book. The first thing was to share with you my favorite plug-ins, because Photoshop is enhanced a lot by other vendors' products. I've included sampler versions of these on the Companion CD, and I'll show you in this chapter what some of the effects can look like.

More important, I'd like to share with you a vision of where the path from the end of this book can lead. I really hate it when I finish watching a movie or reading a book, and *bang!*—all of a sudden the story is over. What was the author *thinking*??? I'm going to leave you with several questions before this chapter is through, and if you can answer them, then you will know what to do after you close this book.

The Author's Favorite Plug-Ins

For the most part, I've never fallen out of love with a Photoshop plug-in (or suite of plug-ins), from the first version on through the years. This is special stuff I'm going to show you, and you will get results that cannot even be faintly simulated using Photoshop without the specific plug-in.

Our first stop is a place called Andromeda Software, and the 3-D and Cutline filter.

Andromeda's 3-D Filter

I realize that a lot of us would like to try our hand at creating 3D models, but the budget is too tight, the time is too short, or you believe that the learning curve is a tidal wave. There's a plug-in that addresses and dismisses all three concerns. Andromeda's 3-D plug-in limits the options you'd have in a modeling program, but does so in such a way that you're not intimidated—the shapes are predefined, and you can modify them. You've got a box shape, a cylinder, and a sphere.

Now, primitive 3D shapes are not artistically expressive unless you add *shading* (I'm calling texture mapping "shading" here) to the primitive forms. It is one spectacular thrill to suddenly see your 2D artwork in Photoshop stretched around a sphere. In figure 15½.1, you can see the interface of Andromeda's 3-D filter, with callouts as to which control affects which aspect of the primitive and the picture:

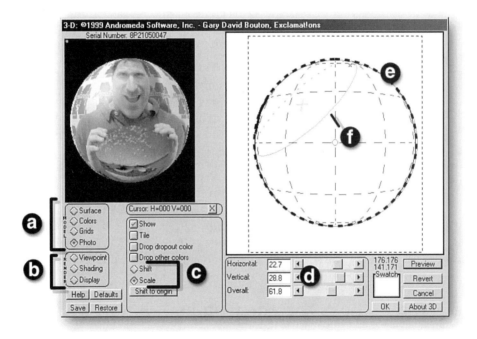

FIGURE 15½.1   *The interface to Andromeda's 3-D filter.*

The controls are less of a challenge than they look. The following alphabetical list tells you about each one:

a.   This is the area that determines what it is you are manipulating at any time in the interface. For example, I've got Photo checked in figure 15½.1, and all the rest of the controls offer me choices on how to scale, move, tile, and set the background color for the finished model. Earlier, I chose Sphere when the Surface button was checked in this area, so both the preview window and the wireframe window are displaying a sphere with the current Photoshop image mapped to the sphere.

b. These are the view and lighting controls. Viewpoint determines your view of the object through the window (the controls for this and other properties are located at *f* in the figure). Shading determines the direction of light that falls on the surface, and when this is selected, the area called *d* in the figure offers controls for soft light, light direction, and how much of the surface or the image is illuminated. Display is the part of the object's surface that is visible to your view; it's not the same as viewpoint—you're moving the object, and not your view, when this option is checked.

c. Shift and Scale are perhaps two of the most important properties you can control when you're mapping a Photoshop image to a shape. Scale controls the size of either the image or the 3D surface, and Shift determines how the image, or the model, faces your view. As with the other controls, the *d* area in the figure changes to offer options when you click on Scale or Shift.

d. This area changes its options, much like Photoshop's Options palette, when a certain aspect of the scene is chosen (such as Scale, Surface, or Shading). In the figure, the controls are for how the photograph scales around the outside of a sphere.

e. Coverage. It's hard to see in this image, but I've created a dotted outline exactly where the extent of the picture lies, which is on the edge of the sphere, so all the sphere is covered with photograph. You have the option to make the image smaller, or to tile the image, but given our picture here, I thought wrapping the image so it takes up the entire front half of the sphere looked the best (or at least, the funniest).

f. Finally, the oval you see on the sphere is where lighting is directly falling. You control where the hot spot is when you choose Shading from the *b* area of the interface, and you can also control the size and intensity of the light source on the object. Unfortunately, there is only one light source in Andromeda 3-D.

I'm looking over what I've written, and realize that this filter is not that difficult a one to use, when weighed against what you can accomplish with it. It took me perhaps an hour or so before I understood not only the sphere, but the other mappings for images across 3D geometry.

It's a fun, unique filter, as you can see in figure 15½.2. It doesn't require a lot of studying, and the 2D Photoshop user can become a bonafide 3D expert in no time, without having to learn a modeling application's mountain of controls.

Unflattering   Unflattering, but
                        interesting-looking

FIGURE 15½.2   *Go from 2D to 3D for very little money, and a very brief introduction period.*

I suspect that some of you think that the 3-D filter is a "one trick pony," and that if you're not interested in placing everything on a sphere, tough. That's why I've dug out a picture from the *Inside Photoshop 3* book, done in 1996. It took me several hours, but *look* at the piece in figure 15½.3. I added the shadows manually (you learned how to do this in this book), worked with different colored wood images, and used Photoshop layers a lot. On the right of figure 15½.3 is a wood sample, and also three different wireframes from the Andromeda 3-D interface that show how the wood image can be mapped along a number of different surfaces, as shown in the image at left.

The 3-D filter is perhaps one of the earliest filters offered by Andromeda Software, but I still have not seen anything like it to date in the plug-ins arena.

In addition to the 3-D filter, I really like the results of Andromeda's Cutline filter (this is currently a Windows filter which should go biplatform at any moment). Let's take a look at that.

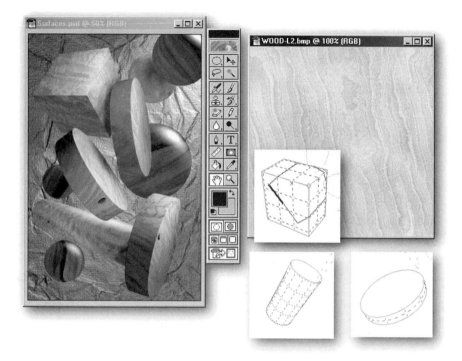

Figure 15½.3   *"Art, using very few materials." If you pick an interesting sample image, and you can spare some time, you can really build up a complex, photorealistic piece.*

The Andromeda Cutline Filter

Corel Corporation had something very close to this filter back when version CorelDRAW 6 was out, but it was a utility that converted halftones to vector art, with three zillion paths in the file, so working with it was, em…a challenge. Andromeda's Cutline filter is very straightforward in its use, and very rewarding in terms of the sophisticated look you can lend extremely simple objects.

The secret? Keep a gradient going on every part of your original design. This will make the Cutline filter draw thick lines that taper off to thin ones. If you're with me here, check out figure 15½.4. I drew a simple button, first by filling a large circle with a black-to-white gradient, and then drew a smaller circle inside the larger one, with the gradient going in the opposite direction.

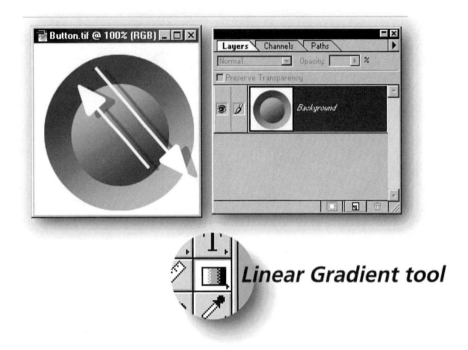

FIGURE 15½.4   *If you make gradients across an image, the effect will be more pronounced when you apply the Cutline filter.*

Figure 15½.5 is the interface of the Cutline filter. If you read the documentation (which is not that long, nor does it need to be) you will be up and running, producing some truly wild line art. In this figure, I've marked the two most important areas of the interface—those areas which provide the most different and stunning results. The first of these areas is the resolution of the effect. Although it depends entirely on how large an image you want to filter, I've found that the lower resolutions (10 is shown in the figure) provide crude but artistic, breath-taking results. In the other area you can choose from one of four Cutline types; you can further refine each Cutline type with the minitoolbox in the center of the interface.

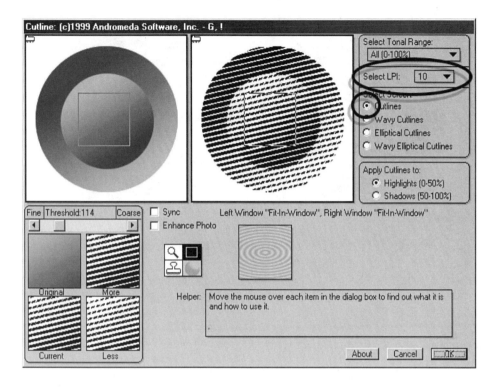

FIGURE 15½.5 *Straight-type cutlines at a low resolution make "High Art" out of a design that took five seconds to create!*

To show you a little variety here, figure 15½.6 shows the straight cutline and the elliptical cutline, both used on the same art. With the elliptical cutline, you determine where the center of concentric ellipses should begin.

The Cutline and the 3-D filter are only two of Andromeda Software's offerings. If you'd like to check out demo filters that are not provided on the Companion CD, the URL is **www.andromeda.com**.

I'd like to move now to a filter that has been offered for a long time on the Macintosh platform, but finally made its biplatform debut with version 2. It's XAOS|tools' Terrazzo filter, and I think you'll get a kick out of how this one works.

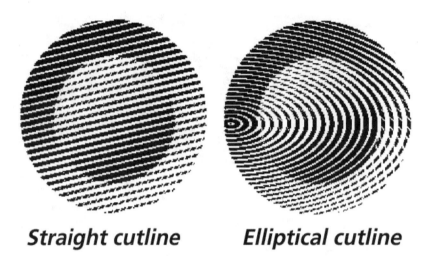

Straight cutline *Elliptical cutline*

Figure 15½.6 *One piece of art, but clearly two different styles of execution. Not bad, beginning with a simple design, hmm?*

A Kaleidoscope on Steroids, Anyone?

The Terrazzo filter is currently being bundled with Paint Alchemy and the new TypeCaster (make 3D type in Photoshop) under the name "Total XAOS." I did the math, and you're much better picking up the bundle than Terrazzo alone, because you're essentially getting three knockout filters for the price of two (Paint Alchemy and TypeCaster are cool, too).

I have a particular fondness for the Terrazzo filter because it can produce not only kaleidoscopic wonders from ordinary image areas, but you can also use it to create seamless tiles from the plug-in to use as Web-page backgrounds.

Here's the scoop on Terrazzo: You have your choice of 17 different pattern templates, upon which you place an area of the current image in Photoshop. You then move a polygonal screen element over the preview of the sample image, enlarging what XAOS calls the *motif* (the polygonal screen control) until you see something attractive in the right window. The Feathering controls are available for some—but not all—of the patterns, but feathering the image area defined by the motif can lead to some wild and beautiful patterns. This plug-in should be of particular interest to textile artists. In figure 15½.7, I've loaded an image called Doodle.tif (it's in the Chap15½ folder), and look what has become of a section of it in the right window!

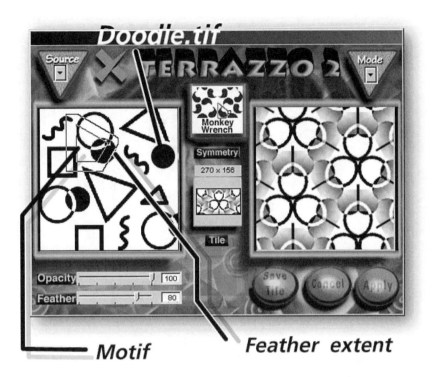

Motif   **Feather extent**

FIGURE 15½.7   *Anything from intricate floral patterns to concrete sidewalk designs can be simulated, using Terrazzo 2.*

Now, the Doodle.tif image is only in black-and-white, but it was carefully designed to provide the greatest number of unique patterns from a single piece of art. What I did was tightly pack together doodle figures, and then I expanded or contracted the motif (the lone control handle on the motif does this) and moved it around a little within the preview window. You should try out your own designs—make sparse, close, bold, definitive strokes, and try your hand at pattern-making.

Color is another aspect of Terrazzo I've not addressed yet. What's the best type of color image to use in Terrazzo? Well, I'll tell you what I did: My spouse took a picture of a plant on a wooden deck, I ran it through Photoshop's Cutout filter (not to be confused with Alien Skin's Cutout filter) to get nice sharp edges and a minimum of different colors. You can see this image in figure 15½.8 (but not in color, so it's in the Chap15½ folder, as flowers.tif).

Filter, Artistic, Cutout

FIGURE 15½.8   *Filtered photographs can often become wonderful Terrazzo creations because the detail in the original photo has been simplified or dropped out. And this makes a pinwheel sort of Terrazzo creation that's easy to understand from an artistic standpoint—and it's easier on the eyes!*

I opened the image in Terrazzo and picked a part of the image, as you can see in figure 15½.9. Now, here's a trick: As you can see in this figure, a seamless tile is previewed in the center of the interface. If you click on Save Tile (left, squishy button on the bottom), you can save a tile in BMP (Windows) or PICT (Macintosh) format(s). Then, cancel out of the filter interface, and go hunt down the seamless tile you created.

What I did with the seamless tiling image might be a crime (against what, I don't know). I embossed the seamless tile, using a color channel in the Lighting Effects filter to bring out certain areas, and then I colorized the tiler, using the Hue/Saturation's Colorize command to reach a monotone but very interesting background for a Web page. The filtered tile will not compete with other elements on the page, as shown in figure 15½.10. By the way, if you'd like to see this site in your computer's Web browser, there's a folder called artpage in the TOYS folder. Double-click on the HTML document title, and you should see something like figure 15½.10.

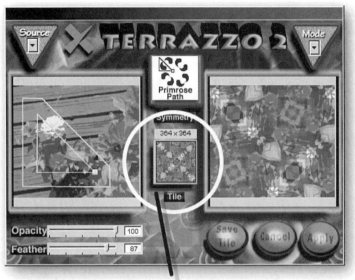

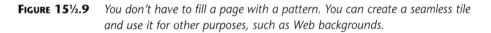

Save as bmp or pict file

FIGURE 15½.9   *You don't have to fill a page with a pattern. You can create a seamless tile and use it for other purposes, such as Web backgrounds.*

FIGURE 15½.10   *Web backgrounds are only one of the scores of uses for original, fresh patterns you can generate from Terrazzo 2.*

Just as a side note here, figure 15½.11 is a scene I created a few years ago, using trueSpace as the modeling program. The cracked surface, which really stands out in the composition, was created by first drawing some black lines on a white canvas, using the Filter, Distort, Glass on the seamless tile, and then using the image as both a surface map and a bump map (so the ridges looked authentic). So Terrazzo is sort of one of those omnibus filters you might find yourself using daily.

FIGURE 15½.11   *The Terrazzo filter provided the cracked land in this image.*

The next "Bouton's Best" filter is currently Windows-only, with a Macintosh version in the works. It is simple and elegant in the effects it produces, yet the math behind the interface must be mind-boggling. You can paint in *3D,* using this plug-in.

Right Hemisphere's Deep Paint

I own MetaCreation's Painter and I like it a lot. But what Painter provides me with, and what Deep Paint can do, are entirely different things. Deep Paint can be run as a plug-in from within Photoshop, or run as a standalone program (it has its own layers, tools, and other options). The thing that had me hooked immediately on Deep Paint is how realistic and *deep* the paint looks when applied to a canvas. It's the closest thing I've ever found that makes a digital paint program feel like an atmospheric artist's loft, with turpentine rags strewn all over! In figure 15½.12, you can see me using the Chrome brush. Tell me that the text doesn't leap off the page!

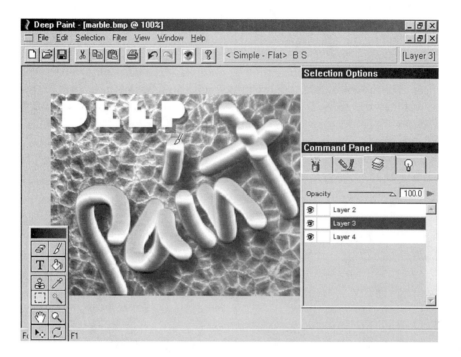

Figure 15½.12   *There's paint, and then there's Deep Paint. Right Hemisphere has captured the look and feel of real paint and other materials you apply to a canvas.*

I found myself so engrossed, working with Deep Paint for the first time, I missed most of my favorite TV shows!

They've landed! They've landed! And they bring with them some truly funky, inspiring plug-ins. I'm going to show you Alien Skin's Xenofex and Eye Candy filters next.

Xenofex Filters: A Weird Kind of Gallery Effects

You know the additional filters that came with version 5 of Photoshop? The Watercolor and Paint Daubs effects, and such? These are terrific filters, and they have been terrific filters for more than four years. They were originally sold as plug-ins by the late Aldus Corporation; skipping over the history part for a moment, these were a collection of small filters that produced natural media effects.

Xenofex is not made by Aldus, and the media it renders can hardly be called natural media. Nevertheless, the Xenofex collection reminds me of Aldus Gallery Effects because each of the 17 filters does only one effect, but does it spectacularly. You have some control over each filter's parameters, but this collection certainly does break away from convention, and conventional thought! In figure 15½.13, you can see that I'm filtering the American Icons picture you worked on back in chapter 6, using the Constellation filter. The background color of the stars must be set from Photoshop's color selection boxes on the toolbox, and black is a particularly effective color. You can't see the colors in this figure (unless you can see something most of us can't), but trust me—the Constellation filter produces fireworks from any image that has strong colors.

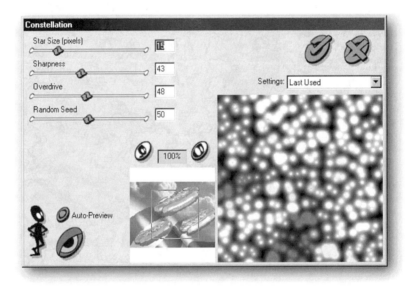

FIGURE 15½.13   *Alien Skin's Xenofex, Constellation filter creates remarkable phenomena from the humblest of source images.*

I also get a charge out of Xenofex's Crumple filter. It really does crumple the visual content of the selected image, as shown in figure 15½.14. And as you can see, it works best with text. I tried out this filter with the Burger King logo, and the result was a totally convincing wrapper just taken off a Whopper.

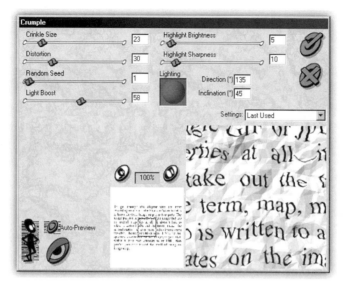

FIGURE 15½.14   *Is your text too legible? Why not muss it up—in a creative way—by applying the Crumple filter?*

In fact, I'd be hard-pressed to pick out my very favorite Xenofex filters, because each one is totally different from the next. I like the Baked Earth Effect for certain things, and I'd be remiss if I didn't mention that the Little Fluffy Clouds filter makes some of the most realistic clouds I've ever seen.

But Xenofex is only one offering from Alien Skin. The aliens also have Eye Candy 3 (going to *Eye Candy 4000* a short while after this book goes to press, so I don't have any info on the upgrade at the moment). Eye Candy 3 is an outgrowth of the classic Black Box filters that created drop shadows, glows, and cutouts (I used the Cutout filter to "sink" the color signature images into the pages in the front of this book). But Eye Candy has matured, and now offers a lot of additional filters that are more enhancers than they are effects. In addition to the shadow filters (which are terrific time-savers), you can produce fur, smoke, fire, glass effects, and my all-time favorite, Water Drops. In addition to the drops rendering to your art, you can specify that the drops refract (bend) light. Look at figure 15½.15. The drops on the text really are bending the text outward, just like *real* H_2O!

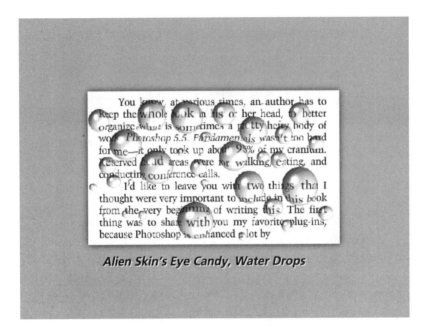

Alien Skin's Eye Candy, Water Drops

FIGURE 15½.15   *Take the plunge without getting all wet! The Water Drops Eye Candy filter creates remarkably lifelike droplets on your artwork.*

Hey, I feel like I'm on a roll now, and would love to share with you 17 dozen useful
plug-ins, but I promised myself (and my publisher) that I'd keep to documenting filters that are on the Companion CD.

What's left? As far as Photoshop and ImageReady go, what's left is what you discover
beyond these introductions. But this is only the design aspect; what's left for *you*, as a
flesh-and-blood individual, might be a little more complex to explain than a plug-in!

Where Do We Go from Here?

I get just enough e-mail from readers each day to make me feel as though I'm at a
cocktail party all day long, rubbing elbows with fellow designers. The only difference
is that the chatter is highly specialized. "It's a bomb," "tanking," "ripping"—all sorts
of colorful language abounds in my e-mail.

But the really nice thing about correspondence is that I can tell what readers want to
know most, and what they want to hear about their future. The top three questions
are

- *What's the right resolution to scan at? I have a lot of family images I want to print.*
  (I answered that in chapter 10).

- *I really want to get into computer graphics, but don't know where to begin.* The answer's Photoshop.

- *Can you make any money doing this stuff?* If you try hard enough and read my equation for success (in the book's Introduction).

Believe it or not, all these questions have something in common. They all ask whether getting into Photoshop is worthwhile, whether it is better to dangle one's toes in the pond, or to go splashing in. Pull up a rock, and I'll tell you...

There are two terms, *half-heartedly* and *whole-heartedly,* that constantly pass through my mind when I hear of the plans of others, and frequently when I examine my own work. Now, if you use a word too many times, its meaning is blunted, so just to refresh for a second, you're *half-hearted* when:

- you're not interested at all in something, but are required to do it.

- you're not trying because you have something else on your mind.

And *half-heartedness* is the step-sister to *mediocrity;* even if you're a practitioner of half-heartedness, being *surrounded* by mediocrity *will* send you up a wall.

In contrast, you're *whole-hearted* when:

- you find that your work is feeding *you* energy.

- you know in your bones that what you are designing is right, and you turn a deaf ear to would-be detractors.

- the guy who buys your piece thinks he's paying you too little.

Serious and Earnest

I guess where you go from here depends on how seriously, how earnestly you approach a medium, specifically that of Photoshop. By *seriously,* I do *not* mean *somber.* There are far too many would-be famous artists who can't be reached because of their attitude—which usually looks as though it was purchased at a drama school. *Serious* simply means that *you* mean what you're doing, that you are committed. You can be *surrounded* by laughter (usually your own) when you create something that really intrigues and excites you. Hence the term "serious fun."

By *earnestly,* I mean that you should not *presume* to be an expert until others have told you that you are one, so many times that you're sick of hearing it. (I'm kidding—you'll *never* get sick of hearing it). I once knew a rock musician who had the audacity to go about criticizing Bach's work as a whole. As though this dude had ever heard even a fraction of J.S. Bach's work, or even understood that a lot of the Beatles' music was based on the structure of Bach's music. No, this is a very nonearnest, ego-salving thing to do, and if you do it in public, you become an ass in public. Do not go tearing down the masters only to make yourself feel larger in comparison. Do you see what a fantasy, what a futile thing this is? You learn from them; you do not hold them in self-righteous contempt. You listen, you read, you learn as you grow. If you do this, there will be little time for ego-flaunting, and you *will* be pursuing your craft in earnest.

How Far Do You Go from Here?

Again—it depends on how serious and earnest you are. I know a lot of hobbyists who would not win an art contest with their art, but are happy with what they accomplish, and therefore are a success. What lies in success is different for every person— I work hard to see myself as a success every day. If this section of the book has struck a resonant chord, then I'm a super-success! All in all, *success* is best left alone. Success means something different to each of us, and it's a waste of time that would be better spent in Photoshop than in trying to define the term.

If you've gone as far as you want to go by reading this book—terrific! That means I did my job. If you're hungry for more and want to become an all-star, my recipe would be equal amounts of

- **Talking.** Talk with others who are more proficient than you, and really pick their intellect for Profound Wisdoms.
- **Practicing.** Lots of practicing.
- **Reading.** It would be nice if your future reading contained a few of *my* titles, but I will understand if you want other point of views. That's what makes the world an interesting place, and why we all feel that need to capture some of it on paper or the screen.

If you doubt for a moment that what I'm telling you here is good, solid advice, I could show you more than half a dozen of my "students" who are currently doing work that is more refined and more soulful than my own. Am I bent out of shape about it? Not at all. I like to see my students graduate. Success comes from nurturing, and nurturing comes from sharing. And I hope I've shared enough with you in this book.

Index

New Riders Professional Library

Bert Monroy: Photorealistic Techniques with
Photoshop & Illustrator
Bert Monroy
0-7357-0969-6

CG 101: A Computer Graphics Industry Reference
Terrence Masson
0-7357-0046-X

Click Here
Raymond Pirouz and Lynda Weinman
1-56205-792-8

<coloring web graphics.2>
Lynda Weinman and Bruce Heavin
1-56205-818-5

Creating Killer Web Sites, Second Edition
David Siegel
1-56830-433-1

<creative html design>
Lynda Weinman and William Weinman
1-56205-704-9

<designing web graphics.3>
Lynda Weinman
1-56205-949-1

Designing Web Usability
Jakob Nielsen
1-56205-810-X

[digital] Character Animation 2
Volume 1: Essential Techniques
George Maestri
1-56205-930-0

Essentials of Digital Photography
Akari Kasai and Russell Sparkman
1-56205-762-6

Fine Art Photoshop
Michael J. Nolan and Renee LeWinter
1-56205-829-0

Flash 4 Magic
David Emberton and J. Scott Hamlin
0-7357-0949-1

Flash Web Design
Hillman Curtis
0-7357-0896-7

HTML Artistry: More than Code
Ardith Ibañez and Natalie Zee
1-56830-454-4

HTML Web Magic
Raymond Pirouz
1-56830-475-7

Inside 3D Studio MAX 3
Phil Miller, et al.
0-7357-0905-X

Inside AutoCAD 2000
David Pitzer and Bill Burchard
0-7357-0851-7

Inside Adobe Photoshop 5
Gary David Bouton and Barbara Bouton
1-56205-884-3

Inside Adobe Photoshop 5, Limited Edition
Gary David Bouton and Barbara Bouton
1-56205-951-3

Inside SoftImage 3D
Anthony Rossano
1-56205-885-1

Maya 2 Character Animation
*Nathan Vogel, Sherri Sheridan,
and Tim Coleman*
0-7357-0866-5

Net Results: Web Marketing that Works
USWeb and Rick E. Bruner
1-56830-414-5

Photoshop 5 & 5.5 Artistry
Barry Haynes and Wendy Crumpler
0-7457-0994-7

Photoshop 5 Web Magic
Michael Ninness
1-56205-913-0

Photoshop Channel Chops
*David Biedney, Bert Monroy,
and Nathan Moody*
1-56205-723-5

<preparing web graphics>
Lynda Weinman
1-56205-686-7

Rhino NURBS 3D Modeling
Margaret Becker
0-7357-0925-4

Secrets of Successful Web Sites
David Siegel
1-56830-382-3

Web Concept & Design
Crystal Waters
1-56205-648-4

Web Design Templates Sourcebook
Lisa Schmeiser
1-56205-754-5

New Riders | We Want to Know What You Think

To better serve you, we would like your opinion on the content and quality of this book. Please complete this card and mail it to us or fax it to 317-581-4663.

Name _____

Address _____

City_____ State_____ Zip _____

Phone _____

Email Address _____

Occupation _____

Operating System(s) that you use _____

What influenced your purchase of this book?
- ❏ Recommendation
- ❏ Table of Contents
- ❏ Magazine Review
- ❏ New Rider's Reputation
- ❏ Cover Design
- ❏ Index
- ❏ Advertisement
- ❏ Author Name

How would you rate the contents of this book?
- ❏ Excellent
- ❏ Good
- ❏ Below Average
- ❏ Very Good
- ❏ Fair
- ❏ Poor

How do you plan to use this book?
- ❏ Quick reference
- ❏ Classroom
- ❏ Self-training
- ❏ Other

What do you like most about this book?
Check all that apply.
- ❏ Content
- ❏ Accuracy
- ❏ Listings
- ❏ Index
- ❏ Price
- ❏ Writing Style
- ❏ Examples
- ❏ Design
- ❏ Page Count
- ❏ Illustrations

What do you like least about this book?
Check all that apply.
- ❏ Content
- ❏ Accuracy
- ❏ Listings
- ❏ Index
- ❏ Price
- ❏ Writing Style
- ❏ Examples
- ❏ Design
- ❏ Page Count
- ❏ Illustrations

What would be a useful follow-up book to this one for you?_____

Where did you purchase this book? _____

_____

Can you name a similar book that you like better than this one, or one that is as good? Why?

_____

_____

How many New Riders books do you own? _____

What are your favorite computer books?_____

_____

What other titles would you like to see us develop? _____

_____

Any comments for us? _____

_____

_____

_____

Adobe Photoshop 5.5 Fundamentals with ImageReady 2, 0-7357-0928-9

www.newriders.com • Fax 317-581-4663

Fold here and tape to mail

New Riders Publishing
201 W. 103rd St.
Indianapolis, IN 46290

Add A Search Engine To Your Web Site In Minutes

Search for FREE!!!!!

Need a way for your visitors to search your web site? Atomz.com Search is your answer. Just sign up at www.atomz.com, add a few lines of HTML to your site, and your site will have a search engine in less than five minutes.

- Customize the look and feel of your search results to match your site design.
- Control how your pages are ranked.
- Index your site whenever your content changes.
- And much more…

It's FREE

Atomz.com Search is free for sites with less than 500 pages and 5,000 searches per month. No banner advertising is required. For larger sites, Atomz.com Search Prime provides support for high-capacity and high-traffic sites, up to over 10,000 pages and millions of searches per month.

See how our members are using Atomz.com Search today at www.atomz.com/gallery/.

Thousands of sites are already using Atomz.com Search. Join today!

atomz.com

http://www.atomz.com

All the graphics on this page were drawn in XARA version 2 for Windows. A fully-working, 15 day trial version of this vector program that thinks it's a bitmap program can be found in the XARA folder on the Limited Edition CD. CorelXARA™ is small (7MB), fast, and one of the perfect companion applications to Photoshop, for the Web and commercial printing uses. For a limited time, you can purchase this amazing program online, for **$99**⁹⁵ U.S., at i/us. **http://www.i-us.com**.
Look in the XaraXone on i/us.

Colophon

Adobe Photoshop 5.5 Fundamentals with ImageReady 2 was layed out and produced with the help of Microsoft Word, Adobe Photoshop, Adobe Illustrator, Adobe ImageReady, and QuarkXPress on a variety of systems, including a Macintosh G3. With the exception of the pages that were printed out for the proofreader, all files used for the final design—both text and images—were transferred via email or ftp and edited on-screen.

All of the body text was set in the Stone Serif family. All headings, sidebars, and figure captions were set in the Stone Sans family. The Symbol and Zapf Dingbats typefaces were used throughout for special symbols and bullets.

The front of the book contains a special 16-page, four-color section, printed on XXX paper. This color signature was printed at GAC in Indianapolis, Indiana.

With the exception of the color section, *Adobe Photoshop 5.5 Fundamentals with ImageReady 2* was printed on 50# Lynx Opaque Smooth at R.R. Donnelley & Sons in Crawfordsville, Indiana. Prepress consisted of PostScript computer-to-plate technology (filmless process).